Frank Lowy
A Second Life

Frank Lowy
A Second Life

JILL MARGO

HarperCollins*Publishers*

HarperCollins*Publishers*

First published in Australia in 2015
by HarperCollins*Publishers* Australia Pty Limited
ABN 36 009 913 517
harpercollins.com.au

HarperCollins*Publishers*
Level 13, 201 Elizabeth Street, Sydney NSW 2000, Australia
Unit D1, 63 Apollo Drive, Rosedale, Auckland 0632, New Zealand
A 53, Sector 57, Noida, UP, India
1 London Bridge Street, London, SE1 9GF, United Kingdom
2 Bloor Street East, 20th floor, Toronto, Ontario M4W 1A8, Canada
195 Broadway, New York NY 10007, USA

Margo, Jill, 1954– author.
  Frank Lowy: a second life / Jill Margo.
  ISBN: 978 0 7322 8778 8 (hardback)
  ISBN: 978 0 7304 9735 6 (ebook)
  Includes index.
  Lowy, Frank P., 1930–
  Lowy Institute for International Policy.
  Directors of corporations – Australia – Biography.
  Successful people – Australia – Biography.
  Success in business.
  Immigrants – Australia – Biography.
338.092

Typeset by Kirby Jones
Printed and bound in Australia by Griffin Press
The papers used by HarperCollins in the manufacture of this book are a natural, recyclable
product made from wood grown in sustainable plantation forests. The fibre source and
manufacturing processes meet recognised international environmental standards, and carry
certification.

Contents

Foreword

I should tell you straight up that I am an admirer of Frank Lowy's and, even if I were not, I would still be fascinated by him.

When I had to move house in what people call my "advanced years", but did not want to lose the extensive library I had built up, Frank Lowy generously funded the relocation of the library to the Sydney Mechanics' School of Arts in Pitt Street. The ambience of the original was recreated and it now serves as a public library. Such examples of Lowy's generosity are so common that there would not be room in this book for all of them.

But I am not writing this because of that previous benefaction. That is not why I enjoyed *A Second Life* or why I admire the gifts of narration and research Jill Margo brings to it. I read it so enthusiastically in part because Lowy seems to me to be an escapee from some phenomenal novel. Unlike Lear, he is no mad old king. Unlike the Buddenbrooks of Thomas Mann's famous novel, his adaptability and acumen mean that his fortunes, and those of his family, abound rather than decline. He has more appetite for life than any single man can hope to satisfy, and he is not finished trying to do so yet. In his case, as Margo says, drive has not dissipated to create a philosophic old man in an easy chair. But he does assess himself, which makes him very interesting. He is not a man of blunt-force, callow ambitions. There are moments when he looks back gratefully on his long years with Shirley, on his family un-fractured by conflict, and on his significance in the community of Australians. There are also moments when he assesses himself and others more critically. Lowy is a refugee who has shaken life's tree. No branch has been safe. Such achievements, of course, are not accomplished without some grief. But Lowy has been throughout his life extraordinarily gifted at absorbing punishment without being deterred from what can justly be called a spectacular course.

Interestingly, Australians as a whole have found it fairly easy to be sympathetic to Lowy; even those who are not tend to be fascinated by him. From the time he first arrived in Australia and took a job as an ambitious delivery truck driver, he has had a capacity to engage with us. As this book demonstrates, Lowy is self-reflective in a way Australians are not used to seeing in their oligarchs. He has achieved what most rich people cannot in Australia: the regard of the punters. With a few notable exceptions, in Australia wealth tends to go to people without a tradition or onus of endowment, and without a tradition of inner self-assessment and self-judgment.

I commend Jill Margo's book to you as one which deals with the complexity, the enigma, the muscular vision and wisdom of Frank Lowy. I enjoyed it. May you as well!

Tom Keneally

Preface

My previous biography of Frank Lowy, entitled *Pushing the Limits*, was published in 2000. This second biography begins where that one ended. Then, he was approaching his seventieth birthday and was widely expected to retire. As this book shows, he never did.

Frank Lowy is an intensely private man. For the first book he resisted his natural inclination and allowed me to see something of what lay behind his public face. Since nothing bad came of that, for this book he allowed me to see more. I have tried to respect his trust while telling the story of his mature years as fully as I can.

For those who never read the earlier biography, I have summarised it in the initial fifty pages of this book and called it 'The First Life'.

Having now written more than a quarter of a million words on Frank Lowy, I have nothing more to say except to thank him, most sincerely, for the uncountable hours he spent talking to me.

Jill Margo

PART 1

The First Life

The story so far ...

1

Early days

When Hugo Lowy carried his newly born son to the synagogue in October 1930, there was joy in his heart. The Great Depression had drained hope from the world and people were struggling, but in his arms was a perfectly healthy boy. He was the future and as the small congregation of men gathered around for the boy's traditional covenant with God and for his naming, so Hugo blessed his son. As both the boy's grandfathers had died before he was born he received their Hebrew names, Pinchas and Jonah; later in life he would be known simply as Frank.

The Lowy family lived in a little house where their four children shared beds and where water was drawn from a pump in the yard. As the late last child, Frank was well loved and spoiled in the limited ways available at the time. His brother John remembered him as an appealing child, adored by all: "He was the apple of everyone's eye – he was a sensation then and never stopped being a sensation." His sister Edith, however, remembered him less indulgently as a pushy child with a shocking temper, quick to throw a tantrum if it would gain him ground and, more often than not, used to getting his own way.

The family belonged to a closeknit community of some two hundred in Filakovo, a small town in southern Czechoslovakia, now Slovakia. Jews had settled there in the early nineteenth century and were largely accepted by the local folk. While they took part in the town's commercial life and their children went to the local school, they were anchored to their small wooden synagogue where every Sabbath they would meet to pray and talk. The Jewish community saw to its own needs and felt secure.

School would finish early every Friday for young Frank and he would run home to watch as his mother Ilona prepared for the Sabbath, knowing that just after lunch the front door would open and his father would appear, a suitcase in one hand and a business bag in the other. Work as a commercial traveller took Hugo away from his family all week and they keenly anticipated his return. Later, towards evening, Hugo would walk to the synagogue with his sons for the Sabbath service.

In those days many poor Jewish men who were jobless and dependent on charity would move from town to town, hoping for a few coins to send home. On Fridays they would go to the nearest synagogue, praying they would be invited to a Sabbath meal. The Lowys would always take in one or two of these itinerants. After the service they would walk home with other families. It was a peaceful group of men and children that gradually dwindled as people went into their houses.

Through the window of his own home Frank would see the light of the candles and once inside would find his mother and sister with the table prepared for the most important meal of the week. Anticipating the meal and a weekend of rest, Hugo would be in good spirits. He would pick up a child, usually Frank as he was the youngest, and walk around the room chanting the traditional welcome to the Sabbath. There was a celebratory feeling in the house. That there were strangers at the table didn't matter. The family was together again and like every Friday night Frank had ever known, they would draw up around the table to sing and pray before eating.

Frank's family were part Hungarian, part Slovak. Hugo was born Hungarian and having served in the Austro-Hungarian army was considerably more worldly than Ilona, who came from the small Slovakian mountain village of Bystra. Hugo and Ilona were both from large families so there were many cousins. Closest to Frank was his first cousin Eva Haupt, who regularly came to the Lowys' for sleepover visits. Frank and Eva would transform their chores into play and go hand in hand on errands. When he did errands alone Frank would use the family bicycle, but, being so small, he would have to ride under the crossbar. By Edith's account Hugo adored Frank and affectionately called him 'Tata'.

While charming and socially successful, Hugo Lowy did not have great business acumen and was forced more than once to turn to Ilona's family or his older brother Leopold for help. Leopold was the 'rich uncle' in town and although Hugo's children never had a ride in any of his three cars, they visited his grand house once a year.

Before Frank's birth Hugo had opened a drapery shop that failed. When he had contemplated declaring himself bankrupt, his father Jonah refused to consider it. "Pull yourself together," he instructed. "No Lowy will ever go bankrupt!" Hugo had eventually paid all his creditors and kept going, but had lost everything, including their home. Jonah's words would resonate through Frank's childhood.

By the time Frank was born Hugo was working for Leopold as a commercial traveller taking orders for kitchenware. To supplement his income Ilona opened a small grocery shop that sold sugar, bread, flour and other staples, boosted by a limited liquor licence. The family lived behind the shop and the children were always in and out, serving customers or helping themselves to sweets from large glass jars. Typically, the family would be having lunch when they would hear the bells tied to the door that signalled someone was entering. Frank would jump up, attend to the customer and grab a mouthful of lollies on his way back to the table. Although the shop did reasonable trade, financial strains on the family were not helped by Hugo's passion for cards. Too often he played with people who were better off, and frequently he lost.

After school every afternoon the Lowy boys had to attend religious instruction. They had to go on Sundays too; for a devout family this was mandatory. The boys were instructed in German and at home they spoke Hungarian or Slovakian while at synagogue they prayed in Hebrew.

Their days were so full that there was little time to stray. Occasionally, however, if Frank was extremely fortunate, Hugo would take him to a soccer match. Hugo was a soccer enthusiast and had to do some fast talking to extract young Frank from his Sunday classes. Their town's soccer team was famous for its prowess in the district and watching a game was a treat beyond words. Holding hands, father and son would walk through paddocks to the makeshift field with its rickety stand. During the week, when Frank and his friends had a few moments, they would make a rag ball from their socks and relive the game.

Life in Europe, as elsewhere in the 1930s, was grim. The Depression had left a legacy of low morale and a fear of the future that fostered fervent nationalism. While anti-Semitism was entrenched in Germany and Poland, Czechoslovakia had remained fairly benign towards its minorities, including the Jews. But by the time Frank was at school the outlook for Jewish families was growing more uncertain. Fear spread through European Jewry when hundreds of synagogues, Jewish shops and homes were destroyed in November 1938 during the infamous *Kristallnacht* or 'Night of Broken Glass' in Germany and Austria.

The division of Czechoslovakia that same year had dark consequences for the Lowys, who found themselves living in Hungary while much of their extended family was across the border in Slovakia. Long summer holidays with their cousins became a thing of the past. Jews were deprived of opportunities to work and could no longer own businesses or property. Ilona was forced to take a Gentile partner in her grocery shop. Jews could no longer keep their heads down, mind their own affairs and get on with life. In a small town they were easily identified. Frank and his friends were harassed on the way to and from school. "You knew you were a Jew and that people didn't like you. It was humiliating," Frank recalled. But though he was afraid, he would never show it.

Hugo lost his job and the family house was at risk of being repossessed. Young Frank listened closely to the discussion. He shared the family's distress about the house and then its overwhelming relief when Ilona's family came to the rescue once again. The memory of that unquestioning family support remained with him. "That image of family unity is imprinted in my mind. My mother's family provided support to each other not just with money, but in all ways, emotionally, morally, whatever. They were continually in contact, writing to each other, weekly and sometimes more often, and any problem for one was a problem for them all."

In 1942 the Lowys received terrifying news. As part of a general roundup of Jews in Slovakia, members of Ilona's family were being taken away. After a correspondence describing fearful deportations, in April Ilona opened a heartbreaking letter from her brother Géza Grunfeld. He was in despair about the plight of the children: "I would very much like to ask you if you could take our dear children to be with you. Although I know you are not in an easy situation, one only pities the little ones, we can manage somehow. We could arrange to get them to [word deleted by censors] and you could come and meet them there, if we are still here at that time." Without a moment's delay Hugo and Ilona despatched an envoy to collect the children.

It was too late. Four families, each with three or four children, had been deported and almost no information was available. Distraught, Ilona spent much of her time crying and praying. Sadness pervaded the house, with each child feeling the immense loss and becoming increasingly aware of the precariousness of their own existence.

Fear was spreading through their already nervous community. Surrounded by threatening events, they felt the world closing in on their small town and their possibilities for escape diminishing. The Nazis were on the rampage in Europe, Poland had fallen and Jews were being deported from nearby Slovakia. How long would the Filakovo Jews be safe?

On the Day of Atonement the community crowded into the synagogue. Pious and deeply fearful, they had come to plead for ultimate deliverance. It is customary on this High Holiday for

Jews to ask God to pardon their sins and not forsake them. Now the synagogue resonated with their impassioned pleas. During part of the service men cover their heads with prayer shawls and turn inwards. Eleven-year-old Frank was standing next to his father when Hugo drew him in under his shawl and held him tight. Close against his father, through the white shawl Frank could hear the rabbi begin chanting, "Who shall live and who shall die ... who shall perish by fire and who by water ..." Frank felt his father trembling. The chant was about their own situation and by the end of it Hugo was beside himself, sobbing and squeezing his son's hand. What would become of them?

After that, Hugo decided his family was too exposed in the countryside. It was time to move to bustling Budapest, where they could disappear into the crowd.

2

To Budapest

Budapest offered a rare haven. Although there were restrictions on Jews, the Lowys settled into a good apartment, Hugo found work as a commercial traveller and for more than a year the family thrived. Frank saw his parents fall in love again, walk hand in hand in the park and pick the best apples in the market. In Filakovo all their energy had gone into surviving. Now they were going to the theatre.

Frank went to a Jewish day school where the boys were passionate about the MTK football team. Within days he too was a devoted fan. He travelled to school by crowded tram, schoolbag on his back, hanging onto the railing with one hand. On Sundays he went to soccer matches and on Mondays he and his friends pored over the sports coverage in the newspapers. More enthusiastic about sport than classwork, he rated his schoolroom performance as 'average'. His teacher would have been less kind.

Meanwhile, he began supplementing his own pocket money with an entrepreneurial venture not uncommon in the war years. Movies were very popular and tickets for weekend shows were much prized. Early in the week Frank would buy a batch of tickets and sell them at a profit on the following Saturday. If the movie was not a hit, he was left with unsold tickets, but mostly his activities were profitable.

Staying with the family was a young religious relative from Slovakia who coached Frank for his bar mitzvah. This traditionally happy event marks a boy's entry into adulthood but by October 1943 no one could muster the requisite joy. Frank's oldest brother Alex was missing, having been drafted as a slave labourer for the Hungarian army. The family worried about his safety. It was increasingly difficult to block out persecution and the reality of loss continually broke through. There were refugees everywhere, and uncertainty was in the air. A mood of sadness engulfed the Jewish community.

As newcomers to Budapest the Lowys did not have friends and family to share Frank's coming of age. Under normal circumstances an impressive contingent of Ilona's brothers and sisters and their families would have made the journey. But they had all been deported, never to be seen again. Frank's Uncle Leopold did come from Filakovo and bought Frank his first wristwatch. Afterwards the family invited their few guests to lunch at their apartment, where Frank gave a speech. A great sorrow hung over them all.

Whatever fragile equilibrium the Lowy family had found was blown apart on Sunday 19 March 1944. Ilona and Hugo had been to a theatre matinee. They returned in high spirits, only to be silenced by the chilling news that Germany had invaded Hungary. Until then Hungary had been an ally; now it was to be occupied. As well as soldiers, a commando unit of German secret police had arrived in Budapest. Headed by Adolf Eichmann, the unit's sole objective was the liquidation of the Hungarian Jews.

Frank recalled the fear in his parents' faces, their anxiety and the premonition of tragedy. Watching them he felt a knot of tension tightening in his stomach. All night the adults talked. Their haven was no longer secure; once again it was imperative to move to a safer place. By daybreak they were resolved. Hugo would go to the main station and buy train tickets to take the family to Veszprém, about 120 kilometres away, where they had relatives.

Every day of Hugo's life began with prayers. He would bind his tefillin[1] to his forehead and right arm, wrap himself in his tallit[2] and turn inwards. This private ritual would provide daily reassurance that he was not alone. There was God. On this morning he prayed with everything in him, trembling before God, asking for help in keeping his family safe. He closed his prayer book and composed himself, then he kissed his wife and family and left for the station.

The apartment was quiet. Everybody waited. At lunchtime Hugo's place at the table remained empty. In the sitting room there was a couch beneath the window. Frank spent the afternoon standing on it, looking out to the street, certain that at any moment he would see his father. That night someone came to tell them there had been a roundup of Jews at the station. Details were scant. Had Hugo been taken? Had he escaped? Nobody knew.

Frank remained at his post by the window as the rest of the family used their limited circle to search for information and

---

1   Hebrew phylacteries, boxes containing prayers which are bound by leather thongs to the head and arm during morning prayer on weekdays.
2   A large fringed prayer shawl.

for any sign that Hugo had survived. Being relatively new to Budapest, they knew few people and no one in authority. Days passed. Some nights later there was a loud knock. Filling the doorframe was a burly, bearded Hungarian. In his pocket he had a letter. Hugo was alive! He was being held at Kistarcsa, a concentration camp for political prisoners about twenty kilometres outside Budapest.

In the letter Hugo expressed his pain at the separation and his deep desire to embrace his family again. He asked for Ilona to send him some personal items. What he most wanted was his prayer bag, which contained his tallit and tefillin. These religious articles were part of him and to have them in the camp would be a great comfort. The Hungarian man agreed to carry them to him, and did. Indeed, he agreed to become a go-between and for about three weeks, he ferried food and letters between Hugo and the family.

The letters were full of love, affection and anxiety, describing their hopes of being together again. Although trapped, Hugo wrote with practical advice to each child, expressing his affection and offering encouragement. Then at the end of April, the Hungarian man delivered another letter. Hugo believed he would be coming home and asked for a suitcase. Then he changed his mind: he would wrap his things in paper.

The family never heard from him again. It was to be nearly fifty years before Frank learned what had happened to his father.

Lost without Hugo, the family took advice from a relative who said it would be safest if they obtained false papers and split up. As there were no papers for Frank, he and Ilona had no option but to go with 220,000 other Jews into one of the Yellow Star houses, so named for the stars marked on each front door. These houses, designated for Jews, were in various parts of Budapest and sometimes twenty people were crammed into a single home. Mother and son went into a house in the old Jewish quarter, the area that would later be walled off as the ghetto. When life there became unbearable they left and went into hiding. But hiding brought new hazards and fear of discovery made them both extremely nervous. They could find no peace and so returned to the Yellow Star house, where conditions had become more desperate.

During those terrifying months mother and son grew close, relying on each other for survival. Ilona nourished Frank on love while his resourcefulness kept them alive. He slipped through the streets, foraging for food and intelligence. With menace around every corner he quickly learned the value of vigilance and developed a heightened aptitude for observation and listening. He said:

> Once father was taken away my childhood ended. I was
> never a child again. In a sense I became more like a father
> to my mother. My days were spent scheming about how
> to live, eat and survive. I was always listening to what
> was said to make sure we could survive. I don't remember
> having any friends. There was continuous bad news and
> fear. My brother John risked his life to bring us food, we
> all risked our lives for each other. We worried about my
> father and brother Alex, hoping they were alive. The joys of
> those days consisted of meeting each other and obtaining
> food.

Those months shaped the man Frank would become. Rather than melting his resolve, the furnace of hardship forged him into steel.

In October 1944 their already precarious situation deteriorated further with a change to a Nazi-backed government. The ruling Arrow Cross Party (Nyilas) marked its accession to power by executing several hundred Jews. Arrow Cross youths would remove Jews from their homes, torture them and then shoot them so they fell into the Danube from the bridges. One of their favoured methods was to tie three Jews together, shoot one and then watch as the dead weight unbalanced the trio and caused them to topple into the icy water. Some 20,000 Jews were shot on the banks of the Danube.

Such events prompted the neutral diplomats in Budapest, representing countries such as Sweden and Switzerland, to make strenuous efforts to protect Jews by providing *Schutzpässe* (protective documents) that enabled the holders to live in embassies, consulates or their annexes under their diplomatic protection. The largest of these buildings, the Glass House at 29 Vadasz Street, was protected by the Swiss government and housed several thousand Jews.

Frank, the assiduous young news-gatherer, learned that Swiss papers were becoming available. He visited the Glass House and saw queues of impatient applicants winding around the block. Waiting in a queue was dangerous because the Germans could arrive at any moment and round everyone up. How could he avoid this and get inside? He watched from a distance and devised a plan: using the few coins in his pocket, he went to a theatrical outfitter and hired the uniform of a telegraph boy. Then, masquerading as a messenger with an urgent delivery, he went to the head of the queue. He had two photographs in his pocket and the passes were duly issued.

An hour later he and his mother were on their way to a protected house close to the shores of the Danube. These protected houses were extremely crowded with people, who were hungry and anxious. With two resourceful sons to find food, Ilona felt blessed. Whatever Frank or John secured, she would share with others in their apartment. Frank would protest: "Please mother, save some for tomorrow, we don't know if there will be more." But Ilona ignored his requests. To her, not sharing was inconceivable.

From mid-November all Jews in Budapest were forced into the ghetto except those in the protected houses. But these were no longer safe either. Under cover of night, the Nyilas entered the houses, dragged the terrified inhabitants to the river bank, lined them up and shot them into the water. Frank and Ilona shared a bed and lay in silence, listening to the shots and wondering if and when their turn would come.

As rumours of the Russian army's approach grew stronger, the Nyilas increased their violence. Plundering of the protected houses became routine and systematic. If mother and son stayed where they were the Nyilas would reach their block. They had nowhere else to go. "We were in about the fifteenth block along and as they were getting closer we knew it was only a matter of days before the Russians would arrive. But who would get to us first?" said Frank.

In the winter of early 1945, the Russians liberated the city, and the Lowy family began looking for Hugo. They searched everywhere, questioning survivors and scouring lists posted by the Red Cross. Every day they woke hopeful of news. Someone said they had heard Hugo was taken to Auschwitz, but there was no confirmation. During this time Alex limped home, having walked five hundred kilometres from Mauthausen concentration camp near Linz in Austria. No one recognised the young man, who was skin and bones and suffering from typhus. When they did, they carried him gently inside, closed around him and wept. When they lifted him into the bath, Ilona said there was so much dirt on his back she could have grown wheat in it. As he slowly recovered the family continued as one to look for Hugo.

But hope ran out. Budapest was a ruin and with heavy hearts they turned for their old home. The Lowys were among the few Jews to return to Filakovo, only to discover that their former community had all but perished and they were no longer welcome.

3

To Palestine

When Frank looked around Filakovo, he knew there was nothing there for him. Memories were terrible and he felt enormous inner pressure to leave. John had made the decision to go to Palestine, and went quickly. The Jewish Agency had sent emissaries to collect strays and displaced persons and move them clandestinely to Palestine. Now Frank wanted to go too.

> I had missed so many years at school, I was not motivated
> to catch up and I had no desire to create roots in Europe.
> Joining the group to go to Palestine was like going to a
> school camp. This offered a new beginning, a new country,
> a new identity, a chance to be part of the Jewish drive to
> create a homeland. I felt I was leaving a place to which I
> did not belong for a much brighter future.

In 1946, Ilona gave her youngest son her blessing to go. Their pain at parting was lessened only by the plan that the rest of the family would follow.

Guided by the Jewish Agency (which had been formed in 1929 to represent the Jewish community in Palestine), Frank boarded an illegal ship in Marseille bound for his new home. The *Jagur* was built for sixty passengers but was loaded with more than six hundred refugees from all over Europe, speaking many languages. Conditions were awful, the ten-day trip interminable. Fifteen-year-old Frank was seasick, desperately lonely and longing for his mother. Then, one evening the lights on the beautiful hills of Haifa came into view. Spontaneously everyone on deck burst into 'Hatikvah', the Jewish anthem of hope.

Suddenly, out of nowhere, searchlights swept their boat and men with loud hailers shouted, "Stop! Stop!" At gunpoint, the refugees were pushed into the hull of a British troopship. A few days later Frank found himself a prisoner in a British intern camp on Cyprus.

> Among us in the camp were people from the Haganah [an elite underground Jewish defence force] who took charge, organising Hebrew lessons, keeping us physically fit and generally keeping our morale high. We didn't know it at the time, but they were grooming us so we would be strong and confident enough to play an active role when we finally were admitted to Palestine. Under the quota system they let the youngsters into Palestine first. Three months later I was among the first to be taken there by ship.

In Palestine, people were waiting at the dock to welcome them. Someone was even there specifically for Frank. A young man from Filakovo had heard Frank had been detained in Cyprus. When he learned the first boatload of children was due, he went to meet it on the off chance. His was the first familiar face Frank had seen in months and the man even had recent news from home.

For the first time in many years Frank could drop his guard. He would work in the fields in the mornings, go to school in the afternoons and spend the evenings singing and dancing with other boys and girls who had found their way from Europe. As the months rolled by the accumulated tension of the past slowly unwound. He was known as Pinchas Levy, and no one was hunting him any more. And he had freedoms. To escape the heat in the fields he would lie under the shade of a grapefruit tree, reach up and pick a piece of fruit.

Frank was in a group of refugee youngsters housed on the moshav Sede Ya'aqov, a co-operative agricultural settlement near Haifa. The Jewish Agency saw to their needs and in keeping with the general style of dress in the country every boy was issued with blue clothes for work, khakis for the rest of the day and a white Russian folk shirt for best. Frank used his afternoon lessons to make up ground in his education. Some of the boys perceived him as worldly. While they had been confined in concentration camps, he had been living on the streets; in some ways his war experiences had been easier than theirs. He had also learned to take risks.

By the summer of 1947 Frank was restless and eager to explore possibilities beyond the moshav. While he loved the community of friends and it was tempting to stay, he wanted to chart his own course. At the age of sixteen he left the settlement. As he owned nothing, the first place he visited was the Haifa labour exchange. There he got day work as a labourer and eventually secured a position as an apprentice plumber. On his meagre wage it was difficult to find accommodation but his boss happened to be working on a building that was nearing completion and arranged for Frank to live on the ground floor. Although the walls were bare and the windows unfinished, Frank made a small corner habitable. To secure privacy and to protect himself from the elements he boarded up the windows with planks, bought a mattress and a small oil lamp and camped there for a few months. At night he would reluctantly go into the little room and lie quietly in the dark, feeling empty. When the building was completed and power installed he remained and augmented his daily earnings by working as the janitor and cleaner. But isolation was beginning to overwhelm him.

He and his friends had arrived at a crucial point in the history of British-mandated Palestine. By 1947, exhausted and depleted by World War II, Britain handed the vexed problem of Palestine to the United Nations. In November that year the UN voted in favour of the partition of Palestine, dividing it into Arab and Jewish states with Jerusalem under international trusteeship. While the Jewish population celebrated, the Arab population declared the decision a tragedy, rejected it and announced its intention of driving the Jews into the sea. Civil war between Jews and Arabs began immediately.

For the youngsters, there was no question about joining up. While on the moshav, they had given a day a month to the Haganah; now they travelled to Tel Aviv, hoping to join fulltime. At the recruitment station they were assigned to a battalion operating in the Galilee and given makeshift uniforms. These included Australian shoes, US army jackets and hats that announced on the rim, in Yiddish, that they were "a gift from an American hat maker". They were told to buy khaki shirts in the market and report to a settlement near Tiberias. Being enlisted filled them with pride. "We got to a checkpoint and the British waved us through. They saw our uniforms and accepted we were in some kind of army unit," recalled Frank.

The battalion was quickly involved in skirmishes and during one exchange of fire Frank was wounded in the head with shrapnel. He was not expected to live but woke in hospital. After some days he rejoined his unit with a bandaged head.

Since he had left Europe, his mother had written to him every week and as regularly as he could he wrote back, never letting her know of the dangers he faced. Her letters were full of love and, at times, regret at letting him fall into such hazardous uncertainty. "My darling beloved Feri," she wrote in one letter, "sometimes I am so disconsolate that I let you leave, even if you don't say so Feri, I know that you have a very hard life and I, here, miss you terribly. We ought to have stayed together ... the time will come when I can hug you close to my heart and never again leave you." She begged him to disclose what he was doing. He could never have told her.

When David Ben-Gurion proclaimed independence for the new state of Israel in May 1948, Frank and his friends were in the trenches listening over a crackling radio. Being on the front and engaged in battle, they didn't feel celebratory. Neither did Ben-Gurion. He wrote in his diary that he had arrived in Jerusalem that day to find the city rejoicing but he knew what was to come – "war with all of the Arab armies". Indeed, within hours of his announcement Israel was under attack by five armies.

The Syrian army began to bombard the local kibbutzim around the Sea of Galilee. This was the territory of the recently formed Golani Brigade and after heavy losses it repulsed the invaders. During an uneasy truce that followed, Rafi Kocer, a twenty-four-year-old army officer, began looking to recruit tough and courageous youngsters to form a commando unit within the Golani. He had heard about a group of refugee boys, including Frank, with a reputation as able fighters, and he planned to take them from their regular unit.

Secretly he sent his deputy to put a plan to the young men. If they were willing to volunteer, they would have to leave their own unit in secret in the middle of the night. If caught they would be punished for leaving without permission from their commanding officer. This test would show whether they were brave enough to join a commando unit. Frank and his friends were keen. As arranged, they left their weapons behind and successfully slipped away at midnight.

Euphoric and proud at having made it, they signed an oath to join Unit 12 in the Barak battalion of the Golani Brigade. Kocer informed their previous commander that they were now under his command. The boys were issued with caps worn by British paratroopers and German guns and were immediately put to training. Their job would be to operate at night behind enemy lines. To the others these silent, strange European boys didn't match their reputation as fearless fighters. Kocer, however, knew their motivation. "In some way I think they were avenging the Holocaust and empowering themselves. They were willing to do anything, to endure any hardship," he later said.

In the early stages the youths acted as a group, but over time their officers realised that the group had a quiet leader: Frank. Because he spoke better Hebrew than the others, initially all communication was through him. Later, Kocer would say that even in times of extreme stress, when some of the boys broke down, Frank never did.

At the beginning he was young, uncertain and mistrusting of the world around him but during the war he seemed to discover a new strength in himself. He learned real trust. One of the most important things for all of us was that we were 100 per cent sure we would each do the utmost to save each other. It was a formative period for all the boys, it made them believe in themselves and in others.

Without this period in his life I believe Frank would not have done later what he was able to do. This experience helped to build the assertiveness of his character. On the battlefield you are with friends, but you have to be self-reliant. You have to keep pace with your group but still survive in your own way, making decisions on the spur of the moment and doing your best to succeed. Frank did this. He built himself and emerged from the war much tougher emotionally.

In the six months between July and December 1948 the unit had been involved in seventy-three combat missions, many behind enemy lines. When their work was done in the north, they had been deployed south and began to operate in Gaza and the Negev. It was in one of these battles that Kocer was so badly injured that his unit had to be disbanded in March 1949.

Frank found himself transferred to train in Morse code and radio. During this course he made his first conscious assessment of himself. "I was picking up the material quickly and it occurred to me that I might have an aptitude for it. This was the first time I recognised that I was a fast learner." A few months later, in 1949, after running communications for a Druse unit loyal to the Israelis, Frank was discharged. He quietly wondered why he had never attained rank. One reason may have been that young refugee boys joined units with home-grown fighters who were older and more seasoned; by the time the new recruits began to excel, their unit was disbanded.

On resuming civilian life, Frank had to find work. Fortunately his communications training helped him secure a job in the post office, sending telegrams in Morse code. Although such jobs were highly coveted, Frank regarded this as a dead-end position and simultaneously enrolled in night school to study accountancy. He was living with his brother John in Haifa and when he mentioned he would like a position in a bank, John laughed out loud: "Who could ever get a bank job?" A few weeks later Frank took a lower-paid but promising position with Bank Leumi.

He was coming of age and enjoying his life in Haifa: "There was a great vibrancy to the place. We more or less lived in the streets, going to the movies, soccer games and singing evenings. There was always something happening. And importantly, we felt optimistic. We were building a new state." Although he thought of Ilona daily, he understood that he could survive without her. Israel served as a motherland:

These were six impressionable years, from fifteen to twenty-one. They opened me up and showed me new ways of being. The sabras [Israeli-born Jews] were free and daring and couldn't understand why we were so quiet and withdrawn. Over time, through exposure to them and through our own growing confidence, we thawed and became infected with their spirit. These years were my introduction into a Western way of thinking. Now, when I think of 'home' before coming to Australia, I think of Israel.

Over these years, however, conditions for the rest of the Lowy family changed and rather than migrate to Israel, they sailed for Australia. Frank and John felt torn. Should they stay and build the young state or go to their family and heal the separation?

4

Early days in Australia

On a clear summer day in January 1952 Frank and John Lowy saw their mother and their brother Alex standing inside the terminal at Sydney's airport. When they had parted, Frank had been a slight boy of fifteen; now a strong young man of twenty-one was hugging Ilona. Back in her tiny living room on a main road in the city's eastern suburbs, Frank looked from face to face and as he did, something inside relaxed. "I had a sense of belonging. I hadn't realised how alone I felt in the world. Now, suddenly I had a mother, brothers and a sister. I had a home." But amid their joy at being reunited, the Lowy family felt the ache of Hugo's absence. They still did not know what had happened to him.

The brothers had to find work quickly to repay the money they had borrowed for their airfares. Frank's first job was in a toolmaking factory, a dank and depressing basement. He watched the clock and dreamed of a job above ground. He answered an ad in the Jewish newspaper for a sandwich hand in a city arcade; his application was written by Alex's wife, Liesel. "It was like coming up into a new world, full of life with lots of attractive girls wanting sandwiches – which I was always very happy to make." The shop was co-run by the Jacoby family, whom Frank observed closely. They were a close, intact family, and replicating what they had became his ideal. Their son happened to be captain of the Jewish soccer team Hakoah, which meant Frank was at the next match.

Life in the new country was opening before him. That year, at a party to celebrate Chanukah, the Jewish festival of lights, he looked across the garden and was captivated by a very pretty blonde girl. She ignored him. Shirley Rusanow, then aged eighteen, felt his eyes on her and remembers thinking, "Gee, you're gorgeous!" The chemistry must have been strong because the next day she told a friend that Frank was the boy she would marry. Shirley had been born in Sydney in 1934, so she was four years younger than Frank. Her mother Golda (née Pynt) was from London and her father Jacob Rusanow had come from Poland. The Rusanows worked hard at their tailoring business to educate their three children, Shirley, Allan and Leonie, but the money could not stretch to sending Shirley to university so she went to work.

A short time later, Shirley and Frank met, and Shirley was smitten. Her mother tried to steer her towards a better match, describing Frank as a poor immigrant boy. "What's he ever going to amount to?" she asked. But Frank was unlike anyone Shirley had met. "He had a little extra quality. He knew where he was going, he wanted better than he had and he certainly wasn't going to be a sandwich hand for the rest of his life. He could speak four or five languages and he liked going to concerts and films. He loved music."

On 7 March 1954 Frank and Shirley married and set up home in a minuscule apartment in Kings Cross. By now Frank had risen in the world and was a delivery truck driver for a smallgoods manufacturer.

> I supplied about forty shops. I had a big bag of coins and every morning I would rise early and call them first thing from a public phone to get their orders. I'd have finished deliveries by noon, then I'd check and see if they needed more and would do an afternoon run. The trick was being first and getting the big order. I used to drive very fast, and whenever I had the chance, at red lights and intersections, I would write out orders and invoices on a clipboard wedged next to the steering wheel.

When they married, Frank's wages were £9 a week plus 2 per cent commission, but such was his drive to succeed that he never brought home less than £100. His determination to save for his own business meant they lived frugally. Shirley, who was soon pregnant, had two dresses: one for home and one for going out. On New Year's Eve 1954, just before the year turned, David was born. The apartment's balcony was transformed into the nursery. It could hold a cot, but not much more.

Frank's delivery round brought him into contact with John Saunders, a Hungarian Jew eight years his senior who was running a hole-in-the-wall delicatessen at Town Hall railway station. Saunders and his wife Eta, both Holocaust survivors, had arrived in Sydney in 1950 with nothing. Saunders, who worked on instinct, could feel Frank's potential and liked him.

"I had many salesmen coming into my shop. Most tended to overcharge and were late," he said. "But Frank was different. His invoices were always correct on weight and price and he was always on time. No doubt he had problems, but I never knew of them."

Theirs was a life-changing contact. Certain that Frank would make a good partner, Saunders raised the possibility of their going into business together. Frank said he would think about it and a couple of days later returned, having formulated two conditions. They would have to be equal partners and their wives would not be involved in the business at all. There was something about Frank's firmness and determination that appealed to John. He accepted.

Their first venture was a delicatessen in Blacktown, thirty-five kilometres west of Sydney. It was brand new territory for them both but the area was teeming with new migrants who had European tastes they knew they could satisfy. Initially Frank deferred to John's experience, but then they hit their first legal issue. "He surprised me when we received the lease documents and started to negotiate the terms with the lawyer," said John. "He had never seen a lease document before, yet he knew instinctively what needed to be changed to get us a better deal. Then, because of his accounting background, he started looking after the finances."

Frank the diligent saver had cobbled together £5000, which he put into the business as initial capital. In 1955, having been in Australia for three and a half years, he put on a white apron and stood behind the counter in his own business. The Blacktown delicatessen was open and ready to welcome the first customers. At the time Australians ate white bread, milk bars sold milkshakes, and a cup of real coffee was hard to find. Whenever a train carrying homecoming workers arrived in Blacktown station, the shop would fill with people wanting salami, rye, olives, salted herrings and pickled cucumbers. While Anglo Australians would buy sixpence worth of devon sausage and a shilling's worth of ham, the 'new Australians' bought salami by the yard.

Frank and John were in their element. They shared a utility and whoever had it for the week picked up the other. Together they would travel to Leichhardt to collect goods and then go on to the Riga Bakery in Hurstville, often arriving so early that the bread was too hot to handle. Wearing gloves, John would throw the loaves to Frank, who would pack them into the utility. By this time they were in an upbeat mood and with their delicious load of fresh food they would sing all the way to Blacktown – Hungarian songs, Jewish folk tunes, whatever came into their heads. When they arrived at about 7.30 am, people would be waiting outside the shop. Their deli became a focal point, with people travelling long distances to buy real European fare. When John and Frank drove home with good takings for the day, they would really sing. This early co-operation marked the start of an association that grew into a remarkable business partnership of thirty years. While their camaraderie was inevitably mixed with a degree of productive tension, they never went home arguing. They always smoothed things over first.

Within a year the pair had recreated another bit of Europe next door to their deli in the form of a coffee lounge with chairs on the pavement, music and real espresso. People flocked. Migrants were pouring into the area, which was already experiencing a critical housing shortage. Then, realising there was money to be made from the mini land boom in the area, Frank and John began buying and subdividing local farmland for housing. Their business was growing so fast that their solicitor, Leslie Winter, suggested they convert from a partnership to a private company.

Winter was impressed by Frank's quick understanding of legal issues. "When I first knew Frank he was a beginner in the commercial field but in no time at all he could master the most complicated legal documents. I always had the highest regard for his intelligence. He made a good impression on the people he was dealing with because he looked honest, he was honest and was always neatly and nicely dressed. He has inborn manners, manners you can't get at Eton or Harvard. He has natural charm that attracts people."

5

Westfield is born

Lowy and Saunders took Winter's advice. But what should they call their new company? One Saturday afternoon while driving home they were throwing names around and hit on Westfield. As they were doing business in the western suburbs, the word 'west' was a natural choice, and as they were subdividing farming land, 'field' seemed appropriate. It felt right, and Westfield Investments Pty Ltd was born.

Around this time, something happened in Blacktown that made them change direction. Another Hungarian émigré bought land near their deli and instead of putting up houses, he built a row of shops. "We can do that too!" said Frank, and in no time they had built and sold their own row of shops around the corner from their deli.

By 1958 John and Frank were ready to take off their aprons and leave the delicatessen business for property development.

The deli was sold for £20,000 and they bought a large piece of land around the corner. Rather than building a predictable strip of shops they created a retail centre, a mini version of the malls that had begun to enjoy success in the United States.

Westfield Place had twelve shops, a small department store and a small supermarket and it was built around an open square. It was not the first mall in Australia: the first one, Chermside drive-in shopping centre, had opened in Brisbane in 1957. Next had come Top Ryde shopping centre in Sydney. Then came Westfield Place. It opened in August 1959 and was an instant hit.

Things were really looking up. Earlier that year Shirley had given birth to their second son, Peter, and Frank had bought a piece of land in prosperous Rose Bay for £4500. On it, he was building a £20,000 house as the first home of their own. This was an enormous leap and now he wanted to stretch the business, too, by moving it into the central business district. John resisted. Blacktown was their golden goose; why move? Frank prevailed and in 1959 they moved. No sooner had they arrived than he was ready for the next bold step, and began urging John to take Westfield public. As this would bring a swathe of regulatory issues, John resisted. He didn't need the headache! But they did need to raise funds for a new centre they were building at Hornsby on Sydney's northern outskirts, and he was persuaded. In 1960 the Westfield Development Corporation Ltd was floated on the Sydney stock exchange.

John also began looking for new ventures. He devoured books on business, architecture and engineering to help him identify opportunities. With his penchant for the legal and financial aspects of business, Frank would assess these opportunities. The two complemented each other perfectly.

When a small supermarket chain that had leased a space in the Hornsby shopping centre was taken over by Coles, an opportunity flashed before the partners' eyes. Coles, a major variety store, was moving into supermarkets! This was their chance. They approached Coles and soon had their first commission for a supermarket. Then they were introduced to Sir Edgar Coles, who was in an extremely expansionary mode. Driving around Sydney in a chauffeur-driven car, Sir Edgar would sit in the front seat, point through the window and say, "Get me a site here, and get me one there." And they did. "It was music to our ears," said Frank. They closed deal after deal.

With a harmonious household, Frank had the family he had always yearned for. That Shirley loved his mother was a great blessing. But Ilona was ill and in 1962 she died, holding Shirley's hand. She was sixty-two. It was a time of immense sorrow, intensified by the sadness that had pervaded Ilona's life. "She had lost the will to live," said Shirley. "She would sit in our house and stare out of the window and think of her late husband, brothers and sisters." Frank too ached with loss as the memories of the times they had shared flooded back. He remembered his mother's spirit as a young woman, with her family intact and her husband by her side, and how that too had died during the Holocaust.

When Frank and his family buried Ilona, they buried an era. Her headstone was engraved with a moving testimony to her five brothers and sisters and their children who had all been lost, and it serves as their sole memorial. Frank struggled with the loss but the cycle of life turned and joy returned to the family with the birth of Steven that November.

With business humming in New South Wales, Frank and John turned their minds to other states in Australia. First in their sights was Queensland, then Victoria followed. From the mid 1960s to the mid 1970s the company opened a shopping centre a year, with Frank and John putting in twelve to sixteen hours a day. Their attention to detail was legendary. Frank read every word of every document and sought advice until he was completely satisfied with its meaning. He also continued to monitor the cash flow, with him and John signing all cheques relating to their part of the business.

But there were tensions between the partners. John's habit was to arrive at the office around ten in the morning. He would come in, plonk himself down opposite Frank, call for a coffee and settle in for a chat. Often he brought in snippets torn out from the newspaper and wanted to discuss new ideas. Frank would be quietly fuming inside; he wanted to get on with work, not become involved in a rambling discussion. To overcome this predictable daily irritation he would get into their shared office at 7.30 am, so that he could clear his desk and do the essentials before John arrived. But at the end of the day there was more potential conflict. John was not ready to leave until eight in the evening, whereas Frank preferred to be home in time to have dinner with his family by seven. Being together was extremely important to the Lowy family but was of less interest to John: his wife worked and at the time they had no children. He had no hesitation in trying to hold Frank back in the evenings or ringing him later at home. He would call freely at night or on the weekends. This intrusion was a source of irritation to Shirley, compounded by the fact that the two men spoke in Hungarian. The closeness of their business partnership could easily leave a wife feeling excluded.

When Sydney's town planners decided to enhance the city by transforming William Street between the city and Kings Cross into a local Champs-Élysées, Frank and John wanted to be part of it. They bought a site in William Street and began building to the vision. But recession set in, the city changed its mind and their building was left as the only commercial high-rise building between the Cross and the city. In 1974 the company moved into the new Westfield Towers, which remained the headquarters for almost forty years.

By 1976 the partners were restless. Australia was getting too small and America beckoned. Taking Australian shopping centres into the home of the mall would require chutzpah, which they had in full measure, and patience, which they would find.

While chatting to a stranger in an airline queue in Las Vegas, the ever-personable John stumbled on an opportunity. Trumbull, a centre in Connecticut, would soon be up for sale. It was perfect for Westfield's 'toe in the water' approach, and they bought it. Frank's eldest son, David, who had just graduated with a commerce degree from the University of New South Wales, was recruited to work there. In reality, David had been with Westfield since boyhood, having spent hours strolling through the centres with John, absorbing the older man's talent for the business. As John loved Frank, so he loved David.

To keep the US business under close scrutiny Frank spent six months of the first year in the United States. He had little difficulty in adjusting. "When I went to the office in Connecticut it was like going to the office in Australia," he said. "I took to the US scene like a duck to water." Out of necessity he began making independent decisions and started to feel a new freedom. Neither he nor John realised this move would be a point of separation in their close partnership. When back in Australia Frank would ring the US constantly and visit regularly.

Several months after purchasing Trumbull, Frank and David spent a rainy afternoon in Connecticut, driving out to explore the area. They stumbled on Connecticut Post, an open shopping centre that was rundown and full of potential. They bought it, hired Richard Green, an expert in the US mall business, and then bought another centre in Los Angeles. The US business was on its way.

By 1979 Westfield had a sizeable portfolio of shopping centres but was laden with debt. The value of the properties was growing faster than its cash flow, which meant it had to keep borrowing against the assets.

Frank wrestled with the problem of how to unlock the value. A while before, Lend Lease had created an independent trust called GPT, and this gave him an idea. He would modify the Lend Lease model and rather than creating an independent vehicle, he would create a trust to own the assets, which Westfield would still control. This could multiply shareholders' money many times and set the company up for further growth.

With a small team of five Frank led this $80 million restructure. For an equivalent exercise today, ranks of investment bankers, accountants and tax experts would be necessary. The small Lowy team hit a few speed bumps but eventually achieved its aim. The Westfield Trust was born, clearing the way for growth and increasing shareholder wealth eightfold.

6

The separation

During a visit to the US in 1984, Frank and David had just returned to their suite at the Pierre Hotel in New York when the phone rang. Down the line came John's unmistakable greeting, followed by words Frank had never thought he would hear: "I want to sell." Although thrilled at the prospect of being independent and autonomous, Frank was less thrilled later when he discovered John had been planning the separation for a couple of years.

With Peter Lowy already in the business and the strong likelihood of Steven joining in the future, John had been concerned about being squeezed out. Westfield's shares were trading at $5.20 and he wanted Frank to buy him out for $8 a share. The risk was enormous, but Frank said, "There are some opportunities in life that are so momentous that you almost have to leap first and deal with them later."

John left Westfield with major assets that grew substantially over time, and which later became the basis of his wealth. But some months after he sold his shares he was furious when Westfield had a bonus share issue to celebrate its twenty-fifth anniversary as a public company. This bonus helped Lowy cover some of the cost of buying out John.

Relations between John and Frank frosted over. After a few years they had a meal or two at their old haunt, Beppi's Italian restaurant in Darlinghurst, but they failed to rekindle the warmth of their earlier association. However in 1997, when heart failure put John into hospital, Frank visited him.

John had always been an indefatigable optimist who ignored any suggestion of bad health; he prided himself on being a survivor. He discharged himself and went to Surfers Paradise for a break. A few days later Frank heard he had collapsed and was in a serious condition in Southport hospital. Frank and their mutual friend Andrew Lederer flew up to see him. A couple of days later, when John was well enough to fly, Frank sent the company plane to bring him home. However, John's heart condition proved fatal at the end of 1997. Frank was on his way to Israel and he only heard the news that John had died when he reached his hotel in Tel Aviv. But there was a general strike, including of aviation, and he could find no way of getting back to Australia. Not being able to go to John's funeral was something he deeply regretted.

7

A passion for football

Hakoah, from a Hebrew word meaning 'the strength', was the first Australian football team that Frank loved. This nomadic, little-known club wore the Star of David and carried the hopes of European Jewish refugees. In 1952, while working as a sandwich hand in the city, Frank had been taken to his first match at Hakoah's home ground in the eastern Sydney suburb of Maroubra. The only structure in place was a small dressing shed and the boot of someone's car was the official club headquarters. Committee members would take home and wash the team's socks and shirts. Spectators stood to watch the games and players received no pay. The club was competing in the amateur division but doing so with panache.

It didn't take long for Frank to become a devotee. Only dire circumstances prevented him attending the matches on Saturday afternoons. The club offered him a pleasurable route to becoming integrated into the new country. It gave him a sense of belonging to a community and soon provided the opportunity to create some standing within that community. Noticing his dedication, the club invited him in. When he joined, he was raw; he didn't know how to speak publicly, let alone in English, and he knew nothing about the formalities of committee organisation. Once part of its machinery, he honed his skills, learning about the domestic politics of the club and the wider forces at play in the state. He kept a close watch as major change moved through the soccer fraternity and a breakaway organisation was formed. Frank listened to everything and stored it away.

As his involvement in the club increased, his business was improving and he was able to contribute more financially. There was a continuous battle to keep the club afloat and it was suggested Hakoah establish an outside source of income such as a social club that could generate support and funds. By the late 1960s Frank was its president. He aimed to build Hakoah into the best soccer team in Australia, supported by the social club. Through the club he had met Andrew Lederer, another Hungarian émigré mad for soccer. The two became very close and worked together on the team.

While not the kind of father to kick a ball around with his sons, Frank infected them with his enthusiasm for the game. Before they could walk they were on the sidelines. Steven doesn't remember soccer being secondary to anything. He would wear his soccer boots when he watched Hakoah play and would sleep in its uniform. "Whether we won or not on the weekend would determine the environment in the house for the week," he said. For Frank, supporting Hakoah was the perfect foil to sitting, well behaved, at his desk. He was up and down the field on the sidelines for the whole match, barracking.

To overcome the lack of public interest in the game, some of the progressive clubs decided to try and create a national league. Rather than having each state run its own competition, where every week ethnic teams settled scores they had brought with them from the old world, the aim was to build a new tribalism by having cities compete against each other. From his own attachment to Hakoah, Frank understood the passion that drove the ethnic teams and that it would take time for new loyalties to develop.

In 1976 the National Soccer League, NSL, was established. With twelve clubs, it fielded the best players in the country and was a turning point for the game. To join, clubs were supposed to modify their names to reflect their location rather than their ethnic background. This didn't quite happen, although Hakoah did become Sydney City.

A couple of years later, Frank became president of the NSL. Soccer was still a game for foreigners and until it became a mainstream Australian sport it would not thrive. To try and drive this through, he considered making a bid to become president of the Australia Soccer Federation. But he was politically outmanoeuvred by Sir Arthur George, who retained the position.

While Frank had built Hakoah's social club into a thriving enterprise, its soccer team was becoming an increasing strain on the club finances. Frank was worried that football would drive the club broke and both would have to close. In 1983 he raised the heretical possibility of reducing the financial support for the team. The team was in its prime and its supporters were stunned. They loved the team and put up so much opposition to the idea that Frank retreated.

By 1987, with financial losses from football threatening to pull down the club, Frank decided to act. The season had already begun, and he pulled out the team while it was on top. The howls of protest could be heard well beyond the eastern suburbs and Frank was subject to virulent personal attack. Old friends wouldn't talk to him. Someone even called the Jewish burial society, reported that he had passed away and requested it collect his body.

With the social club successfully saved, the football team was pulled out of the competition and closed down. With no role in soccer administration, Frank walked away from the sport.

8

Setback and restoration

During the worldwide bull run of the mid 1980s, Frank couldn't put a foot wrong. Westfield was riding high. Growth was off the chart: between 1985 and 1986 investment in Westfield appreciated by 111 per cent. The Lowy family held 46 per cent of the shares and with the core business secure, Frank began looking to the wider horizon of commerce. It was the era of merciless corporate raids and underperforming companies had good reason to feel vulnerable.

In 1986, the Sydney Stock Exchange declared that Westfield had outperformed all other listed shares available to the public in 1960. And by 1986 investment of $1000 in Westfield's original shares was worth $4 million, provided that all dividends and other benefits had been reinvested in additional Westfield shares. From such a position it seemed nothing could go wrong.

At the time, cashboxes were fashionable and Westfield decided to create one. It would put its non-core assets into the box and then use the cash to invest in the lucrative equities market. This would offer investors a specific vehicle for investment, separate from Westfield's shopping centre company. By then, Frank was on the boards of both Coles-Myer and Bridge Oil and the plan was to use Westfield's shares in these companies as seed capital for the cashbox.

The concept was worked up by David Gonski, a high-profile corporate lawyer, and Peter Lowy, who had gained merchant banking experience on Wall Street and in London. In Gonski, Frank had found a person with whom he could synergistically build ideas. It was the same synergy he had experienced years before with Saunders. Then they had been building tangibles – property and shopping centres. Now, with Gonski, he was building intangibles – financial concepts and structures. As a problem-solving duo he and Gonski sparked off each other, reaching solutions they could not have reached alone. Gonski explained:

> As a lawyer I was taught to solve problems, not to tell
> people they couldn't do something, but to help them do it
> while complying with the legal requirements. To achieve
> this you have to be inventive, proactive and think laterally.
> The marvellous thing about Frank is that he knows where
> he wants to get to. Lawyers are not strong on that – we are
> not taught that. Frank would typically say, "I want to go
> from A to B." I would then look at it and ask, "What road
> are you going to take? If you take this one, you've got this
> bridge to cross." He would reply, "No, I don't like that, I
> could fall into the river." And then I would probably say,

"Well, how about this way?" And he would say, "It's a long way round, couldn't we take a short cut?" I would think about it and say, "Yes, let's take a helicopter." Then Frank would say, "Let's take a Learjet." We would build on each other all the time. It was a wonderful thing.

A cashbox was a major deviation from Westfield's core business and from the outset there were rumblings of discontent in the boardroom. Tremendously optimistic, Frank drove the project to completion. In April 1986, Westfield Capital Corporation (WCC) was launched. Gonski, having given up his partnership at Freehills, was managing director with Peter as his deputy. As executive chairman, Frank was suddenly rubbing shoulders with the major entrepreneurs of the day.

Media were the stocks *du jour* and in 1986 WCC had taken a large stake in a company called Northern Star, which went on to buy Channel Ten and turn it into a national network. Frank was unfamiliar with the glamorous world of media and suddenly he found his name mentioned in the same breath as Alan Bond and Christopher Skase. They were the three new media moguls of the era – all having wildly overspent on television networks.

Northern Star had bought Channel Ten with a parcel of other media assets from Rupert Murdoch for $842 million. But much of its management had gone and no matter how hard Frank tried to attract fresh expertise, he was left frustrated. The network struggled with ratings and when the stock market crashed in October 1987 the network was overexposed.

For the first time, Westfield had an asset in its stable that threatened the standing of the entire enterprise. There was negative press and whatever Frank tried didn't work. The Bridge Oil shares had been sold at a profit and now, with reluctance, he sold the highly valued Coles-Myer shares that supported his seat on that company's board. From the surplus of the sale he planned to inject $200 million into the network, hoping this would enable him to sell it.

With this, he all but gave away the network. In September 1989 it was sold to the media company Broadcom for $1. But the problems were beyond repair and Broadcom couldn't make a commercial success of it either. The network went into receivership. This foray into the world of media was Lowy's first major public failure.

Having digested the failure, Lowy began planning his recovery. Foremost was the need to rescue his reputation. This could be achieved by returning to core business and performing so strongly that the television debacle would be dwarfed by subsequent success. Westfield had been growing steadily throughout, but reasserting its dominance in the market was a matter of urgency. Together with David, Frank devised a strategy to lift the company to a new level. Then he called the top executives together. "Fellows, we've got to make $100 million from development this year," he said.

In the meantime, to show he was still standing, he hosted a cocktail party at his Point Piper home, inviting influential political and business figures. He spent a few uncomfortable moments worrying whether they would come. In the end they all did and Frank felt reaffirmed.

With the help of the Lowy sons, Westfield powered into the 1990s. By June 1991 its shares had surged to a four-year high, by 1994 it had tripled its space under management in the US and by 1996 it had established the Westfield America Trust. The following year it listed on the New York Stock Exchange.

But this successful decade was not without controversy. Details of a $25 million family settlement with the Australian

Tax Office was leaked and brought bad publicity. So did non-transparent activities Westfield used in a campaign against a retail centre being established in its trade area. It was an embarrassment and Frank apologised publicly for the campaign.

For a man with no formal education beyond primary school apart from night classes in accountancy, Frank's appointment to the board of the Reserve Bank of Australia in 1995 was a key moment. Initially there had been some internal opposition to his joining the board but his opponents changed their view when they came to know him. By the time he left a decade later he was regarded as an outstanding director. He had a reputation for having perfected the art of the obvious question. When talking to people schooled in a particular subject, there is often a reluctance to ask basic questions for fear of appearing ill-informed. Lowy asked anyway, which sometimes had the effect of unmasking common assumptions that were incorrect. His interest in getting the answer was greater than his need to protect his standing.

As the century drew to its end, Frank was deeply grateful. His family of seventeen was the source of his spiritual strength. Shirley was healthy, Peter and his wife Janine had four children, David and Margo had three as did Steven and Judy, who would soon have four. Frank was approaching the biblical lifespan of three score and ten but didn't feel anywhere near the end. He had much to do.

PART 2

A Second Life

In 2003, the stars were aligned for Frank Lowy. This was the year he turned seventy-three, and the year he made three decisions that would alter the course of his life. While he continued at the helm of Westfield, which was in a growth phase, he took on three unrelated new pursuits. These were not for commercial gain or charity: these were passionate matters of the heart. He ran these activities in parallel to his business life, as if he was growing a second life alongside his first. When he stepped out of his executive role at Westfield, it was seamlessly into this other life.

Those close to the older Frank describe him as an alloy of warm understanding and steel that can freeze to the touch. They say people who experience only the understanding Lowy find it difficult to imagine the toughness within him, just as those who cross him find it difficult to imagine he is capable of compassion.

A complex character, Lowy is both generous and has a strong sense of entitlement. With his level of wealth he is expected to be philanthropic, and he is, but in business he never shies away from taking his full share and perhaps more. His style is to cut off questions about the large salaries the family draws from the business by saying, "We're worth it." He never has a problem looking after his own and expects others to do the same. If they stand around waiting to be recognised they could wait a long time. While he admires strength and self-reliance, weakness makes him uncomfortable.

The Dutch press once tried to explain him to their readers. After a high-profile commercial battle in Holland in 2002, the publication *FEM de Week* described him as a short man who mostly had a smile on his face. While he was "charming, modest, thoughtful and not a shouter", it said, he can be as hard as nails if he considers it necessary for business. "As a landlord he has no sympathy for retailers and resists legislation that is intended to provide shopkeepers with more protection. But in person he doesn't give the impression of being a shark; he is approachable and modest in a way one seldom sees in people at his level of business."

When Lowy was in his early seventies, an Australian newspaper columnist described him as being "as fit as a mallee bull". But when he looked around the city he was almost alone. Most of his contemporaries were no longer there and it was largely the presence of his three sons in the business that kept loneliness at bay. David, Peter and Steven also kept him up to date. All three were in their forties, all had extensive experience at Westfield, and their mutual respect got them through the inevitable family tensions.

For many years the four Lowy men were the core of the business. There is always a risk when families work together – if it goes well it can produce powerful synergies, but if it goes badly it can do irreparable damage. Ever conscious of this, Frank maintained it for at least two decades and was then perplexed when his oldest son wanted out. David wanted to diversify, to become non-executive, to run the family's private wealth and to pursue his own interests. After several discussions, his father gave him his blessing.

When Frank reached the age of sixty he was asked all the predictable questions about retirement. By the time he got to seventy people thought retirement must be imminent. However, by the time he reached eighty they just assumed he was one of those characters, such as Rupert Murdoch or Warren Buffett, who would continue to continue. Frank, however, had charged a trusted colleague with the task of tapping him on the shoulder: not when it was time to go but just before. For the colleague, it was a weighty responsibility.

In his later years there were times when Lowy was so swept up in his activities that he felt ageless and would make plans with long horizons. "While I live I work," he told the *Australian Financial Review*. "The shorter the real horizon, the longer view you take. When I was young and in business with older people I thought, 'What the hell is he worrying about? He's not going to be here to enjoy it.' Yet I keep doing the same thing. It's the nature of the beast."

He was a man who did not want to or know how to stop. Although he dreamed of relaxing and would organise long glorious vacations, with some regret he would admit that his head never went on holiday. "I work every day of my life. I can't think of a day since 1960 when I have not thought about Westfield and how I can improve the company." This unrelenting focus on work has been his strength and his weakness. Shirley, who has been at his side for more than sixty years, knows he has no 'off' button. She watched him go full bore until the age of eighty, when illness pulled him up short. Coming face to face with his mortality was a brutal shock, but he got through it and kept going.

In the year he turned eighty Frank Lowy also finalised some unfinished spiritual business. He had been just thirteen years old when his father, Hugo, was taken away. Since then, he had longed to stand at Hugo's grave, pray for his soul and weep for what had been lost. But Hugo had perished in a death camp that had no graves. With a great deal of thought, imagination and work, Frank Lowy created a way finally to bury his father.

Personal Matters

9

The machinery of family

Mark Bieler was in bed in New York when his phone rang. The caller was Frank Lowy. Bieler, an adviser to Westfield and the Lowy family, was used to receiving calls at odd hours but now it was past 11 pm and he was slightly annoyed. He listened to Frank and formed the view that the problem could have waited for daylight. Because of their relationship he wouldn't disclose his irritation at the timing but he did say, "You know, Frank, I would have thought that at the point I was worth $6 billion, I wouldn't be bothered by such insignificant things." Without missing a beat, Frank shot back. "You might stop to think that it is only people who are bothered by such insignificant things that make $6 billion."

Frank Lowy has never run on conventional time and anyone who works with him has no choice but to follow. Work is one long continuum, broken occasionally with recreation and irregular sleep. He has kept this up for more than sixty years and when asked if he had any misgivings, he said he would have liked "to have done it all with less anxiety, less stress and less pain."

This drive was not evident when he arrived in Australia in 1952. He knew little about the country except that it had taken in the surviving members of his family and would welcome him too. He arrived with no grand dreams, just a mixture of relief and gratitude at being reunited with his mother. At twenty-one he was looking for no more than to share her one-bedroom flat on a main road in an eastern suburb of Sydney.

He had arrived in time to catch the huge boom of the postwar era and with his partner John Saunders watched in amazement as their little business flourished, surpassing any expectations they might have had. As it flourished, so Frank grew in sophistication, ambition and audacity. He was ambitious for his sons too. All three seamlessly entered the business and, with some chutzpah, Frank elevated all three to the board while they were still in their twenties. It was an era when board members had deep experience and tended to be greying at the temples. But Frank had other youngsters on the board too, reflecting his belief in the brainpower of youth. From his own experience, he knew what switched-on young people could achieve.

As each son joined the board of Westfield there were suggestions Frank might be laying foundations for a dynasty. He shrugged this off. He had no interest in building the House of Lowy or in encouraging subsequent generations to enter the business. Pragmatic and without pretension, he was intent on keeping his immediate family together – preferably in the family business – and on preserving its wealth. Anything else was a bonus.

The third generation spans twenty-three years. While the oldest grandchildren grew up in relative anonymity, by the time the younger ones were growing up the Lowy name was well known in Sydney. For one or two of them it could sometimes be a burden. Teachers would occasionally make remarks and in the playground other children could sometimes be heard repeating their parents' opinions about the Lowy family and its business. In Sydney it wasn't possible to look at the city skyline without seeing their grandfather's signature in the sky: from the classroom window they could see the large red Westfield sign on the shopping centre in Bondi Junction and from another vantage point they saw the oversized sign on top of Sydney Tower. The family knew the children needed ordinary lives and consciously worked at achieving this. Each child was repeatedly told there was no expectation they should or would enter Westfield.

Although Westfield had been a public entity since 1960, it was run much like a family company for almost the next forty years. As long as it continued to generate wealth, only a few objected. In Westfield's earlier days annual general meetings were tribal gatherings where the family's leadership was respectfully acknowledged and the Lowys mingled in the foyer afterwards for the ritual tea and sandwiches. Corporate governance was not a burning issue and the family's passion for the business was perceived as an asset. In response to rumblings about nepotism, the sons said it was obvious they had enjoyed privileged access but once they were in position they had to prove themselves capable of remaining there. Their father took a different view: "Should Westfield be denied their talent just because their surname is Lowy?" He would explain that family members add something to the business. "It is continually in front of us."

While Frank never overtly pushed his sons into the business – "he was too smart for that," says David – they had been prepared for it their whole lives. Apart from the example Frank set, he would take them to the office, to malls and to building sites. But he made sure he was present at the table most evenings to share their day and his. Research consistently shows that the dinner table is the ideal venue for the transmission of values. It may be politically incorrect these days, but then when a man arrived home at night he not only benefited the family by his presence as another adult, but symbolically added the paternal order that balanced the maternal order. He brought worldliness and the opportunity for a different kind of discussion.

Indeed, once the Lowy boys were a bit older the two main topics at dinner were business and soccer. Although there must have been times when Shirley wished she had a daughter, she says she was content to be a homemaker and would listen to the conversation without comment. She was the constant in all their lives, ready to patch them up and do all that was necessary to keep them going. While Shirley might not have been a 'modern' woman with her own income and a life outside the home, she was deeply bound to Frank as his life partner, providing the stable suburban base from which he could build a global empire into which their sons could follow him.

With Shirley, Frank had the home he had always yearned for, and he was acutely aware of his place in it. He remembered how his own father had been away all week as a travelling salesman and how his chair stood empty at the table. He remembered how on Friday afternoons he would rush home from school in anticipation of his father's return for the weekend. When Hugo was in the house the family was complete and there was joy in young Frank's heart. Then came the terrible rupture. Hugo was taken away. The family was broken.

Over his own growing family Frank held tight central control. He was devoted but demanding. While his sons didn't have to pick up their socks or wash their plates, participating in family activities was mandatory, starting with being at the Sabbath table every Friday night, regardless of what else was happening. Frank was determined to build a unit so cohesive and so strong that it could withstand outside forces. Over time, however, he learned he had to accommodate inside forces too.

When his sons graduated from university he encouraged them to work overseas. When the eldest returned with his wife Frank provided the young couple with a brand-new house built in his own front garden. It was beyond his comprehension that they would not want to live side by side with him. He was dreaming of Camelot, of a compound to keep the family together. When David and Margo eventually moved away with their new baby, Frank felt the rupture. He missed popping in to see the baby every morning before work, but gradually came to recognise that his dream was not possible or healthy.

In many families the firstborn faces the most challenges. The first child has to forge a path through the parents' resistance that the other children can later follow with far less stress. Close observers of the Lowy family say that in forging this path David forced his father to a new understanding of the world. First he demonstrated that it was possible to move away while keeping the family intact. Then, after some time he and his wife had marital difficulties and separated for a period of time. To Frank, this was emotionally catastrophic because it threatened to fragment the family.

To deal with his anxiety Frank turned to a family adviser in Sydney who happened to have a background in psychoanalysis. The adviser pulled the curtains back and showed Frank internal forces he had never thought about. They talked for hours about patterns imprinted from the past, about the power of the unconscious and the way it influences behaviour. Frank began to see his own history in different terms and to understand why this event in David's life should have had such a dramatic impact upon his own. While these insights made the family rupture less overwhelming, they didn't take away the pain (which he tried to keep to himself). Only David and Margo getting back together could do that. When they did of their own volition, Frank could breathe freely again.

For Peter and Steven life was easier. By the time they were ready to move away their father had adjusted to the realities and knew the only way to keep them close was to let them go. Like any family, the Lowys had their tensions but the point of difference was that in the early years Frank remained hypervigilant about anything that could threaten the unity of the clan.

By 1997 all three sons were managing directors of Westfield. With Frank as executive chairman, the family was clearly running this public company. But knowing this needed to change, Lowy was quietly working behind the scenes with Mark Bieler with the aim of shifting Westfield to a professionally managed company. The process was slow but inexorable.

By the late 1990s and with ten grandchildren, Frank moved to protect the family wealth. All their eggs were in the Westfield basket and it was time to diversify by selling a large slice of the family's shares in Westfield Holdings. "This will relieve family members of any pressure," he told the *Age* newspaper in 1998. "I want to avoid the thought there's a place here for anybody in the family. This company is a meritocracy and this [sale of shares] gives a chance for family members to do something else." The sale raised almost $500 million, enabling the family to tap into its wealth without disturbing the stability of Westfield's share register. At the time, that left the Lowys with $1.2 billion in Westfield shares.

Lowy had carefully observed how other rich families managed their wealth in subsequent generations and had learned what to avoid. No grandchild would be encouraged to enter the business and any who wanted to do so would have to earn a place. This was in sync with corporate governance changes sweeping through publicly listed companies. The old days of privileged family access were ending. There were also questions about a conflict of interest inherent in one person being both chairman and chief executive of the same company. This was exactly the role Frank held as executive chair. In the closing years of the century Westfield was criticised for its corporate governance.

As it happened, the family executive contingent was about to be reduced. David never aspired to take over the leadership of the family and wanted to explore interests beyond Westfield. Flying was his passion and for most of the 1990s he had been a serious aerobatic competitor. The sky was his territory, where everything he did depended on his skill. Aerobatics is a high-risk sport and he would not stop until he had won the national championship. In 1998 – the year of the family share sale – he finally became Australian Aerobatic Champion. Then he promptly retired from the sport to look for a new challenge.

He owned an ageing war bird, a Cessna A–37B Dragonfly, and thought he would buy a few more warplanes and build a hangar at an old RAAF base as a dedication to the veterans who had flown in defence of Australia during World War II. There was space at the base at Temora in NSW and he planned to invite a few flying mates for weekends. Perhaps people would come and watch (and hear) the odd Spitfire or Tiger Moth winding overhead. Soon he and his friends were staging impromptu air shows and drawing crowds. In 1999 his Temora Aviation

Museum was incorporated. It would eventually attract 40,000 visitors a year.

Frank took a while to adjust to David's desire to follow his own interests but eventually things worked out well. The funds from the selldown of shares were put into a new entity, LFG, the Lowy Family Group, and needed to be managed. Until then David had been looking after the family's interests and so the job of running LFG naturally fell to him. He took the job and in 2000 stepped down from his executive duties at Westfield, though he remained on the board as deputy chairman, a role he shared with Fred Hilmer.

Never happier, David returned to his other passion, music. He grew his hair long and joined a rock band. Years later he curated an all-star band, the Dead Daisies, that included musicians from INXS and Guns N' Roses. He was the songwriter and rhythm guitarist. He was also the driver because he piloted the plane on its world tours. When the Dead Daisies performed in Israel, Frank and Shirley were rocking along in the audience. That they were four times older than those sitting beside them seemed irrelevant.

Meanwhile LFG achieved stellar results. In the first fourteen years, despite the global financial crisis and despite always retaining a large cash balance, David achieved an IRR (internal rate of return) greater than 13 per cent a year. The investment business suited him. He loved the way he could apply his time and his intellect to making money rather than dealing with the nuts and bolts of business. "It's very scalable," he said. "It's possible to manage a large amount of assets with a very small number of people."

Separate from its investment division, David runs the 'Family Office', which is responsible for tax, treasury, finance and administration. It also administers all the family's activities from its research institute to its museum and think tanks, including real estate, boats, planes and other possessions. It employs some twenty people and is a small corporation itself. "There's no dynasty here either," says David. "This just represents four men who get along, who have worked together as a unit for a long time and have a partnership. My father is the senior partner and it works because our economic interests are aligned, our emotional interests are aligned and we are prepared to accept each other's faults. It's a happy accident rather than a dynasty. Will it continue? I don't know. There is no plan."

Frank consciously worked at building a model for the family that would preserve as much harmony as possible and protect its wealth. The model was constantly evolving, but for most of his later years he said the individual families were like four independent silos with little spillover. Frank explained:

> Each family is unique with its own characteristics, outlook,
> social life and friends. There is no regular social contact.
> Friday nights used to be mandatory but now it's all much
> looser. But if we miss once or twice, it will happen the
> third time because we are all aware of the value of it.

The families bring up their children differently and each deals with its own issues but often when the men are together, if there's a problem they will discuss it. Frank added:

> While the women look after the welfare of their own
> families and have their own work and outside interests,
> they have no role in the business and are not involved in
> the family's finances. The four men take care of the larger

unit. It is very male but the relationship between us is strong. Compromises are made all the time to keep this relationship intact. Nothing interferes with it.

Financially we are all locked in. We have common interests and any of the four of us can have what we need or want. It all balances out over time. There are no financial issues between us. While the model works well, it is not as sweet as it appears to be and everyone makes concessions. There are tensions and differences of opinion but these don't last. Everyone finds their place. We strive to keep the unity above all else.

I expect that my sons offload their frustration about me to one another. Of course, they have their disapprovals about each other too and in a way I am the sponge. I absorb the disapprovals from one to other. The test will be what happens when I am gone.

Frank's attitude to the use of money within the family is drawn from his experience growing up in the aftermath of the Great Depression. When one part of the family was in financial distress, others came to its rescue. He remembered when his father was unable to meet the mortgage payments, his mother's brothers arrived with a suitcase of notes to save the house from being repossessed by the bank. The brothers were small-time grocers in a village some fifty kilometres away. They didn't have much to spare.

Even in Sydney, when the newly arrived Lowys had virtually nothing, there was always a small family bank. It was housed in an old soup tureen on top of his mother's wardrobe. If anyone had spare coins or notes they would put them in. Whoever needed money took it out. They would just say, "I took so much" and would put it back when they could. It was there for the whole family.

Fifty years later, so was LFG. It was there for the family's needs but it also had the capacity to fund other businesses should someone in the next generation want to begin one. If it was business, however, they wouldn't get a free ride. "If the kids want to do any activity within the LFG umbrella we will evaluate it on its business merits and whether they have the capacity to do it," says David. "We will treat it just the same way we treat other potential partnerships."

Acutely aware of his responsibility, David takes guidance from Nathan Mayer Rothschild, who at the beginning of the nineteenth century wrote: "It takes a great deal of boldness and a great deal of caution to make a great fortune; and when you have got it, it requires ten times as much wit to keep it."

10

A private matter

One Monday afternoon in November 2003 Frank was alone in his office enjoying the glow of the weekend just past. His grandson Josh had celebrated his bar mitzvah and the family had travelled from near and far to be present. Josh had acquitted himself admirably; everybody was well: there seemed every reason to celebrate. The weekend's festivities had ended with a party at Farm Cove on the edge of Sydney Harbour, where, through the transparent walls of the marquee, the Lowy men could be seen, ties loosened, dancing and singing late into the night.

Now his office door opened and Steven walked in. The pleasure from his son's bar mitzvah was absent from his face. He pulled up a chair. "Dad, the results are bad," he said. "I may be losing my vision. I could be legally blind in five years, maybe ten." As Steven explained the rarity and apparent incurability of his eye condition, his father listened in silence. When it was over, he made a solemn promise: "Steven, we will find a way. We'll use our family and financial capacity to solve this issue." With that, Frank got up and put his arms around his youngest son.

Frank described this news as a tremendous shock, but his mind immediately went into overdrive. "In my mind, very quickly I played out the scenario of us running around the world, from doctor to doctor, with no satisfactory resolution. I know of people chasing non-existing cures and we were not going to take that route. At that moment I knew what we would have to do. We had been heavily involved in medical research for many years and now we would have to extend it. Steven couldn't be alone in this. There must have been others with the condition who needed help too. With full belief, I promised Steven – and myself – we'd do whatever was humanly possible to solve this."

Frank was echoing the words Steven had spoken thirty minutes earlier after retinal specialist Mark Gillies had delivered the diagnosis. Steven had said he would need to go away and absorb this bad news and then added, "In the meantime, maybe you could think about how to solve this, because my family has the experience and resources to attack problems like this." Gillies, a professor at Sydney's Save Sight Institute, had never heard of the Lowy family and was taken aback by his new patient's response to the prognosis. Knowing how much money and infrastructure are needed to conduct research, he thought the sentiment was fanciful.

A decade later Gillies would say that the model the Lowy family created to deal with this disease was without match. He described being part of the process as "probably the greatest medical undertaking" of his career and said the research had electrified the whole field of retinal medicine.

For some time Steven had been aware that he had a problem with his eyes, particularly when reading with changes of light. If he looked to a light source such as a window and then glanced back at the page, many of the words would have vanished. After a while they would come back but he had noticed that their reappearance was taking longer than it had done at first. He kept this largely to himself and tried to manage as best he could until a problem in synagogue made him act.

During the day, Sydney's Central Synagogue is flooded with light. It pours in through the transparent centre dome and filters through large lightly coloured windows around the sides. In accordance with tradition the men sit downstairs and the women sit in a gallery upstairs. By sitting opposite each other the Lowy men and women remain in visual contact across height and space. But the minute Steven looked up to the gallery, his eyes filled with light. When he returned his gaze to his prayer book much of the small Hebrew text was invisible. When this happened once too often, he made an appointment to see the family ophthalmologist, Professor Frank Martin.

The Martins were old family friends, connected through geography and business. Frank Martin's late Hungarian father had been in the delicatessen business in Sydney and had also been one of Frank Lowy's partners at cards. His sister Claire was married to Fred Hilmer, who had been on the Westfield board for many years. The families were comfortable with each other and there was an easy rapport between them.

Frank Martin examined Steven and found that although his field of vision was abnormal he could pass any test on the chart. Martin couldn't pinpoint what was wrong, but he floated the possibility of a brain tumour. This jolted Steven but he duly had a brain scan that found nothing. Something unusual was probably occurring in the retina, the light-sensitive layer at the back of the eye, and Martin referred him to Gillies.

The next day Steven's wife, Judy, sat in the waiting room while Gillies conducted numerous tests on her husband. They took so long that eventually she had to leave to do the school run. She was in the car when Steven called. It was the first seriously bad medical news he had ever received and his voice was trembling. "It was hard," he said. "There is no known cause, no known cure." Judy pulled over. Until this time she hadn't really given the issue much thought, assuming that all would be well. While the Lowy men tended to inflate their medical concerns and worry about them, she tended to deflate them and not react until there was something really to worry about. Now, sitting in the car, she was in tears.

In the meantime Frank Martin had flown to Bangkok to attend an international ophthalmic symposium. Between sessions he picked up a message that Frank Lowy was looking for him. He called back. A very upset Lowy wanted to discuss the diagnosis. As Martin wasn't up to date, he called Gillies. To his dismay he learned of the diagnosis made earlier that day.

Steven had macular telangiectasia – 'mactel' – a disorder so little recognised and understood that it rated only a couple of paragraphs in ophthalmic textbooks. While many people knew about macular degeneration, a not uncommon eye condition in the elderly that causes progressive, painless loss of central vision, mactel was significantly different. It was extremely difficult to diagnose, had no known cause and could affect younger people. Steven was then forty-one.

With mactel, minute abnormal blood vessels grow over a crucial area at the back of the eye called the macula. This area is responsible for central vision, and anything that damages it damages that too. At the centre of the macula is a tiny spot the size of a pinhead called the fovea. This is where all the nerve endings are concentrated and where vision is at its absolute best. With mactel, vessels begin to grow towards this prized spot.

Being at a symposium with world leaders in eye disease, Martin was well placed to get expert guidance, and he sought advice before flying back to Sydney. From the airport he went directly to lunch with Steven and Frank at Westfield. The first thing they needed to do was confirm the diagnosis. Martin had the contacts and made the arrangements.

Two days later Steven and Frank were on a plane to the United States. They planned to visit two centres of excellence in treating eye disease, one on the west coast and the other on the east coast. The uncertainty about what they would discover was making Steven anxious. While confirmation would be confronting, the lack of it would create more uncertainty. On arriving in Los Angeles they went directly to UCLA's Jules Stein Eye Institute.

First they met emeritus professor Bradley Straatsma, a founding director of the institute and a towering figure in ophthalmology. He sat them down and spoke to them kindly and at length. Then he and another retinal specialist, Professor Allan Kreiger, examined Steven together. It didn't take them long to confirm the diagnosis. He had mactel in both eyes and it was much worse in the right eye than the left.

Wasting no time, father and son flew east and arrived jetlagged and worried at the National Eye Institute in Bethesda, Maryland on a wet and wintry day. They sat in a packed waiting room to see Dr Emily Chew, who had agreed to fit them into her busy schedule. When she eventually ushered them into her room Frank felt they were in blessed hands. She treated them with a graciousness they could not have anticipated and after examining Steven, she wanted him to meet the director of the National Eye Institute on the other side of the campus. "Seeing our exhaustion and knowing we would not find it easily, at considerable inconvenience to herself, she took us almost by the hand and led us there, through the rain," Frank said. That afternoon, Steven's diagnosis was reconfirmed. He and Frank now really knew what the problem was, and the certainty calmed them a little.

Although there was some comfort in the fact that the disease would not affect Steven's peripheral vision, there was the real fear that it could take out his central vision. This would leave him legally blind, able to read with difficulty and unable to drive. Along the way there had been some suggestion of a link to diabetes, which Steven didn't have. Little was known about the natural history of mactel and there were differing views on the timing of the decline. On the flight home, they were still in the five-to-ten-year mindset and feeling the urgency. By the time they landed, saving Steven's sight had become a family priority. As Steven explained: "If one of us cuts a finger, we all bleed."

What should they do next? Should they hire an expert to go around the world to see if anything was happening in this field? Should they do what other wealthy families do and fund a reputable scientific institute to research the problem? Frank called an old friend, Larry Horowitz. They had known each other since the late 1980s when Lowy had travelled to Los Angeles to try and buy programs for his television network. Horowitz was a medical doctor turned banker with an interest in biotech and research.

He suggested they approach the renowned Scripps Research Institute in La Jolla, California, which had a reputation for good basic biomedical science. Lowy knew it; some years before he had been invited to join the Scripps board and had visited the campus a few times. While impressed with what he had seen, he had been unable to accept the invitation because of his other activities. Now he held discussions with Scripps while simultaneously putting out feelers into the rest of the global ophthalmic community.

After months of consultation a consensus was finally reached. An array of scientists and researchers would be needed to crack this complex condition, and it was unlikely that any one institute would have all the necessary expertise under its roof. Frank had been concerned that if the family took the traditional path and funded a single institute they would likely become passive donors. As the clock was ticking so loudly, the Lowys were keen to drive the process.

While the Scripps option was kept open, Frank and Steven began developing an alternative plan. Why not amass the world's brightest minds on this issue and use the family's wealth, leadership and organisational skills to drive them as a team?

As far as they knew, this had never been done before. It would be a unique model. While the Lowys knew nothing about collaborative international research, they knew they would have to find someone who did. They needed an impeccable scientist whom they could trust.

Professor Robert Graham, director of the Victor Chang Cardiac Research Institute, had been a family adviser during the months of consultation. The Lowys knew him well. Steven had sat on his board for many years and as the family had been major donors to the Victor Chang Institute, Frank knew him too. Apart from Graham's international reputation in cardiology, he had spent a sabbatical working with a Nobel laureate on the biochemistry of vision. He agreed to help in exploring ways of creating this new model and soon became a regular visitor to HQ, as the family called Frank and Shirley's home in Sydney's Point Piper. From this point onwards Graham would be at the family's side.

On visiting HQ visitors typically parked in Wolseley Road and enjoyed an uninterrupted view of the Opera House and the Harbour Bridge as they walked down the long driveway towards the house on the water's edge. Shirley was usually at the door to welcome them. While not directly involved in the discussions about Steven's vision, she was always present and ready to help. One Sunday afternoon early in 2004, Bob Graham and Frank Martin visited. Their goal was to find someone who could lead this project if it went ahead.

Given the thinly veiled rivalry between the European and American scientific communities, it was thought they would need an esteemed but geographically neutral figure. Professor Alan Bird from London's renowned Moorfields Eye Hospital seemed the perfect choice. Being English and possessing an encyclopaedic knowledge of retinal eye diseases, he would satisfy people on both sides of the Atlantic. It was said of Bird that there was probably no one in the world who knew more about retinal disease than he did.

Bird accepted an invitation to fly to Sydney and on a Sunday morning soon afterwards he and Bob Graham walked down the driveway at HQ. If Bird was a little nervous because Graham was obviously evaluating him, he was about to be intimidated by the unfailingly polite Frank Lowy. Over tea and cake he talked about the issues with Steven, Frank Martin and Graham. After a while Frank Lowy cut in and delivered a series of rapid-fire questions. As Bird recalls, the conversation went like this.

Lowy: What's the treatment?

Bird: There is no treatment.

Lowy: What's the cause?

Bird: We don't know.

Lowy: What research is going on?

Bird: None.

Lowy: Can you think of any research that might be done?

Bird: Yes, several things.

Lowy: So why aren't you doing them?

Bird: Well, we haven't thought about it. Most of the research we do is derivative, by which I mean it is determined by what we did yesterday. It is not innovative and, in fact, it is quite unusual to start something new.

Lowy: As you can think of what should be done, how can it be achieved?

Bird: Well, if you offer grants and call for applications, it could take eighteen months before any work is done. Why don't we invite people to a meeting who we think can contribute, people who know each other very well and who will exchange ideas freely. This means forgetting about intellectual property, but it will be much quicker.

Lowy: How would we structure it?

Bird: We'd get everyone together and have two strands. One would be a clinical strand that collects patients to conduct a natural history study to see how the disease develops over time. The other would be a research strand, where laboratories are established to investigate what the clinicians find.

This seemed a good plan and Bird reeled off a list of names of people who might contribute. The Scripps option was temporarily shelved and the top names in retinal vascular disease from around the globe were duly invited to an inaugural meeting in Baltimore in October 2004. They came willingly.

"When someone like Bird or Straatsma calls and says, 'We are having this meeting, I think you'll find it interesting and I would appreciate if you join us' – that carries a lot of weight," said Professor Marty Friedlander of Scripps, who was on the list. He didn't know his institute had recently been in the frame. He just knew a wealthy Australian family was interested in this disease and there was a possibility of a research program being established in some way.

Friedlander expected a small gathering in Baltimore. He had been down a similar path several times before and each time it had come to nothing. "I probably get a call every couple of months from a wealthy family that has an afflicted member and wants to do something. It usually doesn't work out," he said. But he was excited to see some twenty-five of his international colleagues in the room; it felt like a meeting of old friends.

By the time the invited specialists arrived in Baltimore, they had heard about Frank Lowy's commercial success and expected that he would be present. They knew someone in his family had the eye condition but did not know who it was. When Steven rose to open the meeting on behalf of the family, he gave no sign.

At lunch on the first day, Friedlander took an empty seat at a table and politely introduced himself to the man next to him. When the man replied that he was Frank Lowy, Friedlander said, "You can't be." He had been expecting a different kind of character, someone with a broad Australian accent, not an elderly man with a marked Eastern European one. They chatted and chuckled for a couple of minutes and then Frank turned to him and asked, "*Redstu Yidish?*" He was asking Friedlander whether he spoke Yiddish. When Friedlander answered in the same language, the social distance between the two men disappeared. Friedlander said he felt as comfortable as he would have been sitting beside his own father. For the rest of the meeting Friedlander was often at Lowy's side, explaining who was who and where necessary translating the science being discussed.

The Lowys were well supported by a large contingent of Australians. Professor Ian Constable from Perth had come along, as had Professor Robyn Guymer from Melbourne. Stephen Johns, a trusted family friend and a long-serving Westfield executive and board member, was also present. He would go on to set up the administrative infrastructure necessary for this research project to proceed.

When business was over, Frank told those present that the family wanted to solve the mystery of mactel. "We want to put our personal and financial resources behind this and if it is achieved, it will be a major advance for retinal science and, of course, our family member will benefit in the process. If it happens that it helps diabetes or contributes to the understanding of other retinal diseases – and not mactel – it would still be worthwhile. I am told scientific exploration can open unexpected doors."

While nothing was formally in place yet, the early foundations of a 'mactel community' had been established and everyone had met the family, including Shirley and Judy, who had been present throughout. People left in good spirits, not certain what would follow but feeling the two days had been well spent. This disease represented a mystery in ophthalmology and, as retinal specialists, they were keen to see it solved.

Knowing how quickly research burns dollars, Friedlander was sceptical about the plan. To fund private research, bottomless pockets are required. More than once he had heard a wealthy family say, "We've put in $10 million, so where's the cure?" But as he liked the Lowy family and was attracted by the science, he remained in the loop. A structure was evolving. At a subsequent meeting, he forcibly realised that the family was serious and that this research was going to happen.

He couldn't have imagined how big a part he would have in the process. Friedlander and the whole retinal community were about to be exposed to a business model of research like nothing they had encountered before. David, Steven and Frank had spent many hours on its funding and with the help of Stephen Johns had decided to commit $5 million a year for five years and then make a decision on whether or not to continue. From Los Angeles, Peter supported the expenditure and the provision was made.

By the end of 2004 the Lowy Medical Research Institute, LMRI, had been formed. A year later it was funding 'The MacTel Project', with Bird as chief scientific officer and twenty clinics in the US, the UK, Australia, Germany, France, Israel and India. In addition, there were five laboratories in the US, the UK and Australia. A little later a genetics division from New York was added.

Father and son were building the organisation with the determination they had shown for developing Westfield. Together with Stephen Johns they were on a steep learning curve, coming to grips with issues of intellectual property (now part of the project) and complex contracts for running clinical trials and laboratories. As administrative director of the LMRI Johns was in new territory, dealing with institutions such as Harvard, Scripps and University College London. He didn't know the norms, he hadn't encountered medical ethics committees before and while he came from a purely commercial background, he was suddenly negotiating on scientific ground. When he explained that a five-year horizon had been set to determine whether the project had merit, one expert told him to triple it.

The LMRI grew into a large virtual research institute over which Frank and Steven Lowy kept close control. Their diaries were peppered with dates for teleconferences, group face-to-face meetings and international meetings where everyone got together for a couple of days in Sydney, Los Angeles or London. Participants were made as comfortable as possible and everyone kept their day jobs while doing this work in their own time. Some were remunerated and some were not. Most who had attended the embryonic event in Baltimore remained involved.

Steven and Frank were at every meeting, almost always with Judy and Shirley. While actively committed to the project, the Lowys placed total confidence in those they had appointed. What gave the project its solid foundation was the family's shared understanding that the expenditure could be considerable and the project could take a long time.

In the beginning, Frank had had trouble grasping the relevance of some of the science. Once he looked at a series of cell culture experiments and asked, "How's this going to stop Steven going blind?" But he soon became acculturated and would sit hour after hour as specialised research was rolled out. "The science meetings are very complex and baffling to me, but I sit through them because I am looking for the essence of progress, where there are holes to fill, people to recruit and organisation to be done to assist the process. That's my role," he said. "The commitment is huge but I have the resources and I make the time – and a little of the science rubs off."

11

A breakthrough

By a stroke of luck, new tools became available to eye specialists soon after the mactel project began, allowing the retina to be seen in greater detail than ever before. While using such a tool, one member of the team saw something quite unexpected. He noticed that a deep, dark hole occurred just beside his patients' central vision. What did it mean? Had anyone else in the research group noticed the same thing? Yes, some had.

Professor Frank Holz from the University of Bonn, Germany, had made a discovery that would change the understanding of this disease. The dark holes had no nerve cells, which are essential for vision. These cells had died and blood vessels had begun growing into the empty space. This is a classic bodily process; blood vessels often grow into damaged areas to try and save them. This is exactly what they were doing in the eye.

Until this point everyone had been thinking about mactel primarily as a disease caused by the growth of new blood vessels in the eye. Now it appeared that the new vessels were secondary. The primary problem was the death of nerve cells. This was a major shift in understanding.

Anxious for further progress and frustrated by the unpredictable course of research, Frank put pressure on those around him. Alan Bird was never quite sure how to handle this. He found Frank a very good listener as long as his patience lasted.

> Suddenly the businessman in Frank would emerge and he'd
> remark that he could have built an entire shopping centre
> in the time we were taking and that we kept changing our
> plans. Intellectually he knew clinical research was quite
> different from building a mall, where there are set timelines
> and certainties. With clinical research there are no definite
> timelines and unexpected findings can cause a deviation in
> the path, which may then reveal more uncertainty. While
> Frank understood this he was frustrated, and at times I felt
> I was being tested.

That said, Bird believed the Lowy model of research, which invited people to work together, was a perfectly viable alternative to the standard model of putting up money for science and asking who could use it.

While the group became accustomed to the Lowys being hands-on and keeping everyone on track, it took them a bit longer to get used to the family's hard-edged business approach to science. Scientists are accustomed to getting funding and then being left to their own devices. In the Lowy model, researchers were only as good as their last six months' results and decisions were made quickly if things were not moving forward. For Frank and Steven, the process was not governed by financial constraint but by perceived need. "Often we were told we were too easy on the scientists because in other places the money is quite restrictive and they are kept hungry," said Frank. Initially the project had been costing $4 to $5 million a year but that soon escalated.

In the early years the researchers were fascinated by the dynamic between the Lowy father and son. Steven was in a difficult position. Not only was he the raison d'être for the project, he was co-running it. While his general approach was measured and careful, his father was in a hurry and could go at issues like a bull at a gate. Once Frank had come to a decision he was difficult to restrain. In front of others the two would have a robust exchange of views and minutes later resume their normal warm concern for each other with no reference to what had just happened. People watched in amazement, not knowing this was the standard family method for resolving business issues. An issue needed to be resolved and when it was, they regarded it as a successful family decision. One observer said at times Frank and Steven were like an old married couple, squabbling but inseparable.

But the family was taking the strain. Steven was working long hours at Westfield and although he knew mental fatigue affected his vision, he wouldn't let up. Judy felt it was time for more support and called David. "We need a fresh approach," she said, explaining that the level of frustration was building. "Steve and your dad are so emotionally invested that an objective perspective would help – it would help to have three of you debate the issues rather than just the two of them." Judy's call crystallised what was already in David's mind. Aware of the strain, he had been thinking about offering to help.

As Frank Martin recalls, David Lowy wanted to meet him. One Sunday morning, a tender picked up Martin from the wharf at Rose Bay and took him out to David's boat, the *Shirley Anne*, which was moored nearby. The two men sat on deck and talked about the project. The load on Steven was too heavy and more manpower was needed. David wanted to be involved, but first he needed to come up to speed. "He caught on very quickly," says Martin.

"It's frightening to think of one's brother possibly losing his sight and I wanted to do whatever I could to help. Whatever it takes and whatever it costs, this is the most important thing for us," said David. He threw himself into the project, read what he could and began attending the scientific meetings. He became part of the core group with Steven and Frank and his commitment was total. "He has an innovative mind and drives things hard. He brought new vigour," says Frank. Several times a week when David, Steven and Frank lunched together, the mactel project was their major topic of conversation. Peter offered his support from Los Angeles but because of the geography he remained on the periphery.

Meanwhile, Steven was living with the realities of his condition. Although his eyesight was not sufficiently degraded to complicate his life on a daily basis, there were times when he felt shaken. In November 2007 he had an awkward public moment. As president of the Art Gallery of NSW he was due to deliver a speech at the opening of a Sidney Nolan exhibition in front of an audience of a thousand. He'd had a busy day and as he rushed into the gallery he was given the notes. "I read them through and thought okay, I can do this. But I was a bit tired and the speech was not that intuitive for me. When I looked up at the crowd, a light caught my eye and sent me temporarily blind in my central vision. When I looked back at the page, the words were not there. This probably lasted fifteen to thirty seconds but it felt like forever. I tried to wing it but I made a few mistakes. No one said I had messed up but I felt terribly embarrassed. After that, I began to prepare a lot better and have my speeches typed in bold on grey paper." Three years later he was reading off an iPad. The back lighting was perfect.

Hearing of incidents like this made his father all the more impatient to find a cure. When the scientists tried to educate Frank about different ways of measuring progress he understood why it was slow, but it brought him no comfort. Steven's vision could remain stable for years but it could also deteriorate without warning.

When Gillies gave the first forecast, the prevailing wisdom had been that Steven could be legally blind in five to ten years. Now the forecast had lengthened from ten to twenty years. As distinct from being totally blind, a legally blind person can read only the top line on a vision chart while wearing glasses. Someone can also be legally blind if the field of vision is drastically restricted, a problem Steven didn't have.

Since the first forecast, mactel had moved from being considered rare to being considered uncommon. With new diagnostic tools in wider use, mactel patients began appearing. As the patient population grew, it was clear many people had previously been misdiagnosed with other retinal conditions.

It was now 2009. The project was approaching its five-year mark and was at a low point. In business, Frank would always say that deals were organic: they had a life of their own and it was important to be sensitive to this. The same applied here. He could see that as the project's costs were escalating, the research was plateauing.

Frank figured that democracy has its limits and privately began reorganising. With thirty international centres administered from Australia and the project scientifically overseen from the UK and the USA, a restructure was needed. The project lacked an overall co-ordinator who could pull all the strands together. Frank wanted one person to take full command.

At the next scientific meeting he was impressed by a consultant from the retinal world who happened to be present. Frank wanted to take him on as a fulltime co-ordinator but the others were unconvinced. Frank dug in. "The majority is not always right and I wouldn't be derailed. I drove it relentlessly. There was a lot of passive resistance to hiring this man but I would not be deterred. I forced him in and although he only remained in place for about nine months, his presence was a catalyst for change in the structure." Back in Australia, control of the project shifted from Stephen Johns to the Lowy Family Group, where it would be backed by a full office under David's aegis.

On several occasions people remarked on the uniqueness of the mactel model and suggested it could set a new template for research. They tried to encourage the Lowys to talk about it in public, hoping to start a conversation about using philanthropy and innovative research models. At the time the family was not keen for such disclosure. The project had been going for five years and its anniversary came and went without note. The family had no option but to continue. However, to get a better fix on this puzzling disease, the project began offering generous grants in the hope that other scientists would join and bring fresh thinking.

Still not happy with the project's structure, Frank began working on a new idea. While a virtual institute had its merits, what the project most needed now was a physical home, a headquarters built of bricks and mortar. It also needed one individual to be responsible for its success. He could picture Marty Friedlander as the fulltime CEO, running the project with a number of other researchers under him, and asked Friedlander whether he would consider this. Friedlander was not overenthusiastic but promised to think about it.

He also promised to keep the whole question of a restructure strictly between himself and Frank. When they had agreed on a plan it would be tabled for debate, but until then Frank wanted it kept under wraps. "I knew there were many problems and I wanted to keep it to myself until Friedlander agreed it was a goer. If he did, then changes could be debated specifically rather than in abstract," said Frank. While Steven and David were aware of this, they were asked not to become involved until the plan was formed.

Unrelated to the restructure, Bird and Friedlander met with Steven in Los Angeles. They had a new idea they wanted to discuss. A biotech company produced a tiny device that could be implanted in the eye, consisting of an immortal cell that produced a protein that appeared to arrest or slow deterioration of nerve cells in the retina. As these same nerve cells die in mactel, perhaps the device might work in this disease too.

Although the device had already passed safety trials in more than 200 patients with other retinal diseases, fresh trials for mactel had to be conducted. There was no difficulty in finding seven volunteers happy to have the device implanted into an affected eye for a year.

Steven didn't consider joining at this point because his disease in both eyes wasn't advanced enough. But he soon changed his mind. His eyes were being tested every six months and with each test there was evidence that his vision was deteriorating slightly –

and there was nothing to hold it back. Time was against him. He could let his vision slip away or he could use this device, which might do him good, harm or nothing at all.

It was an agonising decision and the family consulted widely. Being present at a debate about his own fate made Steven, normally controlled and deliberate, unusually unsettled and tense. Eventually the advisers reached a consensus. He should have the device in his worse eye so as not to risk the better one. Then the opinion changed: as he needed to save his good eye, it should go in there.

Steven was stalling. "The whole issue was whipping up a storm inside me," he said. "Dad and David were pushing me hard to do it. Judy was more conservative after one consultant scared the life out of her. I really felt I was between a rock and a hard place. Eventually, everyone told me to get on with it. So I decided to take a punt. I'd have it in my good eye. Once I had made the decision, I felt afraid of it."

In June 2012 a small contingent of Lowys arrived in Atlanta, where the device would be implanted. As always, Judy was at Steven's side and Shirley was at Frank's side. Peter came too. "It must have been a royal pain in the arse for them but it shows the family support I was getting," said Steven, who was so full of anticipatory dread that the minute they got to their hotel he rushed to the bathroom to throw up.

The procedure at Emory Hospital was nerve-racking but successful. Afterwards, rather than being holed up in a hotel room, Steven and Judy decided to fly home. "I remember sitting in the Qantas lounge with a patch over my good eye and not being able to see much out of my bad eye. This brought home for the first time the enormity of the problem with my bad eye and what could possibly be ahead for me."

No one on the safety trial suffered any side effects from the implant and after a while, some could read a few extra letters on the bottom line of the eye chart. Steven suffered no side effects either, and also began doing better at the eye tests. He didn't know if this was a genuine improvement or a result of becoming more familiar with the test.

While this drama was playing out, Frank and Friedlander were developing a new structure for the project. In July 2012 the *Ilona* berthed at Canary Wharf in London. It would be Frank's base for business and entertainment during the Olympics. Friedlander, who was in London too, spent much time on board hammering out the new plan, which would see the LMRI's headquarters built next door to his laboratory on the Scripps campus. Although on campus, the project would be entirely independent of it. Friedlander could keep his day job and run the project at least one full day a week.

This new model would streamline the organisation and, Frank hoped, re-intensify its focus. Both Steven and David agreed an adjustment was necessary but questioned how to make a change while keeping everything that was good about the existing organisation. A period of turbulent family decision making followed: with a few concessions, Frank prevailed.

In September Frank sat down with the key participants and announced that he wanted to accelerate the process. One of Westfield's strengths had always been its ability to pull together the decision makers without notice to act quickly; now he wanted this research institute to be able to do the same. When there was a breakthrough he wanted it to be clean, without being caught in a tangle of process: he wanted it to be translated quickly from the bench to the bedside. In 2013, the LMRI in La Jolla opened its doors.

By then the project had an established place in the world of retinal medicine. It had taken six years to change the disease paradigm from a blood vessel disorder to a nerve disorder. The same was now happening with diabetic retinal disease, but this had taken sixty years. Although researchers in both conditions came to the same conclusions at more or less the same time through separate paths, Bird says the mactel research was an impetus in the diabetic research. Given that some 350 million people in the world have diabetes, this small piece of research could have a considerable impact.

Meanwhile, laboratory research showed that the protein from the device appeared to cause upper parts of the nerves to grow back again. Whether this could be replicated in humans was not known. In one or two subsequent clinical trials Bird said, "There was a very slight chance that vision might even improve. People who were said to have no usable vision seemed to regain some after treatment. They started seeing the edges of the letters. It was tempting to believe they were improving, but we always fear we are overoptimistic." Once the safety trial had been done, work began on the next trial to test its efficacy. It would be a two-year program with sixty-eight patients. This was a major escalation and the family spared no expense. "What else is the money for?" asked Peter.

By 2014 the rate of deterioration in Steven's good eye had apparently slowed and he was considering having the device implanted in his bad eye, too. Whether this improvement might have happened naturally remained unknown. But he regarded the decision as a good one. He had come to no harm and might even have benefited. The only two downsides were that he couldn't rub his eye for fear of dislodging the implant and when he played soccer he had to wear goggles.

Even if the worst came to the worst and Steven became legally blind, Bird believed he would always be able to perform his job. As his peripheral vision would remain normal, he could surround himself with technological and human help to continue working actively. By 2014, off-the-shelf technology such as iPads, Kindles and large-screened smartphones were meeting his needs. If he had to read a ledger with small print, it could be done with a sophisticated digital magnifying glass or an app on his phone. In synagogue he used a prayer book with large print, a gift from his rabbi.

Most people around town didn't know about Steven's condition and he never made it weigh on his family. His children took their cues from him. While he loved to play cricket with his youngest son, Jonah, if the ball was coming straight at him, sometimes he could not catch it. "I guess Jonah probably thinks I am a big klutz," said Steven.

His oldest son, Josh, could tell when Steven was bothered visually. "I don't put him into situations where he is going to struggle, like reading something small on my phone," says Josh. "I know he doesn't like others to see him struggle so if I am present, in a subtle way, I try to help. Once we were at Westfield Labs in San Francisco and I knew a presentation was about to be given in red with white writing and that he wasn't going to read it easily on the screen. So I printed it out in black and white beforehand and gave it to him without explanation. That said, the subject is not taboo; we talk about it. And personally, I am not going to get terrified by something that hasn't happened yet."

While the ultimate prize would be to identify this condition early enough to stave it off, the family target was to halt Steven's disease and perhaps reverse some damage. By 2014 the Lowys had spent in excess of $50 million on the project and anticipated it would cost a lot more. "We are ready for it," said Frank. While Steven was uneasy about such expenditure, his discomfort was mitigated by the knowledge that although he was the focus, public good could come from the project. It is common for research in one disease to add to research in another, and he was hoping the ripples from this would spread. Neither he nor his father had forgotten the prediction that it would take fifteen years before they knew if they were on a fruitful mission. Five years to go.

12

'What gift should I give?'

When Frank Lowy opened a think tank in Sydney in 2003 his friends were puzzled. They didn't quite know what it was but they had heard it cost $30 million to establish and that it was his gift to the nation. Lowy explained the decision by saying that a think tank is a factory for ideas. His particular factory would focus on foreign policy, with the aim of strengthening Australia's voice so it could be better heard on the world stage. The think tank would also provide a forum for world issues to be better heard at home.

The friends were still puzzled. Why should a businessman like him be concerned with geopolitics? Frank pointed out that his early years had been entirely shaped by the foreign policies of several countries. During his boyhood, borders had changed so often that his small town was in Czechoslovakia, Hungary and Slovakia. Each change affected the population. Then the family moved to Budapest, where they felt the impact of Germany's brutal foreign policy. In 1944 the Nazis occupied the city, took away Hugo Lowy and filled the rest of the family with such fear that they would never feel secure again.

In occupied Budapest, however, Frank had also felt the benign effects of Switzerland's foreign policy, when its embassy provided him and his mother with documents that allowed them to enter a protected house. This was similar to the protection offered by the Swedish diplomat and businessman Raoul Wallenberg, who had saved tens of thousands of Jews by offering them protective passports as Sweden's special envoy in Budapest. Jews were being hunted on the streets and such documents helped them survive until the Russian army marched in. By the age of fourteen, Frank had been affected by the foreign policies of five countries.

After the war, when he left Europe and attempted to sail illegally for Palestine, Frank Lowy had felt the effects of Britain's foreign policy. The British navy had intercepted the rickety boat and sent all its refugees to Cyprus, where they were interned. The British behaved humanely and after a few months they allowed the youngest members of the camp, including Frank, to go to Palestine as part of the Jewish quota.

A year after his arrival, Frank would experience global politics on the grandest scale when the United Nations voted to partition Palestine. After debate on the issue, the voting procedure was broadcast live around the world. In the end thirty-three countries voted for partition, thirteen voted against and ten abstained.

This was a lesson in international policy that Frank never forgot. The Jewish population of Palestine – then 600,000 strong – had erupted in joy, but the mood among the 1.4 million Arabs had been grim. For them it was the beginning of *al nakba*, the catastrophe, in which hundreds of thousands lost their land and their homes. They hadn't wanted partition; they felt the split was unfair and that they were unjustly being made to pay for the Holocaust. War broke out. Frank enlisted to fight for the Jewish state. Having been battered by the policies of other countries all his life, he was finally in uniform, fighting for what was now his own country. As multiple Arab armies lined up against Israel, he felt a strong sense of purpose. So did the other refugee boys in his unit.

With him was his friend Yona Sommerfeld, who remembers lying behind rocks, shooting at the enemy some 1500 metres away, when he felt the soldier next to him tugging at his arm. He looked around and saw a young boy crying. "What's the matter? Just shoot," he barked in Hebrew. "*Ich vais nit, Ich vais nit*," the boy sobbed in Yiddish ("I don't know how, I don't know how"). He had come off a refugee boat two days earlier and had never handled a gun before. "So in the middle of the exchange of fire, I instructed him in Yiddish, step by step, how to use it," says Sommerfeld. "Then he was so excited he could shoot that when the order came to halt fire, he wouldn't stop! The orders came in Hebrew, Yiddish, Polish, Russian and Czech, but he continued."

After the war, Frank was ready to remain in Israel to build the young state. But the pull to join the surviving members of his family in Australia was stronger. Australia's tolerant policy about refugees meant that like his family, Frank would be welcome.

Half a century later, when he reflected on the events that had shaped his life and saw the patterns behind them, he was impelled to create an institution dedicated to encouraging enlightened foreign policy.

In 1999 the University of NSW conferred on Frank an honorary doctorate of letters. At a luncheon to mark the event he delivered a speech about the role of population in underpinning prosperity. He used international comparisons and economic theory to build a convincing case for Australia to open its doors to greater immigration. Over the preceding years the issue had been stirred by the controversial politician Pauline Hanson, who had appealed to the community's basest instincts by speaking out strongly against Asians. Against this background Lowy argued that a much greater number of immigrants was the only thing that would secure Australia's future in the coming century. The speech became a national conversation point, and to harness the momentum Lowy decided to establish an institute to develop policies for encouraging immigration.

Preparations were underway when fresh controversy about refugees and border protection swept the country. In October 2001, as part of its election campaign, the Liberal–National Coalition government whipped up antagonism against asylum seekers, claiming it had evidence that passengers on an illegal ship off the Australian coast had thrown their children overboard. Although this was untrue, it exploited voters' fears about people smuggling and illegal immigrants and the government, which had been shaky in the polls, comprehensively won the election the following month. In the wake of the election result, the issue of immigration was so politicised that Frank decided to put his population institute on ice.

But January 2002 would mark the fiftieth anniversary of his arrival in Australia, and he wanted to make a gesture to the country in appreciation of the opportunities it had afforded him. What should that be? It can be difficult enough to find a gift for a friend, how do you find one for a country? He, the Lowy family and the Westfield Foundation had already bestowed many buildings, halls, research grants and scholarships. Frank Lowy wanted to do something different, something that would make a difference to the country and continue to do so after he had passed on. Leaving a legacy that had intellectual power would be ideal.

For the past two decades, Lowy had spent one-third of his business life abroad and he knew the value of international exposure. While he had encouraged his sons and executives to gain such exposure, he wished there had been a better appreciation of Australia overseas. "When I am overseas and read newspapers, sometimes the only references I find to Australia are about shark attacks, bushfires or tennis. We are perceived as small and geographically isolated and frankly, I find that condescending. Australians have distinguished themselves in so many other ways," he said at the time. He believed Australia had much to contribute to the international community and that its location in the Asia-Pacific region was one of its strengths, enabling it to bring a unique perspective to any international exchange of ideas. It was time to throw out the tired notion of the tyranny of distance and start exploring the potential of proximity. The so-called 'Asian century' was dawning and over the next decade Australia's neighbourhood would steer global politics.

Working in the United States with executives from all countries, Lowy would often say that pound for pound Australians were the most accomplished. So why, he asked, was Australia was not properly recognised on the world stage? Why was its voice not heard on global matters? These thoughts were floating around his head when his son Peter made a suggestion that crystallised them.

Peter had lived in Los Angeles for about fifteen years and was a keen follower of American politics. His involvement with the Democratic Party deepened and he became more interested in policy, spending time in Washington DC. Think tanks are usually headquartered in national capitals and DC was no different. In fact, a newspaper columnist once commented that DC "has think tanks the way other towns have firehouses".

Washington DC is home to about one-fifth of the think tanks in the USA. Peter had visited one or two and was interested in their ability to devise policies that shape the lives of millions.

There are different views about the origins of Western think tanks. Some say they began in Britain in the early 1830s when the Duke of Wellington – wanting some research on defence and security – founded the Royal United Services Institute. Others say think tanks are essentially an American innovation that began in the early twentieth century, when Robert Brookings and others formed a private institute to take a clear look at public policy and analyse it objectively. After World War II more think tanks were formed, in all shapes and sizes. Think tanks had first appeared in Australia in 1924 and while they existed in various forms they didn't have much public profile, including the oldest, the Australian Institute of International Affairs (AIIA).

One evening as Frank and Peter Lowy were flying to DC the conversation turned to the issue of legacy. Peter explained that in the US people who make great wealth create think tanks to facilitate the discussion of public policy. He suggested that if his father wanted to make a lasting contribution he should follow the American example and build an international think tank, but base it in Australia.

As they talked over dinner, Frank became convinced that a think tank could be a perfect ongoing gift to the nation. It could incorporate aspects of the population institute he had originally envisaged, but with a broader reach. He saw no reason why Australia wouldn't be as capable of first-rate thinking as any other nation on earth. But it was more likely to be heard if it had something powerful to say. Excellent scholarship provided by a dedicated think tank could empower this voice.

The role of such institutions in forming a bridge between knowledge and power appealed to Lowy too. They exist in the middle ground, between universities and governments, drawing from both and using scholarly muscle to form public policy. Think tanks exist on a broad spectrum. At the low end they appear to be centres for research into important public issues but are really self-serving talk shops, promoting the interests of their sponsors. At the high end they are distinguished institutions that provide brainpower to drive policy improvements affecting the lives of many. Obviously Frank was interested in the high end, but investigation was required into whether his plan would work in Australia.

On his return to Sydney, Frank Lowy tested the idea with his adviser Mark Ryan. As corporate director of Westfield Ryan had an office four doors down from Frank and the two men debated issues daily. With his background as a journalist and with a decade in the political sphere including a stint as a senior political adviser to former prime minister Paul Keating, Ryan was able to provide opinions that others might have been nervous to offer. He knew that Frank cannot tolerate thoughtless agreement and needs to be challenged.

Ryan listened to the idea, loved it and undertook to find someone to conduct a feasibility study. He called Michael Fullilove, a Rhodes scholar who had also worked in Keating's office. Coincidentally Fullilove was tossing around the idea of establishing a small think tank himself. He had imagined a brains trust of three that was nimble, lively and quick to respond. Frank's thinking was on a much grander scale and a meeting was arranged, where Fullilove was able to explain the unique culture that exists in think tanks. He described how it would need the depth of a university, the pace of a newsroom, the policy nous of a ministerial office and the business efficiency of a corporation. There was excitement in the air and Fulliove was commissioned to investigate the possibilities.

After interviewing two dozen experts in Australia and overseas, by August 2002 Fullilove's report was ready. At the time there was limited awareness about the country's three main think tanks; the Institute of Public Affairs, the Centre for Independent Studies and the Australia Institute. But Australia had no foreign policy think tank of international standing. While a number of organisations were already examining Australia's relations with its region, no one was examining its relations with the world.

The intellectual topsoil of the country was thinly spread between newspapers and academics. (In 1957 this had been skewered by an Australian Nobel laureate, the novelist Patrick White, who had written that Australia was a place "where the journalist and the schoolmaster rule what intellectual roost there is"). There was no dynamic middle ground with people who could do 'blue-sky thinking' but also knew what was feasible. Fullilove saw an opportunity to establish the country's first world-class, non-partisan foreign policy think tank. It had the potential to pull Australia into the mainstream of international thinking, generate concrete, workable policy options and educate a new generation of leaders.

It sounded perfect. Ideas are expensive and risky and if this worked, it would be a gift to the nation that would go on giving. As no one else was in the space, it could own the market and develop a distinctly Australian view of the world. But there was also sharp warning about politics. Such a think tank would need to protect itself from becoming a vehicle for domestic political agendas.

Frank bounced the idea around with a select group of people, among them Rob Ferguson, the former head of BT Australia and a long-standing member of the Westfield board. He also sought the opinion of Ian Macfarlane, then the Governor of the Reserve Bank, on the board of which Frank sat, and sought the advice of Professor Robert O'Neill, chairman of the Australian Strategic Policy Institute and a world expert in security and strategic studies. The general consensus was 'onward'.

As Fullilove had delivered the report during a particularly busy period for Lowy, he expected he would have to wait for a reply. But the next morning Frank called him on his mobile: "Michael, I was up all night reading your report. I want to do it. Come in and see me. What do we do next?"

Lowy could picture himself on quieter days spending hours at the think tank as new intellectual vistas opened before him. At this point he did not know that he would have to exercise considerable self-discipline because he would be required to have nothing to do with the scholarship involved. Of course, he would be hands-on in the planning, the structure, the execution and the promotion of his 'ideas factory', but the choice of issues, the manner of their exploration and the conclusions drawn from them would have to be the domain of the professional staff.

In the first twenty years of Westfield's existence Lowy or Saunders had signed every cheque and known the price of every paper clip. Lowy often said that no one detail is more important than another. In his later years, as he became more fully occupied with the company's worldwide strategy, he would still descend into minutiae if an obstacle needed to be overcome.

He got almost as much pleasure from details as from being in control, espousing the view that a proprietor has rights over his enterprise. In the case of this think tank, as he would be spending his own money there was an expectation that he would have at least some say. When it was explained why independence was vital for success, and why he should have no say at all in its intellectual business, he stepped back and let it proceed.

Lowy had received a similar check in the 1980s, when his television network had a current affairs program over which he was informed he would have no influence. If it wanted to run an anti-Israel piece it had to have the right to do so, no matter how painful this might be for the chairman. "Non-interference is not in my blood," said Lowy. When the network planned to run a favourable interview with Yasser Arafat he went through personal turmoil, fighting himself to let the interview run. When it ran, he could hardly watch.

The chairman did, however, have the right to expect good ratings from the television program and to investigate when these were not forthcoming. So it would be at the think tank. There would be no interference from the board but it would expect success. While there would be ongoing debate about how to measure success it was Lowy's clearly stated aim that as a bipartisan institute his should be one of the best in the world.

In September 2002 Lowy announced his gift to the nation. "I arrived here in 1952 with a small suitcase. This country has given me so much, I want to give back something of real value," he told the *Australian Financial Review*. At the time he was the country's highest paid chief executive with his incentive-based salary for 2002 expected to be above $11 million. He would give the bulk of this pay packet as his first instalment on the gift.

Meanwhile many decisions needed to be made, starting with what to call it. Lowy preferred a serious generic name that could be condensed into a memorable acronym to emphasise its independence. But he was persuaded that this would be lost in the alphabet soup of think-tank acronyms. His surname, on the other hand, had become a brand. It would be distinctive and identify the institute with one of the great names of Australian business. It would also be consistent with the philanthropic practice in countries such as the United States, with its Carnegie Endowment for International Peace and the Brookings Institution in DC.

He agreed on the Lowy Institute for International Policy. Known simply as the Lowy Institute it would try to put issues on the national agenda, get people thinking about them and draw up effective policies. But how many people would be listening? The traditional audience for think tanks is the informed public – perhaps 5 per cent of the Australian population.

Lowy wanted to broaden this by having the institute located in Sydney, his home town and Australia's most internationally known city. As the country's business capital Sydney could also attract interest from the business sector, from people simply looking for another dimension, wanting to network or just curious about international affairs. There might also be some with a commercial interest offshore keen to understand the impact of foreign policy decisions on their trade in Australia. He could see this institute providing a much-needed venue for business to promote its ideas or support research not taking place elsewhere, research that might be to its advantage.

Another way to broaden the base would be to engage with the great Australian diaspora, Australians living overseas who felt tremendous goodwill towards home but had no intellectual outlet for expressing this. Indeed, in its second year of operation, the Lowy Institute would produce a report on the 'worldwide web of Australians' living offshore and what an underappreciated and underused resource they were. At any one time a million Australians are living or travelling away from home, not driven out by conflict or economic depression but rather obeying a sense of adventure.

The next debate was about the institute's home. Some said it didn't need a trophy building; it was primarily about ideas and as academics didn't need to be housed in a great edifice, a warehouse fitted with computers and benches would do. The money saved could go into research, the institute's core business. Others said appearances were important and the building should be an expression of everything that the institute is about and over time become its symbolic home.

Lowy sought advice from Martin Indyk, an Australian who had founded the Washington Institute for Near East Policy and who knew his way around the US think-tank scene. He had also recently completed his second stint as US ambassador to Israel and knew the diplomatic scene. "Martin told me we needed a high-prestige building, preferably with a wood-panelled interior and a sense of place. It should be imbued with history, stand in the central business district and have sufficient grandeur to make an immediate and powerful impression on anyone entering it." Others concurred that to be an influential foreign policy think tank it was best to look like one. Frank wouldn't want to invite visiting prime ministers and ambassadors to a warehouse in a less salubrious part of town.

One Friday afternoon 31 Bligh Street, a classic sandstone building nestled in the city's business district, unexpectedly came on the market. Lowy dashed to see it and by Monday he had bought it. "It fitted Martin's description exactly and was what I imagined too," he said. Classified by the National Trust and listed for permanent conservation under the Heritage Act, the building gave the institute instant gravitas. It had been built in 1886 by one of the most distinguished architects of the colony to house the New South Wales Club and had several gracious rooms, ideal for hosting dinners and meetings. Although a restoration in the 1970s had won the Royal Australian Institute of Architects Merit Award, work was still required to mould the building to the institute's needs. The end result was a beautiful building that couldn't fail to make an impact. Jonathan Lusthaus, an intern there in the early days with the responsibility of assisting with research and other tasks, said each day his spirits would lift at the sight of the building. Interns are not paid but the sheer pleasure of working in that environment was compensation enough.

The Lowy Institute's core business was to generate original research that could be used to inform or influence policy. Its thinkers publish papers, write opinion pieces in newspapers, comment on geopolitical events in all media, run blogs, give talks, hold public forums and discussions with government, and provide an Australian voice at international conferences. When foreign visitors push their way through Sydney's hectic traffic to the solid doors of the institute and are admitted to its quiet interior, they sense they have arrived at a destination of consequence.

Frank Lowy was opening Australia's first independent foreign policy think tank at the start of a decade of immense international change, much of which was occurring in the country's region. China was inexorably rising as a global power and becoming Australia's major trading partner, the first time that the country's largest trading partner had not belonged to the same security alliance. New Islamic fundamentalism was becoming obvious, and there were concerns about nuclear weaponry in Iran, India and Pakistan, all of which affected the whole region. There was ongoing conflict in Afghanistan and Iraq, with little resolution in sight.

The Lowy Institute opened in April 2003, a month after the invasion of Iraq, an action that immediately complicated Australia's foreign policy. In the previous century Australia had loyally allied itself first to Britain and then to the United States, both of which had been committed to preserving the existing order. But early in the twenty-first century, when things in Iraq went awry, issues had arisen about the previously unquestioned US–Australian alliance. There was a new tension between Australia's need to support a powerful long-standing friend and its need to maintain its autonomy, while adjusting to the rising importance of China as a regional power.

While Frank's most obvious contribution to the institute was financial he brought much more than money. He attracted a board of directors, eminent in their own areas, who would not otherwise have joined. The line-up was formidable. He started with Ryan, who had played a crucial role in building the institute. Macfarlane and Ferguson came on board and so did Indyk, who held a senior position at the Brookings Institution. To this founding board he also drew Robert O'Neill, the former chair of the Council of the International Institute for Strategic Studies in London and retired Chichele Professor of the History of War and Fellow of All Souls College, Oxford. Ross Garnaut, former Australian ambassador to China and professor of economics at the Australian National University, also accepted an invitation. Frank was chair and Steven and Peter were board members too.

Following the Brookings model, an international advisory board was appointed too. It included two former Australians;

Rupert Murdoch, the most powerful media figure in the world and James Wolfensohn, former president of the World Bank. Other eminent figures included Professor Lord Robert May, the Australian-born past president of the Royal Society, London, Sir Lawrence Freedman, Professor of War Studies at King's College London, Dr Rita Hauser, chair of the Hauser Foundation NY, and Dr Pervaiz Iqbal Cheema, president of the Islamabad Policy Research Institute, Pakistan.

In his report Fullilove had emphasised that a think tank's greatest asset is its people and that the best writers and thinkers in the world had to be recruited. But before any of this could be done, the position of executive director needed to be filled. This appointment was critical. Lowy was told they could get every other aspect right but if they chose the wrong executive director, the whole enterprise could be doomed.

13

Frank's ideas factory

When Allan Gyngell received an invitation to come to Sydney for a cup of coffee with Frank Lowy, he never thought of it as an interview. Allan, a well-known figure in Australia's foreign policy community, had started working with the Department of Foreign Affairs and Trade in 1969 and had served successive governments at the most senior level in Australia and abroad. He'd also been the principal foreign policy adviser to prime minister Paul Keating. With his impeccable qualifications and connections, Lowy thought Gyngell would be ideal as director of the institute.

Years later, at a lunch to celebrate the institute's fifth birthday, Gyngell confessed that when offered the position he had pretended he knew precisely what a think tank was and how he would go about building one. "I knew nothing of the sort, but I really wanted the job. And after a long career working on Australian foreign policy I felt absolutely confident that Australia needed something along the lines Frank was proposing and reasonably sure, one way or another, that with a lot of help from others I could make it work."

At the time, Lowy's pledge of $30 million was said to be the largest single commitment to any such organisation in the country, but he hoped the institute would eventually earn such respect and standing that it would attract support from a broader base.

For a man in a hurry, Lowy was putting his money into a slow machine. He would have to adapt to the pace of intellectual exploration. The last time he found himself in an unknown culture had been in the 1980s with his purchase of a television network. During the first lunch with the network's senior staff he had listened to the gossipy chat around the table and his heart sank; this was nothing like the pragmatic, reality-based business discussion he was used to. But this time it would be different. There would be the comfort of knowing his investment would be controlled and he was looking forward to the conversation around the table.

When Gyngell left the public service for Lowy's employ, a new culture awaited him too. Early in the piece he made an attempt to impress his new boss:

> I remember going up to him soon after the first conference
> we held within four months of being established, on
> Australian foreign policy and the age of change, and
> saying we were going to write about it. As most academic
> publications take about two years to come out, I thought
> he'd be very impressed when I said it would be published
> within three months. I thought, How good am I? But his

face dropped. He was probably thinking, "What have
I done?" Then he said, "Allan, why not publish it next
week?" Thereafter we increased the speed with which we
did things.

Some years later Lowy told a gathering that when he was getting
to know Allan, his only lingering doubt had been that he didn't
seem aggressive enough. He seemed too much of a nice guy. "I
needn't have worried," he said. "Yes, he is a nice guy, but he is no
pushover. He can stand his ground in the nicest possible way –
there's real steel in him and he uses that steel whenever necessary
to advance the cause of the institute." Lowy was impressed at
Gyngell's ability to take a long-term view, to look at trend lines
rather than headlines. He particularly admired Gyngell's ability
to put the enterprise before his ego.

Gyngell understood what a rare opportunity he had been
handed and later explained:

When we say this is an independent, non-partisan
empirically driven think tank, it's true. I've never shown
Frank anything before we published it and I've never had
to seek permission or even get a nod about things that we
write ... What he wants for the institute is to develop a
high reputation for the quality of our research and events,
and as long as he believes that is happening he is non-
interfering.

While disciplined about not meddling with the agenda, Frank
found the board meetings an irresistible smorgasbord. Each
member had expertise in some area and he was hungry for
discussion. But the intellectual thrill did not divert him from the

main game. He constantly wanted to know whether the institute was performing. Was it making a difference and if it was, where was the evidence? He pushed and pushed for tangible markers of success.

One of Gyngell's innovations was to take an annual poll designed to capture Australians' opinions on a broad range of foreign policy issues. This would be the first attempt to track over time what Australians thought of the world. It would also serve to examine claims by politicians that they were in tune with what Australians thought. When this was done for the first time in 2005, it generated wide interest in Australia and abroad. It was the most comprehensive single survey of the public's view on foreign policy and showed that the vast majority believed Australia was "a good international citizen" and was "vulnerable to external threats". Some two-thirds saw Australia as "a follower not a leader". The idea was that every year, the Lowy Institute Poll would take a snapshot of Australian views and uncover shifts in attitude.

The inaugural poll, however, was not without its critics. Greg Sheridan, the foreign editor of the *Australian* newspaper, described it as "very nearly meaningless". He said it showed how narrow sets of views held by foreign policy academics in Australia will inevitably replicate themselves in answers to questions designed by such folk. "In other words, the poll tells us little about public opinion but a great deal about think-tank opinion." While the Lowy Institute was a good thing and full of conscientious folk doing useful work, he said it didn't look as if it would inject any fresh thinking into foreign policy.

Sheridan was not the first to criticise the institute. Early on, people accused it of being left-wing and biased towards Labor with Gyngell, Fullilove and Ryan all having worked for Keating. There were also mutterings that it was a plaything of corporate interests and the Jewish lobby. The institute had to work hard to make it clear that there was no Lowy Institute view of the world. It provided well-researched, well-tested analysis and people could make up their own minds about it. Had there been no disagreements with the positions it took, Frank would have worried about what impact it was having.

There was also an understanding that not everything it produced had to be brilliant. Although think tanks operate in a rarefied sphere, often they are staffed with ordinary smart people who know how to turn theory into policy. Even high-calibre think tanks often produce material that just fills gaps. In government people typically work on a day-to-day basis. They're under pressure and do not have the time to stop and think strategically about issues. Academics have the time, but their work tends to be more theoretical than practical. Think tanks sit perfectly between the two. Their researchers have the luxury of time and can select issues less to do with immediate policy and more to do with evolving policies for the future. As many participants have a background in government, they can talk the language of policy and as no one else is producing for this space, they have a licence to produce anything – as long as it meets a certain standard. Sometimes the material is excellent and sometimes it is just something no one has written before, not groundbreaking but something that fills a hole.

When the institute opened there were already some organisations dealing in regional policy, and the well-established Australian Institute for International Affairs was fostering debate on international relations. The recently established Australian Strategic Policy Institute (ASPI) was in the space too and producing high-quality, expert advice for Australia's strategic and defence leaders.

Jonathan Lusthaus, who did an internship at the Brookings Institution before completing one at the Lowy Institute, said that in Washington there was vibrant debate outside of government. In Australia, before the Lowy Institute opened, there had been little outside debate. The foreign policy community was small, comprised of people from the public service: the Department of Foreign Affairs and Trade (DFAT); the intelligence agencies; international and national security divisions and the Department of the Prime Minister and Cabinet (PM&C). "That all changed with Lowy." Lusthaus remembers going to a 'new voices' conference for people under thirty-five at the Lowy Institute and chatting to young public servants from DFAT who all wanted to secure a job at Lowy. Among students, the institute had gained the reputation of being a superstar factory.

Prime minister John Howard delivered the inaugural Lowy Lecture on 'Australia and the World'. Howard, routinely criticised by foreign policy wonks, drew plaudits for his speech on rebalancing foreign policy to reflect better Australia's history, geography, culture and economy. It was a genuine Australian view of the world, delivered in an authentic Australian voice, and was very pleasing to Frank's ear – but he was not yet comfortable.

Although Frank was hearing that the institute was a triumph and could stand shoulder to shoulder with the world's top think tanks, he couldn't be sure. At every board meeting he would raise the question of measuring its success. "We can refurbish a fine building and hire the best researchers in the country and publish serious material that is regarded as academically sound and relevant but at the end of the day – so what? It doesn't mean we are successful," he would tell the board. Where and what was the hard evidence?

While success was reflected in the fact that the institute had drawn in philanthropic partners including the Myer Foundation, the MacArthur Foundation and for a period the Bill & Melinda Gates Foundation, Lowy wanted to see evidence that it was influencing public debate. Gyngell would explain that influence is extremely difficult to measure. "Ideas are intangible and fast-moving. How sure can you be that your work is the source of change? Sometimes ideas are specific but often what you are trying to do is to reframe the way in which an issue is seen. It is hard to chart between an idea and an outcome." The institute was nevertheless trying, by noting reactions, tracing impacts and undertaking surveys which asked audiences what they thought.

There was also the complicated issue of disclosing influence over government. Influence often needs to be invisible and it is inappropriate for an institution to crow about a policy victory. It could be counterproductive for it to be known that government was influenced by an outside organisation. This meant that some of the institute's most influential moments went unreported. In the context of real change, however, one unseen moment of influence might be worth a year's worth of coverage in newspapers.

Despite this, influences could be tracked in some cases. Through its annual poll the institute was credited with changing the nature of the domestic debate on foreign affairs. By providing an empirical foundation to the debate it provided data that could up-end preconceived notions, and it tracked changes in Australia's attitude to the world.

When the institute decided to make Australia's diplomatic service a priority, the lines of influence seemed clearer. In 2009 it produced a report arguing that the diplomatic network was seriously overstretched and hollowed out. It recommended a major staged reinvestment to ensure Australia was in a position to prosecute adequately its international interests. The report, the first of its kind in more than two decades, prompted wide discussion and in the next federal budget funding for diplomacy was increased. It looked like a link. Then in 2011 the institute followed up with another report demonstrating that despite some positive recent developments, Australia remained one of the lowest-performing OECD nations in terms of its diplomatic networks abroad. It warned that Australia's future prosperity, security and standing in the world were at risk unless the overseas diplomatic network received a sustained funding boost. A few months later a parliamentary inquiry was announced into the work, structure and geographic spread of Australia's diplomatic representation overseas.

Under Gyngell the institute steamed ahead. By 2009 it was outperforming all reviewed international marker think tanks in terms of media coverage per researcher. But Gyngell was leaving. The then prime minister Kevin Rudd wanted him to return to Canberra to take up the position of director-general of the Office of National Assessments, which brings together the information of various intelligence agencies such as ASIO and ASIS and provides advice to the prime minister and cabinet. Gyngell accepted.

Just before he left Gyngell caught a glimpse of his chairman that remained with him. It was March 2009 and he was attending a dialogue between Australia and the United Arab Emirates to reshape attitudes to the Gulf. Australia's interests in the Gulf had emerged ahead of its policy and there was a need to refocus. Gyngell was attending the inaugural meeting of the dialogue in Abu Dhabi with Lowy and a small party of Australians:

The Bolshoi Ballet was performing in the hotel and one
evening Frank, Geraldine Doogue and Orietta Melfi and
I went down to watch a performance. We hadn't eaten
since lunch and at interval we looked for something to
eat. Food was available but could only be purchased with
vouchers that had to be bought with local currency. A
couple of us went off to buy vouchers but couldn't persuade
the attendant to take a credit card or Australian money.
We returned crestfallen. We would just have to wait until
after the performance. Frank listened, told us to wait and
zoomed off to one of the food stalls. From a distance,
we could see a very intense negotiation going on. Three
minutes later, he was back, triumphantly waving a book of
vouchers. I've seldom seen him as happy. It didn't matter
what the negotiation was, it mattered that he could do
it. I was astonished and we were all fed. The capacity to
overcome obstacles gives him great satisfaction.

Over the years Gyngell had become a keen observer of his
chairman and at his final board meeting, when he noted how
Frank combined passion with a light touch, the others around
the table erupted in laughter. It wasn't ironic. The lightness
was a mark of Frank's absolute confidence in him. Lowy would
say, "What Allan has achieved in just five years can take a
generation."

Gyngell found it hard to leave. It was like parting from one
of his children. "But I said to myself that anything worth doing
has to be able to survive transition." He described his successor,
Dr Michael Wesley, as "prodigiously clever and energetic". One
of Australia's finest international relations scholars with deep
experience in government and practical policy, Wesley had been

professor of international relations at Griffith University and assistant director-general for transnational issues in the Office of National Assessments. His job was to take the institute to the next level and broaden its message so it would become known outside the foreign affairs reading and thinking literati.

Over his career Wesley had noted that while the Australian government became more international in its outlook, the public had not followed suit. "We've grown rich and confident over the past twenty years, but also complacent and very uncurious about the rest of the world." His appointment represented a generational shift. He was just forty and while he had attended the same high school in Queensland as Kevin Rudd and had been a leading figure in Rudd's 2020 summit, he was viewed as an impartial analyst of global issues. Earlier in his career he had reported directly to prime minister John Howard and his book *The Howard Paradox: Australian Diplomacy in Asia, 1996– 2006* had challenged the academic orthodoxy that had often been stridently critical of Howard.

When Wesley had his first interview with Lowy, he was not quite ready for the charisma and charm. "I liked him enormously. His style of personal politeness reminded me a lot of my father, who was an immigrant from India and had that old-style gentility to him. There's a restless intelligence inside Lowy and most disarming is his ability to break the rhythm of a conversation with a personal anecdote." Wesley was taken by Lowy's interest in him and his family – where they would live, the children's schooling – and the invitation to come and talk whenever he needed to. He would later describe how the institute was itself part of the larger informal Westfield family. There was nothing to indicate that the relationship between Lowy and Wesley would fail to be a long and healthy one.

To Wesley, Frank had created the first modern think tank in Australia. For a major business person to make such a substantial investment in ideas and intellectual infrastructure was extraordinary: "What differentiates Frank Lowy from a lot of powerful wealthy people is that he has real social vision, a sense of rich healthy societies and what is required to keep them going. What he did in setting up the institute is unprecedented in Australian history."

Lowy had also been effective in getting outsiders to invest in the institute. His initial capital had not been in the form of an endowment, because he wanted the institute to be hungry. Even though his sons were committed to it for the long term, it had to be entrepreneurial. By 2010 the institute had moved past total dependence and 50 per cent of its funding was from non–Lowy family money. But it wasn't just the "outside" dollars that mattered to Lowy: "I've always had the view that the institute should be owned in the broader sense by the community because with one dominant supporter it could be guided to self-interest."

Indeed, from time to time there had been some sniping about self-interest. In 2009, the blog *Middle East Reality Check* said the institute's elephant in the room was Israel. And there were other criticisms too. In 2011 *The Conversation*, an independent online news commentary service sourced from the academic and research community, criticised the methodology used by the Lowy Poll.

Under Wesley the institute moved towards a more strategic approach to research, becoming less reactive to policy agendas and setting its own for debate by looking over the horizon at bigger issues. By then if the Australian government had an idea for a piece of research or an event it wanted to sponsor, it often approached the Lowy Institute as a partner organisation.

That said, when the Coalition was in opposition, the institute struggled to get close to it because of a residual suspicion that it was a Labor-leaning think tank. Dispelling this distrust was high on Wesley's agenda.

On Wesley's watch Frank finally got a satisfactory indication of how well his think tank was performing. In January 2012, when the latest league tables on global think tanks were published, the Lowy Institute was rated fifth in Asia and in the top thirty outside America. The survey, conducted by the University of Pennsylvania, had looked at some 6000 think tanks, a third of which were in North America – hence the methodology of ranking outside of this group.

A couple of months later the institute emerged as a founding member of the Council of Councils, a network designed to connect leading foreign policy institutes from around the world. Its aim was to find common ground on shared threats and to inject remedies into the public debate. Its founding members roughly tracked the countries involved in the Group of 20 (G20).

By 2012 the institute was a permanent part of the Australian international policy landscape. It provided platforms for ideas, generated public debate and was useful in enabling ideas to be tested in the way the academic community could not do. But the relationship between Lowy and Wesley was deteriorating. The contention between them was never disclosed but when it was announced Wesley had decided not to renew his contract after three years, there were mutterings in the corridors that he had been pushed. For his excellent scholarship Wesley had received unconditional accolades, leaving some to assume that the reason he left was a basic incompatibility between him and the chairman. However the parting, announced in August 2012, was gracious, with Lowy praising Wesley for making "an enormous contribution to the intellectual life of Australia" and saying he had "built its national and international profile, bringing in substantial new research funding". Wesley declined to comment to the media and in November 2012 was appointed as Professor of National Security at the Australian National University.

Michael Fullilove's time had come. Since writing the feasibility study for the institute, helping to establish it and then working there for almost a decade, he finally got the top job. Fullilove wanted to see a "larger Australia". In his first address to the National Press Club in March 2014, he attacked comfortable old clichés about Australia and said the country punched at its weight and needed to move up a division. As to the tyranny of distance, he noted that while the country had once been remote from the world of Europe, the focus had now shifted to Asia and it was in the neighbourhood. "We are closer to the world's booming markets – and closer to the world's developing crises. We are less isolated – and less insulated."

As the institute matured, examples of its influence on public policy became more obvious. One related to its work in urging Australian political leaders to pay more heed to China, establishing a more structured bilateral relationship similar to that with long-term ally the United States. When prime minister Julia Gillard went to China and signed a strategic partnership agreement, the Lowy Institute's contribution was officially recognised. It had written a paper outlining what such a strategic partnership should look like.

Another example of influence concerned terminology and the reconceptualisation of Australia within its region. Rory Medcalf, director of the International Security Program, wrote that Australia's region should be described as the Indo Pacific instead of the Asia Pacific. Australia should look west as well as east and as the Indian Ocean had become the world's primary waterway for commerce, the new term better recognised Australia's two-ocean geography. While defence minister Stephen Smith adopted the term to describe Australia's region in 2012, the switch became official in the 2013 Australian Defence White Paper. Medcalf's work also helped shape government policy on India, particularly in expanding the bilateral relationship beyond sport and trade into new areas such as defence co-operation.

Yet another area of influence was the way the institute's Melanesia program director Jenny Hayward-Jones helped shift the Australian government's approach to Fiji. She highlighted how the Australian government's initial attempts to isolate the island after the 2006 coup had failed to deliver any return to democracy. Her advocacy of engagement with the Fiji government was reflected in the new approach adopted by Coalition foreign minister Julie Bishop and saw the bilateral relationship improve and Australia make positive contributions towards the restoration of democracy in that country.

Before its first decade was out, the institute had also become the venue of choice for important policy announcements. In late 2012 Julia Gillard chose it to announce the release of the Asian Century White Paper. As it happened, back in Canberra Gyngell had helped to draft it. Whenever world and thought leaders came to town, a stop at the Lowy Institute was high on their agenda.

By 2012, for a number of reasons, Australia's profile was changing and its voice was being heard around the world table. After an absence of a quarter of a century it had been elected to the UN Security Council and was also part of the G20. Australia was to chair the G20 in Brisbane in 2014 and to prepare itself for these meetings the government turned to the Lowy Institute for assistance. This was Australia's opportunity to make a visible contribution to international issues and the government funded the institute to establish a G20 Studies Centre to generate new ideas and policies. Frank's factory was in full production.

In his guide to Australia's think tanks, journalist Robert Milliken noted that in recent years Australia has seen a mushrooming of think tanks. Published in the blog *Anne Summers Reports*, his guide suggests this has been spurred by the shrinking influence of old media, the inward turning of universities and cutbacks in the public service that have seen many policy functions outsourced. Think tanks have filled the space and are now part of a more public debate.

As the institute prepared for its tenth birthday celebrations in Sydney, not many knew Frank had set up another such ideas factory in Israel. It was planning its seventh birthday. The Institute for National Security Studies (INSS), the leading think tank in Israel, was planning to celebrate with an intellectual feast to which the Israeli president, the prime minister, the minister for defence and the head of intelligence would all speak as part of an international panel.

The Sydney birthday was different, a black-tie affair celebrated by 700 people at Sydney's Town Hall. Having produced millions of words in its first decade, Fullilove decided the institute should treat its audience to a silent movie about its achievements. Frank then invited Rupert Murdoch, one of the most powerful citizens in the media world, to describe how he saw Australia. At the podium the two octogenarians gave each other a bear hug. Then News Corp's executive chairman praised Australia for having moved on from a "sentimental economy" to one that embraced disruption with vigour. It was late 2013 and he encouraged the country to seize its place in the world.

That same year, at the launch of an anthology comprising the best of the institute's work over its first decade, former foreign minister Gareth Evans told the audience that the Lowy Institute "has become a simply indispensable player in the Australian policy landscape".

He spoke of the institute's contribution to the intellectual life of Australia and also praised its founder. "Frank has made many investments in the course of his journey from running a thinking man's delicatessen in the western suburbs to the head of the world's largest retail property group, but this 'grand investment in ideas' as John Howard described it, may well be the grandest of all, with the most lasting impact."

By 2014, the core of the institute's board with the Lowys, Ryan, Indyk and Macfarlane was still in place. The new faces reflected broader views, with ABC chairman and former chief justice of NSW James Spigelman; free market economist Professor Judith Sloan; businessman and philanthropist David Gonski; former ambassador of the Republic of Singapore to the United States Chan Heng Chee; and Air Chief Marshal Angus Houston (Ret'd), former chief of the Australian Defence Force.

The following year, for a brief period Australia found itself simultaneously president of the United Nations Security Council and president of the G20. During this period Lowy found himself on the stage introducing the eleventh Lowy Lecture. It was to be delivered by Germany's chancellor Dr Angela Merkel and it was her first public lecture in Australia.

From the podium, he spoke directly to her. "World War II had a profound effect on both our lives," he said. "For you it led to the partition and the unification of your homeland. For me, as a Holocaust survivor, it was the reason for my immigration to Australia. I appreciate the leadership you have shown in rejecting racism and prejudice, especially anti-Semitism. I respect the way Germany has reconciled itself with its history." He explained that one mission of the Lowy Institute was to project Australia's voice to the world. Another was to bring prominent international voices like hers to an Australian audience.

But this occasion achieved more. Merkel had just come from the G20 in Brisbane and in the lecture she delivered that day in Sydney she abandoned her caution about Russia, sending headlines spinning around the world. In German she delivered a carefully worded attack on Russian president Vladimir Putin over his country's activities in Ukraine. She accused him of outdated thinking which trampled international law underfoot. This was a major geopolitical statement that made people sit up everywhere.

Sitting in the front row, listening to a live translation through headphones, Frank could feel the waves of history. He remembered how, at the age of fourteen he had been trapped in Budapest, hunted by the Germans and counting the minutes until the Russians arrived. He hadn't known about foreign policy then, he had known only fear. Now here he was, at eighty-four with no fear, sitting comfortably and seeing foreign policy in the making, except this time Germany was seeking to curb Russia's ambitions.

14

Closing a circle

Australia was Frank Lowy's real home, but not his only one. His other was the country that had given him refuge as a youth. When he stepped ashore in Palestine aged fifteen, the country embraced him. There were no questions, just complete acceptance. In the first few months, as the darkness he had escaped receded behind him, a new world was opening before him. No longer hunted, he could begin to belong.

As an older man he wanted to recapture that sensation of belonging. He wanted to return to that country, now modern Israel, and make a place for himself close to her heart. This time he didn't want to come empty-handed, and he didn't just want a comfortable house in Tel Aviv where he could quietly pass the years on the terrace with friends. Rather, he imagined making a substantial investment in a commercial enterprise of national significance. He was ready to take something on and make more of it. It would be his contribution to the country that he felt had given him so much.

As they age people often turn to the place of their birth to try and reconnect with the meaning of what was once there. For Frank Slovakia held no such meaning and although he visited it often, he felt no real connection; Israel had been the first country to give him a legitimate place. He would often say that at the age of fifteen he had been "reborn". Although his loyalty to Australia remained unwavering, his soul was drawn to Israel.

Since leaving the country at twenty-one he had remained attached, reading about it wherever possible and nervously following threats to its security. He would make donations for its welfare and visit as a diaspora Jew, but could never quite touch that sense of belonging. The country had changed dramatically since he was there as a young man and so had he. But by his mid sixties, the pull was becoming stronger and, no longer wanting to be just a tourist, he decided to establish a presence in the country.

He had a few connections to work with. From the 1980s there had been a constant march of Israeli fundraisers through the well-to-do Jewish communities of Melbourne and Sydney. They would usually be brought to Frank's door by his neighbour Joseph Brender, who was known as Australia's unofficial ambassador to Israel. Many of these fundraisers were on their way to becoming prominent figures in Israeli politics. Always happy to speak Hebrew and chat about Israel, Frank would entertain them at his home or on his boat. Through this process he spent time with Ehud Barak, Benjamin Netanyahu and Ehud Olmert, three future prime ministers of Israel. They drew him into a deeper involvement with the country and incrementally he began building connections to the higher echelons of its society.

One evening Brender and the then president of the University of Tel Aviv came to Lowy's house for an after-dinner drink. Professor Yoram Dinstein, renowned for his lack of tact, put the hard word on Frank. "My problem is that when I do something there is an expectation that I will do something big," said Frank.

"Excellent!" replied the president. "We expect something big." He then offered Lowy naming rights on a range of buildings.

"All my life has been about buildings. I want something with intellectual content, something to do with learning not building," said Frank. They settled on assisting a school for overseas students on the campus.

As regular visitors to Tel Aviv the Lowys would take a suite at the Hilton while looking for a place of their own. In this endeavour they were helped by Brender, who happened to have a house close by. He also happened to have a friend who was a developer. Alfred Akirov's prominent apartment blocks towered over the Tel Aviv skyline. Would the Lowys be interested in a spacious apartment in one of his towers? When Frank called Akirov to inquire, he got an invitation to lunch.

Not knowing what to expect, he arrived to find Professor Itamar Rabinovich at the table. They had met briefly before. A figure of considerable standing, Rabinovich had been a former Israeli ambassador to the United States and was the new president of Tel Aviv University. The ensuing discussion was so electric that by 4 pm, when Rabinovich pushed his seat back and rose, Frank was unaware the afternoon had passed. He suggested they meet again that night. As dinner could only be arranged for the following night, Frank delayed his departure. Akirov said he felt he and Frank had known each other for two hundred years. He understood the kind of company that would interest Lowy and proceeded to introduce him to his own circle. Over the next few years this would become Frank's circle too.

In 2001 Brender found an old office block opposite the Hilton that looked perfect for the Lowys. It was in Hayarkon Street with a view of the Mediterranean and when he described it over the phone, Frank asked him to begin negotiating immediately. When a head cold prevented Frank from flying he asked Brender to buy it. But he arrived in Tel Aviv just before the contract was to be signed and when he saw the property he was thrilled.

For many years the Lowys had run a second household in Los Angeles so Frank could be on the ground as Westfield's American business expanded. But over time as Peter took more charge they had found themselves visiting less often. There was less need for a big house in Beverly Hills and rather than pointlessly holding an unused asset, they sold it.

The timing was convenient and the contents of the house were shipped to Tel Aviv to await the completion of the new home, which would take years. It would be constructed to accommodate the entire Lowy family, with separate floors for parents, children and grandchildren and common entertainment areas. Frank's vision was to create an appealing base for the rest of the family to visit and from which they could each form their own attachment to the country.

During the long building process the Lowys continued to bunk down at the Hilton and there were times when they almost had the run of the empty hotel. Whenever Israel was involved in hostilities foreigners stayed away and the economy dipped. The family visited regardless and on a couple of occasions found the hotel with ten per cent occupancy. When Shirley's seventieth birthday fell in the middle of an Intifada, the whole family arrived in Israel to celebrate.

Akirov, who never did business with Frank – "I don't need him and he doesn't need me" – quickly noted Frank's inability to deal with small talk and observed him shamelessly napping whenever the conversation did not interest him. Against this background Akirov tells the story of a dinner in his home with several luminaries including Shimon Peres, later to become president of the state of Israel. The dinner lasted five hours with a crackling discussion across many issues. The following morning Frank called to say, "It was enthralling. I didn't sleep a wink."

In this circle Frank quickly connected with Bolek Goldman, a Holocaust survivor and professor of medicine. Goldman had been only a year old when World War II broke out and had spent the next three years hiding in the woods of Poland with his family. After most of them perished, his grandmother took him to Warsaw with false documents, where they lived as Poles until the end of the war.

Like Frank, Goldman had experienced the power of hardship and its potential to drive performance. The two men had similar experiences on arriving in Israel, both feeling the need to outperform the locals to gain acceptance. Just as the skinny young European refugees in Frank's army unit would be first to volunteer for dangerous missions, so Goldman had to be best in medical school. In those early days of statehood, there was marked tension between the local sabras and the newcomers from Europe, who were perceived as feeble and passive. It was not until the trial of Adolf Eichmann, the Nazi mastermind of the Holocaust who had been captured by Israelis in the early 1960s and who was tried in Jerusalem, that a full understanding emerged among Israelis about what it had actually meant to survive the Holocaust.

Goldman had achieved extraordinary success and over many years as co-head of Tel Hashomer Medical Center in Tel Aviv had seen the hospital grow from a few scattered prefabricated buildings into a major institution. He had been the personal physician to many prime ministers, including David Ben-Gurion, and by the time Frank met him, he was the doctor of prime minister Ariel Sharon. Frank held Sharon in high regard and was keen to meet him. Goldman obliged and took Frank and Akirov to Sharon's farm for lunch one Saturday:

> Sharon had been one of Frank's heroes in 1948 and he was
> very excited to meet him in person. I had never seen Frank
> so animated. He asked many questions about the future
> of Israel and the Palestinians. Arik [Ariel] told him the
> truth, what he feared and what he thought would happen.
> In those times Frank was naive and was sure the peace
> process was going well. Sharon told him, "No way, not in
> this generation or the next." He explained although he was
> trying to give things away and make sacrifices, it would not
> happen in his lifetime. On the drive back Frank was in a
> black mood. He had never expected the situation to be so
> bleak and was very pessimistic.

When they first met, Goldman noticed Frank tended to ask many questions. Initially he put this down to politeness but then realised the interest was genuine. Frank wanted to understand. They would discuss diverse aspects of medicine, from the way cancer spreads to the usefulness of stem cells, and Frank would ask for references so he could read further. He would also draw Goldman into metaphysics and question why he was not a believer. His own Judaism ran so deep that he couldn't grasp the concept of having nothing to believe in.

By 2004 Frank had begun upscaling his philanthropy. That year Shirley turned seventy and rather than receiving a personal gift she wanted to give one. By now the Lowys and the Olmerts had become friends and through them an ideal opportunity arose. Ehud Olmert had recently completed a ten-year stint as mayor of Jerusalem and while he was regarded as a right-wing nationalist his wife Aliza, an artist, photographer, author and social worker who disliked the political limelight, was known for her left-wing views. Among other things she was involved with Orr Shalom, an organisation that took care of children who had been removed from their homes because of severe abuse or neglect. Rather than place these children in institutions, Orr Shalom placed them in small community houses where "house parents" took care of them.

This cause appealed to the Lowys, who arranged a house in Jerusalem for a group of such children. They called it Golda's House, after Shirley's mother. "Shirley took this seriously and, without ceremony or glamour, was generous beyond the call of duty," says Aliza. "She made personal contact with the managers, would write to the children and send them gifts on their birthdays." Then the Lowys helped to renovate another home that was called Jacob's House in honour of Shirley's father. After the age of eighteen the government no longer subsidised homeless children and Orr Shalom now gave them the possibility of graduating to Jacob's House where they would have lodgings, support and more opportunity to prepare for adult life.

A decade later, on a visit to Golda's House, Frank was talking to the children when he noticed a slightly built boy of about eleven, smaller than the others, standing to one side.

He engaged him in conversation. The boy was withdrawn and answered quietly until Frank mentioned music. "Are you interested in music?" he asked. The boy switched on. Yes, he was. "Do you play any music?" Yes, the boy was alive with interest. He led Frank and Shirley to his small room where on a table he had a keyboard. "He sat down and, with his little face a picture of concentration, played 'Für Elise' for us," said Frank. "He was playing by heart and for two minutes or so, as his tiny fingers flew over the keys, we stood transfixed. Then he played another piece." Before they left the Lowys undertook to nurture his musical talent. Later, a place was secured for him in a conservatorium in Tel Aviv.

While Frank had met Ehud Olmert a few times in Australia and London he had not known Aliza previously. Not drawn to fashionable society she often declined invitations, but accepted one from the Lowys because she had heard that Frank had used his own boat to re-enact a traumatic childhood voyage after the Holocaust. These few elements made her curious and the story stayed with her. "This was a man with something extravagant about him, who was searching for symbols. He was trying to wipe the misery of the past by redoing it, under a new flag, in a glorified way," she said.

In 1946 Frank had been on an unseaworthy, overcrowded boat sailing illegally from Europe to Palestine. Scared and lonely he lay on his narrow bunk feeling seasick. Eventually, when the lights of the Israeli shore came into view, the refugees including Frank had broken into 'Hatikvah', the Hebrew song of hope. But their boat had been quickly identified as illegal and barred from entering the harbour. With all hope extinguished, the refugees were forced into the hull of a British warship and taken to an internment camp in Cyprus.

Eventually the children had been taken from the camp, repacked into a British warship and delivered to Haifa. Some fifty years later Frank wanted to relive this part of the journey on his own terms. On his magnificent yacht *Ilona* he sailed from Cyprus south-east towards Israel. As it neared her shores, he stood on the bridge remembering the medley of voices from 1946 as they joined in hope and song. Then he heard the coastguard calling on his boat to identify itself. This time the caller had a distinctly Israeli accent and the official response was, "Welcome to Israel". As *Ilona* navigated her way into the Herzliya marina and docked, with a sense of pride and completion Frank hoisted the Israeli flag. When he had stepped ashore as a youth, he had been a British prisoner. Now, with a sense of exhilaration, he stepped ashore as a free man. The circle was closed.

When the Olmerts were invited to Herzliya marina for dinner on this same boat, Aliza's curiosity overcame her natural resistance. "I don't usually go to those dinners because I find the yacht culture empty, but I recalled the story and thought it would be interesting to meet him," she said. She was seated next to Frank at the table and they quickly fell into a private conversation. "It was one of those conversations when you know from the first minute that you are talking clearly and honestly," she said. "As he talked about his life, it occurred to me that a very dear friend of mine, Tommy Lapid, had exactly the same history. There were so many similarities between them that I said, 'Listen, if you are still young and ready to do something socially unexpected, let's go to Tel Aviv straight after dinner, and I will introduce him to you.' Ehud and I had planned to meet Tommy after dinner for coffee."

The guests were still at the table when Frank got up, excused himself and left with the Olmerts. "We went to a coffee shop in Tel Aviv and Tommy and Frank linked in such a way it was unbelievable," said Aliza. "Their personal histories were so similar that the other three of us around the table listened transfixed." Lapid was a well-known broadcaster and journalist who went into politics and later became the minister for justice.

His early life mirrored much of Frank's. A year younger, he had been in the Budapest ghetto and had lost his father to the Nazis. While Frank's father had gone to the eastern railway station in Budapest to get tickets to get his family out, Tommy's father had gone to the western station to do the same. Tommy had survived with his mother and eventually the two of them had made their way to Palestine. Aliza's friendship with Tommy gave her insight into Frank. In both men she saw a wounded child fighting back.

As minister for justice Lapid had been invited to Budapest as a guest of the Hungarian government. He later told Aliza that when he arrived to a military ceremony at the airport he felt the same dread he had experienced as a boy when he encountered military force in that occupied city. He was conscious of the duality of the experience and as he sat in the back seat of a large Mercedes, the small boy in him was hiding from those who were driving him.

"Frank is also touching the past and becoming friendly with his fears," said Aliza. As their friendship grew, she saw Frank become more reflective and interested in issues many of his contemporaries no longer felt the need to deal with. Because he had never had a normal adolescence or young adulthood, he had lacked the luxury of wrangling with the meaning of life and asking all the important questions. He had just been trying to survive.

Frank was still fighting to survive, Aliza thought. She recognised in him personality traits similar to other Holocaust survivors who had gone on to do well on the world stage:

Frank and Shirley at her seventy-fifth birthday party, Sydney, 2010. *(David Mane)*

Frank Lowy drives the tender out to *Ilona IV* on the Mediterranean, 2013. *(Martin Chaffiotte)*

The family grows. Clockwise from top left: grandson Daniel and his wife Elana at their wedding in New York, 2009; their twins Honey and Ayal in Sydney, 2014; Frank holding their just-born son, Ranan, in New York, 2015; granddaughter Simonette and her husband Leo at their wedding in Los Angeles, 2014. *(Top two images: David Mane. Bottom left: Peter Halmagyi Photography)*

In March 2014, Frank and Shirley celebrated Shirley's eightieth birthday and their sixtieth wedding anniversary with a party in Sydney. Friends came from abroad for the occasion. Clockwise from top left: Alex and Shula Ceder; singing with Aliza Olmert at the party; with former Israeli ambassador to the US Itamar Rabinovitch; Frank and Shirley farewell guests at party's end.

In Israel, Frank Lowy has found a society of men. Here, left to right, in Tel Aviv: former political adviser Yoram Turbowicz; former Prime Minister of Israel Ehud Olmert; prominent physician Bolek Goldman; and international businessmen Alfred Akirov and Rami Unger.

Prime Minister Kevin Rudd opens the Lowy Cancer Research Centre at the University of New South Wales, May 2010. *(UNSW/ Grant Turner: Mediakoo)*

In conversation with the Chancellor of the University of New South Wales, David Gonski, at a Philanthropy Australia event held at the university in November 2013. *(Andy Baker)*

The wagon in Birkenau beside the gravel ramp specially built in the spring of 1944 to speed up the extermination of the Hungarian Jews. The Gate of Death can be seen in the distance.

Some of Hugo Lowy's descendants at the wagon dedication service in 2010.

Frank and his older brother Alex recite Kaddish, the Jewish prayer for mourners, for their late father Hugo Lowy at the memorial ceremony in Birkenau, April 2010.

Frank's blue prayer bag rests in the wagon to replace the one torn from his father. Greg Masel, director-general of Keren Hayesod–UIA, looks on as Frank slides the heavy door closed.

Frank and his siblings. Left to right: John, Frank, Edith and Alex at the wedding of John's daughter Rebecca in March 2001.

The bat mitzvah of Steven and Judy's daughter Rina in Sydney, 2009. Back row (l to r): Frank, Josh, Noah, Shirley, Margo, David, Simonette, Daniel, Jacqui, Benjamin, Jonah, Steven, Judy, Peter, Janine. Front row: Caroline, Amelia, Claudia, Rina. *(David Mane)*

The Lowy family in Budapest, 1943. Left to right: Frank's sister Edith, mother Ilona, brother John, Frank (in school uniform), brother Alex and father Hugo.

Seventeen-year-old Frank in army uniform in Israel, 1948.

At a young age, everything collapsed around them and there were no rules to the game. It was up to them to survive in their own way. They did and they emerged highly motivated. They were going to recreate themselves, gain an identity and a sense of belonging. These men are in perpetual motion and no matter how much money and recognition they have, they remain hungry for something. Once Frank said to me, "You are richer than me because you can be easily satisfied, I am always hungry."

When Frank was in Israel he and Aliza would often meet in a coffee shop in east Tel Aviv. "I love listening to his philosophical view of the world. He has been through so much there's a depth and a resonance, a different dimension to his conversation. I am a generation younger than him and when we talk, I hear echoes of many of the voices I heard at home because my parents are Holocaust survivors too. I love the way he fights physical decay, the way he is fussy about his looks, the way he listens when you talk and that you can have an intimate conversation with him and he'll tell you frankly what he thinks. He's not someone who just wants to please you and I appreciate that.

The Lowys pressed the Olmerts into their social circle and three or so times a year, the Olmert calendar was marked with "Frank is in town", which meant dinner at the Akirovs'.

Around this time, Itamar Rabinovich, who was in his last year as president of the University of Tel Aviv, suggested Frank take an interest in a think tank called the Jaffee Center for Strategic Studies. Given Frank's attachment to Israel and his preoccupation with the country's security he wasn't difficult to persuade. Rabinovich, an experienced fundraiser, understood that a man like Frank "knows how to build his fences so he is not solicited day in and day out" but he also understood Frank's belief in the power of ideas and his confidence in his institute in Sydney.

Frank wasn't ready for such a role but he liked the idea of re-energising the think tank. Israel's legitimacy was always being questioned and its security constantly challenged. Perhaps a freshly invigorated think tank could enrich public discourse on national security and contribute to decision making. As Frank didn't want to brand it with the Lowy name, it was decided the Jaffee Center would be folded into the newly independent Institute for National Security Studies (INSS).

Frank accepted the challenge of chairing the INSS which would itself become independent of Tel Aviv University. It would aim to have its own building and its own governing board. Through this he hoped to become more engaged with Israel's existential issues. If he couldn't find a commercial investment to connect him to the society, perhaps this would do that.

Around the table at the INSS people noticed a characteristic of Frank's for which he was known in Australia. Unafraid of revealing gaps in his knowledge, he would boldly ask basic questions. Rabinovich described him as having no false modesty. "Most of our discussions are about issues. We begin in Hebrew but move into English. Although he speaks English with an accent, his language is layered and rich, it is not an immigrant's English. His command is impressive."

But Rabinovich did find dealing with Frank on the INSS tough going. "We negotiated and we remained friends but the negotiation was not easy. He knew what he wanted and there were moments of make or break. Wealthy people resent it when they suspect others are taking advantage, when others have the attitude, 'He's so rich, what's another few million.' When they negotiate a gift like this it is not business, but they want to feel it is a businesslike transaction." The negotiations were difficult because Tel Aviv University didn't want to let go of the institute. Lowy thought it was essential for it to be freed from the university's bureaucracy and constraints and he was prepared to fund the transition. He was also prepared to fund its future needs, mostly but not entirely because he wanted the public to take some ownership too. More than anything, he wanted it to be entirely independent.

The negotiations with Frank were also challenging for the director of the new INSS. During their discussions Dr Zvi Shtauber identified a tension between Frank's humanity and his business instinct and could see him shuttling between being tough and being considerate. Shtauber's background as a brigadier-general in the Israel Defense Forces' intelligence service and as Israel's ambassador in the UK had seen him appointed head of the Jaffee Center in 2005. He remained at the helm during the transition and led the INSS for a couple of years. Shtauber understood Frank in the context of his history:

> My impression is that he is looking to leave something
> for the future and it is not in the malls. He wants to do
> something that will inform the decisionmaking process in
> Israel. There is a great need for fresh thinking. His idea
> is to create a market place for ideas on strategic thinking,
> a place to shop for ideas. Many times, people from the
> outside have changed the course of history.

Shtauber believed that if Lowy's funding led to a fresh insight that, in turn, led to policy that protected Israeli's security, he would "leave fingerprints by providing the means to make change".

15

Reputational risk

It is not unusual for wealthy Jews in the diaspora to donate to Israel and have their names splendidly displayed on the object of their donation. Although Frank Lowy was one of the largest donors to the country he was discriminating about the use of his name and was little known to the general public. When he was described in the press, it was simply as an Australian real-estate magnate.

In his push to participate in Israel's economic life, Frank worked closely with his son David. The two hadn't worked together for some time and tension arose. They had different objectives. David wanted to invest with the primary aim of creating business opportunities. Frank was more focused on the contribution an investment would make and the engagement it would bring. Another layer of complication was that Frank had all the connections and understood the language and its nuances.

Meetings would begin in English for David's benefit but would invariably move to Hebrew.

David was uncomfortable, and rather than being involved in a complex partnership that would be difficult to manage he wanted to make a simple investment that he could control. Eventually he created a small hedge fund, Ion Asset Management, which was domiciled in the Cayman Islands but focused its investments in publicly traded Israeli and Israel-related securities. David based it in Tel Aviv and his own son Daniel worked there for some time. Realising he needed to get a better grip on Hebrew, David later immersed himself in the language and gained basic competence.

For the Lowys doing business in Israel required an adjustment. Business practice was culturally different and they found it difficult to cope with the 'Don't worry, it will all be okay' style of business characteristic of the Israelis. Nevertheless, they decided to push into the banking sector and almost bought a majority shareholding in the Safra National Bank, but they shied away at the last minute. Other options were considered and when the opportunity arose to buy a 5 per cent block of shares in Bank Leumi, David was keen because it meant the family would hold a sizeable parcel on its own and could deal with it as it liked.

Frank was less interested because it was not a major stake and didn't carry much clout. It didn't fit his style of investment or suit his objective. While the offer appealed to David's head, it didn't appeal to his father's heart. They pursued it anyway. Funds were set aside, a special bank account was opened and David and his advisers flew to Tel Aviv. They did their due diligence and set about working through the night. It was expected they would sign in the morning. But late that night Frank called David: "Look, five per cent is not enough – it doesn't do anything for us. I want a meaningful stake that would give us influence." David responded that if they wanted a controlling stake they would have to join a consortium because it would require more money than they wanted to invest.

The next morning when David met with officials there was shock in the room as he announced the family was not proceeding with the 5 per cent block. He explained his family would rather bid as part of a consortium in the tender for the sale of the controlling interest of the bank. The family was looking for a long-term investment and believed the controlling stake would be available.

On hearing this Dr Yaron Zelekha, the accountant-general of the state of Israel who was leading the tender, became suspicious. The fact that there had been no serious bidder for the controlling stake had been kept confidential, but the Lowys seemed to have wind of it. Zelekha assumed the information had been leaked and he had his suspicions about the friendship between Frank and the then acting finance minister Ehud Olmert.

Unaware of this suspicion the Lowys continued to press ahead with others to purchase a parcel of shares, constituting 20 per cent of the bank, which would provide a controlling interest. They had no intention of trying to buy it alone. They also had no idea that Zelekha, who believed they wanted it alone, was working behind the scenes to try and stop this happening.

When the draft documents for the tender came out with a request for comments the Lowy camp suggested changes. "This is standard commercial practice and any changes we suggested would flow on to all the bidders, creating a level playing field," says Frank. "There were many meetings in Israel and New York, with and without us. At one point David and I were in Israel and we went to dinner at Akirov's place. Olmert was there. I raised the issue with him, saying the criteria for a long-term investor are different from those who want to make a quick turnaround – and for us to be interested, it would need to be suitable for the long term."

By now the Lowys were in a consortium with Joseph Safra of the Safra Bank and Mort Zuckerman, publisher of the New York *Daily News*, editor-in-chief of the *US News & World Report* and a real-estate developer. The Lowys left it to their lawyers to represent them. In the end their consortium withdrew before the closing date and never bid. The hedge fund Cerberus-Gabriel won from six other contenders. Its win was announced in November 2005 and Frank Lowy, no longer interested in Bank Leumi, moved on.

In his career dozens of deals have come to nothing and he never gave this one a second thought. But it was still front of mind for Zelekha. He had been brooding on it and in early 2006 he made an official complaint about the transaction to the state comptroller, alleging that Olmert had interfered in the award of the tender. This was a serious allegation at any time but was particularly so because by then Olmert was acting prime minister of Israel. Ariel Sharon was in a coma, having suffered a severe stroke and Olmert had stepped into the breach. In May 2006 Olmert became prime minister.

By October 2006 the comptroller had recommended to the attorney-general that a criminal probe be started. As one journalist at the time noted, all recent prime ministers of Israel "have known the insides of police investigations rooms": Benjamin Netanyahu was involved in a case about gifts, Ehud Barak in a matter of non-profit organisations and Ariel Sharon in a case concerning Greek islands. Now Olmert had become the fourth to be investigated, a phenomenon unprecedented in any other democracy and not well understood outside Israel.

When, that October, an Israeli website linked Frank with the Bank Leumi scandal he wasn't concerned because he "didn't think the allegations had any legs". A few weeks later, however, the story hit the international press. In Australia the ABC reported that Lowy was embroiled in a high-level corruption scandal involving Israeli prime minister Olmert.

Australians were told that as finance minister Olmert had allegedly advanced the interests of Lowy and another man in the privatisation of Bank Leumi. It was also alleged that Olmert had a conflict of interest through the law firm that dealt with Lowy's affairs. The ABC said Israel's attorney-general confirmed he was investigating claims that Olmert had accepted bribes from two international businessmen in this matter. Lowy rejected all suggestions of improper activity.

The matter went quiet until January 2007, when Israel's state prosecutor announced that a criminal investigation would begin into allegations that Olmert had intervened in the sale of Bank Leumi. The press was full of reports, some factual, some speculative and many commenting on the events. The London *Financial Times* asked the governor of the Bank of Israel, Professor Stanley Fischer, for comment. He said all the facts he knew indicated that the differences of opinion were solely professional. "I'm not saying there is no corruption, but I think there's a tendency to read too much into so-called corrupt incidents. In the British tradition, civil servants recommend and the minister decides. In Israel, I read that if a minister makes a decision that goes against the recommendation of a civil servant, it is corruption."

When locals asked Frank about the controversy his answer was always the same. "I never came to Israel to make a fortune. I already have a fortune. I came to make a contribution to the country's commercial life through a solid, safe investment." But some remained sceptical and Frank was determined to clear his name.

He prepared for battle. Apart from lawyers on two continents the family employed consultants in Israel and Australia to track all media and where necessary have broadcasts and articles translated into English. "It was a major exercise. The reputational risk was huge and we were on full alert," says Frank. "The allegations were outrageous but I was worried something may have occurred that I didn't know about. I also didn't know, if the worst came to the worst, how I would cope with the state of Israel prosecuting me. How would I cope with the conflict of being such a passionate Zionist and being prosecuted for nothing?"

During the nine months of the formal inquiry, David and Frank were advised not to go to Israel because they might be asked to give evidence in a police station in accordance with Israeli practice, which meant no lawyers would be present. "We wanted to give evidence and were anxious to do so because we knew it would clear many of their questions, but we were not prepared to do it under Israeli law without legal representation," said Frank. "We wanted the kind of representation that was allowed in Australia." The Israelis would not agree and the matter went backwards and forwards until eventually the Israelis decided to fly to Sydney and conduct the interviews under Australian conditions. Two high-ranking police officers and a policewoman arrived for the event, which was to be held in a suite in a Sydney hotel.

The Sheraton on the Park was five minutes from Westfield's head office, and Frank remembers the atmosphere as relaxed: "Both our Israeli and Australian lawyers were present and there was no tension." The police interviewed two or three executives from the Lowy Family Group, LFG, who had been part of the due diligence team for the deal, then David and finally Frank. "By the time they got to me, I think they knew all suspicions were baseless and when we finished the interview, I said, 'What now?' They replied that as far as they were concerned, I was free to come to Israel. There would be no more questions. They were very polite and friendly and said when I come to Israel we should have lunch. Then they qualified it saying, 'We can't have you buy us lunch.'" The lunch never eventuated.

Although his Israeli friends accustomed to the country's culture of controversy had supported him throughout, the allegations had hit Frank like a typhoon. Goldman thinks he was hit so hard because "he came with clean hands". Rabinovich saw Frank as an innocent bystander in the affair "as if a car drove past and splashed him with mud". When Frank returned to Israel at the end of 2007 people were embarrassed for him and tried to make him feel welcome. "I was upset about it all and I got a lot of sympathy. Although my belief in the country is still unshakable, I look at it somewhat differently now," he said.

But he was there in time to launch the first major conference for the revitalised think tank, the INSS, and despite his mixed feelings he was gracious. Significantly, among the dignitaries were prime minister Olmert and Aliza. Frank told the gathering the conference was personally symbolic and explained how, some sixty years earlier he had left the ruins of Europe and made his way, lonely and afraid, to Palestine.

When I arrived something unexpected happened. The darkness of the Holocaust closed behind me and a new horizon opened up. The people embraced me. They fed me,

they clothed me and they gave me a sense of belonging.
For the first time in years I had friends, I had work and
I had time to play. This country gave me a home. It also
gave me a sense of something very precious that needed
to be defended, at all costs ... So here I am, some sixty
years later, at this conference on Israel's security which will
focus ... on keeping Israel safe. I now have a home in Israel
again and through the INSS, I feel I can once again make
a small personal contribution to the country. I feel I have
come full circle.

It was a healing evening and nine months later, when Zelekha published a book that reignited some interest in the Leumi affair, Frank was indifferent. He said he never read the book, which was about Zelekha's four years as accountant-general. Called *The Black Guard*, it described various scandals that had thrown the country into turmoil during his term of office. Two chapters were devoted to the Leumi affair in which Zelekha did not directly criticise the Lowy group. He portrayed it as a business entity interested in winning a controlling stake in the bank at the cheapest possible price, using whatever means it could. If its requests to and alleged contacts with Olmert were against the law, he blamed Olmert and not the Lowy group.

In December 2008 the state attorney Moshe Lador announced he was closing the case against Olmert due to the lack of evidence for pressing charges on counts of fraud and breach of trust. In a forty-three-page public report he said, "Even if Olmert acted in a conflict of interest in this affair, it was of a relatively low degree, and even if he deviated from proper conduct, it was pretty limited." He did, however, note that the probe left "a number of question marks" regarding Olmert's conduct during the sale of the controlling shares and his attitude towards his ties with the Lowy group and its representatives. In the end he said Olmert's contacts with his associates did not result in any significant change to the conditions of the process and did not weigh significantly in favour of Lowy's group of investors.

As often happens, when it was over the media reports of Olmert's exoneration were not commensurate with the reports of the allegations. The same was true for Lowy. While headlines in the Australian press had shouted his alleged involvement, they reported the dropping of the allegations much less prominently. The record was corrected. Although relieved Lowy remained vigilant, alert to the fact that in an era of global media cultural nuances don't always translate. People outside Israel who read about the affair would not have grasped the difference between an investigation in Israel and one elsewhere.

Lowy had a sentimental attachment to Bank Leumi, having worked for it as a clerk when he was twenty. The interrogating police had known this and had tried to twist it, suggesting he would have attempted anything to own part of the bank because of its symbolic value to him. This supposition turned Lowy off. "I went to Israel to make a safe and solid investment. I wanted to use some hundreds of millions of dollars to do this and be involved in Israeli economic society, but it was not to be. I suppose in time the sour taste will go away."

While resolute about not getting involved in business in Israel, Frank would continue to chair the INSS and enjoy his extensive social network in the country. He also decided to upscale his charitable activities. While it may not be readily understandable to others, his sense of responsibility about Israel was heightened by the fact that he was living outside it. He felt both obligated and motivated to contribute in tangible ways. Frank had become a donor of note when he used surplus funds, amounting to US$68 million from the sale of US shopping centre assets, to create the Pa'amei Tikva Charitable Foundation. It contributed to education, health, medical research, strategic studies and community charities across Israel.

In 2008, however, this US$68 million would become the subject of international interest when a US Senate committee alleged Lowy and his family had concealed it from US and Australian tax authorities in Liechtenstein. Lowy rejected the allegation and the matter was dealt with by mediation in Australia. In the US, the matter was vigorously investigated by the Senate and by the Internal Revenue Service, but no action was taken.

Most of Lowy's and Pa'amei Tikva's charitable contributions were channelled through Keren Hayesod – United Israel Appeal, a national institution in Israel established almost a century ago. It works closely with the government of Israel and the Jewish Agency to further the national priorities of the state. Based on the concept of collective responsibility, it acts as a bridge between Israel and Jews in the diaspora. While fundraising is central to it, its role is broader. "It creates a partnership between Israelis and the global community of Jews," says Frank. "While the lives of Israeli Jews are on the line all the time, Keren Hayesod provides the means for us in the diaspora to participate in a material and spiritual way. However unbalanced this may be, maintaining this partnership is crucial because it connects us as a global family and brings us closer together."

The highest honour a philanthropist can achieve in Israel is to be given the title of 'nadiv' or benefactor. This title was first held by Lord Rothschild almost a century ago and has rarely been bestowed since then. In 2013 Frank received it "for decades of leadership and boundless care of the Jewish people". The award was made at a world conference of Keren Hayesod in Jerusalem, in the presence of the then president of the state of Israel Shimon Peres. "I have received some accolades in my life but this honour tonight supersedes all. That it comes from your hand, Shimon, makes it all the more significant," he said on receiving it.

Occasionally Lowy allowed his name to be used in relation to his philanthropy. A concert hall for the Israeli Philharmonic Orchestra was one such exception. As a long-standing subscriber to the Sydney Symphony Orchestra and with his deep but unschooled love of music, he was pleased to see his name on the wall of that Israeli concert hall. In addition to contributing to the hall, the funds from Pa'amei Tikva also covered a program designed to give 25,000 children and young people the opportunity to learn the basics of classical music.

As Frank stood with Shirley at the door of the Lowy Concert Hall in Tel Aviv in 2013 and welcomed guests for an inaugural concert conducted by Zubin Mehta, he felt another circle closing. He remembered that during their courtship he and Shirley had queued for hours at Sydney's Town Hall for tickets to a free youth concert and had rushed inside full of anticipation. That had been his first concert and a new world unfolded before him. These days, if his head wasn't too full and he wasn't too preoccupied, a concert could still take him into another realm. When the last of the Israeli guests had filtered in, the Lowys followed and took their seats. As Mehta lifted his baton Shirley took Frank's hand, just as she had done sixty years earlier in the Town Hall.

Most of their friends were at this concert. Forming new friendships late in life takes a special talent; for Frank this group in Israel is precious and he goes to great lengths to keep the connections. He and Shirley go to concerts with Arik and Shula

Ceder and explore art with David and Carmela Rubin. Carmela, who is the director of the Reuven Rubin Museum, helps the Lowys curate their Israeli art collection. Once at a business conference outside Israel the Lowys met Hanina and Jenny Brandes, established a rapport and then re-established contact in Israel, bringing the Brandes into the circle.

In Israel Frank has found a place in the company of men from all walks of life who are tied by companionship, not business. When he is visiting he joins them for lunch several times and the conversation is informed and vigorously uninhibited. No subject is off limits in the company of Akirov, Goldman or Rabinovich. It's a movable feast, takes place in various restaurants and the faces around the table change. The philanthropist Morris Kahn from the huge software firm Amdocs or Dan Propper, the founder of the food conglomerate Osem, may be at one meal. Like Frank, both are boating enthusiasts. At the next meal there may be Brandes or Ido Dissentshik, the former editor of the national Hebrew-language newspaper *Maariv*. When shipping magnate Rami Ungar is there Frank enjoys commonality of background, and the two of them sometimes reminisce about their shared roots in Slovakia.

While Frank thrives on the masculine energy he also enjoys the change in dynamic when they all meet as couples at night or on the boat. Although these friendships are comparatively recent there is a relaxed intimacy between all involved. But as is inevitable, the circle is shrinking. He already feels the loss of Dov Gottesman, who was president of the Israel Museum and a good friend. He also misses Tommy Lapid.

By 2013 Frank was also quietly enjoying the success of the INSS, which had become the leading think tank in Israel. According to the global gold standard for think tanks, it ranked among the world's top hundred outside the United States and among the top fifty in the world in the field of national security. It had taken a few years to emerge from its previous identity and establish its own culture. Now it was in the hands of Major General Amos Yadlin, the third head of the institute to be appointed under Frank.

For Yadlin, a former fighter pilot, deputy commander of the Israeli air force and the Israel Defense Force's chief of military intelligence, the offer to head up the INSS had come out of the blue. To mark his retirement after forty years at the IDF he had planned a long sabbatical and bought two tickets to South America. On the first morning of his retirement in November 2010, he woke feeling unburdened. He had no secrets to hold safe and there would be no telephone calls from high places. So he wheeled out his bike and went for a free, relaxing ride. Then his phone went. It was Frank Lowy asking him to lunch. He had never heard of Lowy and quickly Googled him. "But you live in Sydney!" he said. Lowy chuckled and gave him the address of his Tel Aviv apartment.

As the former chief of intelligence, Yadlin could be expected to be observant and to have done his homework before lunch. Later he would say he had been impressed by the apparent organisation and efficiency of Lowy's apartment. "I thought this is someone who cares about details, aesthetics and things being clear. The apartment was simple and clean and not over-extravagant." Yadlin liked Lowy from the first moment and saw him as "a man who cares about Israel, and is very warm, while showing quiet leadership in a way that is both effective and straight to the point".

Lowy asked Yadlin whether he could start work the following day as head of the INSS. It was out of the question. Yadlin needed a break and would not be available for twelve months. He planned to be back from South America around August 2011 but would not be doing any work until November that year. The two men parted amicably, and that was that. Lowy, who forgets very little, made an entry for August 2011 in the diary he keeps in his head. True to form, in August 2011 Lowy called Yadlin, who happened to be in Washington. Lowy happened to be in New York and they met at his Park Avenue apartment.

By then Yadlin had completed due diligence on the INSS and had three issues to clear. First, he wanted to get a fix on where Lowy stood politically. Was he on the extreme of the right or left? "I care about the state of Israel, its security, its welfare, its economy and its position in the world," said Lowy. "Whatever you do to support good policies for the country, I will be behind you and I will not interfere."

Next Yadlin said to become first-class the INSS needed more funding. This was a tough discussion, but not as tough as the discussion over the third issue, which concerned Yadlin's role as a fundraiser. He understood it was part of the job description but Frank wanted him to spend 50 per cent of his time on it. Yadlin said no, it would be a waste of his capacities and anyway, it would require too much time overseas where the real sources of funding were. Yadlin said, "So we negotiated and, as you know, Frank Lowy is not an easy man to negotiate with. But we ended up meeting halfway, and have not had any reason to complain ever since. After we closed these three points we shook hands and the partnership started. Since then, neither of us has any reason to complain."

Under Yadlin's watchful eye, the INSS's financial base increased, it took in young researchers and had a stronger mix of academic and practitioner experience. It also started to engage with the public in a different way. Apart from its work with policy elites it became a place where the enquiring public could go for a clear understanding of the issues. Yadlin made an early impact with security concerns about a potentially nuclear-capable Iran. Until 2011 this subject had been discussed behind closed doors, in small government and security groups. Yadlin's arrival at the INSS coincided with the eruption of public discourse on the issue. The timing was good and the INSS offered the credibility that politicians didn't have.

In Australia, whenever his local think tank was mentioned in the press, the Lowy name was prominent. It would be seen and heard repeatedly. In Israel it was absent. Yadlin was the face of the INSS. This was apparent in 2013, when it hosted a debate on what had gone wrong in the Yom Kippur War of 1973. This war had caught the over-confident young state by surprise and changed its perception of itself as idealistic. Citizens had been shaken by the realisation that their military, their intelligence gatherers and their political leaders were not invincible. Even worse, because communication between these entities had been poor, their decision making had left a lot to be desired. This war destroyed the heroic legend of young Israel.

To mark the fortieth anniversary of the war the INSS provided a platform for two surviving leaders of the period to fight for their legacy. These controversial figures, both in their late eighties, held the population in thrall as they slogged it out. The encounter was tense and probably the last opportunity for Eli Zeira, the head of the Israel Defense Forces intelligence division during the war, and the then Mossad chief Tzvi Zamir, to offer their versions in the same forum. That it became a major talking point in the country reflected the INSS's position in the society. Lowy's name was not seen or heard.

When Lowy bought his land in Tel Aviv in 2001, it had been with the hope of creating a hearth around which the family would gather in Israel. This happened, and the apartments became the family's headquarters in that country. In 2013 Frank was particularly pleased when his granddaughter Jacqui dropped in for a visit, on leave from the Israeli Army. At that point she was the only one of the grandchildren to have volunteered for military service and her grandparents saw more of her than they would have done had she remained in Los Angeles.

Unlike the Sydney-based grandchildren, Jacqui never had weekly contact with her grandparents.

> We used to have fly-in and fly-out visits and my contact was as part of a family group. I saw my grandfather from the outside but now I have a more interior view and more understanding. Often, we have breakfast together. It's valuable time. And, of course, with me being in the army, we have this commonality. We discuss things and I am much closer to him than before. He wanted me to go to the officers' course but I wanted to be a combat soldier. There is always so much for us to talk about when I get home from a mission. He understands what I am struggling with and helps me to think about things differently.

For Jacqui it is also a mark of honour to have a grandfather who fought for Israel in 1948. "In the army all my friends talk about their parents and family who are generals or hold high office. It's a proud thing for me to say that my grandfather was in the first battalion of Golani." Seeing her in uniform made Frank proud of the continuity. He never forgot how that uniform had transformed him from a refugee boy into a fighter.

Late one night he was sitting around a dinner table with friends when the conversation turned to the Israeli War of Independence. The discussion was heated and characteristically loud but for a moment Frank disengaged. He looked from one grey-haired man to another and then it dawned on him that he was the only one present who had actually participated in that war. The others had not been old enough. He had never thought about the ten-year age gap between him and his friends. Now he felt it and it gave him pause.

Sixty-five years had passed since that war and only a few participants remained who were still sharp and active in public discourse. For Yadlin such people provided an important perspective as they had "one leg in history and one leg in the future". At the time, Yadlin had three such men from whom he could gain a sense of the old values. They were his eighty-seven-year-old father Aharon Yadlin, who had been a government minister for education, President Shimon Peres aged ninety, and Frank.

During the 2015 Israeli elections Yadlin took leave from the think tank to stand as a candidate for defence minister on behalf of the centre-left party should a new government win office. When it didn't, he returned to the think tank.

As former head of military intelligence Yadlin had earned the moniker 'the nation's assessor', and when asked if the Bank Leumi episode had stained Lowy's record in Israel, he said it hadn't. "In the three years I have been working with him, no one has approached me about it." But he did think it might have been one of Frank's better decisions not to become involved in business in Israel because in the last few years big businessmen had been the target of negative media.

Despite the controversy, Frank had achieved his dream. He had done the emotional work and recaptured a sense of belonging. With Shirley equally keen and with a home that gave them a sense of place, they were able to stay in Israel for extended periods. "It made us semi-locals. We invite and we are invited. When Shirley gives a lunch for fifteen or so women, they come readily. From my study I can hear the laughter and I love it. Sometimes, one or two of the women come up to say hello. I feel we have been embraced," says Frank. Shirley's guests were usually the wives of the men in their circle. Curiosity about the Lowys coupled with Frank's extraordinary ability to reach out, make contact and include people in his world, made it possible. His disregard for age also helped.

Israel is a high-octane society, intellectually driven with a strong appetite for art, music and dance. Although Frank has found a place in it, after a couple of months in Tel Aviv he is usually ready to change pace and return to his other home in Australia.

16

Touching the past

In the first half of his life Frank had no interest in returning to Slovakia. Members of the small Jewish community of Filakovo had all but perished in Auschwitz and the town had been 'ethnically cleansed'. As Frank's adult life was packed with activity, he found it relatively easy to block out his early European years and think back only as far as Israel, which had given him a fresh start.

But this comfortable internal arrangement was not sustainable. The pain kept breaking through. In his early fifties, plagued by incapacitating stomach pain, he went from doctor to doctor looking for an explanation. Eventually one made him sit down and trace its origins. Frank remembered it from his boyhood. Whenever he felt threatened, a knot of tension would form in his stomach. For the rest of his life, this knot became his barometer of safety.

The doctor referred him to a clinical psychologist and with some reluctance Frank went. Over the next few weeks, through a series of discussions, the psychologist helped to open the vault of his memory. "I broke down and I told him the stories that had been long buried," he said. Memories of the terror of persecution, of living on the margins, of hiding and of being chased were overwhelming. Forty years later Frank was shuddering at the terror of being caught and of living with constant fear about the safety of his family. This unearthing was so powerful that he called his wife and children together to share it with them.

Used to knowing a dominating man, always in command of himself, his family had never seen him like this. As he struggled through the story of how his father had been lost and how he and his mother survived, they had a view into his soul they could never have anticipated.

Afterwards, Filakovo remained on his mind. It was the place where the family had been intact, the place where he had felt secure and happy before the great rupture. Now he was ready to visit and made arrangements. With Shirley at his side he slowly navigated his way through the town to the old family house. It had been modernised and the street sealed and tarred. They stood on the pavement and looked. Frank felt nothing. They wandered around a bit but he couldn't find what he was looking for – not that he knew exactly what it was.

The disappearance of his father had remained an open wound. While Frank had learned to live with it, he never forgot that it was there. For all his skill and power in worldly matters, there was one thing he could not achieve. It was to stand at his father's grave and grieve. No grave existed.

Frank's attachment to the memory of his father was so deep that for his entire adult life he had carried a photograph of Hugo in his wallet. After his mother Ilona died he carried a picture of her too. As he became more successful in business, he would make donations to various causes in the name of his parents. It warmed his heart to see their names in print, on buildings and plaques, but privately he was still waiting – for a sign about what happened to his dear father.

In 1991, out of the blue, it came.

At the time Peter Lowy had moved to Los Angeles with his wife and two daughters. As newcomers they knew few people and decided to spend Passover that year in a kosher hotel some two hours away by car. The hotel, in Palm Springs, was hosting a few hundred guests over the Passover period. During the day there were prayers, talks and activities followed by a traditional seder on the first two nights and communal meals thereafter.

On his second morning, Peter went down to the kiosk in the foyer to collect his newspaper. Standing next to him was an elderly man also waiting to be served. When the assistant asked the man's surname, he replied, "Lowy," and was given his paper. Peter remarked that his surname was also Lowy. Thinking they might be related, they engaged in conversation.

"Where are you from?" the older Lowy asked.

"Australia," Peter replied.

"No, no, no," said the man. "I mean where you are really from?"

"My father was born in Czechoslovakia but he lived in Budapest during the war."

"What was your grandfather's name?"

"Hugo."

Hugo Lowy! The old man, Meyer Lowy, said he had known him. They had been arrested together at Budapest railway station on 20 March 1944 and had spent the next five or six weeks together in Kistarcsa, the camp outside Budapest. Meyer Lowy explained that they had initially been drawn together by their shared surname and had grown close over those weeks.

Peter stepped back, barely able to absorb what he was hearing. He checked the story again and called his father. In Sydney, Frank called his brothers and sister with the news. Then he and Shirley flew to California. They wanted to arrive in Palm Springs before Passover ended and Meyer returned to reopen his bakery in New York. The coincidence was extraordinary. Peter was new to Palm Springs and this was the first and only time Meyer had taken his family there for Passover. That instant in the kiosk could easily have slipped away.

But the coincidence ran deeper. At the seder the night before this kiosk meeting Meyer had been saying to his own family that although Passover is about a momentous event – the liberation of the Jews from Egypt – he thought the liberation of the Jews from Nazi oppression had been historically as significant and should have a place at Passover too. This led him to talk about his own experiences under the Nazis and for the first time in forty-seven years he felt compelled to tell his family the story of a man called Hugo. Meyer spoke with such intensity and so movingly about his attachment to this older man it was almost as if he were feeling Hugo's presence again. Around the table, his family was surprised they had never heard of Hugo before.

During that meal Meyer noticed two little girls sitting at an adjacent table with their parents. He waved and they waved back, smiling. After watching them for a while, Meyer commented on how beautiful they were. He didn't know he was looking at Hugo's great-grandchildren. The very next day he encountered Peter.

When Frank and Shirley touched down at Palm Springs airport Peter drove them directly to the hotel, where they met Meyer Lowy. Churned up and not sure what to expect or say, Frank embraced Meyer. Then he opened his wallet and took out his father's photograph. Meyer took one look. "That's him," he said.

When they met, Meyer was eighteen and Hugo was fifty. The day after the Germans occupied Hungary, Meyer had been in a long line trying to buy a ticket at the eastern railway station in Budapest. A guard, who knew there were soldiers inside the station, repeatedly tried to dissuade him from entering, but he persisted. He continued:

When I got inside, I saw a couple of hundred people waiting to one side. The secret police and the SS were checking identification papers. In those days Jews were easily identified by a big Z for Zsidó [Hungarian for 'Jew']. I was put with them.

We were marched to the police station a couple of blocks away. There, we were packed chest against chest, like herrings, and were not allowed to move or even go to the bathroom. They kept us like that overnight. It was a very bad introduction to the Germans.

The next morning we were taken to Kistarcsa, less than twenty kilometres from the station. We were left in the yard. It was freezing. Snow was falling. We were scared because we had heard stories about what was happening to Jews in Poland. Around the yard there were high guard towers with soldiers, their guns pointing at us. Whenever a phone rang in one of the towers, we thought we would be shot and began reciting 'Shema Yisrael' [a central prayer in the Torah, declaring that "the Lord is our God, the Lord alone"].

It was bitterly cold. When it was dark, the Germans came and let us inside the barracks. That was much better. That's where I met Hugo. I recognised his name and since I was alone, I went to him to see if we were related. We weren't.

Hugo was one of the older men in the camp and as the youngest Meyer looked to him for support and stayed close. When the Hungarians were in control of the camp, food trucks from the Jewish community would be allowed in and everyone had enough to eat. When the Germans took over the men starved, except for occasional food parcels sent by families. Meyer had no parcels and three men would share their food with him. One was Hugo.

Some women and girls were arrested, brought to the camp and housed in a separate building. At night the SS would go into the building and the men heard screaming and crying. This enraged Hugo. He would go wild and the others had to calm him.

After a few days Meyer was ordered to wash floors in the police barracks. To do this he had to get a pail of hot water from the boiler in the basement. At the boiler, there was a large gruff man whom the Germans forbade him to talk to. On account of his beard, Meyer thought the man might have been Jewish. Eventually they talked and the man began questioning him. Where did he and the others come from? When Meyer explained, the man said he was not Jewish himself but he felt bad hearing what was happening. He also mentioned that he went home to Budapest every night. Meyer told the others about this and on the next occasion asked the man whether he would take letters in exchange for money. The man said they need not pay but Meyer insisted. Eventually Meyer became a go-between, giving the man money to take letters to relatives. This was how Hugo Lowy's family found out where he was.

The men had been in the camp for about five weeks when one of 'the big leaders' of the orthodox Jewish community of Budapest came to visit and made an announcement. According to Meyer, he said:

> "Jewish brothers and sisters, tomorrow they are going to take you to a small town, to a brick factory, where you will survive the war and even get paid for your work. So nobody should worry."
>
> So we waited to go. We were packed up and very early the next morning, while it was still dark, we walked back into the big station where we had been arrested in the first place. On that walk through Budapest we could have escaped. It was dark and for the whole group of us – the whole prison community of Kistarcsa of perhaps a couple of thousand people – there were maybe five or ten Hungarian guards. We could have just walked away from there but we believed the Jewish leaders.

At the station they waited for the train. Unexpectedly, the train that rolled in was German, guarded by the SS. Between the wagon's slats they managed to talk to the people inside, who believed the train might have been heading for Auschwitz.

Meyer and Hugo were forced into the same wagon. Before they closed the door the Germans appointed one man to be leader and warned that if anything untoward should happen or if anyone escaped, he would be held personally responsible and shot. There was a dull clang and the wagon was in darkness.

On the train ride some Slovakians used a kitchen knife to remove part of the wooden floor and when the train was travelling very slowly up a hill, they slipped out onto the tracks below. When they first began hacking at the floor, the 'leader' started to scream, but others in the wagon hit him to make him be quiet. He fell down.

The train was going through Slovakia and we were talking in the wagon that to be a Jew in that country you didn't have a chance of survival. The population there, the first thing they did when a Jew escaped was to call the Germans.

It was very bad in the wagon because we had not even a place to urinate. The train stopped here and there and the Germans opened the doors and looked in. Then we got a little fresh air to breathe. There was no water. That was the biggest thing. We were asking the Germans please let us go for water and they just slammed the door back. Once they hosed water in.

After some days, the train came to a halt. Dehydrated and distressed, the men were finally allowed out. They were dazed. Most were carrying only small items of luggage that they were ordered to leave in a pile beside the train. Meyer remembered the men being sorted into two groups. The strong younger ones, who would be good for work, went to one group and those who were judged too weak went to the other. Meyer was placed with the workers and because he was fit and healthy, so was Hugo.

Meyer noticed that despite the orders Hugo had hung onto a little parcel. The Germans had promised that everyone would get their possessions back later. Hugo didn't trust them. He needed the parcel and would not relinquish it. An SS officer came up to him, reprimanded him, grabbed the parcel from under his arm and threw it onto the heap. As the officer turned around, Hugo went to retrieve it. A guard noticed, pushed him aside, beat him and threw the parcel back on the pile.

Hugo then made another attempt. This was extremely dangerous and those watching implored him to leave it be: "Hugo, *bácsi*, don't do it! Hugo, beloved uncle, don't do it!" Perhaps they were also afraid there would be collective punishment. But Hugo was determined to have that parcel. This time more guards came, pushed people aside and with their rifle butts began to beat him, on his back, on his head, in his stomach. Hugo collapsed onto his knees but continued to hold onto his bag. Everyone was watching. They kept beating him. He was terribly beaten up, bloodied and shaking. Then they tore the bag from him and opened it. And the others moved on.

Hugo's torn parcel contained his tallit or prayer shawl and his tefillin, the small leather boxes with black straps attached that contained verses from the Torah and were worn by observant Jews during weekday morning prayers.

As Meyer Lowy told his story Frank became overwhelmed and had to leave the room. He was absent so long Peter was sent to look for him. He found his father weeping uncontrollably in the men's room.

The story left Hugo's children in emotional turmoil. For decades they had lived with the ache of not knowing what had happened to their father. Now, rather than soothing them, the knowledge brought fresh pain. They talked among themselves and each in their own way tried to absorb the account. Some weeks later Frank realised he was no longer dreaming about his father, after almost fifty years:

> While my memories of my father had always been vague it was extremely important for me to know what happened to him, in a sense more for my mother's sake than mine. During so much of my time with her in Budapest she was so scared about what could have happened to him and in such constant pain over his absence. The consuming sense of loss I saw in my mother and experienced in my own way has been a great motivating power for me with my own family. Not only did I not want them ever to experience anything like that, but my family is almost a validation of having survived. It gave and still gives me the sense of belonging I lost during the war years. This is not easy to express, as so much understanding is required. The burden of this understanding is not something I necessarily want to pass on to others. Bearing it alone seems less complicated.

Although now calm, Frank was not at peace with the past. He needed to do something to honour it. At Sydney's Moriah College, he dedicated a beautiful synagogue in his father's name. It wasn't enough for him. While others had visited Auschwitz-Birkenau, he could not go. He could not visit this greatest Jewish graveyard on earth until he knew where his father had perished, until he had a place where he could stand and touch something representing him. More than this, he wanted to mark the place for himself, for his family and for generations to come.

*

A couple of years later, Frank and Shirley went back to Filakovo, knocked on the door of the former Lowy house and were invited inside. The house came alive for Frank. He remembered where he had slept and where as a boy he had been bathed in a tub on the kitchen table. In the yard he showed Shirley where the old water pump had stood. With the new residents they had tea where his family used to have their treasured Friday night dinners. Frank could feel a connection stirring. He wanted to bring the rest of the family too.

A few years later he brought his sons and their wives to Filakovo. While this generation would see the modest dimensions of the family's origin they would have no sense of the rich communal life that had once flourished there. There was only the stark fact of its annihilation.

Just outside town they stumbled on the derelict Jewish cemetery. While the women waited in the bus the men climbed a high fence to get in. It was overgrown and stones had long fallen. For an hour in the heat they searched, clearing weeds and turning over headstones.

Just as they were about to turn back David called out, "Dad, is this it?" The Hebrew writing was weathered but the name of Jonah Lowy could be deciphered. He was the grandfather Frank had never known but had been named after. They set the headstone upright and as is customary placed a few stones on the grave. Then they stood in silence. It was a solemn moment, each aware that four generations of Lowy men were in one spot – only Hugo was missing. Frank, David and Steven started to move off when they noticed Peter was not ready to leave. They walked back to him and together they all spontaneously began to recite the Kaddish. This prayer for the dead would not have been heard in that cemetery for fifty years.

Now Frank wanted to take all the grandchildren back too. First he took the oldest, Daniel. Then he took six others: Noah, Josh, Benjamin, Simonette, Jacqui and Claudia. It was a profound and unforgettable experience for them all. Benjamin, then sixteen, said, "It was a moment when I was growing a lot and many things in my life were changing. As I stood in the cemetery in Filakovo, I felt the history. As we said Kaddish, I felt like a living link between the past and the future. I will be the link for my children and their children, all the way back to my great-great-grandfather. I have stood at his graveside and I have felt the responsibility."

The trips back to eastern Europe with the grandchildren were not all sombre work. Although there was a planned educational itinerary, Frank would break it whenever he saw they were overwhelmed. He'd forgo a museum for ice-skating and whenever their guide was over-explaining, he'd cut across with, "Okay, okay, we get it ..." And he understood when the grandchildren let loose at night. "We needed a counterpoint," said Benjamin. "When we played ding dong ditch in the hotel passages he watched us and laughed. He had never had that as a boy himself."

Some years later it was Caroline and Rina's turn to make the journey. On these visits Frank would walk with them to the house, sit on a bench in the railway station where Hugo had arrived home on Friday afternoons and pray at Jonah's grave in the cemetery. He wanted every member of the family to touch their origins so they could bear witness for future generations.

Although the whole family except for Amelia and Jonah had gone back – it was hoped those two would go later – Frank hadn't yet closed the circle. He didn't know what it would take and he began making the trip alone. It wasn't as if he just dropped in on his way to somewhere else. Filakovo has no airport and is a two-hour drive from Budapest. Each time he arrived it was with the unrealistic hope that there would be a sign of the community that had been there since the early 1800s. But there was nothing and there was no one to sit with, to remember what had been.

Through these visits he became known in the town. When the locals Googled him they were pleasantly surprised to discover who he was, and claimed him as Filakovo's famous son. After all, he'd spent the first eleven years of his life there and spoke both Slovak and Hungarian. Over time, Frank's visits and their curiosity about him awoke in the town an awareness of its lost Jewish community.

17

Burying a father

The one place Frank never went and never took his family was Auschwitz-Birkenau. He could not visit until he knew where his father had perished, until he had a place where he could stand and touch something representing him. More than this, he wanted to mark the place. Thousands of people who visit Auschwitz-Birkenau have the same impulse. They want to leave a personal memorial, a plaque or a note that speaks of their private loss. And often they do. The authorities usually allow these symbols to remain for a couple of weeks and then remove them. Their aim is to keep the death camp as close as possible to its original condition at liberation – empty.

Hugo's death had a profound effect on the man who had befriended him, Meyer Lowy, and it continued to reverberate through his life. After he met Hugo's family, Meyer talked about that time in his life so often and with such warmth that his own wife and children became entirely familiar with the story. It became part of their family narrative and they would tell it to others. As Meyer grew older, the fact that he had borne witness to Hugo's death and had personally been able to transmit the knowledge of what he saw held great meaning for him. As a religious man, he felt he had performed a sacred duty.

After Palm Springs, Meyer formally retold the story twice for the record. In January 2004, I went to see him and his wife Katy in Miami. In common with other snowbirds, every winter they would leave New York and migrate south to the warmth of Florida. By then Meyer was not well and his voice was soft, but he sat for a few hours in his apartment, looking out to sea and talking about the time he spent with Hugo. More than half a century had passed but his memory was clear and his richly detailed account was full of affection.

With his charismatic presence, he said Hugo soon emerged as the leader of the barrack of some 200 men in Kistarcsa. He led them in prayer and represented them to their captors.

"Hugo was in charge of us. He was the one who did things for the group. We called him 'Hugo bácsi'. He was an organiser, always active, arranging and doing. We formed a davenning [prayer] group. He gathered people for prayer and led them. We prayed all day."

Somehow Hugo had the resilience to lift himself above their circumstances. Meyer said his religious conviction was so strong that, at times, he was even joyous. People were drawn to him. His warmth helped to ease their distress and his faith gave them comfort. "He had authority over us. He was the baal tefillah [the person who reads the liturgy during the worship] and we loved him. Davenning was our only hope and we prayed Thilom [psalms] because only God was going to help us."

Meyer's words, which I transcribed, were a revelation for Frank. In Palm Springs he had heard every word of Meyer's account of Hugo's death, but not the details of the six weeks they had spent together in the camp. Frank had not known that his father was a leader. He hadn't known that his father had been held in such esteem. For decades Frank had struggled with a few bare facts that he'd heard about his father. He had heard Hugo was a good man and an appealing personality but that he lacked commercial skill and the family had struggled to make ends meet.

Until Meyer spoke there had been no one to correct his lopsided perception or give a fuller account of Hugo. As Frank absorbed this information, his thinking about his father began to change. While Hugo might not have been good at business and might have liked to play cards, there was another dimension to him. He had been spiritually powerful. In desperate conditions his strength had enabled him to inspire people and draw them to him. He had led them, negotiated for them and comforted them.

As Frank began to understand more about Hugo he began to feel an unfamiliar emotion. At the age of seventy-three he felt proud of his father. More than ever he began to sense the urgency of laying him to rest. Was this magical thinking? Would it be possible to bury Hugo? Frank began to read about the concentration camps. He learned while Auschwitz was a prison camp, Birkenau, about three kilometres away, was its death camp. Hugo had perished in Birkenau; whenever Frank came across photographs of people arriving there, he would search the faces in the hope of seeing his father. But so many had passed through this vast desolate place that Frank would never find him. Until he could find a way to mark Hugo's death, he wouldn't step into that graveyard.

There is no comfort in Birkenau. There is nowhere to sit and nowhere to lean. The soil is soaked in sadness, the lake is full of human ashes. Terrible memories hang in the beautiful birch trees under which families with children once sat waiting to enter the gas chambers. Bare railway tracks now run down the middle of the camp, from the gate to the gas chambers.

These tracks and a new ramp were specially built in the spring of 1944, to rush the Hungarian Jews to their deaths. The trains had previously stopped outside the camp and people had been marched in or taken in trucks. But that had been too slow. During the spring and summer of 1944, day and night, trains went through what the prisoners had called the Gate of Death and rolled down the new tracks. They stopped to unload at the freshly graded 'new ramp'. Within hours most of their human cargo had vanished into smoke.

In 2006 a Holocaust historian happened to be in Australia for a lecture tour. Dr Gideon Greif had detailed knowledge of the Hungarian transports and if anyone could help Frank in this quest, he was the man. In a private meeting at Frank's house, Greif described the new ramp and how it had been constructed with the express purpose of receiving the Jews of Hungary. This was where they disembarked and where the SS performed selections, deciding whether they lived or died. It was a clearly defined place, and it had been kept exactly as it was after liberation in 1945 – empty.

To the meeting Greif had brought a copy of the 'Auschwitz album', a collection of photos taken by SS photographers on the ramp during the Hungarian transports. As he and Frank looked at the photos, it became clear that Hugo must have met his death close to this location.

This too was a revelation. Greif's help in finding the likely location of Hugo's death inspired Frank. In his mind's eye he could see a wagon standing quietly beside this ramp. It would be of the kind used to transport the Hungarian Jews. He saw it standing empty as a memorial to those 400,000 men, women and children who stepped onto the ramp, exhausted, hungry and afraid, and were then turned and made to walk deeper into the camp towards the birch trees.

For more than sixty years the ramp in Birkenau had stood empty; the Auschwitz-Birkenau State Museum kept it bare as an eloquent reminder of what had taken place. During those decades, placing a wagon beside the ramp would have been unimaginable. Now, as Frank raised the possibility it could serve as a memorial to the Hungarian Jews – one of whom was his father – a new approach was evolving at the museum where a young director had been recently appointed.

A historian by training, Dr Piotr Cywinski believed in the importance of maintaining the authenticity of the camps and in the value of educating future generations about them. The idea of having a wagon struck a chord. By seeing and touching a real boxcar from the era young people would better understand the transportations and the tragedy of what had happened. He supported the idea of allowing a wagon into Birkenau provided it was fully authenticated. It would stand as a memorial to the mass murder of the Hungarian Jews in the spring and summer of 1944.

Frank spent many hours reflecting on what it would mean to put a wagon there. He saw it as a monument to Hungarian Jewry, rich in collective meaning, and he also wondered what meaning it might hold for him personally. After so many decades of not knowing where his father had perished, and now knowing, could such a wagon also stand as a private memorial? Now he yearned to stand under the same sky as his father, and to perform the ancient mourning rituals, at least in his own mind. He could stand in the place where his father had drawn his last breath and perhaps feel a sense of him again. While this boxcar would be a public symbol, for Frank Lowy it would be a private spiritual one.

He began looking for a wagon. It would have to be original, used to transport Hungarian Jews to Poland in spring and summer of 1944. When the war ended most of the wagons resumed carting goods for the German and other railways. Any day of the week until the 1970s they could be seen crossing the countryside on routine business, their sinister past unacknowledged. But by the time Frank was looking for one they had not been in use for well over thirty years.

A small taskforce headed by Greg Masel, director-general of Keren Hayesod – United Israel Appeal, was established to find a wagon. Masel would handle the logistics while Gideon Greif dealt with the historical issues. The pair's first stop was the Transport Museum in Budapest, which has the largest collection of wagons in Europe. The men walked for hours through the open-air collection, looking at lines of historic wagons. The curator showed them two that had transported Jews from Hungary to Auschwitz-Birkenau. These were in good condition and after establishing authenticity the two men selected one. But after complex negotiations, the Hungarian government decreed that the wagon could not leave Hungary. The official reason was that the weather conditions in Poland, especially in winter under an open sky, might endanger it.

Masel and Greif later returned to the museum in Budapest and viewed other wagons that could be exported. Protracted negotiations followed, but these proved fruitless too. Then they heard of a private collection on the outskirts of Budapest.

There they found a wagon in poor condition and brought in conservation experts from the Auschwitz-Birkenau State Museum to check it. They removed small pieces of wood and metal and tested them in the museum's Polish laboratory. Two weeks later they announced that the wagon had been built in the twentieth century and its parts were original. Further investigations using old photographs, documents and the work of train experts confirmed it was one of the models of wagon used to deport Jews to Auschwitz. Negotiations progressed quite far, but ultimately they failed too.

And so it went, through Hungary, Poland and Germany. Masel and Greif conducted endless negotiations with private collectors and made no progress. But then Israeli journalist Micha Limor joined their search team. Friends in Germany had told him about a wagon collection near the Dutch border. The team went to investigate and saw two wagons that looked promising. Limor was acquainted with the professional German reconstruction and conservation laboratory, Die Schmiede, and two of its experts viewed the wagons. One was selected. It had a little braking hut, a small wooden structure attached at the back, where one or two employees would apply brakes when necessary to stop the train.

This wagon was standing in a field in a state of disrepair and was being used for temporary storage. It belonged to Dr Roland Hüser, a medical doctor and railway enthusiast, and he was asked whether he would consider selling it. Hüser was sceptical about the request. He had heard of fellow enthusiasts who had given their wagons for such projects only to find that once they had served their purpose the wagons had gone to scrap. The projects were rich in emotion but there was little understanding about their value as museum pieces.

But Hüser was keen to see the wagon professionally restored and as discussions continued it was closely examined. The originality of the parts and model were compared to historical and archival photos and documents. Then experts from the Auschwitz-Birkenau State Museum authenticated it – human remains were found between the slats – and declared that it belonged to the group of wagons used to transport Hungarian Jews to Poland.

When Hüser better understood the reason behind this flurry of interest in his wagon, he changed his mind. He could make a contribution against 'the forgetting' and in the process help an Australian man, by the name of Frank Lowy, 'with an affair of the heart'. But there was a condition. The wagon had to be conserved at Die Schmiede, which had a fine reputation for the restoration of historical wagons. Hüser had never considered the wagon as his private property but had intended over the long term to preserve it for the public. If he donated it to the Auschwitz-Birkenau State Museum its restoration would happen quickly and at the highest technical level.

What for Hüser was a fine museum piece was for Frank Lowy a spiritual symbol. During the negotiations, neither realised that together they were preparing an emblem that would come to represent Birkenau. On entering the camp, the eye would immediately be drawn to it. In that bleak expanse, it would become the point of focus.

Hüser had bought the wagon in 1994 after the Royal Corps of Transport announced it was selling some freight wagons it had taken over from the German railways in 1945. In the early postwar days the British had commandeered four of the wagons and assembled them into a service train designed to restore and rebuild damaged tracks. Each wagon in the train had a different function. One had been a sleeping car, one a kitchen, one a workshop, one a washroom. Hüser had viewed the wagons at the Wulfen ammunition depot and selected four. His goal was to have the sleeping car professionally restored to its original condition. This was the very wagon the experts had selected to stand in Birkenau. Hüser wanted no praise for his gift, he just wanted to savour the preservation process.

> I was able to experience its full restoration at the highest technical level. Worldwide no comparable model of this type of wagon has received such a high-quality, complete and contemporary restoration. For one who would like to preserve the technical, cultural heritage of the wagon there is no equally appropriate way of displaying and preserving such a technical cultural asset as in Auschwitz-Birkenau. I am highly grateful and proud to be part of this project. I would never have imagined that I would ever have the opportunity to contribute with modest means against oblivion. This thought will always connect me with this wagon.

After months of work, under the supervision of the museum, the wagon was ready to be transported to Poland. Three years had passed since the search began and on a grey day in September 2009 the wagon arrived outside Birkenau, a piece of the past returning. It had come by road train on an articulated truck and was unhurriedly unloaded onto tracks that had last been used some sixty-five years earlier. A group of workers slowly pushed the wagon under the brick archway and through the Gate of Death. Rain was drizzling and the air was misty as they moved it almost a kilometre along the track deep into Birkenau. At the ramp, they stopped and locked the wheels.

The recognition was immediate. The wagon fitted naturally into position, and new visitors to the site thought it had always been there. A brass plaque from the museum affixed to its side explained its presence in English, Polish and Hebrew:

> This freight car has been placed here to commemorate the
> Jews deported from Hungary who were murdered by the
> German Nazis in the Auschwitz-Birkenau death camp.
> More than 400,000 Jewish men, women and children were
> deported from Hungary in similar freight cars, in more
> than 100 transports during the spring and summer of
> 1944. On arrival, most of them were murdered in the gas
> chambers here.

Recognising the wagon's significance, the museum agreed that a smaller plaque could be affixed in a less conspicuous position at the back, saying it had been conserved by the family of Hugo Lowy who had died in these transports. But Hugo's story had to be verified. There were no official records of his presence in Birkenau and the only known living witness to his death was Meyer Lowy, who was by now critically ill in New York.

Greif was assigned the task of taking Meyer Lowy's testimony but on the day he phoned Meyer was weak and hardly able to speak. The call was difficult, the long-distance line crackled, and when the conversation ended Meyer worried that he had not given a full account. He could not rest until he had given a proper testament and urged his wife and son to locate the historian so he could try again. This time his wife helped to interpret and after a two-hour interview Meyer was satisfied. His work was done. Two weeks later, on 31 October 2009, he died.

Meyer Lowy had been told about the wagon's restoration and it held deep significance for him. As his life was drawing to a close he told his family that part of the power behind his survival had been his mission to bear witness. He told his own son that beside the train, Hugo Lowy had looked at him and said, "I am not going anywhere without my tallit and tefillin." In that moment Meyer had understood that for Hugo these religious items were essential for life. With the spiritual strength he drew from them he had been able to lead men in prayer and sustain them. In Kistarcsa they had been under constant threat and had nothing to depend on but the protective power of prayer. In Auschwitz-Birkenau Meyer Lowy believed Hugo intended to continue his work. And in full view of the men he had led he had refused to relinquish these items. The men would have known what the little parcel contained, and in the heightened terror of those moments Hugo's act of spiritual resistance would have made a lasting impact upon them.

Sixty-six years later, in the northern spring of 2010, Hugo's last moments were finally relived beside the railway tracks at a ceremony to dedicate the wagon. Meyer's testimony ensured that the smaller plaque would be in place. Hugo's children would have a mark for their father but only Alex and Frank would see it; Edith had since died and John was too ill to travel to Poland for the ceremony. The surviving members of the family and many close friends made the journey. Those who arrived the day before brought their prayer bags containing their own tallit and tefillin, knowing that prayers would be held early the next morning.

Alex led the men in prayer at the hotel where they were all staying. In a quiet moment, Masel came over to Frank. A thought had flashed across his mind, and he asked: "What would you say to placing your prayer bag with your tallis and tefillin in the

wagon? Symbolically, to replace the one torn from your father?"
It was an inspired idea and seemed absolutely right. All that
was needed was for Masel to get the blessing of the museum
authorities.

As Frank dressed for the ceremony he picked up his own
prayer bag and felt its weight. He remembered the first letter
his father had written from Kistarcsa in 1944, thought of the
comfort his own prayer bag must have brought Hugo in the last
weeks of his life and imagined him holding it in the darkness
of the wagon. But his imagination couldn't stretch to what it
must have been like to stumble weak and disorientated onto the
ramp, after days confined without food, water or space, and still
be determined enough to hold onto what was so important to
him. Frank left the hotel for the ceremony with his own blue and
silver prayer bag under his arm.

It was a dull and overcast day at Birkenau with no shelter
from the persistent drizzle. As the guests passed through the
notorious gate the first thing they saw was the wagon in the
distance. Silently, under black umbrellas, they made their way
towards it. They had come to commemorate almost half a
million people who had disappeared as smoke into the grey skies
above. Profoundly solemn, the ceremony nevertheless had within
it an element of celebration. Not only was the late Meyer Lowy's
family there, but so were more than twenty-five of Hugo's
descendants and 100 guests from the independent Jewish state
of Israel.

Addressing them all, the museum director said the deep
memory of what happened at Auschwitz-Birkenau lay within
them. But their presence that day was not just about memory: it
was about victory, the victory of survival. Holding Frank's blue
and silver prayer bag Levi Wolff, a young rabbi from Sydney's

Central Synagogue, explained that it would be placed in the wagon as an everlasting memory of Hugo's soul. Two of his sons would replace the bag that had been torn from him.

The sky above Birkenau remained leaden as cantor Shimon Farkas, also from Central Synagogue, rose to sing a holy song of hope and longing that had been sung by the Hungarian Jews in the camp. In a mixture of Hungarian and Hebrew the song, 'Szól a Kakas Már', expresses a deep yearning for redemption and for the return of the Jewish people to the land of Israel. As his voice lifted, so the skies began to clear.

Standing in front of the wagon Rabbi Yisrael Meir Lau, the former chief Ashkenazi rabbi of Israel who had been a child himself during the Holocaust, described how as a young boy he had travelled in such a wagon and what a traumatic impact it had had on him. Even as an adult, he said, the sight of a wagon would make him quake. But this day, standing next to this wagon, he was no longer trembling. To him this wagon no longer spoke of the suffering of those crammed inside with no air and no water. It had become a holy monument – a monument of Kiddush Hashem, a sacrifice for the sanctification of God's name. In almost every generation individual Jews and entire communities have sacrificed themselves for the sanctification of the holy name.

Since hearing Hugo's story Rabbi Lau had often asked himself what Hugo Lowy could have been thinking in those last moments. Why had he done what he did? Perhaps the contents of the prayer bag had been his link to life. They had been his Jewish heritage, his tradition, the education of his father and his mother. Rabbi Lau now wanted every boy and girl of the Jewish world, "to know the story of how a Jew, Hillel Zwi Lowy [Hugo], sacrificed his life and was ready to go on the altar of history, of Jewish tragedy, because he understood that without his, tallit, without his tefillin … this was not a life for a Jewish man". He also wanted everyone to understand the importance of children honouring their parents, not only in life but in death, too. In his death, Hugo had left a heritage for his own family.

Three of Hugo's great-grandchildren, Daniel, Simonette and Joshua, stood in front of the wagon and in turn read from the final letter Hugo had written home sixty-six years earlier. Then the Lowy brothers Alex and Frank stood together to recite the mourner's Kaddish for Hugo and for all who had perished there. The words of this ancient Aramaic prayer drifted through the barbed wire fences and over the broken barracks. Their faces bathed in tears, the brothers could scarcely get through it.

To mark the passing of so many hundreds of thousands of Hungarian Jews a large pile of white stones had been brought from Jerusalem. Everyone present was asked to place a stone inside the wagon. While flowers are a metaphor for the brevity of life, stones represent the permanence of memory. As people silently gathered around the open wagon the brothers placed the prayer bag inside it. Slowly Shimon Farkas began singing the song that has become known as the Hymn of the Camps. Others joined in, and the air was filled with the Hebrew refrain of 'Ani Ma'amin' – "I believe …". Then the heavy wagon door shut with the same dull clang that must have reverberated across that ramp in 1944. In that year, most of the Jews leaving the ramp would have walked down into the camp towards death. Now the guests turned towards the gate.

In the presence of family and his friends, Frank had finally touched the past. "It is the closing of a certain stage for me," he said. "I was thirteen years old when I lost my father. Today I am eighty."

Having come to peace with his loss, Frank was able to accept an invitation to return in 2013 as one of the leaders of the annual March of the Living, in which some 14,000 young people from all over the globe march from Auschwitz to Birkenau in a symbolic reversal of the death marches that took place at the end of the war. While David and Peter stood on either side of Shirley and supported her on the march, Steven accompanied Frank at the front. With them, together with dignitaries and military personnel, was Rabbi Lau. Not far behind were Judy Lowy, Dr Hüser and Meyer's son, Allan. As he marched Frank was conscious that somewhere in the throng behind him was his granddaughter Rina, marching with the Australian youngsters.

At the formal ceremony in Birkenau Lowy spoke to all the youngsters about his father and how, even though he was now eighty-two, he still missed him. "I want to say that your mother and father always matter – even when you get to my age. And honouring your parents matters very much while they are alive ... and when they are no longer." He explained how he had longed to stand in the place where his father had been to see if he could feel him. "So here I am, with you all in Birkenau. And I know he was also here, under this same sky. Just like almost half a million Hungarian Jews, he came to this place in a wagon, and almost immediately after arriving, disappeared as smoke into this sky."

He told them about the wagon and how he placed his prayer bag inside it, symbolically to replace the bag torn from his father's hands. "For me, this helps to heal the brokenness of the past. Some two centuries ago, Rabbi Nachman of Breslov taught that if you believe the world can be broken, then know it can also be fixed."

Afterwards he attended a small gathering of Australian youngsters who were holding an additional memorial among the birch trees and who were addressed by Rina, among others. It had been a day of heightened emotion and as Frank listened to his granddaughter's soft, clear voice he felt his eyes filling. Here she was, generations after Hugo's annihilation, standing under the same sky, a beautiful embodiment of his spirit.

There was one more thing Lowy needed to do. After two decades of visiting Filakovo intermittently, he wanted to go again and make a mark there too. In a small park on the site where the synagogue once stood he placed an obelisk dedicated to the memory of the two hundred souls who had constituted the now-lost Jewish community. The town was enthusiastic about it and organised a ceremony to which a small crowd came. While Frank could have flown in five hundred people to share the occasion, he wanted it to belong to the town. "I needed to formalise the existence of the community. With this column the townsfolk know there once was a Jewish community among them. They now also know what happened to it."

Back in Australia in 2013, Frank was at his desk when two emails arrived in quick succession. One had a photograph of flowers placed around the wagon in Birkenau. The accompanying note explained they been placed there by footballers from Berlin who had been moved by Hugo's story. The second was from a woman in Filakovo he had engaged to maintain the memorial site surrounding the obelisk. She wrote that the locals had placed flowers around it. While Lowy would never allow himself to think such gestures were universally representative, the fact that the two floral tributes came together made an impact on him. So did the fact that the townsfolk of Filakovo had dedicated museum space to a few artefacts someone had saved from the synagogue before it was destroyed. Among the bits and pieces was a seating plan showing where Hugo had sat.

Lowy would make one more trip to Filakovo, to put in place a formal long-term agreement with the town to look after the memorial site and to maintain the Jewish cemetery. He went alone and found the town had organised another dedication ceremony. The locals were there, so were a few Jews who had been discovered in the district. A small group of klezmer musicians had been invited too. One sang a Hebrew song that hadn't been heard in those parts for seventy years. As he observed the impact this had on the gathering, Frank let go. His work was done. "I felt an inner glow. Something in me was validated."

18

A dark year

By his eightieth birthday Frank Lowy was the wealthiest man in Australia. After hovering near the top of *Business Review Weekly*'s Rich List for many years, 2010 saw him in first place, with a fortune exceeding $5 billion. While naturally pleased, he dismissed the number as "the usual overestimation" and didn't believe he would hold the position for long because of fluctuating currency values. He was correct.

With age his priorities had shifted. At sixty he had hosted an all-star birthday party accompanied by a full orchestra with fireworks on a barge anchored in front of the house. At eighty he wanted to mark the day privately, surrounded only by the immediate family. They met on the water in north Queensland and with two of the family's boats moored alongside each other they created their own world. On 22 October 2010, everyone gathered around as Frank quietly blew out the candles on the past decade. It was a time of reflection and thanksgiving. The twenty family members around the table were in good health and the family was in a state of sufficient harmony. Collectively they had brought him a gift: a painting by Monet of his garden at Giverny. No one at the table that peaceful night in the Whitsundays could have imagined that Frank was entering the most challenging year of his adult life.

Although more impatient with almost everyone, Frank kept his physical frailties to himself. As he observed his contemporaries becoming more cautious and sedentary he pragmatically defied age. Every time he opened the front door at home he saw his tennis court, now idle, spread out before him. Rather than indulging in nostalgia for an activity he could no longer do, he redeveloped the court into a gym with a lap pool: he could still swim and exercise, and expected to do so for a long time.

Although he took longer to fire up in the morning and arrived at work later, he continued to present to the world as a man in command. Ironically, the better known he had become, the less connected he was. When he walked through Sydney's Martin Place almost everyone recognised him. Through football he had gained folk hero status and people who would never have approached him previously, now did. But most of his business acquaintances had long since left the city and he missed the comfort of his own generation. There was less incentive to go to business drinks or dinners. At business meetings he would scan the faces around the table and calculate how many decades separated him from them.

At meetings, most people deferred to him. Gratifying as power can be, he preferred to be stretched and challenged. Fortunately his sons felt no inhibitions and debated him rigorously.

A couple of weeks after the gathering in the Whitsundays Frank and Shirley flew to Israel, where their life moved at a different pace. No sooner had they touched down than their friends sped them to Jerusalem for a high-spirited party, where they danced deep into the night in celebration of Frank turning eighty. In Israel he is usually able to loosen a little and enjoy the Middle Eastern way of life but on this visit he was preoccupied. His mind was already in Zurich where in a couple of weeks a prize of inestimable value would be in the offing.

The prize was winning the right to host the FIFA World Cup in 2022. If Australia could grasp this opportunity the country would have a permanent place in the world of international football. Faith in Frank was strong. He was the man who had led football out of the wilderness and he was the man who was now trying to bring the greatest footballing prize home, although he had his doubts it was possible.

Steven and David flew into Zurich for the event in early December 2010. "It was going to be a great day or a terrible day, and either way we wanted to be there with him," says Steven. "Dad takes on high-risk things to achieve what no one else can achieve and he puts in a Herculean effort. But this time we had lost before we even got there. I say 'we' because we live and die together. The loss was terrible and he was publicly embarrassed on a global scale. He's not a good loser, none of us are."

While Lowy had endured losses in his business career this loss was unprecedented. That afternoon in Zurich, in front of the world media, the ground disappeared from underneath him. That Qatar won was beyond his comprehension, as was the shock of Australia getting only one out of twenty-two votes. There was no comfort to be had, just the reality of the loss and the unrelenting criticism that followed. No one in Australia had been as invested in winning as he had. He had used everything at his disposal and it wasn't enough.

In the larger scheme of things, of course, this had been simply a procedural loss. Countries often bid several times before they win the right to host major events. For the Olympics, Australia bid three times before it was successful. But Frank felt this was different. Although this had been Australia's first tilt at the FIFA World Cup it had been given an inordinate amount of attention. Perhaps the audacity of the attempt caught the public imagination. Perhaps culturally cringing Australia had never perceived itself as a possible contender and watched with dread as the predictable loss unfolded.

Lowy held himself together and the day after the loss flew directly to Sydney to face his critics. That he was emotionally spent was a private matter. Before he walked into the first press conference at the headquarters of the Football Federation of Australia, there was an undercurrent of hostility in the room. The journalists were restless, anticipating blood and speculating how many heads would roll. After all, Australia had spent $46 million on the bid and there were some bad rumours around. Lowy walked up to the microphone, took charge and soothed the meeting. He accepted full responsibility for the failure, put it into a different perspective and explained that, in fact, something had been gained.

The press saw a man moving smoothly through the agenda, admitting things had gone wrong but reasonable and confident of recovery. "Don't worry, the sun will rise tomorrow," he told one doomsayer. Most important for him was to keep his desolation from view and maintain authority. He told the gathering that Qatar's win had come out of the blue and, in his opinion, the last word had not been heard on this matter.

Again he was looking to the horizon, to the next significant football event in the shape of the Asian Cup, just over a month away in January 2011. That it was being held in Doha was not great, particularly in light of Qatar's contentious win. But Lowy summoned the grace and attended the requisite round of social events in Doha, watching hopefully as the Socceroos won all their games and reached the finals unbeaten. For the final David and Steven flew in to be at their father's side again. Australia was up against its old rival, Japan, and while a victory would not redeem what happened in Zurich, it would be welcomingly sweet. And it almost was, but for the fact that one unfortunate error by a defender in the last few minutes of the game allowed Japan to score the only goal.

When Lowy's jet took off from Doha, he was feeling battered. Finally by himself, he no longer needed to put on a brave face. More than anything, he needed a tranquil place to make sense of the events and restore himself. He was beyond exhaustion as he and Shirley spent the next week alone on the *Ilona*.

Few would want to pay the price for his wealth that Frank Lowy has done. In the past fifty years he can hardly remember sleeping a full eight hours without a sleeping pill. Although he leads a glamorous life and smiles for the camera he rarely experiences lightness of being. Achievements bring gratification but not sustained joy because there is always the next challenge. While he is an aggressive commercial animal, his internal gauge of achievement does not register the competition. When he played tennis, he would pit himself against his own last best performance. Winning was important but what mattered more was that he had put in maximum effort and excelled. He had no difficulty congratulating an opponent who was a better player. Congratulating himself was much harder.

Now he allowed himself little latitude. Casual observers would have seen a billionaire on a beautiful boat in the Red Sea. No one but Shirley saw him awake through the night, raking over events, berating himself for not having seen what was happening in the 2022 bidding process and entirely unable to unwind. As he went through hell, she was quietly at his side. Things improved when they went up to their apartment in Tel Aviv. Friends came around, listened to his account of the events, discussed the issues and over the next weeks, slowly replenished him. By the time he was homeward bound, he was back in charge of himself.

Lowy and his sons meet regularly away from the office to discuss Westfield, the family and their finances. In this way they keep a close watch on how the greater family is functioning and how their assets are working. But these meetings have another dimension too. There is an understanding that any issue, no matter how uncomfortable or how raw, can be aired. The rule is that no one takes offence and decorum is maintained. Such a meeting was arranged for early February 2011, to begin the morning Frank arrived home. It would take place on his Sydney boat, *Ilonka* (the diminutive of *Ilona*), moored in Rose Bay. For two and a half days the Lowys would lock themselves away and take no outside calls.

This year Mark Bieler was with them from New York. He had been working with Westfield for more than a decade to guide the company as it evolved from a family-based enterprise to an institutional–professional base while not losing its entrepreneurial edge. For some time he had also been retained by the Lowy Family Group as a private adviser. It was the height of summer and the five men sat barefoot in the salon. Their casualness belied the seriousness of the issues about to arise. As they hadn't met for a while, there was much to discuss.

Although the issue of age was very much in Frank's mind, it wasn't on the table as they began tracking through various business and family issues. They talked about corporate governance and discussed Peter's pet subject: how restrictive regulation was strangling the country's entrepreneurial spirit. They discussed how institutional investors were wielding more power than ever and were voting with proxy advisers who had their own agenda.

Then they turned their attention to the fact that the noise surrounding their remuneration had been getting louder. Frank's annual pay of $14.9 million had been repeatedly singled out and there was a tendency in the media to lump the pay packets of the three Lowy executives together, with complaints that they took home in excess of $30 million a year. At the last shareholders' meeting only 16 per cent of the shareholders had voted against the company's remuneration report – a percentage most companies would be happy with but a figure that made the Lowys uncomfortable.

As the discussion flowed back and forth, Frank suddenly said, "Perhaps it's time to make a major change here." Everyone stopped and looked at him. "It's not easy for me to tell you this," he continued, "but I have been thinking about it for quite a while. I know it has to be done sooner or later and even though it is painful for me, I have to do it now." The time had come, he said, to move from being executive to non-executive chairman, that he was ready to take his hands off the levers. The room fell silent. No one was expecting this.

Later Frank said he was taken aback by the boldness of his own decision. "I used to resist it because I was afraid of being irrelevant or of accepting that age is limiting. But I always maintained I wanted to go a day before I had to. The idea had been swirling around my head for some time and my gut told me this was the moment. I usually like to talk and talk until a decision emerges, but this just came out."

"We had discussed this possible move many times over the years and Dad was not ready but in the end, he changed on a dime," says Steven. "Something in him that day made it possible. The noise level was rising and he felt in his bones that it was a good thing to do." David knew the time was getting close and that his father needed to ensure he was in control of the situation rather than the situation controlling him. "I thought it was a good thing overall although not necessarily for him personally. We only owned 7.5 per cent of the company and had to take cognisance of the environment. We all felt this was the right time but when he actually said the words, we were taken by surprise. You could see he was not happy about it."

While Frank would no doubt have appreciated someone in the room opposing his decision, he knew he had expressed the general feeling. His words were immediately recognised as right. But the decision needed to be double checked and an hour later two trusted advisers were in a tender crossing Rose Bay. Simon Tuxen, the Westfield Group's general counsel and Mark Ryan, the head of the group's corporate affairs, had been called in because they could be relied on to say what they thought. Both agreed that Frank's was the right choice and a natural decision in the succession process.

As the strategy for Frank to step back had been prepared long before, it was now just a matter of following it through at his own pace. As Frank moved back Peter and Steven would move in. There would be no pressure on his tenure as non-executive chair and the consensus was that not much would change regarding his workload. He would still be involved with strategy and the big picture, but be paid much less. This did not worry him, but the possible consequences of his decision did. He had seen men wilt in retirement and feared the same might happen to him.

On the boat that day David made a significant decision too: he would step away from Westfield altogether. This meant giving up his position as non-executive deputy chair and not being in line for chair should something happen to his father. He had been thinking about it for a long time. "If I had been needed for Westfield I would have done it and done it well, but my philosophy is that the money should work for you and not you for the money ... and that's the business I now run [i.e. the Lowy Family Group]. In my opinion, the risks of being on a public company board are not commensurate with the rewards," he said.

In the ensuing debate about his decision David argued that he could still have the same influence, perhaps more, as a true investor in Westfield than as a family member. A couple of years later he would say as an outsider that his perspective of the company's strategy had changed. "As an external investor I read things in the paper. At LFG we dissect their accounts apart and know them pretty well just as any other company we invest in. We see ourselves as similar to an institutional investor, we tell them things we don't like and that need to be changed."

Back on shore the men hugged each other, got into their cars and went their separate ways. Frank went home to try and sleep off his jetlag and absorb what had happened. In early March 2011 the press announced his decision. The formal transition would take place in front of shareholders at the Westfield annual general meeting on 25 May. Lowy wanted no fanfare. He would enter the meeting as executive chairman and leave as a non-executive chairman. Although many wouldn't register the difference – and he would still be in the chair at the next AGM – it would be a landmark event. In the meantime, he kept his mix of feelings to himself.

Diligent about his health, he would have regular blood tests and check-ups. In early May his otherwise good blood results showed an abnormally elevated liver enzyme. The doctor told him not to worry but he did. Although he was feeling well, a week later he repeated the test. This time the enzyme level was down. While relieved he was not relaxed. He and Steven were slated to fly to Brazil immediately after the AGM to look at new business opportunities, and he didn't want any health complications.

Spooked by the earlier result, a few days later he did the test again. Now the enzyme count had shot up and was even higher than the first time. It was a flashing red light. His medical team shared his concern and wanted to investigate but the AGM was two days away and Frank wanted to be in good form. The investigation would have to wait.

On the morning of the AGM he woke before it was light, thinking about the early days of Westfield. Some fifty years had passed since he and John had floated the company. There was so much to remember but in a few hours the story of his involvement in Westfield would begin to taper. Allowing himself no more nostalgia, Frank got out of bed and went down to his gym where his trainer was waiting. After some exercise, some laps of the indoor pool and a massage followed by a warm and a cold shower, he was ready for the day.

He made a point of treating this AGM no differently from all the others and worked efficiently through the agenda, batting away the difficult questions and enjoying the expressions of appreciation. There was no sentimentality and those who observed him closely could see no hint of dejection about the change.

The moment his formal commitments were over, he went directly to St Vincent's Hospital. More blood was taken. This time there was a check for cancer markers too. With his bags packed for Brazil, Frank was impatient and wanted everything done in quick time. He paced up and down. When the results returned they were mixed. There was no concern about cancer markers but frustratingly, the enzyme result was still high. So were Frank's expectations of flying out.

But he had to delay as the next few days were filled with scans, consultations and investigations. There was clearly a problem. A small blockage had been detected in a bile duct. At best it was sludge, at worst it was a cancer. If it was cancerous it could move swiftly into his pancreas with critical consequences. The prospect of pancreatic cancer is frightening and the family gathered as an attempt was made to get into the duct and take a sample of the material. After what seemed like a very long procedure, the attempt failed.

Steven flew out to attend to business in Brazil and Milan while Frank went home to recover before the next attempt was made. It failed too. Physically spent but on high alert, Frank prepared himself for the third attempt. This represented an unimaginable strain on his eighty-year-old body but there was no option. This attempt would be made at Westmead Hospital on the other side of Sydney. This time it was successful. A sample was taken and a stent was placed in the duct to keep it open.

Only a week had passed since the AGM but it seemed a long time away as Frank waited for the pathology results. He had been on the operating table four times, once for diagnosis and three times for samples. More than anything he craved a long rest. But later the same day the results came back. They showed cancer in its very early stages. The next step was surgery. Steven remembers picking up the phone in the middle of the night in a town outside Milan. It was David to say their father had cancer. Steven got up and began preparing himself for the worst.

The next morning Frank was up at first light, dressed and assembling a private medical panel to help him navigate what lay ahead. The panel included friends such as Larry Horowitz, a doctor turned investment banker from New York, Professor Michael O'Rourke, his cardiologist from St Vincent's Hospital and Professor Bob Graham, head of Sydney's Victor Chang Cardiac Research Institute. They had seen the pathology report and when Lowy asked Graham if he absolutely needed to have surgery, the answer was blunt. "You don't need to, but if you don't, you'll die." With that, they started scouring the field for expert surgeons, consulting nationally and internationally. If the expertise abroad was superior, he would go there.

After many calls to New York and much discussion they decided there was enough expertise in Sydney. There were many advantages in having the operation in the comfort of his home city surrounded by family rather than recuperating in relative isolation in a foreign hotel. In Sydney Frank also had the services of a health professional who knew the local scene and could navigate him through the medical maze, make his appointments, keep notes, explain things and be at his side. Together with her, David and Shirley, Frank visited a couple of Sydney surgeons and settled on Koroush Haghighi, a man of Iranian extraction whom he liked immediately. A date was set for the operation.

He began meeting with Haghighi to prepare himself. The operation he was about to have evokes such dread that people whisper its name. Called a 'whipple' after Allen Whipple, the surgeon who devised it early last century, it is said to be the most radical of all operations. Brutal on the body, it involves the removal of the head of the pancreas, the duodenum, a portion of the common bile duct, the gall bladder and sometimes part of the stomach. Afterwards, the remaining organs are reconnected and for this skill, experience and meticulousness are essential. Less than perfect stitching can lead to leakage with life-threatening consequences. Frank's fear on grasping the details of a whipple was mitigated only by the fact that the procedure had been continually refined over the past seventy-five years. While it was still drastic, survival rates had greatly improved.

Faith is central to Lowy's being and on the second morning of the Jewish festival of Shavuot, on 9 June, he and Shirley planned to go to the synagogue for Yizkor. This memorial prayer is recited by those who have lost a parent or other loved one. Frank wanted to be present in synagogue but he had had a particularly bad night without sleep. Attributing it to strain he suggested Shirley go alone, knowing Steven would be there. She went and as he dozed on the sofa in the salon adjoining their bedroom, she told the housekeeper he didn't want to be disturbed.

That morning illness overtook him so rapidly that he was past helping himself. When instinct brought Shirley home early, she walked in to find him in a high fever with rigors. He was freezing and shaking so violently that she called David and then the doctor.

David was there in minutes and was shocked at his father's state. Having consulted the doctor, he put him in a car and they went to St Vincent's Hospital. Steven joined them. "For a couple of hours we were not sure what was going on and we were quite scared. The situation had become much graver than we anticipated. A friend of mine, a radiologist, X-rayed Dad just before he went to intensive care and later told me Dad's fever was so bad he thought he was going to expire in the room. He'd seen people die of this before," said David. Later, another specialist would comment on how, at this point, he thought Frank's life was over.

The situation was dire. Frank had contracted a hospital super bug during the stent procedure and given his already weakened state it was not certain he could survive. The stent had to be removed and replaced with a smaller one to keep the duct open. This was the fifth time on the operating table in two weeks and he was extremely weak. As he lay in intensive care, he was told the whipple had been delayed for a fortnight.

Eventually he was moved to a private room where the family could visit at will. Shirley was there several times a day and brought warm homecooked meals. She laid a small table with their own linen, crockery and cutlery and would eat with him. He was as comfortable as he could possibly be. The sole focus was for him to rest, recover and gain some weight for the big operation ahead. Steven visited on his way to and from work and at lunchtime too. David was there most of the time: "We were in the loop with him immediately and began dealing with this in a technical way. We were a little nervous but it was a process, we had a problem and we had to solve it. But when he got this infection, it suddenly went from being something mechanical to being something emotional. He was in danger. We were scared."

Frank had a week at home before the operation and much time was spent with his surgeon, who went through the details, explaining the steps, never attempting to gloss over anything. By now Frank had a new vocabulary and a good working knowledge of what he was facing. Haghighi had assured him that apart from a little bloating and discomfort from time to time, he would return to a normal life. With complete faith in this surgeon, he had stopped worrying: "Not once did I waver in my conviction that I had made a good choice. I trusted the surgeon and when he told me I would make it, I believed I would. Of course I was anxious about the recovery but I had no fear of dying. In his hands, I knew I would be all right."

Given his age and the recent medical mishap, his family didn't feel as confident. By now, Peter had arrived from Los Angeles. The whipple was booked for Saturday 25 June and the evening before, just as they had done hundreds of times, the family gathered around the Sabbath table. That night the ritual was rich with meaning. Sitting at the head of the table and not permitted to eat, Frank looked at each face and thought it was not possible to have more love and support.

Early the next morning hospital staff watched as Shirley, David, Peter and Steven escorted Frank down the corridor to his private room and stayed until he was taken away from them. Then the family went to the synagogue where Peter led the congregation in the morning prayers. Everyone present knew Frank was unwell and that the family had come as one, to pray.

As there would be no news until the nine-hour operation was over, the family went back to the Point Piper house to wait for the phone call. "I was really worried we were going to lose him from the operation," says David. "The wait was nerve-racking. It was good in the beginning because the fact that there was no early phone call meant they hadn't opened him up and closed him. It meant they were going through with it." Finally, around 6.30 pm the phone rang. The operation had been a success and Frank, who would be kept asleep for another day, was all right.

19

A pragmatic decision

As Frank emerged from prolonged sedation he began hallucinating. When the family visited him in intensive care he complained bitterly that the hospital hadn't fixed him. "No one does anything around here. All the nurses do is carry pillows from one place to another. Don't pay the bill, I'm not better," he instructed his sons.

While his focus had been on the operation, he hadn't prepared himself for its aftermath. There would be three weeks of intubation, no eating and no drinking. Never before had he experienced such a lack of autonomy, and he fought back wherever he could. Within a couple of days he had shed the hospital gowns and put on his own tracksuit and shoes. He had his own nursing staff and despite the tubes coming out of his nose, mouth, abdomen and arms, and being instructed not to attempt to use the phone, he somehow got hold of his mobile and managed to make a few calls.

At night he couldn't move or read. A prisoner in his bed and thrown entirely on his own resources, he went through dark times. There were moments when he felt lost and questioned the meaning of fighting on. But morning always came, with the bustle of hospital business and the sun streaming in through the window.

From his window Frank could see the top of the Sydney Tower in the Sydney CBD, on which Westfield's neon sign was then being installed. The night it was lit up, Steven was at his father's side. "Look up there, Dad," he said pointing to the huge red letters spelling out the word 'Westfield' on the skyline. But to Steven's disappointment his father was feeling so low he couldn't summon genuine joy.

Only the immediate family was permitted to visit and they came from Los Angeles and New York. As the family wanted to manage the situation and participate in all the decisions, they decided someone had to be with Frank almost all the time to hear and learn as much as possible. Steven came several times a day, so did Shirley, and David virtually moved in.

Frank continued to push every barrier. When after three weeks they let him have his first solid food – a plain sandwich on white bread – he was ready to go home. When hospital staff exhorted him to stay he insisted on going, saying he had other pressing business. His surgeon Haghighi had been warned Frank would be a difficult patient but personally found him to be "possibly the easiest" patient he'd ever encountered. "He was smart. He wanted to get better, he asked for advice and he followed it 100 per cent. We got on very well indeed." It had helped that physiologically Frank was some twenty years younger than his chronological age. As he was doing well, Haghighi agreed Frank could have an early discharge. He would visit his patient at home.

Frank wanted to be home for a week to normalise before participating in two days of meetings that he would not postpone. The subject of the meeting had been preoccupying him for several years and now was his chance to put it all to rest. He would take no advice on rescheduling.

The issue under discussion had silently originated in Liechtenstein more than a decade earlier, and had proceeded to cause him and others around the world considerable distress. In the 1990s one of its citizens, Heinrich Kieber, had left Liechtenstein to go travelling. He spent time in Australia and loved it. In 1995 he popped up in Barcelona where he was involved in a half-million-dollar real-estate fraud involving an apartment. A couple of years later he was in Argentina, where he claimed he was kidnapped by people linked to the Barcelona apartment.

By 1999 he was relieved to be home in Liechtenstein. As a computer programmer his skills were needed because the principality's banks were busy digitising their records to meet new European compliance procedures. Kieber secured a job with LGT, the principality's largest bank owned by the royal family. His task was to convert the paper records for its 1400 clients into a digital format.

As he would later explain, he was in charge of handling all the clients' files to make sure they were properly scanned. Apart from formal bank records, these included a vast array of internal documents such as handwritten notes, memos, comments and recorded telephone conversations. As he worked through this process he saw an opportunity. He quietly made copies of all the bank's files. By December 2002, having smuggled out the copies, he left the bank.

The following year Kieber wrote to the prince and the chair of LGT requesting help for the fraud charges he was facing in

Barcelona. He disclosed that he had taken client data from LGT and threatened to release it if assistance was not forthcoming. The prince handed the matter to the chief prosecutor of Liechtenstein, who considered it attempted blackmail and responded by prosecuting Kieber on charges of theft and coercion. Eventually he was sentenced to four years in jail.

When Kieber appealed, however, it emerged that LGT was funding his defence. In the end, he agreed to destroy the stolen data, his prison sentence was converted to twelve months of probation and he walked free. LGT thought the case was closed but Kieber had made copies of the copies. These were locked away in a Swiss bank vault.

In 2005 Kieber began trying to sell the information, and he set his sights on Germany. It was a good target because the Germans had long tried to persuade Liechtenstein to disclose details of the billions of euros it held in German funds. Kieber contacted the German secret service, the Bundesnachrichtendienst (BND) offering it the material. He was keen to return to Australia and as part of the deal he wanted the secret service to arrange Australian residency under a new identity for him.

Negotiations were slow and eventually in 2006 the BND met Kieber. It was reported that soon senior figures from the Australian Taxation Office (ATO) met him too and he was invited to Australia. According to press reports, by May 2007 the ATO had extensive details of twenty Australians who were believed to have LGT accounts.

While the German government was said to have paid Kieber €4.2 million for information about German investors, the Australian authorities reportedly denied paying for information. Kieber did, however, receive a visa to travel to Australia and the ATO was reported to have shared his material with its tax treaty partners, including the Internal Revenue Service (IRS) of the United States. All this occurred behind closed doors.

Out of the blue, in July 2007, Lowy received a letter from the ATO requesting information about his offshore activities. The family was under a 'risk review' and information was duly supplied. Lowy says the ATO asked numerous questions and in October 2007 the review escalated into an audit of the Lowy family. It focused on US$68 million that had been held in Liechtenstein's LGT bank. These funds had come from the sale of US shopping centres that had been held by the family.

Being audited is an ordeal and at the age of seventy-seven Lowy found himself preparing for a protracted engagement with the tax authorities. "This issue was between me and the ATO and in addition to accountants and lawyers, I recruited my son David to join me. He and I spent countless hours and nights on the issue. I felt under pressure and while I didn't think it would turn nasty there was always a chance it could," he said.

According to press reports, that October Lowy's lawyers wrote a letter to the ATO saying the Liechtenstein entity had been wound up in 2001 and what remained had been "donated for the benefit of Israeli charities". The letter said that "no amount was distributed to Mr Lowy or any member of his family or any privately controlled entity".

Lowy says the existence of funds in Liechtenstein was not the issue and that from previous tax returns the ATO was aware that a Liechtenstein entity owned the shopping centre assets. Rather, the issue arose because the ATO had not been notified that the money had since been transferred to an Israeli charitable foundation. There was now a difference of opinion over whether this money was taxable.

His lawyers worked with the ATO and went through the Liechtenstein structure. The funds had been held in a hybrid foundation unique to Liechtenstein. The lawyers argued that under Australian law this foundation would be classified as a company, not a trust, which meant no tax was payable until or if the funds were distributed. As the funds had been distributed to a charitable foundation, the lawyers took the view that no tax was payable by Lowy. This was going to be a long and arduous argument.

It had hardly begun when the family learned that Peter, who lived in Los Angeles, had come to the attention of the tax authorities over there too. Late that same month, October 2007, he received notification from the United States Internal Revenue Service that his tax accounts had been selected for examination. Was it coincidental that both Peter and his father were being examined simultaneously or was something more sinister going on?

While tax inquiries can be intense and intrusive, there are prolonged periods of inactivity when all is quiet and the issue appears to have receded. This was the case with the Lowys and nothing much happened until February 2008, when the impact of Kieber's activity caused a shudder around the world.

It began with an explosion of publicity in Germany. With press cameras rolling, German tax authorities conducted raids on the offices of dozens of prominent businessmen for allegedly using Liechtenstein bank accounts. This generated global interest and authorities in Britain, Spain and France began investigating their citizens. The veil over Liechtenstein's banking system was being pulled away and the principality couldn't stop it.

A couple of weeks after the German publicity, the Australian authorities announced that twenty audit cases were underway relating to funds in Liechtenstein. At the same time the US Internal Revenue Service announced it was taking enforcement action against 100 taxpayers.

While disturbed by this news, Frank had much else on his mind. The global financial crisis was taking hold and with Westfield operating in four countries, he was dealing with the different impact this crisis was having in each of them. While Australia and New Zealand appeared to be holding up the USA had begun sliding into recession, as had the UK. He was concerned about the impending opening of the new £1.7 billion centre, Westfield London. It was to be Europe's largest inner-city shopping mall and it looked as if it would be opening its doors as economic gloom was settling on the city.

In June 2008 Frank and his sons spent four days in formal interviews with the ATO in Sydney. Peter had flown in from the US and voluntarily joined the interviews. All seemed in order and Frank and Shirley departed for their usual European summer vacation.

By July 2008 they were on their boat in the Mediterranean. Frank always works on holiday and typically spends part of each day working with his PA in his study before rejoining guests on deck. While obviously troubled by the tax issue, he says it was not front of mind – until the phone went.

It was Peter. He told his father he had been called to Washington to appear before a Senate committee examining the use of tax havens by US citizens and corporations. Frank's stomach twisted into a knot – an old sign that something unpleasant was building. Many things flashed through his mind. Would this harm Westfield's American business, which had taken thirty years to grow? Would it damage Peter or him personally?

Peter explained that this committee was driven by a group of senators who claimed that $100 billion in revenue was being drained from the US Treasury every year through the use of tax havens. For the past four years or so, this committee had conducted in-depth investigations into tax havens. Formally, it was a subcommittee of the Senate Committee on Homeland Security and Governmental Affairs. The group had introduced the *Stop Tax Haven Abuse Act* and this latest inquiry was part of the political push to get Congress to pass it. Now Peter had been called to appear before it on 17 July.

Frank listened in silence. He was out of his depth. He quickly understood that this Senate inquiry was separate from the inquiry conducted by the IRS and the audit by the ATO. When the German authorities launched their spectacular raid in February 2008 these US senators had been watching. In fact, the raid had spurred them to investigate Kieber's material to see what it could yield in the context of their political push to get the Act passed. The senators were given more grist for their mill when, following the German raids, a witness from UBS came forward and disclosed secret details of that bank's dealings in Switzerland. The committee included UBS in its investigations.

After some months the inquiry's findings were compiled into a 114-page report focusing on the abuse of overseas bank secrecy laws by Americans. The material made for sensational reading and was slated for release to the media on Wednesday 16 July: a day before the hearings were due to commence.

As it happened Peter had pre-existing business commitments overseas and delayed his Washington appearance until 25 July. When his representatives offered to make available a knowledgeable person to brief the Senate staff on the Liechtenstein structure, the offer was declined.

At the time, Frank and Shirley were entertaining four or five couples on the boat and rather than pretend everything was fine Frank explained that a pressing matter had arisen and that he would be absent for longer each day. He was relieved that friends were aboard because they helped to diffuse the tension. Everybody had meals and sometimes went ashore together, but when the others retired to watch a movie or go to bed, Frank went to his study. Being in Europe and working with advisers in both Australia and the US meant little sleep was possible.

When the Senate report went public on 16 July, news of it flew around the world. Frank was among several people named. Bloomberg announced that US lawmakers had accused him of hiding money in Liechtenstein. The lawmakers claimed he had set up a secret Liechtenstein bank account to hide at least $68 million from tax collectors. On Thursday morning Australia's newspapers carried the same story. They reported that the Lowy family was under investigation by the US Senate for allegedly using "a complex web of financial transactions and shelf companies in the world's exotic tax shelters" to conceal money.

From his boat, Lowy put out a press statement and then declined all interviews. That Australia's second richest man, with an estimated wealth of $6.3 billion, had become a victim of a name-and-shame campaign by US senators attracted a great deal of interest. It also created much distress for Frank Lowy, who fiercely guards his reputation. This was his first encounter with a Washington-style inquiry and he was unprepared for it. He was used to the Australian federal model of commissions of inquiry, where people were questioned first and the findings followed. Here, the report came first and the questions followed. "It felt like the US Senate investigators had shot first and were preparing to ask questions later," he said.

From the Liechtenstein data, the senators had selected seven case studies. Peter Lowy was included because his case used a mechanism not seen by the investigators before – the use of a US corporation to name the beneficiaries of a Liechtenstein foundation. The report described this foundation as having a convoluted ownership of five companies whose ultimate owner was the Lowy Family Trust. The US corporation, Beverly Park, was registered in Delaware with the Lowy family members as its shareholders and Peter, an American citizen, as its president and a director.

The report was scorching. While there was no suggestion that the family had actually avoided any tax the report suggested that it used Beverly Park to hide its identity. Frank was incredulous: how, he asked, could he use Beverly Park, of which his son was president and a director, to hide an association with the family? Australian tax authorities knew it was part of the Lowy business group. Frank claimed the report had drawn inferences from the documents and stated them as facts without verification.

While the report never stated the money in Liechtenstein had an illegal or undisclosed source, Frank believed this was implied. He said the source of the money had been disclosed in a public prospectus and there had been no attempt on his part to cover its tracks: "The convoluted internal procedures for transferring and managing funds were a construct of the LGT bank itself. It was the way LGT managed its accounts and it was not necessary for it to consult with its clients on the complex steps involved."

But as he paged through a printout of the report, he realised it would not be possible to undo the damage it had caused: "This report encouraged the public perception that all these offshore transactions are suspicious and are being used for tax avoidance. The fact is that they can be used for legitimate transactions, and that was how we used them. No money went into the Lowy pocket."

No one disputed the facts of the Lowy investment in LGT; they were clear from the formal bank documents. The case that the family had conspired to hide money had been built from informal material generated by and exchanged between LGT bank staff, including handwritten notes, comments, memos and records of telephone conversations. The US investigators relied on this material to construct a back story of collusion and had concluded that Lowy wanted to shelter assets from tax authorities.

The investigators determined that special measures had been taken to keep secret the foundation's existence and the Lowy's relationship at LGT. They thought the measures were aimed at distancing the family and its entities from the foundation. They quoted one internal memo that read, "The Lowys have decided they never want to travel to Liechtenstein or Switzerland in connection with these companies again."

While the investigators had seen all the informal material, the family had not been given access to it and the Lowys and their lawyers questioned its veracity. Frank had many questions. Were the notes accurately translated? Were they selectively used? Were the authors interviewed?

Just as the report *Tax Haven Banks and U.S. Tax Compliance* had made world headlines, so did the hearing that began the next day. Senator Carl Levin, chair of the panel, explained that about fifty tax havens were operating in the world and were essentially "engaged in economic warfare against the United States and honest, hardworking American taxpayers".

Having his family business aired in this Washington forum made sleep almost impossible for Lowy. He believed they had been ambushed to serve the senator's political agenda and there was nothing he could do. His family was being held up as prime examples of tax cheats and he could find no opportunity for recourse. He just had to cope: "I have coped with adversity my whole life and I have learned how to deal with it. I box it in and get on with other aspects of my life. To the outside world I don't appear too stressed but in my private time, at night or when I'm alone, I let it out. That's when I try to deal with the emotional impact."

That Peter was now in the Senate's crosshairs caused his father considerable anxiety. The last thing he wanted was for Peter and his family to be the face of a tax controversy in the US. Peter had carried the can once before over the failure of a major investment in television, and it had taken years before the blame shifted rightfully to his father and Peter's role was forgotten. Now he could be in the firing line again. "The fact is that Peter had been caught up in this without knowing much about it all," said Frank. "He was the president and director of a company – Beverly Park – that had no activity. It was a real-estate holding entity and held a house in Los Angeles and an apartment in New York."

As Peter was in Europe before his scheduled appearance in Washington, he joined his father on the boat to talk through the issues. His characteristic jocularity had given way to a deep seriousness. Frank wasn't feeling particularly lighthearted either as the two of them sat down to digest the proceedings. Peter was used to stress but this was way beyond anything he had experienced. The discussion focused on whether he should or should not answer questions put to him by the committee. Should he 'take the Fifth' – assert his rights under the Fifth Amendment of the United States Constitution to remain silent on the grounds that his response might incriminate him? This privilege can be as much a refuge for the guilty as a safe harbour for the innocent, and invoking it carries a stigma. Proud of his personal record, Peter didn't want to plead the Fifth.

While Peter had already appeared before the ATO in Sydney, where under oath he had been questioned about the Liechtenstein entity, he was concerned that the US committee had prejudged the case. As its report had been circulated internationally, judgment had effectively been passed. Nevertheless, he wanted the opportunity to clear his and the family's name.

The lawyers saw it differently. This was not Peter's forte. As the committee had already shown disregard for the rules of natural justice, they said it would control the public examination process and he might well not have the opportunity to make his case. Besides, Peter was not sufficiently familiar with the details of the foundation or the intricacies of the case. Peter fought back. He declared he would get up to speed.

"Peter argued his case strongly," said Frank. "But in front of the committee he would have needed to make intricate points and the advice was that he wouldn't be given enough oxygen to do so. By now we had heard enough about these committees to pick up the Star Chamber echoes, and I was worried for him."

The weight of advice was against Peter being examined, but the argument went back and forth until his lead counsel Robert Bennett cautioned strongly against it and ended the debate. Bennett, who had famously defended President Bill Clinton during the Monica Lewinsky scandal, said after-the-fact corrections to the record, no matter how significant, usually received little attention and had little effect. It was not possible to unring the bell.

Peter was stuck. He ran the risk of being damned if examined and damned if he took the Fifth. The consensus view pushed him to take the Fifth. With a heavy heart he agreed and left the boat for home. From there, he and his wife, Janine, flew to Washington. "Peter really took the brunt of issues that he had nothing to do with," said Janine. "I didn't really understand what was going on and Peter was only tangentially related to the issues. To take the Fifth was a terrible thing for him." In the hearing room in Washington, Peter's face did not reveal much. One news report said he looked as if he had the weight of the world on his shoulders. Another said he seemed upbeat. When called, Peter apologised and politely declined to answer on the advice of his counsel. His appearance was over in minutes.

While his appearance generated international headlines, the Senate committee wanted little more to do with him afterwards. But the IRS still had work to do, to see if any US tax was due from Peter or the Lowy family. "It was a hard time," says Janine Lowy. "Events we couldn't control were swirling around. But we went through this together and we knew we had to put it in perspective because people go through much worse. It was a surreal experience to see your name suddenly in the newspaper and see your address made public." Friends emailed asking what was happening and Peter and Janine found themselves writing to explain.

Afterwards, Peter had a mission. He wanted to right the situation and in October 2008 he began a long legal quest to get hold of the documents and records used by the committee's investigators. He asserted they had relied on incomplete and "likely inauthentic" information and he wanted to view the material himself. Frank was requested to provide information to the Senate panel in writing after it had published its findings. He was advised not to, and he declined.

*

In Washington the family had been caught in a political process in which they had no ability to steer a course. It was a wild ride of a kind they had never encountered before. In Sydney the experience would be completely different.

This would not be the first time that the Lowys and the ATO had been involved in a dispute. They had settled an earlier dispute in 1995 for $25 million. Tax staff had been unhappy with the settlement and the quantum had been leaked. There was speculation in the press that the current tax issue was connected to this previous one.

According to Lowy, the audit was conducted formally and confidentially. After three years of investigation it was suggested that because of the complications of the case, mediation might be the best way to settle it. Frank agreed, the ATO nominated an independent mediator and the hearing was set for 26 and 27 July 2011.

Then Frank fell ill and in late June 2011 was admitted to hospital for that major cancer operation. It required four weeks' recovery in hospital but intent on attending the mediation he managed to negotiate it to three. "It involved so many people – two sets of lawyers, a mediator, tax officers and associated staff – that finding another date when all could be present could have meant a long delay. We had lived with this for such a long time and now that the opportunity was in front of us we just had to take it," he said.

As he couldn't walk any distance or sit comfortably for any length of time, others tried to dissuade him. "So what if I'm sick, this is not going to kill me, if anything kills me it will be the illness," was his standard response. But he had to gather all his resources to attend. "I had no problem other than my health and as far as they could, my doctors had promised I would survive.

I wasn't so certain and was very motivated to finish this chapter and if possible, clean it up and not leave it unresolved should my illness overwhelm me."

On 26 July, Lowy had assistance getting dressed and was driven to town. Helped from the car, he was assisted up a few stairs to the lobby. To make sure he could last the two days, a hotel suite was booked close by so he could lie down during the breaks.

As the Lowys had not yet received a tax assessment, this would not be a conventional mediation. The foundation was a hybrid, a round peg that did not fit the square holes of Australian tax law. One set of Australian laws applies to foreign companies and another to foreign trusts. But such foundations contained a mix of features from both.

It was reported the ATO conceded this in its submission to the US Senate panel, noting it had encountered difficulties in applying Australian taxation laws to non-common law entities such as Liechtenstein foundations. "These hybrid entities possess characteristics of both a common law trust and a corporation and they may not fall squarely within the anti-deferral of tax provisions," was the report. "Until legislative or judicial clarification is provided on this issue, the ATO will continue to characterise these hybrid entities on a case-by-case basis." Frank was told this was the issue on which the case turned and that this kind of hybrid was unlikely to be used again.

The Hon. Michael McHugh, a former Justice of the High Court of Australia, was the mediator nominated by the ATO and agreed upon by Lowy. Novel legal issues not previously subject to any judicial determination were raised. The lawyers for Lowy and the ATO debated the matter but could not persuade each other of their positions. They did, however, agree on the question of penalties, there being no suggestion of intentional disregard of the law or recklessness. Lowy said, "I had to make a decision. Fight this case all the way to the High Court on a matter for which there was no precedent, or without admission accept the figure arrived at through the process of mediation."

He decided to accept and pay the requested sum which included tax, penalties and interest, but which is the subject of a confidentiality agreement and cannot be disclosed.

When asked why he accepted Lowy answered that it was a pragmatic decision. He had been ill and he wanted his decks cleared. "Litigation is a waste of human and material resources and over a long period it becomes destructive in every aspect. I realised the process could take ten years and at the age of eighty my remaining years are very precious. Given my recent illness, I didn't know how long I had. So I wanted my affairs to be clear of this issue and having regard to our family's financial position, I felt it was worth compromising. Whilst we had no benefits from that money, I wanted to spend my remaining time productively."

With the documentation completed, the Lowys signed. Frank celebrated by going directly back to bed. David was relieved that after so many years of dealing with the matter, it was finally resolved. "It was complex, difficult and emotionally draining," he said. "From our point of view, the matter was a technical one." David and Frank had carried the burden of the tax saga, Peter had been embroiled along the way and while Steven knew about it, he was not on the front line.

Some technical issues remained to be sorted out in the US. It took six to eight weeks to have the IRS accept that Peter owed no tax. He testified before the IRS and received exoneration. It was only when he received a 'no change' letter meaning his previous tax returns were in order that the family felt cleared and relieved.

The Washington experience cut right through Frank. He became interested in the concept of natural justice and how it could be absent from an official process of inquiry in a place like Washington DC. "It was a political stunt for political ends and had no regard for personal privacy. As a family, we were vilified and in the end, when it was understood no offence had been committed, the whole thing just fell away. Where was the natural justice in that?" he asked.

As for Kieber, although his revelations triggered an international revolution in tax haven disclosure rules, he disappeared from sight in early 2007. He was later discovered by the *Australian Financial Review* living under a series of false names on Australia's Gold Coast waiting to testify in a tax case unrelated to the Lowy family. In his absence his old bank LGT was renamed Fiduco Treuhand and sold. Had Kieber returned home to Liechtenstein, he would have faced arrest. The press reported that a $10 million bounty had been placed on his head by unknown individuals. Some said he was a thief. Others said he was a whistleblower of sorts.

By the close of 2011 the Senate committee had long since lost interest in the Lowys, the IRS had accepted there was no tax outstanding and the ATO had banked its cheque and closed its case.

Once the tax issue was settled, Frank began to recuperate. He ate four or five small meals a day. Haghighi visited twice every day and kept watch as his patient gradually grew stronger and started going to work for a few hours at a time. Then, in late August, exactly two months after the operation, Frank opened his email to find good news. His results had been sent to Harvard and Stanford for assessment and there was a note giving him a clean bill of health.

A couple of weeks later he was on his way to London to open Westfield's new shopping centre at Stratford, the site of the forthcoming 2012 Olympic Games. As his wounds were still fresh, Haghighi wouldn't let him fly for more than eight hours at a time. Two stops had to be made en route and each one had to be at least a couple of days.

For such an opening Lowy would usually arrive early with a small entourage to press the flesh, talk to shopkeepers and generally enjoy the occasion. This time he went straight to the podium. As he stood next to the mayor of London Boris Johnson and opened the centre, no one in the capacity crowd could have imagined what this eighty-year-old man had just been through. Adrenaline kept him pumping as he faced a bank of television cameras, did press interviews and shook hands in the crowd. When his immediate duties were over, he and Shirley slipped out and were taken directly to their hotel. He fell onto the bed exhausted. Shirley covered him and as he slept she sat reading by his side.

Football
Matters

20

A telephone call

When Frank Lowy slammed the door on Australian soccer in the late 1980s and walked away he couldn't imagine ever wanting to return. He was fed up and believed the game had no future. It operated in ethnic enclaves and unless it was lifted out of these and blended into a mainstream sport, it would never thrive. Like others before him, Lowy had tried to achieve this but the ethnicity was so entrenched that it was impossible. Frustrated and angry at not succeeding, he wanted nothing more to do with the domestic administration or politics of the sport.

But his love of football remained strong. He would still watch the national team play and if an interesting match was being played while he was abroad he would watch that too. Football, inextricably linked with the memory of his father, was part of his being. As a boy he would hold his father's hand as they walked across paddocks to see their local team play on a makeshift field.

These outings were the high point of Frank's childhood. Later, he replicated this love of football with his own sons. The Lowy boys grew up in soccer uniforms – Steven actually slept in his – and football was the family's conversational currency.

Through the 1990s the game struggled in Australia and whenever there was a crisis Lowy's name came up. Would he help? He was not interested and never responded. When direct approaches were made, he would listen politely and turn them away. "I'd made a clean break. I don't give up easily but once I do, that's it!" he explained.

Without his knowledge, in 2001 a process began that would culminate in his taking full charge of the sport in Australia and unleashing his enthusiasm. Under his aegis, soccer – or football as he called it – would be transformed domestically, regionally and internationally. At home he would restructure the sport into a new national format. Regionally, he would reposition Australian soccer as part of Asia and on the global stage the Socceroos would fight their way to the finals of three successive World Cups.

In commercial terms he would do for football what he had done so often for Westfield. When Lowy took charge, the governing body of soccer was turning over $10 million a year and was insolvent. A decade later it was turning over $100 million and was in surplus. But this wasn't good enough for Frank. Although he had achieved his goal of making football a mainstream sport, he remained frustrated that it hadn't yet reached the level of its major competitors, Rugby League and Australian Rules. Had the turnover been $200 million, he would have been more comfortable.

*

The process that led to Lowy's re-involvement began in early 2001, when Soccer Australia lurched into yet another crisis. With an unworkable constitution, no organisation, no management, no money and no prospects of getting any, it was no longer capable of functioning as a national sporting organisation. There were also fresh allegations of corrupt practices in transferring Australian players abroad. The soccer community was distraught.

In April that year activists began an email campaign to politicians in Canberra complaining of the parlous state of the game. It was one of the biggest orchestrated public-letter-writing campaigns about sport to hit the national capital. The issue was soon raised in the Senate where a call for an inquiry into the governance of soccer was put on notice. A short while later the activists called on Lowy. He heard them out but declined to help, saying the politics of the game were too toxic.

Later that year Ian Knop, a respected company executive and Liberal Party lobbyist, bravely took over the chairmanship of Soccer Australia. After years of mismanagement the dysfunction ran deep and the organisation was technically insolvent. Knop asked the government for financial help and a deal was struck: Soccer Australia would receive salvage funding, but only on condition that it submitted to a full inquiry. It had been through several inquiries before, but this one would be different. Rather than delving into its dark past, the inquiry would assess the game's governance, management and structure, with the aim of developing a 'big picture' plan for its resuscitation.

The inquiry didn't have the blessing of the full board of Soccer Australia and some board members were incandescent with rage. "I wasn't surprised by the vitriol and fury," says

David Crawford, a former chairman of KPMG, who led the inquiry. "Having been involved with organisations in chaos over the last thirty years of professional practice I was relatively used to it." To stop anyone making wild allegations he insisted that all verbal submissions to the inquiry had to be accompanied by written ones. In the 230 written submissions ultimately received, there was not one positive comment about Soccer Australia.

As the inquiry progressed, a new structure for the game began to emerge. It became clear to Crawford that a senior person with the ability to make things happen and who had an interest in the game was needed to implement the reforms. He had met Lowy before and made an appointment to see him, ostensibly to tap his knowledge:

> I thought if I put it the right way, he might be interested. He
> knew the inquiry was on and knew much more than he was
> letting on but he gave me the impression he had an interest
> in seeing the game succeed. Although I went away thinking
> he might be a possibility for the position, it would have
> been inappropriate for me at that stage to raise it with him.

With his soft spot for soccer well defended, Lowy's resolve was firm. He was comfortable talking to Crawford but didn't get involved. He did, however, agree to think about the issues and meet a couple of weeks later. Crawford believed he had identified a thread of possibility in Lowy but didn't push it at their next meeting. In his view Frank would be ideally suited "because of his fundamental interest, his past association and his capacity to bring people into the fold".

To a later meeting Crawford took along Mark Peters, chief executive of the Australian Sports Commission and a member of the committee of inquiry. Peters had pushed for the inquiry and says that, sitting at the same table as Frank, he could feel his intense though unexpressed commitment to the game. "Lowy sat poker-faced, principled and non-committal but there was a sense in the room, a sense of passion and unfinished business."

As the inquiry drew to a close there was talk of a 'wow factor' to get soccer up and running. There was also discussion about how sport is essentially business and that passion and emotion are not enough. Add commercial expertise and there could be a winning formula. Peters explained: "Frank was the person we really wanted. He brought an incredible reputation, from being a working-class boy to running an empire and having the respect of people across the board. When we talked in government about the possibility of Frank Lowy taking the job, people went 'Wow!' He was in the business community; he could get through doors, sit down and share the vision – it was the key." The only problem was that Frank gave them no sign that he was particularly interested.

Soccer in Australia had long had a messiah complex, perpetually looking for a public figure to lead it into a glorious future. David Hill the former head of the ABC had tried, so had former state premiers Neville Wran, Nick Greiner and Jeff Kennett, but none had managed to lift the fortunes of the sport. The question was why the Australian government would care about redeeming soccer, particularly as the country had other powerful football codes, including the home-grown Australian Rules. There were compelling reasons: domestically soccer enjoyed great popularity at junior and amateur levels, with more than a million Australians playing the game. It had the potential to be an important nation builder, to create heroes and open pathways for young people to represent their country.

Besides, given the multicultural nature of Australian society, reviving soccer would be a popular political move. Soccer was the only football code played across the world, giving Australia an opportunity to position itself internationally. The game's stature was reflected in the fact that more countries belonged to the Federation Internationale de Football Association (FIFA), the body that governed world football, than belonged to the United Nations.

The courtship of Lowy was measured but forceful. Not only was he being wooed by Crawford and by Australian soccer legend Johnny Warren, but he was told that the prime minister John Howard wanted him to take the job. When Frank heard that Howard was on his case he replied, "Well, I would like to hear it from him." The minute he uttered these words, he realised what a dangerous request he had made: if the PM did personally ask him, he would be unable to refuse. He decided he would not think about the issue seriously until he had heard from Howard. Some days later the phone rang. His secretary said it was the PM's office.

After the call, Lowy sat for a long time looking into space. What would taking on Soccer Australia mean? What could be achieved? At seventy-two, did he want such responsibility? There were no satisfactory answers, but he could feel himself being drawn in.

David Crawford let it be known that as far as he was concerned, Frank Lowy had the authority to push through the painful reforms that Soccer Australia needed, and was the right person to do so. When Frank finally agreed to an interim leadership position he joked that this was his way of being enlisted in national service. In early April 2003, a letter from John Howard landed on his desk, stating that should Lowy accept the leadership position he would have Howard's total support.

Having been led thus far by his heart, Lowy now let his head take over. Those who had wooed him were about to see an independence they might not have anticipated or welcomed. If they wanted to hand him the levers he would take them, but only on his own terms. He would not campaign for the position, he would be funded, and he would act only when the old board had entirely gone. By this stage Ian Knop had resigned as chairman of Soccer Australia and Remo Nogarotto was warming the chair until the government appointed its own administration.

All details of Lowy's appointment were kept quiet until Crawford's report was tabled in early April. Its fifty-nine recommendations pointed to a radical overhaul of the sport. Peters recalled the media conference that followed: "We sat down and said, 'Here is the report, here are the recommendations, the present board has to step down and an interim board headed by Frank Lowy should take over.' You could just see people went, 'Wow! Frank Lowy!'"

Soccer had all but secured the services of a high-class fixer, about to astonish the soccer community with fast-paced dramatic change. Behind the scenes Lowy had been at work drafting two of the five members for the interim board. Ron Walker, a prominent Australian businessman renowned for his work in managing sporting events, was also a former Liberal Party treasurer and former lord mayor of Melbourne. John Singleton was a widely recognised advertising guru, a radio personality, sports enthusiast and entrepreneur. Their lack of soccer pedigree was a clear sign that Frank was doing away with convention and the announcement got enormous attention. One media outlet described the new trio as a "triple-A team".

In his press statement Lowy explained that he was prepared to be involved in an interim board with the express purpose of driving through important changes within the sport. "It is now up to the stakeholders of soccer in Australia to make a decision on whether they would wholeheartedly support the proposed changes and my involvement," he said. While most of the soccer community loved the Crawford report, several members of the Soccer Australia board loathed it and refused to make way for the new order. To them, a major injustice was being perpetrated. They felt unfairly portrayed and that all their efforts had been trashed.

For a while there was a pale hope that some of them might occupy one of the three remaining seats on the interim board, but Lowy would hear no discussion on the subject. One of his conditions for taking the job had been that he would start with a clean slate. He wanted no baggage and made it clear that he alone would handpick the new board. Eventually some old board members agreed to step down, but four remained obdurate. This disaffected group managed to delay the handover to Lowy by three months. During these months Lowy remained publicly silent.

There was a fear that if the stalemate continued, Lowy would walk. He didn't, but neither did he stand by passively waiting for the political endgame to unfold. He wrote to John Howard in May outlining key conditions that would have to be met before he and the interim board made a final commitment to lead the reform process. He wanted an assurance that the recommendations of the Crawford Inquiry would be embraced, that a new board selected by him would replace the existing one and that his board would not be encumbered by liabilities presently attached to Soccer Australia. Finally, and most importantly, he needed to be sure that funding would be available to implement Crawford's reforms over the next three years.

Crawford had warned that federal funding of $2.3 million could be at stake if the inquiry's recommendations were not implemented. Lowy told Howard he expected it would take $10 million over the three years to appoint quality staff, build coaching infrastructure and secure commercial contracts. Howard said that $10 million was a very large amount and that the government could consider that level of funding only after due diligence to determine the true state of Soccer Australia's financial position. The disaffected members of the old board refused to hand over the books. Insiders thought this a blessing because they feared the contents might have dampened Lowy's enthusiasm. And indeed, when the auditors finally examined the books they found financial disaster.

While publicly Frank was silent, privately he was hard at work. He appointed an emissary in the form of Robin Graham, a Zimbabwean with an accountancy background, and had him criss-cross the nation to gather information about the state of the game. Graham became his legs throughout this period of protracted negotiations with the Australian Sports Commission and during the lead-up to Frank's appointment as Soccer Australia's chairman. Lowy was also hitting the phone. One of the first people he called was Frank Farina, Australia's national coach. "Tell me please, how many people have you got on your staff?" The answer made him gulp. "None, it's just me but I pull in people when there's a match." Later, during Lowy's reign, more than forty people would be employed just to handle the Socceroos.

Lowy began filling the other potential board positions. For deputy chairman he needed someone with excellent finance and administration skills. He called his close friend David Gonski who suggested he go no further than Brian Schwartz, CEO of Ernst & Young. Lowy knew Schwartz professionally but was unaware that he too was a 'soccer tragic' and would be willing to do whatever he could for the sport.

In his earlier days at E&Y, Schwartz had had a few friends at Westfield and would try and secure some of its work for his firm. "Every so often they would throw a little something at me," he said. Over time more work came until one day Schwartz knocked on Lowy's door and asked whether there was any chance E&Y could do the Westfield audit. Lowy explained that Greenwood Challoner had always been its auditors and the company remained loyal to this firm. Some years later when Deloitte bought this firm, Schwartz knocked again: "Surely your loyalty doesn't apply to Deloitte!" He was right. The audit was put up for tender and E&Y won. Soon it was doing all Westfield's work.

When in 2003 Lowy called Schwartz to sound him out about joining the interim board and taking the position of deputy chair, Schwartz didn't hesitate. He also didn't quite realise what was in store. Lowy and Schwartz began working together almost immediately and became a highly effective duo. "We had complementary skills and quickly became a good team," said Lowy.

At this stage they had no infrastructure, just ideas and plans. They needed manpower. Within days Richard Johnson, a chartered accountant, walked into their lives. He had just stepped off the boat from London with his family and was looking for work. Back in the UK he had been an accountant with Arthur Andersen and then moved on to IMG, the world's largest sports marketing corporation. Now in Sydney, he was making contact with old mates from Arthur Andersen, one of whom was at E&Y.

Johnson was sitting in E&Y's boardroom having a cup of coffee and explaining his sports background when his contact said, "You should talk to Brian Schwartz because he's about to become the deputy chair of football." Schwartz soon joined them. "You're just the person we need," he said. The next day, Johnson was sitting across the desk from Lowy. It all happened very fast.

However, when offered the job of chief financial officer Johnson was sceptical because he knew Soccer Australia was in deep trouble. "Pardon me, but you don't really have a job for me yet!" he said to Frank.

"Well, that's a minor detail. In the unlikely circumstance of my not becoming chairman, you can come and work for me, or Brian will give you a job," replied Frank.

A few days later Schwartz asked whether Johnson would mind also being the acting CEO. Johnson replied that as there was actually no management team at all, he assumed he would be doing everything for the first few weeks.

Working side by side with Lowy and Schwartz gave Johnson an extraordinary introduction to Australia. It also shattered his stereotypes about ageing, for Lowy's unceasing energy and view to the future were a revelation. When focused on football nothing seemed to distract him. He was tough, driven and would not take no for an answer. It seemed everything was possible. He was a master at getting 'the right people on the bus'.

For the fourth seat on the interim board Lowy wanted someone with football nous. This person should know about its management, understand the international game, be passionate about the sport and have a good business head. It was a tall order. He settled on Phillip Wolanski, a successful property developer whom he'd known for decades. Phillip was a close friend of Frank's son David and knew all about soccer. "He had good people skills, soccer knowledge and the intellect to devise policy and build a new culture. He understood the foreign coaching scene and the larger world of the sport. He fitted the bill," said Lowy.

For the final board seat Lowy needed legal expertise. He called John Coates, president of the Australian Olympic Committee, who recommended he approach Suzanne Williams, who had been general counsel and corporate secretary of the Sydney Organising Committee for the Olympic Games for five years. She was also a senior partner with the international talent recruiting business Korn Ferry International. "While she had no soccer knowledge, with her corporate and HR skills, I guessed she'd make an excellent contribution," Frank said. She joined the board willingly.

While the board was taking shape, the big question was who would run the day-to-day business of soccer. As executive chairman of Westfield Lowy couldn't do it himself. He needed an outstanding chief executive, and when he looked around the soccer world he could find no one with sufficient knowledge of the game and executive capacity. He had to find a solid sports administrator and he began looking overseas. He also called Coates to see if he had any suggestions. He did. How about John O'Neill, the chief executive of Australian Rugby?

In his autobiography *It's Only a Game* O'Neill described the Lowy approach. On 3 July 2003 he took a call from David Lowy. They knew each other reasonably well as David had been a board member of the State Bank during O'Neill's tenure as managing director. David explained that his father had agreed to assume the role of chairman of Soccer Australia and wanted to have a cup of coffee with O'Neill:

The motives Lowy might have for wanting an audience
with me, a Rugby Union manager knee deep in preparing
for a World Cup on Australian soil, were largely irrelevant.
My thought process was far more simplistic: you never
turn down an invitation from a figure as powerful and
influential as Frank Lowy.

O'Neill and Frank met two days later at Westfield headquarters.
Lowy said he was going to take over the chairmanship of
soccer and he wanted O'Neill to run it. He said he intended to
be a non-executive chairman. He complimented O'Neill on his
ability as a sports administrator and explained that their mutual
friend Coates had suggested they get in touch. Taken aback and
flattered, O'Neill replied it was out of the question at that time:

"Why?"
"I'm running the World Cup."
"What's that?"
Frank was genuinely unaware that the showpiece event in
Rugby Union was heading Down Under in three months.
Even when he did comprehend the enormity of what I
was currently engaged in, he refused to take no for an
answer ... In a smiling and very courteous manner he said
he would stay in touch and try and persuade me to change
my mind. It was my first up-close glimpse of the Lowy
determination.

Before Lowy left for his usual European summer holiday he asked
Coates whether he could arrange an introduction or perhaps a
lunch in Zurich with Sepp Blatter, the president of FIFA. "This
was my first step into the international arena of soccer. I knew no

one in this world and so I decided I would start at the top," said Lowy. As Coates knew Blatter through the Olympic Committee, it would be useful if he could be present too. From that point on Coates became Lowy's adviser in international sports politics, and through this process the two men became friends.

In 2003 Blatter was enjoying a fine reputation and although there was some unease about his practices, his largesse easily covered them. Having worked in the game most of his life he was knowledgeable about all its aspects. He also knew something of Australia as his daughter had worked in the country for a few years and he had visited her. Frank's intuition told him that Blatter could help the cause of football in Australia.

21

Dismantling the old, building the new

As his car wound up the hill to FIFA's headquarters, Lowy turned to look back at Lake Zurich. While he had often been in this city for business, this was his first visit for soccer and his first visit to the traditional residence that housed FIFA. He wouldn't be coming to this charming building for long. A few years later, reflecting its growing might and global power, FIFA would move to a spectacular glass and steel edifice that locals called the 'underground skyscraper' because most of its executive offices were below ground.

Sepp Blatter had already been through Lowy's CV and said within ten seconds of seeing each other face to face, they connected. Said Blatter: "We had a direct communication. Actually, it was more than that. It felt like a brotherhood. We have the same physical constitution, smiling and reaching forward … For us in FIFA it was such a change. All of a sudden we had a chairman facing us with personality and charisma, who was well accepted in all circles in his own country, left, right, up and down." Lowy represented the new breed of football leaders. Although many federations were still headed by traditional figures, Blatter believed that with their growing economic, cultural and political clout, federations needed to be led by entrepreneurs.

For Lowy, the lunch was congenial and he found Blatter very likeable. "Coates was there and we all got on well. My agenda was to establish a relationship and learn as much as possible. We talked about the expertise Australia needed and I said I would approach him in future for advice on restructuring the sport back home." Afterwards Lowy returned to his boat in Monaco. On this trip he set a new template for the governance of soccer in Australia. While it was expected he would give his time freely, he would pay his own way. He would cover his own travel, accommodation and entertainment expenses incurred in the service of the sport.

Later that week, on Saturday night 12 July an extraordinary general meeting of stakeholders in Sydney voted to appoint Lowy as head of the troubled Australian Soccer Association. The next day Blatter made an announcement. In his view Lowy was the best man for the job. "Chairman Lowy is the most credible person in the southern hemisphere to take the helm at Soccer Australia and set its course for future success. He has my full confidence and support." Lowy held a press conference via a video hook-up from Monaco saying he was pleased to be confirmed as chairman and that the task ahead was tough but not impossible. He took questions and was emphatic that the basis of success for soccer domestically and internationally was a strong national league.

When he sat back and contemplated what lay ahead, the enormity of the task dawned on him. When the old structures were wiped away, he would have to start from scratch and build brick by brick. With his day job as executive chairman of Westfield, his time and capacity would have to stretch.

On his return to Australia Lowy set about formalising the new board. When the government said they wanted a representative on it he said, "I thought I was your representative!" Then he changed tack, saying a representative was welcome providing he or she had all the standard liabilities of a board member. It emerged that legally a governmental appointee would mean that the responsibility for Soccer Australia would be sheeted back to the government. The idea was dropped.

Lowy's board of five was designed to cover five disciplines. Singleton would provide marketing skills while Walker would see to government relations and major events. Schwartz would contribute governance and financial skills while Wolanski would bring football know-how and Williams would supply legal expertise. "Frank would be the conductor of this small orchestra," says Schwartz. "At the time we had no management, unsustainable contracts and an organisation that was clearly insolvent. In addition to his day job Frank was working on football thirty hours a week and once I got involved, I wasn't doing much less."

As one of the most pressing issues was funding, Schwartz found himself working intensely with Lowy and had had a close-up view of his modus operandi. Apart from discovering that Lowy's overriding focus was on cash generation and cash flow, he noted how proper he was in business dealings and how he observed traditional business values and was conscious of details, from where people were seated to paying them appropriate respect. "His attention to detail is remarkable. It is unusual for someone at his level to be able to do both the very big picture and the detail. He is strategic as all hell, but on any number of occasions will do a deep dive and go through the numbers line by line."

Range is a Lowy hallmark. In the 1950s when he and John Saunders were beginning in business they were running a delicatessen while doing property subdivisions. Frank could be serving a customer in his white apron one minute and sitting across the desk from lawyers or bankers in a suit the next. One transaction was worth a sixpence and the other £10,000. Both were important and he learned to value the small transactions as well as the large.

Meanwhile negotiations with Canberra were becoming difficult. Johnson had drawn up a business plan showing that $10 million would not be enough. Another $5 million was needed. The Sports Commission baulked. In terms of sports funding $15 million wasn't just out of the ballpark, it was off the continent. The commission was prepared to stretch to $10 million – an extraordinary amount of money in itself for a single sport – and no more. Lowy wouldn't budge. The job couldn't be done for less. Eventually radio broadcaster Alan Jones intervened. As deputy chairman of the commission he suggested an arrangement that allowed $15 million to be dispensed, partly through a direct grant and partly via a loan. It seemed a good solution.

At a meeting in Melbourne to finalise the structure the prime minister, minister for sport Rod Kemp, Walker, Lowy and a couple of others were chatting before they sat down. The proposal was to provide $11 million in a grant and $4 million in a loan. Seizing the moment, Lowy turned to the PM. He wanted to make a serious point in the nicest possible way: "John, of course you know I will take the $4 million as a loan but you will see it will never be repaid." Everyone laughed. Eight years later the loan was forgiven.

There was less laughter later when Lowy declined to accept the proviso that $15 million would be forthcoming only if an observer nominated by the government was invited to attend board meetings. Lowy objected in principle; he would not operate with someone looking over his shoulder. If the government wanted to entrust his board with the future of Australian soccer, it should at least trust the board to look after itself. In rigorous correspondence with the sports minister Lowy threatened to walk away. He said he would manage the position for a while, until someone else was found. The government capitulated.

Much work was needed. An old public business had to be closed and a new one opened along different lines. Lawyers and receivers were called in to close the old and more lawyers and public relations experts were called in to create a fresh constitution. Everyone was working to try and save Soccer Australia's assets, dispense with existing contracts and extinguish its obligations. Lowy pulled in help from people with expertise and many, such as Max Donnelly from the insolvency and turnaround firm Ferrier Hodgson, gave their time gratis. Others worked at reduced rates. Lowy's approach impressed Richard Johnson. "I remember sitting in his office one afternoon and discussing sponsorship opportunities and he just picked the phone up to Margaret Jackson at Qantas, followed by Bob Mansfield at Telstra to see if they were interested in supporting the new venture."

They settled or wound up commercial arrangements with speed. Just as Peters had predicted and Johnson had observed, Lowy was able to move through the stratosphere of Australian business, sharing his vision for the game, building confidence for the future and persuading companies with existing commercial rights to relinquish them. A deal was done with Kerry Stokes, the chair of Channel Seven, that allowed the network to exit smoothly. Frank's approach was rational. The sponsors had been tied to a losing game and there was no value for them in keeping those old contracts. "I called up Kerry and said, 'You have an obligation to sponsor the national team to the tune of some $500,000. We need to tear it up. It's worthless to you and it's not sufficient for us. Let's call it a day.' He said, 'Fine.'" In his discussions with Margaret Jackson, Lowy explained why the national carrier should relinquish its rights. Qantas later returned as a major sponsor for a decade with naming rights under a new contract.

Frank Lowy has a reputation for being masterful at making a request in such a way that rather than feeling the weight of it, the subject feels privileged to be doing him a personal favour. But he is not averse to asking directly either. Robin Graham remembers Ron Walker going off to New Zealand at Frank's request with almost no notice. It was for a meeting of the Oceania Football Confederation. "He went for a whole bloody weekend. I just couldn't believe that Frank could phone him up on the Thursday and say, 'Ron, what are you doing on Saturday, 'cause I'm afraid I need you to go' – no; he didn't say, 'I'm afraid', he said, 'You have to go to New Zealand.' He doesn't apologise for too much, Frank."

With the old Soccer Australia wound up, Frank became chairman of the new entity, the Australian Soccer Association, ASA. By now he had grown very close to Schwartz, who was sharing the burden and would frequently deputise for him. "I recognised what a hardworking decent man he is and practically didn't do anything without fully consulting him; we were as one," said

Lowy. They began bringing in more expertise. Former diplomat Ron Harvey became the ASA's "international ambassador" to repair bridges with FIFA and Australia's neighbours in Oceania. Ian Frykberg, the sports rights negotiator who helped change the global TV sports landscape, was retained as a consultant to explore commercial broadcasting opportunities for a domestic league. Czechoslovakia's former coach Dr Jozef Venglos, an expert on technical development and former Socceroos coach, was hired to advise the national and other senior teams.

But there was still no chief executive. By September Frank got word that O'Neill's future in Rugby might be less certain than it appeared. He picked up the phone. O'Neill was sensing his job was tenuous and said he expected to be in a better position to discuss a move after the Rugby World Cup. Disappointed, Frank said he had to move on. He approached two or three other sports administrators in Australia and overseas, to no avail.

Then, several weeks later, on the day before the World Cup final, John Coates invited O'Neill to lunch. According to O'Neill's autobiography, it was a private affair in honour of visiting IOC president Jacques Rogge. It was 21 November 2003, a beautiful day on the harbour with only eight people seated around a table at the Royal Sydney Yacht Squadron. One of them was Frank Lowy. "Was it planned?" O'Neill wondered. "I have no idea. But Frank was there coincidentally, in the chair beside mine."

Lowy grabbed O'Neill's hand and said, "John, I haven't filled the CEO position at the ASA yet. It is still open and I want you to take it. The Rugby World Cup is over tomorrow, so what about it? You told me before to wait – and I've been a patient man."

O'Neill promised to make a decision after the Australian Rugby Union board met on 12 December. Ever impatient, Frank rang on 27 November to remind O'Neill of his promise. On 3 December he called again. On Saturday morning, 13 December, O'Neill's first call of the day was from Lowy in Los Angeles. "John, what happened? Are you free to negotiate?"

"Yes, Frank, I am."

By the end of 2003 the mood among stakeholders in soccer was upbeat. They were anticipating change, particularly in the insolvent domestic league. While there was tremendous passion and commitment, this National Soccer League, NSL, had no co-ordinated management, marketing, television coverage or financing. For the pleasure of playing at home players had to endure appalling conditions. Now there was an upwelling of good faith, and as a mark of it the Professional Footballers Australia, PFA, and players agreed to waive more than a million dollars they were owed by the new ASA. According to Ross Solly's book *Shoot Out*, they knew that dealing with the new administration would be challenging but they trusted it would be on business not political grounds.

The PFA had already written a wish list and plan for domestic soccer. Many players would have to go and only the elite would survive. It wanted to build eight or ten teams that were capable of capturing the hearts and minds of fans. Its preferred model was an English-style Australian Premier League.

The Crawford report had recommended that the domestic league be entirely separate from and independent of the Australian Soccer Association. Lowy argued against this, saying there was no one on the horizon who could organise it, raise sufficient funds and who had the capacity to run it. "So I decided to take it under the ASA's wing. I called up Crawford and asked what he thought of the idea. He said he'd prepared the report and if I wanted to make changes, it was up to me."

Lowy went ahead and opened discussions with the PFA. He heard them out but decided the ASA would do its own investigations. Andrew Kemeny, a past president of Hakoah, was asked to chair a new review of the NSL. Notwithstanding its lack of success, its lack of a major sponsor and a lack of a television partner Kemeny found the NSL had been remarkably resilient. This was the result of the passion and commitment of club members and benefactors rather than a successful club business model. Indeed, in the preceding three seasons alone the NSL had haemorrhaged $52 million. Acknowledging this, Kemeny recommended drastic change and a tough new model.

The NSL would cease to exist in April 2004. The bloodletting would be swift. The NSL's thirteen teams would be terminated and a new league of ten teams would be established. To join, a team would have to pay $1 million upfront. It would also need to have $2 million in capital and run its affairs on an annual minimum budget of $3.5 million, with a salary cap of $1.5 million. Stakeholders gasped.

A short while later Lowy conceded that the ASA would financially assist clubs that wanted to be part of the new league. It would hopefully do this through sponsorship and the sale of live television broadcasting rights. This would be left to the new CEO, John O'Neill, to manage when he came on board in March 2004. No sooner had O'Neill arrived at his desk than he was handed this job.

Although he didn't pretend to know anything about soccer, O'Neill was seen as a prize acquisition. He had increased Australian Rugby Union's annual turnover eightfold in his eight years at the helm and had raked in $45 million in profit from staging the 2003 Rugby World Cup. But O'Neill quickly bumped up against the legendary Lowy determination. As he worked on the new domestic league, he found himself increasingly anxious about its financial viability. Mistakenly, he thought it was negotiable and when he took his chairman a copy of his analysis, which argued the pros and cons of a new national competition, it was unceremoniously tossed into the bin.

For Lowy it was unimaginable not to have a national championship and he never wanted to hear mention of such doubts again. Club football was the shopfront of the game and O'Neill should go back to the drawing board. He did and over the next three months built himself a high-calibre management team, poached mostly from Rugby Union. This led to rumblings about people with soccer expertise being left in the cold.

There was a lot of discussion about how many teams would be optimal and how many would be possible. Lowy asked Singleton to come in on this. From Lowy's office Singleton called a football mate from the Special Broadcasting Service, who recommended a league with no more than one team from each major city and one from New Zealand. That meant seven. To bring it to eight, the highest bidder from another city would be included. This seemed an excellent idea.

O'Neill set to work building the foundations of what would become the A League, so named after the J League in Japan and the K League in Korea. The concept of one team per city would leave no room for ethnic enclaves. Fans from all nationalities would enter through the same gate. Gosford on NSW's central coast filled the eighth spot. Clubs would have a roster of twenty players and a salary cap of $1.2 million. Each club would also be permitted to have a marquee player whose salary could fall outside the cap.

He cut a deal with Fox Sports to air up to four live games a week covering the eight teams, bear all production costs and pay a rights fee of $500,000 for the first season. This exposure would make it possible to bring in sponsors, and first through the door for the A League was the Korean car manufacturer Hyundai. It was a major sponsor of football worldwide and in particular backed the game throughout Asia. The league would become known as HAL or the Hyundai A League. With that, the ASA was in a position to assist clubs in the new A League slated to kick off in August 2005.

To ensure Sydney had an iconic strong team the Lowy family took a share in Sydney FC. This was controversial and people complained it wasn't right for the impartial chairman of the peak body to have a financial interest in one team. Lowy agreed there was a conflict of interest but argued the circumstances were extraordinary. "We got money together for Sydney FC but it wasn't enough so I bridged the gap. I didn't really want the stake but without Sydney the league would not get up. I did, however, make a point of taking no part in its management." People continued to object and over time the family's stake was reduced to a residual percentage with no rights.

With the A League, the ethnic warlords would finally be replaced with multicultural ownership, and the game would be televised nationally. In the first years it often attracted crowds of ten to fifteen thousand a match. This 'new football' would represent the New Australia. It was fine to call it soccer, but football was the term used in the 'world game' and by FIFA. Conscious of the power of language, in late 2004 the board of the Australian Soccer Association decided to change its name to the Football Federation of Australia, the FFA. It was a bold move, given that it took the number of football codes in Australia to four.

By the time the A League kicked off in 2005 with an opening game between Sydney FC and Melbourne Victory, the teams were playing new football. Lowy was in the corporate box with tears in his eyes. More people showed up than had bought advance tickets and it took a long time for the 25,000 spectators to file into their seats. Steven, who was at his father's side, said they couldn't believe how the stadium kept filling. When Dwight Yorke, the former striker from Manchester United, kicked the first goal of the A League the crowd went wild. He was the marquee player for Sydney FC which, that season, made it all the way to the finals.

The first season was an unqualified success. It concluded with a full house for the grand final with almost a quarter of a million people watching the broadcast from home. But the league had fragilities and it would take several seasons for the old passion to return and for the new tribalism to build. As this was happening, there would be tectonic shifts in the sport regionally and internationally.

Lowy's dream was that one day Australia would play in Asia. Given the history of Australia being repeatedly rebuffed by Asia, people thought he was indeed dreaming.

22

Joining the Asian family

When Frank Lowy went knocking on the door of Asian football in 2004, he was unknown in the region. While some might have been aware of a new force emerging in the Australian game, this would have been of little interest because Australia belonged to a different group: Oceania, the smallest of the six FIFA confederations. As long as Australia remained there, it was of little concern to anyone in Asia.

Because of its geography, Australia had been subsisting in Oceania with only New Zealand and a group of Pacific island nations for competition. It needed to break out and the most logical place to go was north, to the powerful Asian Football Confederation, AFC. Australia had knocked a few times before but the AFC had never invited it in.

Geographically vast, the AFC stretches from the Middle East to Japan. It has forty-six member organisations representing more than half the world's population and a formidable mix of cultures and religions. It also has the greatest potential of all FIFA's confederations. While it was predictable that Lowy's government mandate, his wealth and his business success would make a good impression in Asia, something else tipped the balance. The Asian powerbrokers detected something of the Levant in Lowy and welcomed him in.

The value to the Socceroos of joining Asia had been apparent for some time, but when Lowy accepted control of Australian soccer in 2003 Blatter wrote to him urging him to work with Oceania to make it more of a force. He tried. "It's in our interest to try and make Oceania a more effective body on the world stage," he told the media. "Basically there is Australia and New Zealand and then there are the island nations. Our objectives are completely different and we need to build a bridge to link us." Within months it was obvious that Oceania could not offer Australia a suitable playground and the differences would never be bridged. Lowy made no secret of his frustration with football politics in the South Pacific.

Australia had made numerous attempts to join the AFC. In 1960 it tried and was repeatedly rejected. By 1966 it had given up trying and put its efforts into creating the Oceania Football Confederation. But six years later in 1972 it resigned from Oceania and again began making overtures to Asia. These were denied and by 1978, Australia was back in Oceania. The knock-backs were not really surprising because Australia, like New Zealand, was perceived as an Anglo-Saxon country from another continent.

The next time Lowy saw Blatter, in Zurich in mid 2004, he explained there would be no progress with Oceania and that Australia needed to be part of Asia. Blatter listened and suggested he send someone immediately to Beijing for the AFC conference and the finals of the Asian Cup. Blatter wasn't sure Australia could join Asia but perhaps they could organise a competition together. Frank picked up the phone and gave John O'Neill his next assignment. It would be at the Beijing Workers' Stadium. "And that was the beginning of the Asian affair," he said.

O'Neill was ripe for a romance with Asia. He had only been CEO of soccer for a few months when he attended the Nations' Cup, Oceania's version of the Asian Cup. Staged in Adelaide over a week, the Nations' Cup had six nations competing and even though the Socceroos played – with almost all of their European-based players present – hardly anyone came to watch. The total crowd for *all* matches would not have reached 30,000. There was no broadcasting contract, no revenue and no major sponsorships. The financial result was a quarter of a million dollars loss. It was a non-event.

In *It's Only a Game* O'Neill described watching the opening of the Asian Cup as his 'road to Damascus' moment. The Beijing Workers' Stadium was packed with 85,000 people and he could see the future all around him. What struck him were the faces in the VIP box. "There must have been two hundred people and they were representative of so many colours, races and religions. Why would we be out of place? It was truly a world game. The top sixteen nations in Asia were involved and it was an enormous celebration. I sat there thinking about the Nations' Cup debacle in Adelaide and how it could never hope to compare."

O'Neill met the president of the AFC, Mohammed bin Hammam, and they talked about Australia's football woes. While there was no reference to Australia shifting confederations, O'Neill left Beijing thinking the idea was plausible.

Statistics showed it was also highly desirable. The Asian Cup tournament drew an international broadcast audience of more than a billion people. In 2004, the final was beamed to 120 countries and watched by 450 million viewers in Asia itself, making it the biggest single television event in the Asian sporting calendar. A move to Asia had the power to transform Australia's international sports landscape.

Meanwhile, Lowy identified the 2004 Athens Olympics as an opportunity to showcase Australia. He moored his boat *Ilona* in Piraeus harbour a few kilometres from the games and set his mind to entertaining the elite of the world's sports administration. With the help of Coates he invited to lunch some members of the International Olympic Committee who were close to football. Many were members of FIFA too. As Blatter would be the guest of honour, he asked the FIFA secretariat for assistance in compiling a guest list and was quietly surprised at how many officials accepted. It was an unusual invitation for the time and people were curious.

The seventy-four metre *Ilona* is immaculately classy and comfortable even with a hundred people seated for lunch on the aft deck. "That lunch was a breakthrough," says Lowy. "I made a lot of friends, made good connections and was accepted as a person of substance who was prepared to work very hard for football." While guests were enjoying the conviviality and the fine Australian wines, Frank rose to his feet. With a classic mix of grace and chutzpah, he welcomed everyone before reminding them that no lunch is really free. Australia was ambitious, it would need a great deal of assistance and from time to time, he would be looking to his guests for help. Blatter delivered an effusive response with which everyone concurred, leaving the host beaming for the rest of the afternoon. Lowy would recall this event as Australian football's unofficial launch into FIFA.

Socialising with intent can be demanding work. During that Olympic season Lowy made a point of engaging personally with as many FIFA delegates and members of the Asian Football Confederation as possible. He worked constantly; while his charm sees him through most situations, his directness doesn't always strike the right note, particularly in some Asian cultures. There were times when people looked at the ground.

When an invitation arrived for Lowy and O'Neill to attend the AFC's gala prize-giving in Kuala Lumpur that December, they accepted with enthusiasm. The two flew up the day before and were met at the airport by a security detail fit for a head of state. That evening Lowy met bin Hammam, then at the height of his power as president of the AFC. It was their first meeting and while bin Hammam understood the agenda he knew nothing about Frank, apart from the fact that he was the new head of soccer in Australia. He says: "But from the first moment I met him we were like two people who have known each other for ages, we talked about everything that night. Maybe this is Frank's strongest point, his ability to enter the heart of his opponent without any invitation. He is there and I find myself thinking: I know this man, I like this man and I would like to work with him."

Had there been no approach from Australia there would have been no invitation from Asia, but once the matter was on the table mutual benefits quickly emerged. Australia had a strong economy, an affluent market for broadcasting rights and was rich in sports expertise that it could bring to Asia, particularly in the form of referees and administrators. Besides, the country had world-class players and a deep sporting culture. With more than half a million players at junior amateur levels, Australia knew how to build infrastructure for youth training and how to encourage young people to participate. Australia could also provide a seasonal advantage by presenting the AFC with two hemispheres, allowing the game to be played in all seasons.

For Australia there were only positives in joining Asia, the biggest and fastest-growing football market in the world. Membership of the AFC would lift Australia into a higher league, provide it with more high-quality games and force it to improve its performance. It would present a better route to qualifying for the World Cup and, were Australia to be successful, joining Asia would ensure its players were better prepared for that. But as Lowy saw it, there were three challenges ahead. Australia had to be invited to join the AFC, it had to obtain FIFA's blessing and it had to exit elegantly from Oceania.

On the second night in Kuala Lumpur and before the prize-giving dinner, Lowy and O'Neill were invited by bin Hammam to a private anteroom where he received special guests. "Frank and I were up and down like yo-yos being introduced to Arab princes and leaders from across the region," wrote O'Neill. "My admiration for Frank grew enormously. He would make an excellent Middle East negotiator."

At the formal dinner Frank was seated at the top table, at the left hand of bin Hammam. This promising sign did not disappoint. In his speech bin Hammam welcomed the two Australians and, to their utter surprise, the rest of his address revolved around Australia and how good it could be for Asian football. Without actually articulating the invitation, he was putting down a welcome mat. "We were killed with the kindness of their hospitality," wrote O'Neill. "We even had an unexpected escort back to Frank's plane at the close of the dinner. More than a dozen Arabs, most of them members of the upper echelons, were interested in checking out Frank's plane." For what became known as the Frankie and Johnnie duo, this was a high point. During the nine-hour trip home they toasted each other with Midleton's Irish whiskey.

Before they flew out, Frank invited bin Hammam to Australia, promising to arrange tours of the Australian Institute of Sport in Canberra and other facilities. There was goodwill in the air and while this relationship was politically important and would be pivotal in Australia's move to Asia, both men recognised a personal connection they wanted to continue.

In some other circumstances they would have been considered enemies. A devout Qatari Muslim, bin Hammam would certainly not have been expected to forge such a friendship with a Jew. But bin Hammam did not see it that way. "Most of my followers are Arabs and we don't see religion as an obstacle," he explained. "We can have political differences but respecting the religion of others, that is part of our culture. I never saw it as a problem and neither did he." When asked about their friendship Lowy responded that reactions very much depend on the circumstances in which people meet. "I could have met someone like him when I was young and fighting in the Israeli Army. In battle we could have shot at each other. But I met him in a different environment and we have become good friends." They would remain firm friends for another four years or so.

In the meantime Lowy began building relationships in the region. It was early 2005 and he was a man on a mission. For him, face-to-face contact is most effective and he was on the ground, meeting as many people as he could. Representing a Western country was generally not a cultural obstacle and Lowy's manner often smoothed the process. Impatient with protocol, he often picked up the phone to call a high-status person himself, as if this person was an old friend.

Bin Hammam did not expect this: "People from the Middle East often feel that Westerners are cold and formal. Frank is not like that. He just picks up the phone and doesn't have a limit to express his friendship, or share his knowledge and experience. There's a Middle Eastern warmth about him. It is in his blood. Without his personality, character and friendship I don't think it would have been easy. He is simple and approachable, has a huge financial background and a big company but when he talks to you, you don't feel any of this. People are very much surprised when they hear about his business background."

Before he was due to meet Frank, Manilal Fernando, one of the AFC vice-presidents, did some homework. He called his brother who had migrated to Australia as a pastry chef and asked, "Who the hell is Lowy?" The answer led him to imagine he would be meeting a large imposing figure. When the relatively unassuming Frank walked in, Fernando thought, "Who is this?"

Fernando, who represented Sri Lankan football, became a key figure behind bin Hammam in pushing for Australia's admission to Asia. He appreciated Frank's casualness, the absence of arrogance and his foresight. "Frank is a weatherbeaten man. In my island country the experienced fisherman doesn't use science, he smells the sea. Frank is a pioneer in soccer and could see the future. We are in for better times with a man like him on the scene. We have lots to learn from him and, of course, he is learning from Asia too. Whether I agree or disagree, I speak frankly with him. He uses few words but you can depend on what he says." Although Fernando would have liked to see Frank elevated to the AFC's executive committee – the seventy-year age limit ruled him out – he was not starry-eyed about him. He thought Frank's focus was too strong on the benefits for Australia and that "he should be like a godfather to Asia".

FIFA's regulations allow a confederation "in exceptional circumstances" to grant membership to an association that belongs geographically to another federation. Now it was up to Australia to build its case. O'Neill gathered a team together and began working on it while behind the scenes Lowy shuttled between Europe, Asia and Australia, deepening relationships in Zurich, working to loosen ties with Oceania and to strengthen bonds with the AFC.

Although Australia had suggested that Oceania would be better off without it because competition would be more equal, its impending defection was viewed as a severe blow to that confederation. Questions were raised about whether New Zealand would follow suit and whether this tiny confederation would even survive. Blatter's experience told him this move would not serve Oceania well. In the end, Australia gave an undertaking to assist Oceania financially. It also promoted the theory that the glass ceiling was being removed for Oceania. Apart from the World Cup, Oceania's teams had automatic entry into global championships at all levels: under-seventeen, under-twenty, women's football and the Olympics. Australia tended to take these spots but once it was out of the way, other members of the confederation would have a better chance.

Football did in fact flourish in New Zealand and internationally. Through participating in Australia's A League, New Zealand was exposed to more competition which helped its national team develop. In 2010 the All Whites played in the World Cup in South Africa. Before this change only NZ or Australia could possibly make it to the finals, but in that year they both did.

Australia was ready to join Asia but had to bide its time so the correct process could be followed. Not all the members of the AFC were keen on Australia and some countries were said to have actively campaigned against allowing it to be a member. But once bin Hammam had met Frank, he said there was a feeling of inevitability about the move. It was just a matter of following the timetable. During this period it was not unusual for Lowy to call with: "What's happening, can we speed the process?" Despite his impatience, the transition was swift and methodical.

In March 2005 the AFC executive committee unanimously agreed Australia could join, pending permission from FIFA. By April, Oceania had given its blessing for Australia to go, and by September Frank was in Morocco for the AFC's official welcome to Australia. The ceremony took place in a tent in the ancient city of Marrakech and saw Lowy hand a folded Australian flag to bin Hammam. The two men kissed and called each other brother. "I thank you from the bottom of my heart that you are taking Australia into the AFC," Lowy said, choking with emotion. When the Australian flag was raised and fluttered among the forty-five flags of the other AFC nations, Lowy couldn't speak.

Back in Australia the achievement was applauded. The *Sydney Morning Herald*'s football writer Michael Cockerill commented admiringly that "a Jew has convinced a region containing most of the world's Muslim population that an Anglo-Saxon nation belongs in Asia". He described the achievement of delivering what generations of football administrators had failed to do as Lowy's eternal gift to the game.

There were echoes of former prime minister Paul Keating's observation that while Australia's history was with Europe, its geography was with Asia. Keating had encouraged a new Asian relationship. Talk of 'football diplomacy' followed, with descriptions of football as a vehicle capable of carrying diverse Australian interests into Asia in the form of trade, politics, art and culture; and vice versa. People discussed the novel situation of Australia being in a position to represent Asia, because if it qualified for the World Cup that is exactly what it would be doing.

Independently, the Lowy Institute for International Policy decided to explore what this first real sporting relationship with Asia would mean for Australia. Following the Marrakech ceremony, in October 2005 it held a seminar drawing together a diverse mix of specialists on this unique subject, from footballers and foreign policy commentators to sports administrators and regional experts. They teased out the opportunities that AFC membership could create in broadening and deepening Australia's ties with Asia – provided, of course, they were grasped. These themes were then captured in a brief publication called *Football Diplomacy* by research fellow Anthony Bubalo. While the commercial potential of this new relationship and its spin-offs in tourism and travel were obvious, there were interesting and less quantifiable implications.

Over the years Australia had built pragmatic ties with Asian leaders, but a popular dimension was always missing. Now there was an opportunity to strengthen people-to-people links and provide a common point of conversation between societies. While sports fans are passionate about their own teams, they also tend to share an appreciation for the game and its players that often crosses national and cultural boundaries. Given this, football could provide a broader and more grassroots level of engagement that had largely been absent in the past. With sport central to the Australian psyche, the development of a sporting relationship with regional neighbours as enthusiastic about their sport as Australians could transform local perceptions and preconceptions of what individual Asian societies are really like.

Bubalo's publication suggested that here also was an opportunity for a more direct use of football as an instrument of foreign policy. There is a long history of using sport in this way, from Germany's unsuccessful attempt to use the 1936 Berlin Olympics to demonstrate racial superiority to America's use of ping-pong diplomacy to break the diplomatic ice with China. While Australia had well-developed relationships in the region and did not need to resort to sport as an icebreaker, each stadium could become a diplomatic forum where business and political elites could network against a background of commonality.

The promise of a populist base in Asia was of considerable interest to the country. Andrew Clark of the *Australian Financial Review* speculated that it "may prove to be one of the more important Australian initiatives since WWII, arguably ranking with the Australian-inspired creation of the Asia Pacific Economic Co-Operation (APEC) group, and of the Cairns Group of agricultural exporting countries". Clark said what made it even more remarkable was that it was envisaged, planned, finessed and executed by one man who was not a politician or even a government official, but an immigrant who trusted his instincts.

Other commentators exhorted Australian business to follow football's example. The 'Asian century' had begun but Australian business was still not part of the region. The Australian Bureau of Statistics documented this, showing that in 2004 Australian foreign direct investment in China was only 0.15 per cent of its total direct investment abroad. Although there were trading relationships there was no real penetration of the Asian market and Lowy's prescience in moving to the region was acknowledged.

Australian soccer had been dormant for a long time. Before May 2004, the national team had not been seen in Australia for more than thirty months. The move to Asia would raise its profile. It was projected that between 2006 and 2009 the Socceroos would play at least eighteen full competition home and away matches against other Asian sides in qualifiers for the Asian Cup, the World Cup and more – should they qualify. There were also many more games for the A League, for women's soccer and for youth sides.

By December 2005 Frank Lowy was back in Kuala Lumpur. It was exactly a year since he first met bin Hammam and he had come to learn exactly where Australia would be placed in the AFC. It had four regions and Australia would be admitted to the ASEAN (South-East Asian) regional grouping. In a speech to the confederation, Lowy expressed his gratitude and predicted that this would expand the landscape for football in Australia.

By then Australia had already grabbed global attention by qualifying for the World Cup in a play-off against the South American powerhouse of Uruguay. Before the play-off the regional view had been that Australia was using Asia as an easier and possibly undeserved route for qualification. This victory signalled something different, making some AFC countries nervous that their talented new member might one day claim one of Asia's future World Cup spots. This nervousness would prove well founded. But Asia also gained another half-spot for the World Cup. Previously, Oceania had a half spot and had to play a South American team to win or lose the other half. Now, with the change, South America's half spot would be moved to the AFC and Oceania would have to play off against Asia. This would later change again.

The ink was barely dry on the official placement of Australia in Asia when Frank Lowy was focusing on the benefits of Australia hosting the next Asian Cup. This event is held every four years and while the Socceroos would make their debut at the 2007 Cup in Asia, he saw them playing the 2011 Cup on home soil. When he discovered Qatar was already planning for this event, he thought it best not to push. "I wanted to win the war, not the battle, so I decided to hold fire for 2015." He didn't know that he would be facing a much bigger battle with Qatar down the track.

He did, however, secure the 2007 AFC Conference and Gala Awards for Sydney. It was November and he took great pride in hosting his new Asian football family and showing them Australia's bounty. Prime minister John Howard, who lost office that month, would later describe Frank's initiative to join Asia as a far-sighted decision and a significant achievement. "Although Frank's past has had a huge influence on him, he is always thinking about the way forward, the next thing," said Howard.

The conference followed a few months after the Socceroos' debut appearance in the 2007 Asian Cup. When they lined up as the favourites they were brimming with confidence, but quickly understood how tough football could be in their new family. They crashed out to Japan in the quarter-finals. The Samurai Blue had taught them a salutary lesson. The Socceroos took the learning and when they returned for the World Cup qualifiers, they found they were up against Japan again. This time they prevailed and became the top seeded Asian team going into the 2010 FIFA World Cup.

For Australian football, the move to Asia was an acknowledged success. Football writer Les Murray has called it the most important of Lowy's reforms.

23

Hear the thunder

In 2005, Lowy found himself in Germany. He was in Nuremberg in 2005 to watch the Socceroos play in the Confederations Cup, which is held a year before the World Cup.

The Socceroos were there because they had topped Oceania in the qualifiers, but they were out of their depth. Frank sat in the Nuremberg stadium with his head in his hands. The team had just lost its second game in a row and he was afraid of what this meant. In five months the Socceroos would have to play two crucial matches to qualify for the World Cup. They would be playing against Uruguay, the fifth ranked team in South America, and given this performance in Germany he was not hopeful.

Steven was with him and as father and son walked back through the streets, rather than mope about the loss, Frank's mind switched to fixing the problem. It was time, he said, for the national coach Frank Farina to move on. Steven was taken aback: "This was a very big call because it meant a new coach had to be found and engaged almost immediately to get the team ready to play in five months." But although it seemed barely possible, the change in coach would prove to be a master stroke.

When they travel together Frank and Steven are usually on business, under pressure and not interested in sightseeing. Now, with time on their hands, they thought they should see something of the city and decided on the rally grounds that once showcased the megalomania of the Nazis. The area is vast and the proportions huge. As Frank stood where Hitler had addressed the faithful he could easily imagine acres of marshalled troops and the lines of red, black and white flags flying the feared swastika. He could hear the rousing music as planes flew overhead and tanks rumbled down the main parade, reinforcing the might of the Reich. But when he opened his eyes he saw no more than a tacky circuit for car racing. It didn't feel right that these grounds had not been preserved as a monument to the failure of fascism.

Now Frank wanted to see more and they went to the court where in 1945 and 1946 judges from the Allied powers had presided over the hearings of twenty-two major Nazi criminals in the so-called Nuremberg Trials. Frank was entirely absorbed. Although it was history he had lived through, he struggled to comprehend it. "I just couldn't grasp how this could have happened with such fervour and been so wrong and caused so much destruction. How could one man stand at the centre of it all and generate so much cruelty?" He was pleased not to be alone, and having Steven at his side was a comfort.

As they were driven around the city they chatted about football. Frank Farina had been national coach for six turbulent years. Lowy disclosed that he had made contact with a foreign coach the previous year and had quietly courted him. The contact had come through one of Westfield's Dutch bankers and a hardened soccer supporter. He had recommended Guus Hiddink and had arranged for Lowy to meet him and his agent in an airport lounge in Amsterdam. Lowy did his homework and showed up at the airport where the three men had dinner. But Lowy forgot to pay. "I just finished and walked out. This became a long-standing joke between us, with the agent saying he considered it a debt. Our discussions continued but I realised we couldn't afford Hiddink. His agent was talking about many millions and eventually we did not maintain contact."

The Socceroos lost their third and final match in that Confederations Cup. Lowy, O'Neill and Wolanski discussed the situation and on his return to Australia Farina was informed that the chairman had lost confidence in him. His dismissal in July 2005 was officially described as a 'mutual separation' but everyone understood what that meant. Farina was philosophical and told the press that once he had lost the support of the chairman "that was that". He went graciously.

Meantime, Frank was feverishly looking for a replacement. "I interviewed other coaches and visited overseas but got nowhere. I was getting desperate and made contact with Hiddink's agent again. By this time O'Neill was with me and joined the negotiation. It was a tough period for the two of us because I wouldn't let go and we got in each other's way. We were almost falling over each other. But we came to terms on what we could afford and reopened negotiations. O'Neill finalised them and signed up Hiddink."

A celebrated figure in the soccer world, Guus Hiddink had a reputation as a transformational coach. After transforming football in South Korea and taking its national team to the semi-finals of the World Cup in 2002, his stature had rocketed.

The Koreans had never won a game at the World Cup and under Hiddink's guidance they beat Italy, Spain and Portugal. Hiddink became a national hero, posters of him went up around the country, his face appeared on stamps, a statue of him was unveiled and half a million copies of his autobiography were printed in Korean. He also became the first foreigner ever to be granted honorary Korean citizenship. Hiddink's appointment to the Australian team brought instant prestige. What, people asked, would this miracle man do for Australia?

When Hiddink first met the Australian team in Holland for a training session he described them as "a bunch of vagabonds" who arrived wearing a motley collection of caps, flip-flops, shorts and Bermudas. According to a press report, on the field they flew at each other, shouting and swearing. After thirty wild minutes Hiddink stopped play and instructed them to be quiet. They should only shout when a teammate was in trouble. While he very much admired the way Australians gave 100 per cent of themselves, he noted that in their enthusiasm tactical discipline was often lost. They needed a balance between brain and brawn, and he soon had them playing Dutch 'total football' in which players keep swapping positions and thinking for themselves. They responded to this new approach with great interest, as they did to Hiddink's determination to get them fit. He got them into such good shape that a year later one newspaper would report that there was not a fitter team in Germany during the World Cup. Psychologically astute, this new coach worked on team dynamics, rebuilt morale and gained the players' full trust. By the time they walked onto the pitch, esprit de corps was at its height.

As the date for the qualifier against Uruguay approached, Lowy was becoming anxious. The World Cup was just two games away. Australia hadn't qualified since 1974 and now the prospect was so close it was nerve-racking. Every decision seemed to matter, even personal ones.

In late 2005 he returned home from a long-haul business trip just as the Socceroos were due to leave for the first match in South America. Deeply tired, Lowy debated whether he should repack his bag and go too. His seventy-four-year-old body might take the strain of another long international flight, but could his head cope? The stakes were so high he feared a loss in Uruguay combined with physical exhaustion might overwhelm him. But perhaps his presence would boost morale, particularly since a loss was likely. Uruguay was unquestionably the superior team.

Yes, he would go. He called his captain to prepare the plane. Then Steven implored him: "Dad, please, it's just not good for you. You don't need to do this." Frank was swayed but when the team took off on Friday, he felt so unsettled he called his captain again. He figured he could go on Saturday and be back Monday morning. The plane was prepared. But over a broken night he changed his mind, got up early and called off the pilots. That Saturday morning he went to synagogue instead, made a blessing for the team and then remained in a state of heightened emotion all weekend. When Uruguay won by one goal to nil the disappointment was much easier to contain in Sydney.

For the return match, Lowy and O'Neill had created a small advantage. Without disclosing it, they chartered a Qantas plane to bring the team home in the best possible condition. It was expensive but the stakes were high. While the Uruguayan crowd was still cheering in the stadium, the Socceroos were whisked to the airport. They flew home immediately, on a flight with masseurs, special food and exercise laid on. Everything was tailored to ensure they would arrive home in optimum form, which would hopefully give them an edge for the return game in Sydney. When they learned about the plane the Uruguayans wanted to hitch a lift. The FFA refused and they had to take the long route on a commercial flight, with many players cramped in economy class. Without special benefits they arrived jetlagged and tired.

Lowy thought it would never be possible to recapture the intense passion he had once felt for soccer. Thirty years earlier his life had risen and fallen with the fortunes of Hakoah's soccer team. Now in November 2005 the prize was greater, the exposure was greater and so was the public involvement. Financially this return game was crucial for the sport. World Cup qualification would see FIFA pour $10 million into the game in Australia. To qualify Australia had to score twice and concede no goals.

On the evening of 16 November 2005, Frank began to condition himself as he and the family were driven out to Sydney's Telstra Stadium. As Steven recalls, the conversation in the van went like this:

"Is it unthinkable that we can get two goals?" Frank asked.

"It's possible," someone answered.

"Yeah, but it's not probable," came another view.

"But is it entirely implausible?"

And so it went until the family agreed it was possible but unlikely Australia would win. David, Steven and Shirley were with Frank, so were some grandchildren. Peter and the Westfield staff were watching from London and periodically Peter talked to his father on the phone. Daniel, Frank's grandson, was calling from New York for updates.

Lowy would later say he went into the box with foreboding that was realistic, but the longer the game went on, the more confident he became. "Our team was quicker and more attuned. Our boys seemed emotionally stronger, without that hot Latin volatility." Still highly nervous, Frank looked at O'Neill who was sitting in front of him. "He was so tense and tight I was concerned for him." He was a bit concerned for himself too and kept asking David what he thought. At one point David remarked, "Is this supposed to be a pleasure?"

By halftime Australia was leading by one goal. Lowy's apprehension was so intense that he couldn't socialise with the important guests in the box. He needed air and alcohol.

In the second half the Uruguayans seemed a little tired; the longer the game went the stronger the Australians became. As the momentum began to build among the 82,000 people in the stadium and knowing eight million were watching around Australia, Frank felt at the centre of the universe.

By the final whistle after extra time the score was one nil to Australia. As Uruguay had beaten Australia one nil at home, the two sides had reached a stalemate. This had to be resolved with a penalty shootout and as the teams lined up to take their five shots at goal, the crowd froze. No one drew breath. Frank was under such pressure that he later said had anyone pricked him with a pin he would have detonated.

Australia's heroic goalkeeper Mark Schwarzer saved two penalties. This was almost beyond belief. Then, at a quarter to midnight Australian champion John Aloisi walked up in silence and put the ball down. From the fans sitting in the gods to the officials on the field, the Olympic Stadium had never been quieter. When he kicked the winning penalty goal for Australia, the crowd exploded. As soccer writer Jesse Fink described in his book *Fifteen Days in June*:

The noise inside the ground was so loud and unearthly it was as if I'd pressed my ear up against the jet engines of an airplane. The stands rippled with movement and colour,

like fields of blooming canola ... high fives were flying
everywhere. Grown men were hugging and kissing. The
flute solo in Men at Work's 'Down Under' filled the late
spring air, along with fireworks, yellow streamers and all
manner of rubbish ... We'd done it! We'd finally made it to
the FIFA World Cup, the biggest sporting event on earth,
after thirty-two excruciating years.

Those calling the game for television could barely contain
themselves. "At long last! At long last!" they cried. The
victory was as intoxicating as it was uniting. "You are, we are
Australian," they told their viewers. "This is a team from every
community in Australia, and it's our team." It had failed to
qualify for the past eight World Cups and now the voodoo was
broken.

Everyone down under could hear the thunder. Lowy was
shouting too as he made his way onto the field to share the
euphoria. Steven and his kids went too and in the middle of
the pitch, Steven bent down and took a small piece of turf as a
memento. In the dressing room Frank took a call from an elated
John Howard, who was overseas on prime ministerial business
but had managed to watch the match on a small flickering screen.
Waiting for Frank in the car park under the stadium, David and
Steven were shaking their heads. "He's not scared of risk. He's
not scared of risk," they repeated. It was a slow crawl home
through the traffic but Lowy didn't care, he was flying.

The next day he tossed away the losing speech that had been
prepared for the media and happily ad-libbed his way through a
public rally in Sydney's Domain, where thousands turned up in a
spontaneous eruption of support. The country was with him, the
press was rapturous and in a first for soccer, major metropolitan

newspapers had celebratory wraparound covers enthusing about the game. Soccer fever had gripped the country, with millions infected. The sleeping giant of Australian sport had been roused.

Aloisi's goal instantly became an iconic moment of sporting history. It would go on to feature in the top ten sporting moments in Australia which included Sir Donald Bradman's 334 not out in 1930 at Headingley, Cathy Freeman's victory in the 400 metre sprint at the 2000 Sydney Olympics, the yacht *Australia II* winning the America's Cup in 1983, and in 2011 Cadel Evans becoming the first Australian to win the Tour de France.

Frank became a folk hero. When he went to the next local soccer game, crowds swarmed around his car chanting, "Frankie! Frankie! Frankie!" At one point they even took up the chant, "Frankie for prime minister". That win had stripped him of anonymity and he could no longer slip into a suburban café unnoticed. Because of the nature of soccer, people felt relaxed about approaching him. If they saw him in traffic, they would tap on his window and wherever he was abroad, Australians would recognise him and come across to chat.

In the detailed analysis that followed the win it was said that Lowy's idea of hiring a foreign coach had been one of the master strokes in getting Australia to Germany in 2006. On their way to Germany the Socceroos stopped in Holland for a friendly match against the national Dutch team organised by Hiddink. They stunned themselves and everyone else by winning.

For the World Cup Australia was drawn in a group with Brazil, Croatia and Japan. Their first match, on 12 June 2006, was against Japan in Kaiserslautern and they knew millions of fans at home were staying awake to watch.

In business, Lowy's poker face reveals nothing but when he enters a football stadium that learned control gives way. The

President of the Korean Football Federation Dr Chung Mong-Joon was surprised when he first sat in the VIP box with Frank and Shirley in Kaiserslautern. While the Japanese and Korean officials sat in respectful silence watching the match, Frank was on his feet, screaming. "He had the deepest voice I have heard and the energy in him just exploded – his voice controlled the stadium," says Dr Mong-Joon. "My impression was this was very Australian, big, wild and straightforward."

Japan had scored twenty-six minutes into the game and Frank was miserable, fearing the Socceroos had collapsed and worrying that Australia would never make it to the World Cup again. Towards the end of the second half the impending disappointment was too much to bear. He got up and paced around the small box. As he sat down, Tim Cahill scored. "Frank went berserk," says Shirley. He had barely calmed down when, a couple of minutes later Cahill scored again. Frank burst out of his seat, willing to hug anyone. Three minutes later, John Aloisi kicked the final goal for Australia, making it 3–1. Lowy thought he was in heaven.

For the duration of the World Cup the extended Lowy family based themselves on *Ilona* off the coast of Sardinia. For each game, they would fly back and forth together. It was a family event and between games they planned to relax on deck and enjoy the Mediterranean summer. Following that game against Japan, the mood on *Ilona* couldn't have been better.

Although Frank was in his element, he wanted more. For him it is axiomatic that with vision, application and adequate resources apparently unachievable things can be achieved. Just prior to the match against Brazil on 18 June, while pushing his way through crowds of fans in a square in Munich, he imagined the same scene in Sydney's Martin Place. Why not?

That private moment was the spark for what would later become an enormously energetic campaign for Australia to host a World Cup. For the moment, however, he would keep that idea to himself.

While the Socceroos lost their next game to Brazil, they drew the following one with Croatia and miraculously made it to the next round. They had gone to Germany ranked 49th in the world. Now, under Hiddink's tutelage they had progressed to the Group of 16 and overnight had become a source of national pride. But to make it into the top eight they had to play against Italy.

Surveys showed that back home 6.7 million Australians got up between one and three in the morning to watch the live broadcast of this game. This meant almost one in three men, women and children in the country was in front of the television. Against expectations, Australia matched Italy consistently through the game. The play was fast and exciting and when, in the second half, an Italian player was sent off Australia's stocks rose.

The Socceroos were on the verge of greatness when, in the last few minutes, a dubious penalty was awarded to the Italians and they scored. There was no time for Australia to recover and when the final whistle went, the country convulsed in pain. Everyone was hurting and although Frank could barely talk, he recognised an opportunity. In the shakeout after the World Cup, top coaches would be on the loose. It had been known for some time that after Germany, Hiddink would be leaving the Socceroos to become Russia's national coach. Although he didn't expect to recapture the Hiddink magic, Lowy's preference was for another Dutch coach.

By now, O'Neill was physically drained and emotionally spent. Apart from football demands he had difficult personal circumstances and needed a few days off. But as he explained in his autobiography the Lowy drum beats relentlessly and there would be no rest.

He didn't agree with Lowy on the issue of a coach. To save money he thought it would be preferable to use a home-grown coach for a couple of years and then hire an international star for the qualifying period of the next World Cup in South Africa in 2010. Lowy wanted star quality for the full four-year cycle and as chairman he prevailed. This was just a flash of the creative tension that had been intensifying between Lowy and O'Neill all year. They had been a highly effective team but O'Neill's contract was coming up for renegotiation.

Back in Australia, O'Neill brought the nation up to date with a speech at the National Press Club in Canberra. He explained that 'new football' was barely thirty months old and although it was not yet set for life, it was certainly a going concern. It was a $60 million business underpinned by major commercial sponsorships, and had grown at close to 100 per cent year on year since 2003. It was almost unrecognisable from the morass that old soccer had been. Although the country was still sore from the loss in Germany, the giant of Australian sport was awake. O'Neill noted that a creature of this size that had been asleep for so long needed time to mobilise and that the repositioning of football was probably a ten-year proposition. "There is a great deal that still needs to be done before it can lay claim to the castle." Although O'Neill had worked assiduously at building football's success, he was not going to be around long enough to lead the charge across that drawbridge.

As alpha males, both Lowy and O'Neill needed to be in charge. Lowy, as was patently obvious to everyone, was not a hands-off chairman and O'Neill had made it known he could see himself in the top job. The role of CEO, which was equivalent to general secretary in other federations, was too limited. As Lowy had no intention of stepping aside, O'Neill proposed that he could become the executive deputy chairman of the FFA and have a seat on the board.

"Whilst he'd done an excellent job I wasn't prepared to cede power to any CEO and wanted to keep the board's authority unfettered so it could do what was necessary," said Frank. "Although O'Neill and I tried other solutions, we couldn't agree. The tension between us was making life difficult for us both and we decided it would be best if he did not renew his contract. I was unhappy about the parting but happy that relations remained cordial afterwards."

Such was the interest in new football that the Lowy–O'Neill split in August made front-page news as the press mourned the end of a wonderful partnership. During the press conference Lowy, aged seventy-five and O'Neill, fifty-five, sat side by side and played down their creative differences.

By early November 2006 Lowy was sitting side by side with the fresh-faced Ben Buckley, aged thirty-nine, whom he was introducing to the media as the new CEO. This former North Melbourne AFL player was leaving the position of the number two administrator of that sport and was described as representing the best of the new generation of sporting administrators. "He impressed me. He was like a breath of fresh air, fair and hardworking," said Lowy.

And there was much to do. The job of establishing football was unfinished and Lowy himself had been re-elected for another four-year term. This would take him into his eighties and hopefully see football on a solid foundation with a new board. He wanted to institutionalise the sport so professionals could come in and run it. He also wanted to see the Socceroos reach single digits in the world ranking. If Australia could achieve this in other sports, why not in football?

At home football enjoyed a brief windfall effect of the World Cup. There was the FIFA prize for making it to round 16, the promise of better sponsorship deals and a steep hike in the price negotiated with Fox Sports for annual broadcasting rights. Australia, however, has four football codes and not all were pleased with football's success. The *Sydney Morning Herald* carried a lead story claiming soccer – football – constituted a 'net loss' to the country, complaining it was the most heavily funded of the four football codes, that taxpayers had been disadvantaged and that it still owed the federal government several millions.

"But what other government program had received more bang for its buck than the investment in the revival of football?" Lowy asked in response. "Our performance in Germany not only boosted our national spirit but gave us a new world presence. What this means for the Australian 'brand' around the world is beyond measure." Football was just a few years into its ten-year journey to establish itself as a viable mainstream sport in Australia.

Although new football had exploded onto the scene, the momentum of the early years couldn't be sustained. There was no lapse in efforts to build the sport but it was largely unglamorous work behind the scenes. Every now and then there would be a burst of brilliance but overall football dropped back in public awareness.

The Socceroos' painful and embarrassing exit from the quarter-finals of the Asia Cup in July 2007 didn't help. They had entered the tournament as favourites but were unprepared for the humidity, heat, crowds and chaos of Asia: the competition was co-hosted by Indonesia, Malaysia, Thailand and Vietnam. Unaware of just how debilitating those conditions can be, they understood too late how much acclimatisation and training would have been needed for them to play at peak levels. By their last game, they were soaked through and exhausted. The team was also ageing and the golden generation of Socceroos was occasionally referred to as 'the greying generation'. But at least the loss shook the sport awake again and made it pay full attention to qualifying in Asia for the next big event, the 2010 World Cup in South Africa.

First, however, the FFA had to get back into the black. Although it had accumulated an $11 million loss in 2006–2007, Lowy was unworried. In his fifty-year career he had recovered from many financial lows, and he now had a business plan for the next World Cup cycle that was predicting positive cash flows and profitability.

Others were speculating about whether Frank would put his hand into his own pocket for the game. It was argued that as he already supported so many causes, from medical research to think tanks, there was no reason for football to be exempt. He explained it would be unhealthy for him to influence the game with his money. If he was tied in financially and he didn't perform, there would be reluctance to replace him. Rather, he wanted to be judged on his ability, and in that regard he was willing to give all he had. He did, however, continue to fund himself in the business of football and at almost no cost to the FFA. The sport was constantly on his mind and, as his position required, he was doing the strategic thinking, planning for years ahead. Privately, he was collecting intelligence about two major events, the Asian Cup and the FIFA World Cup. His dream was to arrange to host both on Australian soil.

Front of mind, however, was ensuring the Socceroos made it to South Africa for the 2010 World Cup. The perception of football had so changed that the Australian public took for granted the team would qualify. Improvements had been so quick and so dramatic that expectations were not tempered by the fact that the Socceroos had fallen to 48th in the world and the team was without a permanent coach.

Graham Arnold, who had been national coach since Hiddink left, had been relieved of the position in July and a frantic search was underway for a replacement. Frank wanted another celebrity coach to take the Socceroos through the qualifying rounds against China, Iraq and Qatar and condition them to survive the Arabian summer, where day temperatures could reach fifty degrees Celsius. He believed he had found such a person in Dick Advocaat, a well-known Dutch coach. After a brief courtship and negotiation Advocaat had signed a contract with the FFA but then reneged. He had decided to remain in Russia where the sport had much deeper pockets. It was a turbulent time and Lowy pushed to sue for damages. The $2 million the FFA received in compensation mitigated the disappointment.

Time was running out and towards the end of 2007 the press began begging for a coach for Christmas. Wolanski had done a lot of work behind the scenes and now he, Lowy and Buckley were in Singapore interviewing another coach from the Dutch school. A few days later Pim Verbeek was presented to the media. He wasn't quite the superstar everyone had been expecting – most Australians hadn't heard of him – but he was from the Netherlands and he did have twenty-five years of experience. He had also worked in Korea with both Hiddink and Advocaat. The public's fascination with Dutch coaching was still strong and Verbeek's promise to provide more 'Dutch philosophy' was what many wanted to hear. As the New Year dawned he had one clear assignment – get the Socceroos to South Africa.

And he did, quickly, with two games to spare. The team was in peak condition and in nine games conceded only one goal. Although the qualifying route through Asia had been tough, it provided the best possible preparation for the Socceroos. The nation was jubilant and for the moment Verbeek was a hero. Tim Cahill, Australia's star midfielder, loved playing for him and said he gave the Socceroos a "club-like" feeling that he personally had never experienced at an international level before. Where Hiddink had been rather imperious and difficult to read emotionally, with Verbeek the players knew where they stood. He spoke to every member and according to Cahill was "honest and trusting".

The country was enthusiastically behind the Socceroos and full of hope. Commentators noted how everything about the sport had changed. New language was used, the sport had become smarter, there had been leaps in thinking, coaching had improved and Australia now even had its own proprietary methodology for play, which could provide a competitive advantage.

When the team left for South Africa, there was an expectation it would conjure magic. But it came up hard against reality. It opened its campaign against Germany, which was in top form. Germany had won the World Cup three times and was fielding a youthful, fast and highly skilled team. In comparison the Socceroos looked worn and tired. They seemed to have run out of stamina. Verbeek had changed the game plan at the last minute and as they struggled with the strange strategy they conceded four goals. Even though Australia was down to ten men – Cahill had been sent off – the defeat was crushing. For most of the match the 10,000 Australian fans who had travelled to South Africa sat in stunned silence. Lowy sat with his head in hands. Afterwards, he swallowed the humiliation and went to talk to the team.

They needed to find the spirit to rebound and five days later, in the match against Ghana, they came alive. But again they went down to ten men when Harry Kewell was sent off. The game ended in a one-all draw, which left the Socceroos in a precarious position. To have a chance of progressing, they would have to win their next match outright and by a big enough margin to compensate for the German loss. They regained some pride with a 2–1 win over Serbia but their goal difference wasn't sufficient to progress, and they packed their bags for home.

The team was in disarray, fans were disappointed and faith in Verbeek drained away. He had taken the brunt and fortunately for him, the end of his contract coincided with the end of Australia's hopes for the World Cup. Frank wrestled with the loss: "We made big strides getting to South Africa but once on the world stage it is unrealistic to expect to succeed with every step. We accumulated the same number of points in Germany, in relative terms it was a disappointment. While it is possible to draw some comfort from the relativities, the game is result-orientated and, in the end, people don't care about sentiments. It's win or lose."

As the Lowy family packed its bags, Frank looked to the horizon. Ahead lay two opportunities. Australia would be bidding to host a FIFA World Cup and it would be playing in the 2011 Asian Cup. There was no time to mourn.

24

The prize beyond reach

Before Frank Lowy took charge of football, Australia would never have considered bidding for the right to host a FIFA World Cup. This is the biggest sporting event in the world and reflecting his unwavering faith in Australia, Lowy believed it could win this right. When critics said the country was not ready to compete at this level, he pointed out that it had already hosted both the Olympics and the Commonwealth Games. It had led the world in swimming, cricket and tennis. Why not football too?

Until he rebuilt the sport, Australian football did not have the consistency of management, the credibility and the funding to dream about hosting a World Cup. In the decade immediately preceding his appointment, the Australian Soccer Federation (later Association) had had eight chairmen, two presidents and six chief executive officers and had undergone four inquiries.

Long before Frank announced his intention to bid, he had been working quietly behind the scenes, building networks and laying foundations. He became a familiar visitor to FIFA's headquarters. He was also in and out of the AFC's headquarters in Kuala Lumpur. Whenever he travelled for business, if there was an opportunity to fit in a football meeting he would do so, if only for a few hours in an airport lounge. He was on a personal mission. For the first time in its history, FIFA was opening the bidding for two World Cups simultaneously – 2018 and 2022 – apparently to generate better revenue streams.

Lowy needed to be certain about two things before he announced the bid to the public. As Australia would be bidding as the newest member of the Asian football family, he needed to know whether China was also a contestant. If so, there would be little point entering the fray. But how could he uncover China's intentions? At the time it was focused on hosting the 2008 Olympics in Beijing and was making no declarations about football.

Several lines of inquiry were followed and an approach was also made to Australia's new prime minister Kevin Rudd, who had served as a diplomat in China, could speak Mandarin and was planning an official visit to Beijing. Lowy asked Rudd whether he could possibly find out whether China was intending to bid for either of the two World Cups on offer. From all the strands of information that came back he concluded that China wouldn't be bidding.

The second thing was to ensure that Australia would have the support of Asia. At this time the view was that both Japan and Korea would bid. Although they had jointly hosted the World Cup in 2002 each now wanted to hold it alone. But as their experience was so recent Lowy figured they wouldn't be major competitors, especially since Australia was the only continent never to have hosted a World Cup and was an emerging force in football. Indonesia had signalled that it too might be interested but there was a feeling it wouldn't go the distance.

As there was no sign from anyone else in the region, it appeared that Australia would be the favourite from Asia and discussions with AFC president Mohammed bin Hammam confirmed this was the case. Lowy listened very carefully and after several discussions understood that the AFC's president would support Australia.

This was the foundation of the decision for Australia's bid: it could rely on the vote of the AFC's president, and Oceania had publicly said it would support Australia. "We would need at least another three votes to pass the first round, and then we would build on that momentum through the efforts and support of the AFC," said Lowy.

With no experience in the machinations of World Cup vote gathering, Australia needed help. Lowy asked Sepp Blatter for advice about lobbying assistance and Blatter suggested Peter Hargitay, a man of Swiss-Hungarian background who had been Blatter's personal adviser from 2002 to 2007. Bin Hammam endorsed the recommendation. This was good enough for Lowy, who then made inquiries. Hargitay appeared to understand how FIFA functioned and seemed able to navigate his way through the complexities of international football politics. As there was no one with the equivalent background in Australia, Hargitay was slated for hire as a consultant to the FFA.

Bin Hammam thought Australia should also employ Fedor Radmann, a German businessman who had good FIFA connections and was also well connected in Europe and Africa. Radmann had been part of the team that won the right to host

the Cup for Germany in 2006 and South Africa in 2010. Lowy
had met him when he came to Australia as part of a German
goodwill team in the lead-up to the 2006 Cup; the team was
visiting all the countries that had qualified. Radmann had
a great deal of inside knowledge about the bidding process.
Importantly, his closeness to Franz Beckenbauer, a towering
figure in German football who also had a vote, would be a plus
for Australia. After some discussion, Radmann was slated for
hire as a consultant.

Every country vying to host a World Cup has to submit a
large and complex bid book. As it happened, the books that
had helped both Germany and South Africa win had been
compiled by one of Radmann's close associates. There was
now a possibility that this man, Andreas Abold, could compile
Australia's book. Lowy was keen on the idea and asked for him
to come to Australia. Abold duly arrived and an aggressive set
of negotiations followed. He wanted $3 million to complete the
book and if Australia found this too steep he would offer his
services to another bidder, probably Russia. As the book was
a crucial element of the bid, Lowy agreed to the price. When
Radmann said he wanted to be paid through Abold, it made no
difference to the FFA.

Another task on Lowy's list was to raise Australia's profile
as a footballing nation. He worked assiduously to build
relationships and began attending AFC and FIFA conferences.
With the help of bin Hammam he secured Sydney as the venue
for the 2007 AFC Conference and Gala Awards. Many in the
Asian football family hadn't visited Sydney before and this was
an opportunity to show off the city.

Then Lowy approached Blatter, asking to host the FIFA
world conference in Sydney in 2008. With all powerbrokers

present, these annual conferences represent the gathering of the international football parliament. It was autumn and Sydney was at its temperate best to welcome the 2500 delegates and media. They fell in love with the city's weather, harbour and Opera House where the conference was held.

By now it was broadly known that Australia would be bidding to host a World Cup. This fitted very well with Kevin Rudd's nation-building aspirations and his international agenda to secure a seat on the UN Security Council. Rudd enthusiastically supported the bid and during a social function in the Opera House chatted to Blatter as if they were old friends. He charmed the conference too. Rudd also joined a congenial meeting with Lowy and bin Hammam. In the wide-ranging discussions bin Hammam asked Rudd for Australia's help with his pet football project, Vision Asia, which aimed to raise the standards of Asian football at all levels, on and off the field. There was a warm feeling between the men and the meeting closed with bin Hammam promising Asia's support for Australia's bid.

The *bonhomie* continued during a private dinner at Lowy's Point Piper home. With the harbour lapping alongside the terrace more than sixty people – FIFA executives, their partners and office bearers – enjoyed Lowy's hospitality. Whatever was at his disposal Lowy put to the cause.

During the evening, while welcoming his guests, Lowy mentioned that Australia would be bidding for both 2018 and 2022. Blatter responded genially, gently suggesting that a 2018 bid might have been a little premature. There was a feeling on the terrace that this date would be allocated to Europe, leaving the impression that Australia would be better off aiming for 2022 alone. Frank heard the message clearly and although he knew there would be a time when Australia would probably have to move to 2022 exclusively, he wasn't budging yet. "You never know how things will pan out and we didn't want to give up the first option too early," he explained. "If we could gather support for both, perhaps we could transfer the support from one to the other and build our position."

But before the year was out, the environment began changing. It became known that another Asian competitor had emerged for 2022. It was Qatar, the homeland of bin Hammam, who was now under considerable pressure himself. One evening in Kuala Lumpur, he suggested to Lowy that they have dinner. No sooner were they seated than he looked directly across the table: "Frank, Qatar is bidding and I have to work for my home country."

Lowy had known that Qatar was in the running but like everyone else had not considered it a serious rival. He did, however, make a note to stop discussing Australia's planning with bin Hammam, as they were now in opposing camps. "Of course bin Hammam didn't expect at this stage that his country would win but he said it was his duty to support it," observes Lowy. "I didn't tell him his duty was to support an Asian country because he was president of Asia, not of Qatar. Those words were on my tongue a few times but it would have been fruitless because, given the system in Qatar, it would have been unthinkable for him to decline support."

At the time no one thought this tiny state with a population of less than half a million could possibly win. Apart from the challenges posed by its climate, size, prohibitions on alcohol, restrictions on women and its small population, it had no football culture. How could it possibly win against countries such as America, Australia, Japan and Korea? The problem was that everybody's thinking was restricted by convention. Qatar, the world's richest country on a per capita basis, was on a different plane.

Qatar is an absolute monarchy that last had legislative elections in 1970 and is therefore not subject to domestic scrutiny. It is home to the news service al Jazeera, the Middle Eastern equivalent of CNN, and celebrated for illuminating darkness in the region and in the wider world. The Emir of Qatar owns and funds al Jazeera and the main criticisms levelled against it is that its light is never shone at home. Before al Jazeera was created in 1996, Qatar struggled to be heard even in the Middle East. This news service gave it a global presence and afforded it prestige, power and influence. Creating it was a master stroke for a small nation.

Meantime, in Australia Lowy had been lobbying for funding and in December 2008 Rudd announced that the bid to host the World Cup would be financed to the tune of $45.6 million. The football community cheered. Now the FFA had the funds to push ahead. Although more than a year's work had already been done, there were two years before the winners would be announced in December 2010.

In his public appearances Lowy tempered expectations and highlighted the benefits of being able to participate. In mid 2009, after the bid was launched at Parliament House in Canberra, he addressed the National Press Club saying even with the worst outcome – failing to win either 2018 or 2022 – the bid would leave a worthwhile legacy. It would place Australia at the epicentre of world football politics. For the first time it would be seen and heard in an international football forum. It was time for Australian football to lift up its head and start behaving as part of the world game. "Being timid in the world of football gets you nowhere and taking the easy option of standing on the sidelines while the rest of the world goes for the big prizes is never going to be an option," he said. "And anyway, standing on the sidelines is not in my DNA."

He described the goodwill Australia had already generated in world football and how, at the last World Cup in Germany, neutral supporters invariably ended up cheering for the plucky Socceroos. The Australians played exciting, fresh football and had shaken up some of the best teams in the world. Of course Lowy had been distraught after the last-minute loss to Italy – which had gone on to win the Cup – but said, "Once I got over it, I could take some comfort from the fact that we had announced ourselves on the world stage and that we could leverage that performance at home and abroad."

By now the FFA had a presence in world football governance, with senior members serving on committees in Kuala Lumpur and Zurich. An Australian woman, Moya Dodd, had even been elected as a vice-president of the AFC. Lowy himself had been appointed a member of the FIFA World Cup committee. He wanted this position because it gave him an opportunity to mingle at meetings with members of this committee, many of whom were also on the powerful twenty-four-man executive committee that would decide which countries would win the bids to host the World Cup in 2018 and 2022.

While Lowy was fighting an intense battle on the international stage to promote Australian football, he was fighting another at home. The other football codes at home had been watching soccer's renaissance with little enthusiasm and they didn't appreciate Rudd's generous support for the rival game. It gave them no pleasure to see television footage of Rudd, Lowy and Blatter kicking a ball around the football field at FIFA's headquarters in Zurich.

If Australia's bid was successful, it was estimated it would leave a $2.8 billion infrastructure legacy for all sporting codes for generations to come. Overlooking this, the other codes used the occasion to improve their own situations by squeezing soccer and trying to extract further promises from the government. The AFL was particularly aggressive, believing a boost in the world game would come at the cost of interest in itself, a proud Australian-grown product. While the AFL mouthed support for the bid, it was working below the radar to undermine it. "That was very difficult to cope with," says Lowy. "It was not enough that we had to impress, influence and inspire FIFA's executive committee members who make the decision, and make the constant effort to travel to Zurich, London or wherever they were, but we had to fight a battle on the home front too."

One commentator spun it differently, suggesting the AFL's shenanigans could be seen as a compliment because five years earlier it would have howled with laughter at the idea of football trying to bid for the World Cup. But privately the concern was that the other codes could complicate scheduling for the stadia and make it difficult for the FFA to meet all the technical criteria for the bid. The disputes about stadia were also causing bad press abroad.

That wasn't the only source of bad press. Australia's media has no qualms about attacking national initiatives. A decade earlier it had generated a storm during Sydney's bid to host the Olympic Games. Now it was whipping up another for the World Cup. It had sensed something inappropriate was happening and was highly critical of the way the bid was using taxpayers' money. It made allegations of poor accountability, excessive payments to foreign consultants of questionable reputation and about inducements made to win favour.

The charge was led by the *Age* in Melbourne, and to try and slow it the FFA sued for defamation. For Lowy, the unrelenting attack was exasperating:

> The media got hold of these issues and rode them to death. This became an energy-sapping diversion because every one of their accusations had to be chased down. Minor things became big issues. The fact that we had given a gift of cufflinks to FIFA ex-committee members was apparently a crime even though it was within the guidelines. All this caused us great angst although reviews and audits by FIFA, the FFA and the Australian government ultimately showed we spent the money correctly.

In order to win the bid the FFA had to demonstrate that the country was behind it. While other bidding nations had the support of their press, Lowy understood that the attitude of Australia's press was a challenge to be overcome. The local press not only attacked the FFA but went for FIFA's executive committee too. These were the men Lowy was trying to woo.

25

Fighting on all fronts

When Qatar entered the race to host the FIFA World Cup it had an advantage that was not immediately obvious. In accordance with the rules all countries had to compete through their football federations. This levelled the playing field because it put federation against federation rather than country against country. It was up to a particular federation to convince its own government to support its bid. As much as possible, this kept the competition in the realm of sport rather than world politics.

Qatar was in a unique position. Apart from guest workers, this tiny nation had fewer than 300,000 citizens and there was no real difference between its football federation and its government. Its bid was run by Sheikh Mohammed bin Hamad bin Khalifa Al-Thani, the son of the emir of Qatar, and was plainly a matter of state, with the full co-operation of bin Hammam. As Frank Lowy explained, "Ostensibly the bid was run by Qatar's Football Association which was effectively merged with the interests of the royal family, the treasury and the AFC president, bin Hammam."

With the full involvement and backing of the government this was effectively a bid by the state of Qatar, and so it operated in the political and commercial stratosphere, way above the relatively humble football federations. It was the equivalent of a country fighting against companies. Qatar could use state power, money and connections to garner votes. Rather than its football association trying to curry favour with other football associations, Qatar was negotiating at the government-to-government level and making commercial deals with a vote as part of the trade. It was a form of political bartering not previously seen in FIFA circles. Initially because it was so new, it went unrecognised.

Countries such as Australia, England and the US had much lower levels of government involvement. They were still working in the conventional model, using figures of state such as President Bill Clinton, Prince Charles and prime minister Kevin Rudd to create stature and marketing fizz. These figures were not used for negotiations because FIFA has clear regulations that there should be no political interference in football. With Qatar going way above the heads of the football associations, the playing field was no longer level.

The most quoted example of this involved the former French football star Michel Platini, president of the European federation UEFA. Both the US and Australia wanted his vote for 2022 and Lowy remembers him saying, in front of representatives of both countries, that he would not promise to favour either. "But one thing he could say for certain is that he would not, under any circumstances, be voting for Qatar. In the end, he voted for Qatar and then confirmed he had done so!" said Lowy.

The press reported that Platini's motivation to vote for Qatar was not a secret. According to the *Guardian* France's president wanted Qatar to increase its order for five Airbus 380s. Another UK newspaper, the *Daily Mail*, noted that immediately after Qatar's bid was declared the winner, Platini set about advocating the tournament be moved to winter to avoid the fifty-degree-Celsius temperatures common in summer in the Gulf. "Do you not find it a little bizarre that a man supports a plan he knows is hopelessly flawed then proposes reforms when it is too late?" the paper asked its readers.

Platini was not the only one to suggest the move to winter. Germany's football idol Franz Beckenbauer did too. The press reported that like France, Germany had been involved in state-to-state deals with Qatar in the lead-up to the vote.

While Qatar was dealing in the higher reaches of government there were allegations that it was also working underground, primarily to buy votes. After it won the bid a whistleblower came forward to expose the passing of large sums of money to two African members of the executive committee. The news organisation Al Arabiya suggested that her allegations could force FIFA to annul the awarding of the hosting of the 2022 World Cup to the Gulf state and call for a new vote. It also reported that the Qatar Football Association denied all allegations of bribery, saying they would remain unproven because they were false. No sooner had the whistleblower's claims been broadcast around the world than she withdrew them, saying she had been acting out of disaffection, was misguided and had fabricated the allegations.

In Australia the press was also looking for dirt. Most of its attention centred on the activities of the FFA rather than those of Lowy personally, but this gave him no comfort. Afterwards he explained he was resolute in his commitment to keep the FFA and Australia's bid clean:

> One thing I was determined about was that, whatever was in my control, I would not be part of any inappropriate behaviour. Many a time things were suggested to me but I would not deviate. I was meticulously careful not to bring shame on Australia. There are no secrets today and if we had won by foul means it would eventually have come out and all the hard work and credit would have backfired.

Infighting with rival codes at home was also creating an impression abroad that the Australian bid was in trouble. The rival football codes didn't intend to stop Lowy making the bid but they did want to extract as much advantage from it as they could. If soccer was going to benefit, so should they. Not only should they be compensated for loss of access to prime stadia and for having their seasons disrupted, they wanted their future benefit enshrined in the agreements that enabled the bid to go ahead. To this end a last-minute clause was dropped into the agreement, stating that if Australia won the bid and the government wanted to give football extra funding, it should engage with the other codes in a constructive discussion so they received the equivalent.

The AFL, which was leading the charge, held the government hostage over a stadium. Australia had to guarantee twelve stadia of particular dimensions. After complex negotiations involving all levels of government and numerous sporting bodies the twelve had been secured. Then, one of the prize Melbourne stadia, the Etihad Docklands Stadium, was withdrawn and reassigned to the AFL. Without it the bid would be invalid. Lowy was caught off guard: "Of course, rival countries will do whatever they reasonably could do to outmanoeuvre us and we were prepared for them. We didn't anticipate having to fight on two fronts simultaneously, at home and abroad, and that our competitors abroad would use our domestic discord against us."

The stadium was pulled as a crucial deadline for the bid was approaching. The bid book, which detailed Australia's proposal, had to be handed over during a ceremony in Zurich. This 760-page book, which showed that the country would meet FIFA's myriad specifications, had taken more than a year to compile. The ceremony was approaching and suddenly Australia had only eleven stadia.

The book also had a huge appendix of contracts detailing agreements with federal and state governments, host cities, stadia and innumerable other organisations. Now it was incomplete. Lowy delayed his trip to Zurich. He would not leave until a solution had been found and the book was in his bag. While keen to get to Switzerland to quieten rumours that the Australian bid was in trouble, having the book in order was paramount.

When it looked as if the government would guarantee a twelfth stadium, it was suggested he leave Australia and that the book would follow by courier. Lowy refused. The stakes were high. The bid was under the control of the Football Federation of Australia and as chairman he was the principal. He told the government that he would not submit an incomplete bid and if the stadia criteria were not met completely he would withdraw the bid. An eleventh-hour drama was played out, with phones running hot between Canberra and Sydney. Lowy's threat was circulated to several people who recognised that the bid was down to the wire. To avert the crisis, the government agreed to guarantee that a twelfth stadium would be available should Australia win. The book was finalised.

When Lowy finally got to Sydney airport in May 2010, the pilots welcomed him with relief. For the past three days he had repeatedly fixed a time for wheels-up and then rung to postpone it. The plane had been waiting for seventy hours and fresh pilots had come and gone. Now they were off.

The bid book got there on time and although FIFA's judging committee declared it technically excellent, the Australian press continued to carp about it and about everything else. They questioned the cost of the book just as they questioned everything about the foreign advisers Lowy had hired. The *Age* delved into Hargitay's background and found much to report on, including the fact that he had been twice acquitted for cocaine trafficking in the 1990s. They also quoted US court documents from 1997 about an alleged link to a securities fraud in Hungary, and questioned his remuneration package of $1.35 million and highlighted his potential success fee of $2.54 million.

Fedor Radmann was under their scrutiny too. The *Age* said he had been implicated in a scheme in 2000 to allegedly offer financial inducements to key FIFA ExCo officials to get them to back Germany's bid to host the 2006 World Cup. Further, it stated he had been implicated in conflict of interest scandals in 2003 that had forced him to stand down from Germany's World Cup organising committee. Through Abold's consultancy, Radmann would earn a fee of $3.49 million with a possible $3.99 million success fee.

Both Hargitay and Radmann denied the claims. There were never any claims against Abold.

The press made many accusations against the FFA. One centred on the Paspaley pearl necklaces that were given to the wives of FIFA executives when they visited Sydney in 2008. Although the exchange of relatively modest gifts is part of the etiquette of international football, the press viewed them as inducements for support. FIFA did not construe them as inducements and Lowy explained that they had been given before the FFA received government money for the bid. "Anyway, as everyone got one, how could it be an inducement?" he asked.

The press pointed a finger at the FFA over providing funds to help football in Jamaica. It provided no help to Jamaica. The press was correct, however, when it pointed to the FFA for assisting the Confederation of North, Central American and Caribbean Association in its plans to extend the CONCACAF Centre of Excellence in Trinidad and Tobago. In its defence, the FFA said it had been caught in an ambiguous position about legacy that was implicit in the bidding process. On the one hand, the guidelines stated that a football association cannot receive any benefit in exchange for a bid advantage. On the other hand, the same guidelines require bidders to have a legacy program to aid social development through football.

In December 2009, with a year to go, the FFA's bid team travelled to Cape Town for the media expo where bidders display their wares to each other and the public. For members of the Australian team attending a FIFA conference for the first time, it would have been an eye-opener. FIFA booked a top hotel with its adjoining conference centre and, for the period, this precinct became the royal court of football.

When Blatter swept in, it was in a motor cavalcade suitable for the president of the United States, with outriders, a security detail and traffic halted the length of the boulevard. He behaved like a prince, FIFA regarded him as such and paid due homage.

FIFA is so wealthy, so hierarchical and so carefully controlled that, wherever it goes it creates its own world. Like an enormous ocean liner at sea it is a universe in itself, with clear demarcations of status and accompanying formalities and customs. In the hotels FIFA establishes FIFA Clubs, floors that are only accessible to important office bearers. According to a description in the *International Herald Tribune*, these male office bearers – and it is a male club – enjoy lavish dinners and cash allowances of $500 a day plus $250 for their wives or girlfriends. Along with other perks, salaries and bonuses, executive members can reap up to $300,000 a year. The luxuries and pampering create an atmosphere in which the elite FIFA family members start to think of themselves in an exalted manner. They travel like diplomats and are protected by security guards.

They also wear a discreetly elegant uniform. At the South African event, all executives and members of important committees were outfitted with finely tailored Swiss suits with ties and shirts to match. This stylish outfit distinguished them as the elite and enabled them to identify each other across a crowded room. Their jackets have four small letters – FIFA – embroidered in blue on their top pocket.

Dressed in such a suit Lowy glided through the court, going from meeting to meeting, from coffee shop to restaurant, talking, convincing, cajoling and negotiating. When others in the Australian contingent wilted after twelve hours of this, he pushed on. Jetlag would not slow his drive for votes. At this stage Australia was still going for 2018 and 2022.

The Australian bid was overseen by a core group known as the A team which would meet about ten times a year and assess the latest intelligence. In Cape Town they gathered in the dining room of Frank's suite and went through the ritual of counting votes, based on the maxim that in politics you can only depend on those who say they won't vote for you. Around the table were Ben Buckley, Brian Schwartz, Peter Hargitay, Fedor Radmann,

Phillip Wolanski and Lowy. For some time now, Lowy had not been intending to bid for 2018 but was remaining in the game.

In Cape Town something unexpected happened. Without informing Australia and with no regard to friendship or their 'warm' history, bin Hammam announced that the AFC would only be supporting bids for 2022. Australia was taken by surprise and any advantage Lowy had of staying in the 2018 game was effectively taken from underneath him. Without the AFC's support, he would be severely handicapped.

That day Lowy withdrew from 2018. The Europeans were grateful and Australia received goodwill as a result. At the time such goodwill seemed important. Australia's strategy concentrated on surviving the first and second rounds of voting and garnering new support for the later rounds. With two World Cups on offer there would be a lot of horse-trading – which was where the goodwill might help.

But Qatar's stakes started rising. In April 2010, eight months before the voting, Blatter endorsed the idea of the Middle East hosting the cup. "The Arabic world deserves a World Cup. They have twenty-two countries and have not had any opportunity to organise the tournament," he said. Three months later bin Hammam – still president of the Asian Football Confederation – officially threw his weight behind his country's campaign. "I have one vote and, frankly speaking, I will vote for Qatar but if Qatar is not in the running I will vote for another Asian country," he said. Qatar had proved itself. It had already hosted the AFC Asian Cup in 1988, FIFA U–20 World Cup 1995 and was slated to host AFC Asian Cup in 2011.

By the end of July 2010 FIFA's evaluation committee was in Australia to assess its capability of hosting the World Cup. Compared to the other bidding countries, it was deemed to be technically one of the best. In its report on Qatar the committee noted that as the Cup was slated for June and July, the two hottest months of the year in the region, it had to be considered as a potential health risk for players, officials, the FIFA family and spectators.

With this report public, it seemed Australia would be the favourite from Asia. Everything was on track and apart from the eroding effect of the continual bad press at home, the bid team were quietly confident of doing well. It later emerged that many of the twenty-four-man executive committee that was due to vote for the winners never collected their copies of the technical report and many others never read them.

An equally huge effort went into Australia's presentation to the executive committee in Zurich. In turn each bidding country trotted out its celebrities, showcased itself in a video and made a speech or two. Australia's video did not do it proud. In consultation with Abold, it had been outsourced to overseas filmmakers who had made winning films for previous bids but which had no insight into contemporary Australia. They created a tired, clichéd image of Australia that failed to capture the country's spirit, its audacity, its diversity or its distinctive humour. At the eleventh hour Phillip Noyce was called in to rework and rescue the video. But Noyce, one of Australia's most successful filmmakers who had directed hits such as *Patriot Games*, *The Quiet American* and the much applauded *Rabbit-Proof Fence*, didn't have much time and was limited in what he could do with the film and with improving the Australian presentation in general.

When Australia's presentation in Zurich was broadcast back at home, people cringed. As one critic said, "The narrative around football in Australia was completely lost." The film was an embarrassment but it was also a sobering lesson about the perils of outsourcing a representation of something as subtle and precious as the national soul. As it turned out, the absence of cultural authenticity was irrelevant. Like so much of the process, it was just part of the mandatory FIFA window dressing and made no difference whatsoever. As with the technical report and the fancy bid book, the boxes just needed to be ticked. As any politician knows, in the end only one thing matters – the number of votes.

26

'This is not the last word ...'

If there is a perfect place for intrigue in Zurich it is the historic Baur Au Lac Hotel. Settled in a private park beside Lake Zurich and surrounded by the Alps, this *grande dame* of Swiss hotels is a seat of power and privilege. It also happens to be the traditional meeting place for the political elite of world football.

In late 2010, despite being filled to capacity for the FIFA bidding season, the hotel's reception rooms remained hushed as people gathered in small groups, discreetly trading influence. Only members of football's aristocracy could stay at the hotel. Their entourages were relegated to modern accommodation up and around the lake.

Although Zurich was teeming with press, FIFA's formidable machinery kept members of the media carefully controlled. Privacy was paramount in these last few days before the voting and the privately owned Baur Au Lac was strictly off limits. So the press camped on the pavement opposite with their telephoto lenses trained on the forecourt whenever a motorcade of Mercedes, with darkened windows, swept into the grounds. Out would step dazzlingly wealthy sheikhs with their robes threaded with gold, heads of state, prime ministers, presidents or princes.

When Prince William arrived to support England's bid he was shown to the corner suite directly below the one occupied by Frank Lowy. Interest in England's delegation was fevered, not only because of the prince but because of the presence of football royalty in the shape of David Beckham. The mayor of London Boris Johnson and British prime minister David Cameron were there too. Football attracts the upper echelons and in the hotel's lifts and salons any number of celebrities could be seen. While there were cordial greetings and silent nods, no one wanted to be overheard. It was deep winter and occasionally small groups involved in the bidding process braved the snow in the park to be sure of privacy.

The Australian team had set up its war room in the Zurichberg Hotel on a hill overlooking the city. Several times a day Lowy would shuttle up and down. Three days out from the bid he described the mood of the Australian team as "cautious optimism with a sprinkling of anxiety". The consensus was that although the United States had been the front runner for 2022, Australia was closing in. Of the five candidates bidding for this event three – the United States, Japan and the Republic of Korea – had previously staged the game. Qatar and Australia were virgin territory and because of the extraordinarily high temperatures in the Gulf in summer, Australia appeared to have the advantage.

That same evening, at a dinner for some twenty Australians at the Dolder Grand Hotel, Lowy talked about why football mattered so much to him. It was tied to the cherished memory of his father and gave him back that sense of connection. He spoke with such heart that people were wiping their eyes. They understood why winning this bid meant so much to him, even though he said he wasn't sure he would be alive to see the event staged.

These final days in Zurich were packed with press briefings, interviews, fraternising with friends and negotiating with the less friendly. At intervals throughout the day the A team would meet in Frank's suite to analyse the latest intelligence and crunch the numbers. If they needed calm, they just had to look through the window to the tranquil lake below.

Australia took a body blow when Oceania's representative Reynald Temarii was suspended from voting after an investigation into allegations of vote selling. He had been caught in an undercover sting by the UK *Sunday Times*. The Australians hoped another Oceania representative could take his place and his vote.

For this to happen, Temarii had to accept his suspension and not appeal against it. Australia fervently hoped he would and frantic phone calls between the FFA team and Temarii followed. He promised to accept the suspension and announce it in Australia. A press conference was arranged, but Temarii never arrived. He flew to Kuala Lumpur instead. The Australians suspected foul play and in an effort to locate him phoned every five-star hotel in the Malaysian capital. "After trying a few hotels, our team rang the Mandarin Hotel. Bingo! He was there," said Lowy. "But by then it was too late and our chances of securing a vote from Oceania were gone."

Later the *Sunday Times* alleged that it had documents showing that bin Hammam had paid for Temarii's flight and hotel. Temarii had also been provided with a chauffeured car. The *Sunday Times* alleged the expenses had been handled by bin Hammam's construction company Kemco and taken from an account in the name of his daughter. The reason for the payment was simply stated as 'business promotion'. The paper also revealed that bin Hammam later paid sums totalling some €300,000, again via his daughter's account, to a Swiss-based private investigation firm, most of which supposedly went to cover Temarii's 'legal expenses' in defending himself against his suspension.

Another voting member of the Confederation of African Football was also suspended following the *Sunday Times* sting. Usually, all twenty-four members of FIFA's executive committee vote and, if necessary, Blatter has a casting vote. Now only twenty-two would be voting on 2 December.

With twenty-four hours to go there was a restless energy in the Australian camp. On Wednesday morning 1 December David and Steven Lowy flew in separately. "We specifically went to Zurich to be with Dad on the day," says Steven. "It was going to be a great day or a terrible day and either way we wanted to be there together." That afternoon, the brothers found themselves squeezed in the back seat of a car with supermodel Elle Macpherson between them. They were part of a small convoy carrying the Australian delegation to FIFA's headquarters. So much was thought to ride on the presentation that Australia's governor-general Quentin Bryce and its minister for sport Mark Arbib had flown in specially to be part of it.

Australia's bid was technically strong but there was concern about the effect of its time zone on television income, particularly in Europe and the Americas. It was reported that income from Asia/Oceania would need to be increased substantially to offset the likely loss. Australia countered with reports by L.E.K. Consulting and PriceWaterhouseCoopers that had analysed the issue and shown the revenue would be strong regardless of the time zone and that the greatest potential to maximise broadcast revenues and viewers lay in Asia.

A small wave of panic passed through the Australian delegation when a report compiled by McKinsey and Company was released that day. It advised FIFA that Australia had the weakest revenue-raising potential of the five nations bidding for 2022, being weakest in ticketing, TV and media rights, sponsorship, hospitality and merchandising. Lowy calmed the troops and the media: "It's okay, the folks at McKinsey are not voting. They are not the deciding factor in this business – there are many deciding factors."

The rest of that final day passed unremarkably except for a change in favourites in online betting. Australia, which had nosed in front of the United States in the betting stakes, was no longer favourite on Sportsbet.com.au. The new money was on Qatar, which had leap-frogged them both and was in the lead. "We have taken a lot of patriotic bets on Australia but the promise of cash and plenty of it from Qatar is our biggest hurdle," Sportsbet told the other media.

The next morning Frank woke with a sense of foreboding. He sensed that something was turning against Australia but kept his feelings to himself. The vote would take place that afternoon and although the morning was busy, time dragged. Frank was worried. The knot in his stomach told him Australia had been double-crossed. But he chatted to everyone, spoke to the camera and dressed for the afternoon's function.

The announcement of the winning bids for 2018 and 2022 were held at the Zurich Exhibition Centre. This was said to be the biggest media event in Switzerland's history, with seventy TV stations reporting live from the exhibition centre, together with

1000 reporters from all over the globe. Swiss precision was on show as every country was given exact details for its expected time of arrival – to the minute – where to arrive and where to go after getting out of the cars. Nothing was left to chance and marshals ensured there was no deviation from the plan.

While the press went in one direction, the international delegations went in another, to a large, lavishly appointed hall where each country was led to a designated open area furnished with comfortable sofas and easy chairs. The centre of the hall was taken up with tables offering fine food and drink.

Soon the hall began to fill with the global stars of football, the performing arts and politics. The space was crowded by Oscar-winning actors, presidents, billionaires and more famous faces than could be counted. Everyone was anticipating the next phase when they would be politely herded into the adjoining auditorium and seated. The suspense was palpable as they waited. There seemed to be a delay. Frank was quiet. His stomach had twisted itself into a knot and he was steeling himself to expect the worst.

When the signal came to enter the auditorium everyone knew the axe had fallen on all but two of the competing countries. As the Australian contingent filed in, Frank's worst fears were confirmed. "I walked past the executive committee members. We had some 'friends' among them but when I looked at them and they didn't look back squarely, I knew we were gone."

Behind the delegates' seats there was a barrier and behind that a sea of press. As the Australian delegation was settling in, Frank's prescience was confirmed. An Australian television journalist fought his way down to the barrier, leaned over it and with tears in his eyes told his country's delegation that Qatar had won for 2022. He said Al Jazeera had received the news and was preparing a broadcast. This was very odd as the formal opening of the afternoon's announcement was still twenty minutes away. Given that the results for 2018 would be announced first, there would be a further twenty minutes before the 2022 bid was reached. It seemed Al Jazeera had the jump on everyone else by at least forty minutes.

Blatter the multilingual, confident and polished prince of FIFA walked onto the stage brandishing an envelope containing the winner for 2018. "We have had four bidders for 2018 and we can have only one winner." He smiled. "Three of the bidding associations must go home saying, 'What a pity.' But they must say football is not only by winning but football is also a school of life where you learn to lose. That's not easy." Then he ceremoniously opened the envelope and announced that Russia was victorious.

England's team, which had believed it was the favourite, was stunned. It had been knocked out in the first round of voting, having gained only one vote other than its own. Its £15 million campaign had led to humiliating defeat. The other 2018 bidders, Netherlands and Belgium, Spain and Portugal, were equally deflated, while the Russians were exuberant. They had won with their pitch to open up new markets.

Then it was time for the 2022 announcement. By now the news had spread through the VIP enclosure and the announcement was no surprise although, on hearing their country officially named, the Qatari delegation exploded out of their seats. The Australians slumped in theirs while the Americans blanched. It was said the Japanese and Koreans would have been less disappointed as they had recently staged the games and knew their chances were low. A beaming Blatter said as the World Cup had never been to Eastern Europe or the Middle East before, it was now heading to new lands. "So, I'm a happy president when we speak of the development of football."

Australia's 'friends' had broken their promise, causing the country to be eliminated in the first round, with only a single vote out of the twenty-two. It was barely believable. Australia's plan had been based on surviving the first round with at least five votes and then picking up support from eliminated candidates in the subsequent rounds. It had been so sure of the first four or five votes that much of its lobbying had been concentrated on later rounds. Afterwards, there were two claims for that sole vote. Word was put out that Blatter had voted for Australia. There was also word that Beckenbauer, who once called the Australian bid perfect, had placed the vote. But none of this mattered as Qatar set an extraordinary precedent by netting eleven votes in round one. It was later said Qatar was disappointed it had failed to achieve a majority in round one and that someone hadn't kept his promise.

Meantime, holding shock at bay, Lowy led the Australians to a side room to console them but found everyone wanting to console him. "They shook my hand, hugged and kissed me. It was wonderful to have such camaraderie among ourselves because it is easy to be on top when you win." Then he went to face the Australian press, where he met with more solidarity. This was not the time for a postmortem and there were no tough questions. He used a line he would re-use later. "The sun will shine tomorrow and I will be there to enjoy it ... This battle has been lost – there are many more to be won."

That sportsmanship teaches people to handle disappointment was abundantly clear when Socceroos captain Lucas Neill took the floor as the people began to drift away. "Wait a moment," he said. "I have something to say." With clarity and perspective, he talked about the work that had been done and about how far Australian football had come. Then he thanked the chairman. While he didn't say anything new, his timing and tone were perfect. People left feeling a little better, almost as if something had been gained after all.

Although Lowy had ordered his team to be disciplined, to swallow its pain and not complain publicly about Qatar or flaws in FIFA's voting system, Hargitay embarrassingly broke ranks. He told the press that Australia's bid had been too clean. Australia had not greased palms and was the victim of a conspiracy to eliminate it from the bidding process as early as possible. Other countries were less restrained. Sebastian Coe from England's bid team said FIFA needed to change its voting procedure. Former United States international Eric Wynalda said Qatar had "bought the World Cup". The head of the US bid, Sunil Gulati, remarked that the process was not about technical merit. "It's politics, it is friendships and relationships, it is alliances, it is tactics."

A few days later Lowy was back in Sydney preparing to address a major press conference at FFA headquarters. "I was ready to face the music and tell the facts," he said. "By that time, the pain was not gone but the recognition of the loss was in me." Before he walked in the room had been almost hostile. Enough time had passed for the shock to settle and the journalists wanted answers. They also sensed blood. As they waited, they freely speculated which heads would roll. The four-year contract held by FFA's chief executive Ben Buckley was soon to expire and the feeling was that he would surely go.

Frank opened by taking full responsibility for what had happened, said no heads would roll and confirmed that Buckley would stay: "I have confidence in him, he works very hard. He puts his life on the line every day, every week and every month."

Frank turned the mood of the room. His life experience told him this story was not over yet: he told the conference that this would not be the last word on the matter.

The carcass of Australia's bid was picked over for weeks. Although it had technically been one of the best, the consensus was that Australia was a neophyte, politically weak with little influence. It had not been a member of the Asian football federation long enough to expect loyalty, it had no one on FIFA's executive committee and any possible support from Oceania had been cancelled out. "We were naive," says David Lowy. "The day Qatar entered that race we should have realised it wasn't winnable. How could we have any chance against a sovereign state bidding with limitless money and blurred governance?" Steven had a similar view. "We lost before we even got there. It was not a fair fight and in hindsight, we probably should have recognised that."

Frank Lowy came to the view that for all the preparation and analysis, in the light of what happened, there was absolutely nothing Australia could have done to beat Qatar. "The infighting at home, the lobbying abroad, the dinners, the networks, the campaigns, the consultants, the travelling, the marketing – in the end, none of these could have made a difference."

For both Lowy sons, the most deflating thing was seeing their father, who acts on trust and expects trust in return, so let down. "Dad takes on high-risk things to achieve what no one else can achieve. He personally took on this herculean task and was publicly embarrassed on a global scale," says Steven, who then watched as his father steeled himself and accepted responsibility. "But, because he believes he didn't lose fairly, he won't let it go. He can't. He's good at moving on, but not if he has been wronged."

27

Mea culpa

FIFA has a history of controversy but the public outrage that followed Qatar's successful bid was unprecedented. Almost immediately, allegations of bribery and corruption were fired from several sources and to FIFA's distress these didn't die down. Four years later there was still no peace for football's international governing body and its president.

Lowy was not at peace with the result either. Although he had moved on, the loss still rankled with him. Closing out the noise of the controversy, he conducted his own postmortem on his management of the bid process and with hindsight understood where he should have acted differently. Whatever he did would not have changed the ultimate result, but it would have changed the impact on Australia and the country would likely have lost with more dignity.

In the months following Qatar's win the British parliament

held an inquiry at which allegations of bribery arose. It was alleged by Lord David Triesman, former head of the British Football Association, that in exchange for his vote Jack Warner, president of CONCACAF (Confederation of North, Central American and Caribbean Association Football), had demanded $4 million for an education centre in his country. Another allegation was that Nicolás Léoz of Paraguay wanted a knighthood in exchange for his vote. Both men denied the allegations.

At the same inquiry two journalists from the *Sunday Times* testified they had been told by a whistleblower that $1.5 million each had been paid to Jacques Anouma of the Ivory Coast and Issa Hayatou of Cameroon to secure their votes for Qatar. Both men denied it.

Conspiracy theories abounded too. A popular one held there had been dark dealings between bin Hammam, who wanted to become the next president of FIFA, and Blatter, who wanted to be re-elected for another term. It suggested the Qataris got their prize in return for another unopposed presidential term for Blatter. Yet another theory suggested that after Qatar secured its prize bin Hammam changed his mind and decided to run for president and as a result Blatter turned against him. Corruption charges were raised and bin Hammam had to withdraw.

There was no proof of any of these theories but in May 2011 the controversy reached a climax when bin Hammam withdrew as a presidential candidate after being accused of bribing twenty-five FIFA officials to vote for his candidacy. Both bin Hammam and Warner were suspended by FIFA in the wake of these allegations. Warner slugged it back to FIFA, telling the world that its secretary-general Jerome Valcke had told him in an email that Qatar had bought the 2022 World Cup. He produced the email. People gasped. Valcke said he just meant Qatar had "used its financial muscle to lobby for support".

And so it went, with one allegation following another and no one knowing what was true but everyone suspecting something fishy had occurred. In response to the growing pressure FIFA opened its own inquiry under the auspices of its ethics committee and chaired by former US district attorney Michael Garcia. It was said that if a smoking gun was found, the bidding for the 2022 World Cup bid could be reopened.

Qatar had surprised the world. In the run-up to the bidding, its multi-billion-dollar bid had been dismissed by many as unrealistic given the country's conservative social mores and lack of soccer culture. Qatar would be the smallest host nation to stage the finals since Uruguay in 1930. It planned to harness solar-powered technology to cool the match venues and build new infrastructure.

Qatar's win had barely been announced when a conversation began about moving the tournament to the northern winter. At first there were just a couple of voices but eventually Blatter was behind the idea too. In 2013 Lowy weighed in. As all the bids had been based on the European summer he asked FIFA to make an in-principle decision that "just and fair compensation should be paid to those nations that invested many millions, and national prestige, in bidding for a summer event if the tournament is shifted to Qatar's winter". He also suggested a "transparent process" be established to look at the implications on scheduling for all leagues – including Australia's A League – and a method developed "for agreeing appropriate compensation for those affected". His comments made global headlines and FIFA moved quickly to mute his call, saying no nation should expect compensation. It claimed the small print in the bidding contracts gave FIFA discretion to make changes.

By now, FIFA's reputation had been severely damaged. The harshest criticism came from England, where in late 2013 Blatter gave an extraordinary speech in defence of his integrity. "What have I done? Why has it come to this?" he asked a full hall at Oxford University. Protesting that he had been made a scapegoat, he said he was not "a ruthless parasite sucking the lifeblood" out of the sport. Then, in a unique bid for sympathy, he said his life had been troubled since birth. Even as a helpless baby people had been against him: "My grandmother advised my mother to let me go." Still, there he was at the age of seventy-seven, going strong and paving the way to run for his fifth presidential term in 2015, despite having pledged not to contest it.

In early 2014, another scandal broke. The ten-year-old daughter of a Brazilian FIFA executive had £2 million deposited into her bank account. Her father, Ricardo Teixeira, had been one of the twenty-two men responsible for choosing the host nation for the World Cups in 2018 and 2022. The press reported the payment was allegedly made through a former president of Barcelona FC, which is sponsored by the state-owned Qatar Airways. As scandals broke around the Qataris, they continued to deny any wrongdoing. Lawyers acting for the former president made a statement noting that the payment to Teixeira's daughter had nothing to do with the country's World Cup bid, and that the president had not given Teixeira any payments to secure his vote.

Then in mid 2014 the British press dropped another bomb. London's *Sunday Times* ran an eleven-page story on the bidding process. It began on page one with the large headline: 'Plot to Buy the World Cup' and documented how millions of pounds had been paid to officials to support Qatar's bid for 2022. The report was compiled by the paper's Insight Team, a specialist investigative unit that has been in existence for half a century.

The unit had accessed a treasure trove of the 'FIFA files' containing millions of emails, text messages, chat logs, hotel records, bank statements, flight details and other documents revealing the depth of Qatar's practices. The files showed how bin Hammam operated ten slush funds to pay officials around the world and to create a groundswell of support for Qatar. Documents showed that he used his daughter's bank accounts to pay people. There was also evidence that bin Hammam had brokered Qatari government meetings through the Thai FIFA ExCo member Worawi Makudi, to push a gas deal that was potentially worth tens of millions of dollars to Thailand. What football officials were doing brokering gas deals no one could explain. Both bin Hammam and Makudi maintained their innocence.

The paper continued to run new evidence over the next few weeks but there appeared to be no move by FIFA's appointed investigator Michael Garcia to follow the trail of evidence. Especially perplexing was Garcia's apparent acceptance of the Qatari insistence that bin Hammam was in no way connected to their bid. To a reasonable observer the evidence overwhelmingly demonstrated that bin Hammam had been a central figure throughout the campaign.

This was certainly Frank Lowy's opinion. He had already told Garcia, in a formal interview in April 2014, that bin Hammam had told him directly that he would have to renege on his commitment to support Australia and work for the Qatar bid. He followed media reports suggesting that Garcia's investigative team had concluded bin Hammam was not part of the Qatari team, and subsequently wrote to Garcia:

Given media reports casting doubt on Mr bin Hammam's role, I feel obliged to share with you information that did not emerge in our interview that further confirms that Mr bin Hammam was indeed working aggressively and energetically for and on behalf of the Qatar bid. At least two other FIFA Executive Committee members told me at various times that they would not vote for Australia in the first round, but in the event Qatar was eliminated they would direct their second vote to Australia. They told me that this was part of a strategy developed with Mr bin Hammam and he had approved of them telling me so.

It was common knowledge and a widely accepted fact among FIFA officials that Mr bin Hammam was working for the Qatar bid, made obvious by his ongoing discussions and lobbying at the many FIFA meetings and events in the two years or so before the vote for 2022.

Garcia's office acknowledged receipt of the letter but that was the last Lowy heard about the matter. He continued to regard Garcia well, believing him to be an independent investigator who had conducted his inquiry in good faith but who had been hamstrung by the limits imposed on his investigative powers.

When Garcia delivered his 350-page report, along with tens of thousands of pages of supporting material in September 2014, it was not made public. While this surprised many, it was in line with the defined process. As head of the investigative chamber of FIFA's ethics committee Garcia was obliged to deliver his report only to the head of the judicial chamber, former German judge Hans-Joachim Eckert. It was then up to Eckert and his panel to determine what action, if any, to take.

Given the public interest in the report Garcia argued for as full a publication as possible, omitting any material that might be sensitive or identify sources. In October 2014 Garcia, in a thinly veiled attack, reiterated the need for greater transparency and said FIFA's investigation and adjudication process operate "in most parts unseen and unheard". He described the current process as "a kind of system which might be appropriate for an intelligence agency but not for an ethics compliance process in an international sports institution that serves the public and is the subject of intense public scrutiny".

In the face of mounting calls for greater transparency, in November 2014 Eckert's panel released what purported to be a forty-two-page summary of Garcia's key findings. It astonished the world. It read as a mishmash of poorly described allegations of wrongdoing at various levels by various bid teams, but failed to provide any evidence or clarity about precisely what Garcia had found.

While it exonerated Qatar and Russia, leaving them free to host their events, it fingered England and Australia for undermining the integrity of the bidding. Critics denounced the summary as a whitewash while Garcia described it as "materially incomplete" with "erroneous representations of the facts and conclusions". Shortly thereafter he resigned.

When Lowy sat at his desk and read the summary, his disillusionment intensified. Soon after Garcia had been appointed, Lowy and his adviser Mark Ryan had met with him in New York to tell him what they knew about the bid. They had been open and relaxed and later the FFA team answered all questions and provided files of correspondence and email traffic associated with its bid. Most other bidding nations had been less forthcoming. It was later revealed that Russia had destroyed its computers. Qatar refused to meet with Garcia in New York or London. Ultimately, the meeting with Qatar took place on neutral ground in Oman. Bin Hammam and other key figures refused to co-operate. As Lowy explained:

> When we saw Garcia and his offsider in Sydney and in
> New York we went on our own, without the protection
> of lawyers because we believed in the process. We just
> sat down and said, "What do you want to know?" We
> co-operated and gave him our whole file. He put it in his
> report. As far as I know England co-operated too. That's
> why the Eckert summary was such an inversion. It was
> mindboggling. And that's why I have some sympathy
> for Garcia. In hindsight no one could have gotten to the
> bottom of it all and until we see the entire Garcia report it
> will remain a mystery.

Lowy's recognition of his naivety in being so open with Garcia spurred him to look back at the entire process and to critique his own role. He was satisfied that the planning had been thorough. Potential competitors had been taken into consideration, China had been confirmed as a non-competitor and the support of the AFC and the Australian government had been secured. He believed he had had Blatter's support too.

But while the plan had been sound, he recognised missteps in its execution. Rather than trying to run the campaign himself he should have created a separate management structure to do it, as he had done for the highly successful Asian Cup 2015 held in Australia. Although such a move would not have changed the ultimate result, he berated himself.

My normal practice over the last fifty years is that I plan, often in great detail. I surround myself with high-level people close to me and expert advisers who are brought in. They become my team and I encourage openness, scrutiny and advice. My strength is in deep and strong consultation and when I'm convinced I go forward hard or I drop the matter. Well, in this case I didn't do that. I didn't follow my own procedures and my fault is that I thought I could do it without oversight.

I was so intent for Australia to win that although I had people around me I called the shots and made the decisions. While I spared absolutely no effort to do what I thought was necessary, with hindsight I recognise it may have become an obsession.

His next insight was about two of the foreign consultants he hired. Being a novice in the forum of international football politics, he had taken the advice of Blatter and bin Hammam at face value. He had trusted them when they both recommended he hire Hargitay. Les Murray, a prominent football identity in the Australian media, had also given Hargitay the thumbs up.

The other colourful consultant, Radmann, had been recommended by bin Hammam. Rather than conducting his own research into the background of these two consultants – which would have been in line with his normal practice – Lowy took them on board. To his detriment he depended on their counsel.

From the outset Lowy had set the ground rules that Australia would run a clean bid, and at no time did he believe his FFA team or the consultants had breached any FIFA guidelines. The problem was that the consultants were perceived as very expensive, they affected the Australian team's reputation and their networking and influence achieved next to nothing.

Lowy also recognised a lapse in his dealings with CONCACAF, which led to allegations of corruption involving its president Jack Warner and the FFA.

Throughout the campaign the Australian team was mindful of FIFA's requirement that each bidding nation demonstrate a commitment to football and community projects, especially in developing countries. Wherever possible the team sought to dovetail its support with the existing international aid activities of the Australian government. In the end support was provided for dozens of projects large and small, mainly in Asia and Africa. For the most part these were uncontroversial. The CONCACAF incident proved an exception.

As it happened, Kevin Rudd's aspiration for Australia to gain a seat on the United Nations Security Council meshed with Lowy's aspiration for Australia to host the World Cup. Rudd had assigned $60 million in aid to the Caribbean region and Lowy hoped to attract some of that money. He wanted to put it towards the design of an extension to CONCACAF's Centre of Excellence for Football. Officials from the FFA had gone to the Caribbean to conduct due diligence and an engineering consultant had prepared a feasibility study. It was decided that a figure of $500,000 would be needed to achieve the task. But Australian government officials had gone to the Caribbean too. They decided it wasn't a good prospect and retreated from providing funds. At this point, Lowy believes he lapsed.

> When staff advised me of this, I asked our accountants
> if we could afford it from FFA funds. When they said we
> could, I said, "Okay, let's go." We'd provide the money

ourselves because if we won it would have been money well spent.

I just accepted the news that the government was not prepared to do it. Normally, I would make a call myself to the government agency to check what the problem was. Well, I didn't. In hindsight, had I heard it personally, I probably wouldn't have just gone ahead and directed the payment be made. This lapse in my usual procedure probably occurred because I was blinded by my desire to succeed.

We wrote a letter to CONCACAF enclosing the cheque and asking for a receipt. We also followed up and asked the bank for a receipt. It duly arrived showing the money had been deposited into CONCACAF's account. Not for a moment did we imagine the cheque could end up anywhere else but in CONCACAF's account. We had no way of knowing Warner would later be accused of siphoning money into his own picket.

At the time of writing this book, investigations were ongoing.

However, the insight that caused Lowy the most anguish involved Qatar's entry into the bidding game for 2022. When he first learned it was going to bid, he shared the prevailing view that Qatar would never pull it off.

No critical investigation took place. I could have called half a dozen independent people together, who knew the region and the politics, and debated how serious a threat this could be. I would do this in other activities of my life but this time I didn't. In retrospect, had we understood that Qatar was going to operate as a sovereign state and not a football federation, there was an outside chance we might have changed course.

Lowy believed that winning the bid would have accelerated the development of football in Australia by up to twenty years. Money would have poured in and the event would have galvanised the sporting community. Just as he would have taken the glory for winning, so he took the pain for losing.

When we came back from Zurich the press suggested Ben Buckley should be sacked. That would have been the most unjust thing to do. The press accused me of protecting him. I didn't. I just knew it wasn't his fault. The responsibility rested with me and I wasn't going to look for a scapegoat.

28

The A League

When Frank Lowy first thought of creating the A League he dreamed of 5000 spectators at every match. But later, when the crowds doubled and often tripled that number, he wasn't satisfied. In early 2014, when 52,000 people packed into a Brisbane stadium for the grand final between the Brisbane Roar and the Western Sydney Wanderers, he was pleased at the size of the crowd but couldn't help noticing that there were a few empty seats in the stands. He rarely permits himself unmitigated satisfaction and when the match was over and the press was full of superlatives about how far the game had come and where it was going, he was quietly frustrated. The A League, then nine seasons old, had grown but in size it hadn't reached the shoulders of the other main football codes. A grand final was expected to draw big numbers but if the game could attract 20,000 to regular matches, that would make him comfortable.

But he did laugh out loud when a letter landed on his desk a couple of days later from Australia's advertising guru, John Singleton, who had been on Lowy's inaugural FFA board in 2003.

Dear Frank,
    Who would have ever thought so few years ago??
    No teams
    No TV
    No sponsor
    No hope
    And now a sold out house in Brisbane (heartland of NRL) ...
    ... You have made wogball part of our social fabric ...
    Love and respect forever,
    Your old Aussie token mate,
    John.
    P.S. Thank Christ you fucked up Channel Ten or I would have thought you were a genius.

Singleton's note took Frank back to the early 1950s, when the game had been fragmented by ethnic rivalries. "Week in and week out it was like World War III between the various factions from Europe," he said. "Football was totally alienated from mainstream sport, with some of the announcements even made in foreign languages. Australians wouldn't come." Not averse to a bit of ethnic rivalry himself, he knew it had been holding back the game.

When he took charge of the sport in 2003, he had been determined to change this. His timing had been excellent: Australia, which had become one of the most culturally diverse countries in the world, had rejected ethnicity and embraced multiculturalism. Wherever people came from, they were encouraged to treasure their heritage but to share one Australian national identity. Although conflict might break through from time to time, there was a new willingness to accept differences between people. It was the perfect time to do away with 'old soccer', but Lowy knew that by rejecting it, much passion would be lost. A new football culture needed time to mature.

During the long hard years of "old soccer", ethnic communities had kept their clubs alive. They had remained loyal in a dying league, and when the new A League came along in August 2005 most had embraced it. The creation of the A League was described by ABC journalist David Mark as "arguably the biggest break from football's past in Australia – a past coloured by ethnic divisions, grubby politics and racial violence". Of the eight clubs in the new league, four emerged directly from the old: clubs from Perth, Newcastle, Adelaide and New Zealand shed their former allegiances. So did a Brisbane team that had also played in the old league for a time.

While ethnic divisions still existed in some second or third tiers of competition at state level, at the national level 'wogball' had gone and a new tribalism had emerged in its place. Now loyalty was to contemporary Australian cities rather than to European countries that had once been at war with one another. This had enabled the A League to become the shopfront for football in Australia.

It had been given a powerful boost by the Socceroos' qualification for the World Cup in November 2005, which released a form of football fever not experienced before. Momentum had continued to build. The A League's first season had been an unqualified success with almost 42,000 fans attending the grand final between Sydney FC and Central Coast Mariners in March 2006.

A new broadcasting agreement was struck. For the rights to the first A League season the FFA had managed to scrape together a deal of $500,000 from Fox Sports. Now it had more to bring to the table with the World Cup, the forthcoming AFC matches and a successful A League season under its belt. A broadcasting deal for $120 million over seven years was signed.

The second season had been successful too, helped again by the Socceroos making it to the second round of the World Cup. There had been other firsts, with two A League teams going to Asia in 2007 for the AFC championships. So much had happened and at such a speed that the football fraternity had been almost drunk with enthusiasm. But the two teams had arrived in Asia over-confident; in unknown territory and unfamiliar conditions they had performed poorly. The loss had sobered them, and the following year Adelaide United had been runner-up in the championships.

Football was the young darling of sport. In 2009 two new teams from Queensland had joined up, boosting the League to ten clubs. Growth, it seemed, was unstoppable. In 2010 another team joined from Melbourne, setting the scene for a high-spirited derby in the nation's sporting capital.

By now the League had good stadia, solid coverage on Fox Sports and some lucrative corporate sponsorship. Lowy attended as many A League games as he could and with his white hair and distinctive features was instantly recognised by the crowds. Rarely alone, he preferred to watch with one of his sons. If they couldn't make it, he liked to sit next to someone with expertise, not just in the game but in its organisation. He was never there for pleasure alone and was perpetually on the lookout for opportunities for improvement.

But the raw enthusiasm that drove new football had lasted more than six years and was dissipating. Having been in business for many decades Lowy knew about cycles and could tell this one was turning. The spontaneous spin-off from the Socceroos was no longer there. They had lost their sparkle and there was less pride in their performance. After Australia's humiliating defeat in its bid to host the 2022 World Cup everyone had been hoping for some small redemption through the Asian Cup in early 2011, but Australia was runner-up. Football was at its lowest ebb since Lowy took over. At the age of eighty, he asked himself why he didn't step down, why he was not living in peaceful retirement.

However, he sensed that the cycle hadn't yet reached its lowest point and when it did, he expected it would show first in the A League. As this started to happen media commentators noted that because Lowy had given the lion's share of his attention to the World Cup bid and the international side of football, the A League, had suffered. When Lowy registered the criticism, he accepted it and rolled up his sleeves. Without a successful and popular national competition the country would not achieve its goal of becoming a mainstream sport. He knew what was needed.

The A League had grown fast – some say too fast – and cracks had begun to appear. There were questions about the commercial viability of the clubs and the FFA. Then North Queensland Fury, one of the new Queensland clubs, collapsed. Attempts had been made to save it with a community ownership model but the support base was small and players were not having much success on the field.

More bad news followed. The other new Queensland team, Gold Coast United, wasn't pulling crowds either and was financially stressed. After sinking millions into the club its colourful owner Clive Palmer turned on the FFA's management, claiming it had done nothing to help his club sustain its operations. Then he began breaching the club participation agreement. Among other things, he had a seventeen-year-old picked as captain on debut and he sacked the coach. Then he replaced the advertising strip on the team's shirts with the slogan 'Freedom of Speech'.

While Palmer's team performed more or less well, the terms of his licence required the club to embrace the local community and gain its support. "But Palmer was just sitting atop his club dictating and directing," said Lowy.

While the FFA tried to keep that club in the fold, trouble was brewing in Newcastle where another billionaire mining magnate, Nathan Tinkler, had just learned to his fury that the sum he had paid for the Newcastle Jets back in 2010 exceeded that of most other clubs. He believed he had been overcharged and wanted the situation remedied. The reality was that the other clubs had come in years earlier and established themselves and he had been buying an established club.

By this time there was also a new push for the clubs to have a greater say in the running of the A League. On this point, perhaps more than any other in football, Lowy was immovable. The only model for Australia was the current one, with an independent board overseeing everything from grassroots to the national team, including the A League. For one thing, the economics of the game in Australia wouldn't support a separate national competition. Most clubs could not survive without the financial support provided via the FFA (and governments), and as the Gold Coast and Newcastle experience had shown, even clubs with billionaire owners could run into strife and need bailing out by the governing body.

Fundamental to Lowy's philosophy was the concept of running the game for the nation. Vested interests, especially at club level, would inevitably drain resources from the grassroots and restore the old political infighting that had ruined soccer for decades. It would put club interests ahead of the national team. Lowy continued to point to England's continuing underperformance at the international level to remind people of the dangers of allowing clubs to chase financial returns at the expense of the game's overall health and sustainability. "If it ever happens the other way, we can kiss goodbye to all the success we have achieved to date," he said.

During this period Palmer and Tinkler got together. A blistering attack on the FFA was released during a meeting of clubs chaired by Schwartz. Lowy was not present but afterwards was surprised when the pair put a proposal to him. Would he join them in a consortium to take over the A League? "They proposed investing a total of approximately $20 million and have the FFA cede control of the A League to the consortium. If they had been willing to put in ten times that amount, I would never have ceded control," said Lowy.

The low point in the cycle had been reached. After ten turbulent days of rebel forces sniping at the FFA, Lowy hit back. At an official football lunch in Melbourne he told Palmer to pull his head in, dismissed claims of misleading Tinkler during the takeover of the Newcastle Jets and said making the A League stand on its own feet would be disastrous. He had seen this model fail before. In a carefully crafted speech, he said the disrespect to the FFA had been breathtaking.

Then he turned both barrels on Palmer. "The very least you could say about Gold Coast United is that there has been a spectacular failure to connect with the local community to get fans to turn out for the game," he said. A short while later he said Palmer's defiance was having a detrimental effect on the League in general. At a press conference in March 2012 he announced that the licence for Gold Coast United had been withdrawn because its terms had been breached. Palmer tried to take out an injunction but it was declined.

A deal was struck with Tinkler because the FFA could not afford to lose the Newcastle Jets. Newcastle is a powerful soccer city and keeping it in the fold was a priority. (In May 2015, however, Tinkler would put the Jets into voluntary administration, prompting the FFA to terminate his licence and take control of the club.)

With Palmer gone, Gold Coast United played on under the aegis of the FFA. At the end of the season it closed, potentially leaving the A League with an unsustainable configuration of nine teams. It urgently needed another one in order to meet its broadcasting obligations of ten teams. A new team had to be created, organised and on the field by October. It seemed an impossible task to achieve in six months.

Lowy closed his ears to criticism and gave the problem the Westfield treatment. Using the "critical path" method that he had successfully used in business for fifty years, he assembled a small team of executives. Each had an assigned area of responsibility and at formal weekly meetings, chaired by him, would report back on what had been achieved and what was next. Between these meetings there would be informal discussions, with each team helping the others to progress. Frank drove the process, with Buckley, Schwartz, Wolanski, Kelly, Jo Setright the FFA's head of legal and business affairs and FFA board member Joseph Healy, a career international banker who had played soccer at youth level for Scotland. "We just bulldozed our way through until we reached our objective," says Lowy.

In this process it was discovered that a federal government grant was pending for the development of football, of which the FFA could use $4 million as seed capital to establish the club. The objective was to establish a team in Western Sydney, the heartland of football in Australia. A handful of teams had existed here in the old NSL and a couple had attempted to join the A League a few months before, but had been unsuccessful. Everyone knew the region was bursting with enthusiasm to have its own team in the A League.

In April Buckley confirmed there would be a team. He made the announcement in conjunction with prime minister Julia Gillard, who had agreed to $8 million in federal funding for all levels of football in western Sydney. This included $5 million to the FFA, of which $1 million would go to women's football and $4 million to the western suburbs. The rest went to redeveloping Football NSW's headquarters.

Again, the timing was good. As the ink was drying on the contract terminating Palmer's Gold Coast United, it was also drying on a fresh contract for the new club. Soon Lyall Gorman, former head of the A League, was appointed to head the new club for the FFA. This was a deeply multicultural area and it was essential to get the framework right and to engage the passion of western Sydney. Under Wolanski's guidance three candidates for coach were put forward but only former Socceroo Tony Popovic was approached. He accepted unhesitatingly; western Sydney was his home. To take the job he had to secure an early release as assistant coach of Crystal Palace FC.

This was a high-energy creative project, meeting weekly to build the infrastructure, the team and the culture. The optimism and fervour of the project blanketed out the continual criticism about the team being fast-tracked. Its time frame contrasted starkly with that of the rival Greater Western Sydney AFL team, which had begun recruiting staff more than two years ahead of its debut that year. Gorman told the press he was stunned by the outpouring of interest. "We're getting inundated by player managers, players themselves and clubs – domestic and overseas – on a daily basis. They are putting players in front of us and it's a massive job to cull and prioritise all that." Such was the enthusiasm that Gorman found himself managing expectations and cautioning that Rome wasn't built in a day.

Through this new club, football fervour that had long been trapped underground would be released. It would be like a Texan oil strike when, from apparently bare earth, a rush of 'black gold' would shoot sky high, signalling great riches to come. It would be Australia's newest, oldest club, reflecting the long history of football in the region. And its name, the Western Sydney Wanderers FC, would link it to one of the first games of football played in New South Wales in 1880 between the King's School and the Wanderers of North Parramatta.

Lowy had an affinity with Sydney's west, the commercial cradle of his shopping centre business reflected in the name Westfield. In his formative Australian years he had spent more time in the western suburbs than anywhere else. When Westfield moved its headquarters to the city he appreciated the proximity to his family home, but missed the community of the west.

He harboured a special affection for the new club, wholly owned by FFA in its start-up phase. Until a private buyer could be found he would treat it as his club. Thousands from the district embraced it as theirs too. During its establishment the FFA had cleverly held a series of community forums across the district and people had been asked to help choose the new club's name and colours. Online surveys had followed. The locals also had a say in the club's culture and playing style. Under Lowy's guidance the FFA was not just building a football club; it was building a community asset.

Lowy's gift is his ability to imagine the unimaginable and to convert others to his cause. Even the sceptical eventually fall in behind him. Despite the risks, he backs his own judgment and the whole project begins to move forward. The ascent of the Western Sydney Wanderers was unprecedented. It was formed in April 2012 and was one of the first entities to call itself 'Western Sydney'. Locals identified with it. Six months later the high-tempo team was on the field for what would be a record-breaking inaugural season. The Wanderers reached the grand final and became the reigning A League premiers, which gave them a berth in the AFC Champions League.

The club's 'black gold' was its support base. The presence of fiercely tribal supporters was so impressive at every match that people flocked to belong to the Red and Black Bloc, RBB, reflecting the team's colours. On match days the main street of Parramatta was decorated in the colours, turning the city into 'Wanderland'. Such was the demand for membership that a month before the next season the club reached capacity at 16,000 and was sold out.

The upward cycle of the A League required fresh energy. After seeing the Wanderers established Ben Buckley announced he would be stepping aside. He had been CEO of the FFA for six years, had weathered the turbulence of the World Cup bid and was ready to move on. Just as his predecessor John O'Neill had come from the rival football code of Rugby Union, so Ben had come from an even greater rival, AFL. When he arrived in 2006, Lowy had hailed him as "the best of the new generation of Australian sporting administrators". With no background in football he understood the complex sports rights market and had earned admiration for his involvement in a record-breaking television deal for the AFL.

Now, before moving on, Buckley wanted to conclude the next broadcast deal providing financial stability to underpin football's next growth phase. Together with chief financial officer John Kelly he negotiated a joint $160 million four-year deal with Fox Sports and SBS. That this would bring in $40 million a year was a measure of how far the FFA had come. Buckley left as a friend of football and joined Foxtel as executive director of Sport. "There was nothing unresolved between us and we parted amicably. It was time to make a change, Ben's contract was soon to be up and by mutual agreement things came to an organic end," said Lowy.

Ben had had both the challenges and the benefits of working very closely with Lowy, who either raises the standards of all those around him or wears them out. He calls when he wants to, makes demands others think impossible and is never off the case. Although loyal and protective of his own, he is tough on them and doesn't comprehend the concept of down time. But people benefit from the proximity and see the grind behind the magic. By the time he was driving football, Lowy was decades older than anyone else in the team – how could they complain about the pace he was setting?

Lowy's appointment as FFA chairman in 2003 was supposed to be a non-executive role. It never was. Initially he took full executive control and was engaged in establishing an administration, making decisions and running the organisation. When John O'Neill the first CEO first came on board, he found less space for himself than he had expected. The creative tension between him and Lowy turned out to be highly productive and in their three years together they prepared the platform for football becoming a mainstream sport. Although O'Neill couched his departure in polite words, he left because two chief executives couldn't sit on the same seat.

Buckley coped better with the active chairman, although by then the FFA was a little older, more structures were in place and he had more autonomy. Before he left he mentioned David Gallop as a possible head of the A League to replace Gorman. By then the blueprint for football was in place. Professionalising the sport had been a long process and Lowy was ready to disengage from the administrative duties. When Gallop was appointed CEO in November 2012, he had autonomy.

With the memory of an elephant – not just for fact but for nuance too – Lowy doesn't forget much. He had approached Gallop before and had sensed something in the man that he liked. At the time Gallop was running the rival code of Rugby League. That Frank was always looking to the leadership of other codes reflected the fact that he wouldn't draw on 'old soccer'. Although the stalwarts of old soccer had come to Australia with the game in their DNA he was looking for a modern professional.

When Gallop left Rugby League amid considerable publicity, Lowy's ears pricked up and he began looking for a way to meet him. He called the then chairman of News Limited John Hartigan and the media industry veteran Harold Mitchell, who both undertook to arrange an introduction. But the matchmaking would have to wait, as Lowy was about to depart for the 2012 London Games.

As it happened Gallop was in London too, in his official role as acting chair of the Australian Sports Commission. Unbeknown to Lowy he was also on the invitation list to a large, lavish function that Westfield was hosting for the Australian team. "I saw him across the room and didn't wait for any introductions," says Lowy. "I asked him to have a cup of coffee with me." Gallop agreed and privately decided to wait a month or so until they were all back in Australia. But when he mentioned this to a colleague he was told, "If Frank Lowy asks you for a cup of coffee, you don't wait a month!"

The next day Gallop was a guest on the *Ilona* berthed at Canary Wharf. They chatted for a long time. Like Buckley, who had been an AFL player, Gallop had been a sportsman, though his talent was for cricket. Growing up he had been a fan of English football but confessed he knew little about the game in Australia. He had, however, been present at the qualifying match against Uruguay in 2005 and told Lowy how he jumped out of his seat like everyone else when the goal was scored: "But I quickly sat down because I realised this was potentially the waking of the sleeping giant that was Australian football. Anyone involved in sport realised that if football got its act together, the global nature of the game and the simplicity of its accessibility to all shapes, sizes and sexes, meant it could make an impact on Australia's sporting landscape – this was not good for Rugby League!"

Gallop had been CEO of the National Rugby League for a decade. On his watch the sport had recovered from the fractures of the Super League and experienced resurgence. Lowy could see a mirror benefit for the A League and was keen for Gallop to take the job. Sitting on deck, the two men got on well and the next day Gallop called to accept the job.

338   Frank Lowy: A Second Life

It required him to cope with a strong chairman but luckily the two men were compatible. "We got used to each other very quickly," said Lowy. For Gallop it was a good relationship: "He trusts my judgment but he likes to be well informed and is never backward in putting his view." He was struck by Lowy's ability to read politics. "If he were a chess player he would be world champion because he sees the play two or three moves ahead of most people I have ever encountered."

Gallop was taking over a well-functioning machine with revenue of around $100 million a year and in surplus. While $40 million came from the broadcast deal another $25 million was from sponsorships, the major ones being Hyundai, Qantas, Nike, TAB, NAB, Westfield and Foxtel. The remaining $35 million came from a variety of sources, including the gate at A League finals, Socceroos' home matches, licensing, merchandising and government funding. And by all reports, the FFA was a reasonably happy family where people shared a vision: for football to become the largest and most popular sport in Australia.

29

Success and succession

No champagne was opened to celebrate Lowy's tenth anniversary in Australian football's top job. He preferred to let the occasion pass quietly but was pleased to observe that, at last, football had connected with the mainstream sporting audience in Australia. "Hallelujah! Now we can talk about football and not the establishment of football. Now our priorities are consolidation, sustainability and growth," he said on reaching the milestone. The FFA had emerged from its low period with reasonable resources and good crowds and TV ratings. Its blueprint was in place and Gallop was on board to execute it.

This didn't mean that all the thinking had been done. There was much to do to see the game secure into the twenty-first century. Lowy wanted to squeeze as much as possible into the next two years before the end of his chairmanship in November 2015. If only he had another decade to make football the top sport in the land. Like rival codes, he could see football with sixteen teams, more supporters and even bigger broadcasting deals. Although he had set the term limit to the position he now occupied, there were days when he toyed with the idea of staying on. There were also exhausting days when he was relieved his term was finite.

Strategising for the future is his forte, and he set about planting seeds that would flourish long after he had left. Although he consults widely, Lowy does not write anything down. Where others would make lists and keep notes, he keeps a mental record. The issues remain alive in his mind, growing and changing, until they are dealt with.

The first seed was women's football. The sport had long been male-centric and it was time for genuine cultural change. In China in 2007 the Australia women's national football team had qualified for the quarter-finals of the FIFA Women's World Cup for the first time. The following year, the FFA established the Westfield W League. Compared to the A League, its broadcasting rights, funding and salary caps had been paltry. It was time to remedy this. While the challenge was substantial, so were the rewards. Lowy had observed that 80,000 people had watched the women's championship at the London Olympics. "The time is ripe, it's just a matter of doing it," he said.

Apart from the commercial and promotional investment, this required serious political work. Earlier in his term he had appointed Moya Dodd to the FFA board. A lawyer who had been the Matildas' vice-captain for five years, she knew firsthand how tough it had been for women in football. At times funding for the women's championship team had been so meagre that the players had been expected not only to sew their badges onto their tracksuits for international competitions but to pay their own way too.

Dodd was the right kind of figure to champion women in football and Lowy helped to promote her into the Asian Football Confederation. She quickly became a vice-president. Then the AFC nominated her to FIFA's patriarchal executive committee. In this highest sphere she was the only Australian and one of only three women on the twenty-seven-member board – although without voting rights.

Another important seed for the new century was the intensification of Australia's football relationship with Asia. While joining the Asian football family had been a significant achievement, Lowy believed Australia hadn't maximised it yet. "That's where our future is. Europe and South America are too far away so we need to integrate and commercialise the popularity of the game in Asia, together with them, reciprocally. This won't happen on its own."

That the sport lacked a deep culture was another aspect to be remedied. The FFA had developed managers and grown expertise, but it would likely be another decade for that ethos to become entrenched. New academies would help to achieve this. Lowy foresaw it being compulsory for every club to run an academy with forty to fifty players who over time would feed about 400 to 500 new recruits to the game every year. These grassroots players, who would go into the A League and then hopefully be recruited to overseas teams, would provide a bigger pool of high-calibre players from which to draw the national team. Growing the current football academy run by the Australian Institute of Sport would also help talented players make it into national teams.

Before his anniversary year was out Lowy was looking to the A League to supply a coach for the Socceroos. It had long been his ambition to have an Australian coach and given the dissatisfaction with German coach Holger Osieck it seemed the time had come. Osieck had fulfilled his mission of seeing the Socceroos qualify for the World Cup in Brazil in 2014 but he had also taken them to two 6–0 losses to France and Brazil. Consequently his fate was sealed and the post was vacant.

One reason Lowy wanted an Australian coach was that he saw foreign coaches as well-meaning experts who were basically mercenaries. "While there is nothing wrong with employing a mercenary – we did it and many nations do – there is a conflict. They have a limited horizon and their task is often just to qualify for the next World Cup. They are not concerned with long-term goals, with overall development and affecting generational change." Now he wanted these issues resolved and to put an Australian stamp on football. "We can't be copycats all our lives. We need to learn from the world and then stand on our own two feet," he said.

Remarkably, there were three potential local coaches who could do the job. All were former Socceroos and all were current A League coaches. In the end Ange Postecoglou from Melbourne Victory was appointed with a five-year contract. Lowy was thrilled to have arrived at a stage where the best-qualified coach for the national team had learned his craft in the country and had both a passion and a sense of mission for Australian football. Personally he was impressed with Postecoglou's emotional capacity, the way he could be reached and his ability to take people into his trust.

And Postecoglou didn't disappoint. With most of the golden generation of players having moved on, he took charge of a young team that had been drawn in a "group of death" for the World Cup in Brazil. Expectations were low but when the Socceroos played in Brazil people took notice. Commentators said the team played enchanting and engaging football, with an honesty and style that were unique. It wasn't enough, however, and the team was on the plane after the group phase. It was not alone in the Asian family. Out of twelve matches all four Asian teams failed to gain a single victory and all endured early elimination.

While the press offered Postecoglou plenty of advice he replied that one of his objectives had been to measure the Socceroos against the very best. This had been achieved and now he knew exactly where they stood. Postecoglou's next test would be on home ground, at the Asian Cup in January 2015 in front of an expectant audience with Lowy in the prime seat. These games would show how much progress the team had made under his tutelage.

Just as the governance of the sport had become professionalised, so too had the game. It was time for Lowy's trusted lieutenant Phillip Wolanski, who had spent so many years intimately involved with the national team, to step back into his conventional role as a board member and chairman of the football development committee. He had played an important role with the foreign coaches, acquainting them with the history and culture of Australian football and helping them to navigate their way through the FFA. By being hands-on, being in the dressing room and on the sidelines, he was also able to keep the board abreast of developments with the national team.

It was an unorthodox position for a board member, but for the formative years Lowy had deemed it necessary. Wolanski had a very close eye on all developments and was first to alert the chairman to the fact that it might soon be necessary to replace Osieck. Said Lowy: "Phillip had dedicated himself to the game, travelled overseas with the team and constantly kept his finger on the pulse. It was an unusual job that he performed very well. I saw him as a safeguard for the board and knew he took a lot of flak for it. But then Luke Casserly came on as head of national performance. He had deep roots in the sport, having played with Australian Schoolboys, the Young Socceroos, the Olyroos and the Socceroos. And he played professionally in Europe. Then, of course Postecoglou was appointed and he was deeply Australian too. The vacuum that Phillip had filled was now being filled with professional management. Phillip accepted the change with grace."

In many ways Lowy did for football what he had done for Westfield. One of the strengths of the mall business was that it was spread over three continents and when trade was slow in one the other two kept the money running through the machine. So it was in football. Initially the Socceroos had been the financial engine for the sport but as they slid into a low the A League flourished and began bringing success. By 2014 two of its clubs were up for sale.

At just two years old, Western Sydney Wanderers was up for sale. The club had been created in a crisis and the FFA had never intended to hold onto it for the long term. The club was on the lookout for new, suitably good owners. In its short life, Western Sydney Wanderers had rocketed to success. Around the same time, Sydney FC signed legendary Italian striker Alessandro Del Piero. The combination of these two events ignited the A League.

That the four-man purchasing syndicate for the Wanderers was led by Paul Lederer closed another circle for Lowy. Paul, who came to Australia at the age of ten, had been a favoured nephew of one of Frank's closest confidants, Andrew Lederer. The two men had been football brothers and would chat away in Hungarian, argue, get upset, forget they had been upset and continue to run the Hakoah football team together. Their commonality of background and their shared addiction to the game had made them inseparable.

Andrew had gone on to manage the Socceroos and his death in 2004 left an unfillable seat next to Frank at football games. Frank had been there as Andrew built up his business, Primo Smallgoods, and he'd been there as the business passed to Paul, putting him on BRW's Rich List. Despite this background, it took an unexpectedly long time to settle a price for the Wanderers. Although it had exceeded all expectations and emerged as the best supported club, Frank battled to achieve $10 million.

The other club for sale was Melbourne Heart. Its owners were reported to be unable or unwilling to cope with the financial burden of running it. When news broke that it was to be bought by the owners of the English Premier League club Manchester City, the football community was amazed. For $11 million the new owners took an 80 per cent stake and rebranded the club Melbourne City. There was some noise about the team's kit with the new boss adamant about replacing its red with sky blue. That was Sydney FC's colour. There was some tension but in the end Sydney retained the exclusivity of sky blue.

With that noise quietened, there was excitement about the new ownership and a hope that this could mark the internationalisation of the A League. How could it not benefit from Manchester City's global expertise? It was the world's richest football club, with owners from Abu Dhabi, managers from Spain, a coach from Chile and players from everywhere. Five months later it was announced that Spain's all-time leading goal scorer, David Villa, would play ten games for Melbourne City. His presence put a rocket under the newly badged team and fired up cross-city competition with Melbourne Victory.

Back in its very first season the A League had established a tradition of using international marquee players to add pizzazz and draw crowds. "These players are expensive investments but they bring favour and colour," Lowy said. "They provide an X factor, a star to pull crowds and promote the game." Former Manchester United striker Dwight Yorke helped to kickstart the League in its first season and, recognising the value such celebrities added, the FFA soon offered to help sponsor them.

For season ten, it was hoped Villa would do for Melbourne what Del Piero had done for Sydney. Such was his marketing panache that the 'DP effect' became shorthand for the marquee effect. Disappointingly, Villa only stayed for four games.

There had always been a yawning disparity within football. While 1.9 million Australians participated at all levels of football games, the combined participation of AFL, ARU and NRL was only 1.6 million. But professional football teams often struggled for an audience. Why were people happy to play the game but less willing to watch it? To try and close the gap the FFA came up with a novel suggestion – the FFA Cup, modelled on the FA Cup in the United Kingdom.

It was an ambitious plan, involving perhaps 600 clubs across the country and requiring significant sponsorship. Not only would it keep the game alive in the pre-season but it would bring engagement and romance. The lowly and the mighty would have an equal chance and all the plucky second-tier clubs that felt abandoned by the FFA would have the opportunity to show their mettle. Some expressed fears that this would give oxygen to the old ethnic rivalries but Lowy wasn't concerned. One or two such teams had attempted to promote themselves to the A League. They were proud, strong teams and he believed that if they could transcend their ethnic allegiances, anything could be possible.

Play-offs for the Cup began in 2014 and saw some David-and-Goliath-type struggles. The Bentleigh Greens, a team of carpenters, teachers, students and bricklayers from Melbourne's southern suburbs, actually reached the semi-final. In the final, Adelaide took the cup from Perth Glory.

Still keeping Lowy awake at night was Australia's failed bid to host the World Cup. He designated the humiliation in Zurich in December 2010 as the lowest point of his decade in football and had still not accepted it. When questioned about it his stock reply was that the last word had not yet been heard on the matter. Beyond that he kept silent, but the words of his astute friend Andrew Lederer, could not have been more apt: "When Frank gets hurt he does not pull back. He's not like a little snail that you touch and it pulls in its head. Oh, no! He's the opposite. Instead of pulling back he will re-energise and go in three times as strong."

He did go in and did a prodigious amount of work to try and understand what had happened. As 2014 closed, it appeared Qatar would retain the right to host the 2022 World Cup, which would be moved to the Gulf's cooler winter climate. "The question is, who will pay for all the upheaval this will cause?" asked Lowy.

Regardless of the outcome of 2022, in his tenure Lowy had turned football into a giant business. When, in October 2014 he officially opened the tenth A League season he was full of optimism. A decade had passed since he had nervously launched the League and stood at the microphone literally begging spectators to come. Since then the League had been through plenty of growing pains with clubs dying, being reborn and relocating along the way. Now he told the crowd that football was just getting into its stride and predicted it would double if not triple its spectator numbers in the next decade.

David Gallop described this as "a golden period" for football in which the A League was the centrepiece. He told those present that football was about to go through the two million crowd barrier for the first time. It was aiming for 660,000 weekly viewers on Fox Sports and SBS, two million web users, one million social media followers and it expected to go through the 100,000 membership mark.

By all accounts the star of the A League teams was the Wanderers. In the team's short life it had won a Premier's Plate and been runner-up in two A League grand finals. Now it had reached the finals of the Asian Champions League and was on the brink of greatness. If it could beat the formidable and extraordinarily well resourced Saudi Arabian team Al-Hilal, it would be king of Asia. It would also receive $1.7 million in prize money.

When the Wanderers narrowly won the home match of the finals at their modest stadium in western Sydney, the whole football community celebrated. They were playing for Australia and supporters of rival A League clubs forgot their differences and fell behind them. As they were playing, a sold-out A League derby was under way in Melbourne. During half-time the Melbourne fans turned their attention to large screens to watch as the Wanderers scored against the Saudis. They cheered and shouted as one.

The Wanderers carried the banner for Australian football all the way to the King Fahd Stadium in Riyadh for the return match without the support of their beloved rowdy fans. Only fourteen were granted visas and they couldn't be heard against the 65,000 Al-Hilal spectators in the stadium. It was a controversial match with fouls not upheld, lasers pointed into the eyes of the Australian goalkeeper and some disturbance after the scoreless draw. The atmosphere was such that when the jubilant Wanderers lined up to get their trophy, the stadium had emptied.

While Al-Hilal claimed that the kingdom had been robbed and called for an investigation, the Wanderers returned to a rock-star welcome at Sydney airport. Some 5000 fans had watched the match in the early hours of the morning on screens in Parramatta town square and were nothing short of feverish when the final whistle blew. One newspaper columnist, who described himself as "a Rugby League man through and through" wrote that nothing he had ever witnessed compared with the hysteria he had seen in the square that morning. He thought nothing could surpass it until two days later he went to the airport and saw fans "climbing walls, hanging from the ceiling and shouting from the rooftops as they awaited their heroes".

Scenes like these struck fear into the hearts of football's rival codes. Where once they had not given soccer a second thought, they were now paying full attention. Not only did soccer have this huge international dimension but it was sucking up the oxygen at home. Previously it would have been inconceivable that two cracking sold-out games in the nation's two biggest cities could be staged on the same night.

Football turned Australia on. Another columnist, an AFL devotee, had been at the Melbourne derby and wrote how the vibe, noise, colour and excitement made AFL games seem sterile. "I've been to something like 1500 AFL games in my life and only a handful of A League fixtures, but the different feel at Etihad Stadium on Saturday night was remarkable. The place simply buzzed," he wrote.

As the victors of the Asian Championship League, the Wanderers were selected as one of eight international teams to play in FIFA's Club World Cup in Morocco. Making it to this select club brought them in excess of $1 million and the possibility of playing against clubs such as Real Madrid. But their first match against ES Setif ended in a 2–2 draw and went to a penalty shootout which they lost 5–4. They headed back to Sydney having finished in sixth place. After all their energetic success, back home their performance fell off, and they did poorly in their next A League season.

Meanwhile Australian football was coming up to the biggest event in its history. In January 2015 it would stage the Asian Cup, the region's most important football competition. When Lowy first lobbied for this event and then won the right to host it on Australian soil for the first time, it was part of a greater plan. Back then, he had been planning a bid to host the World Cup and thought that hosting the Asian Cup beforehand would be an opportunity to condition the country and build momentum. His ambitious private plan had been to host the Asia Cup in 2015 and then the World Cup in 2018 or 2022.

As the Asian Cup approached there was concern about the state of the Socceroos. The team, which was in the process of being rebuilt, had only won one of ten matches in 2014 and had plummeted to 102 in the world rankings, but because it had made second place at the previous Asian Cup in Qatar in 2011 it was regarded as a favourite. Japan was hot favourite. As host, Australia had qualified automatically and when asked about its prospects, Lowy was publicly circumspect. Privately he was praying.

His prayers were more than answered, not only by Australia winning but by the country staging the most successful Asian Cup ever. There had been fears that, in the early rounds not involving the hosts, the stadia would be empty as one Asian team played another. Could the tournament possibly reach the

350,000 ticket sales necessary to break even? For more than two years Asian Cup CEO Michael Brown and his organising committee had assiduously planned the off-the-field event, enthusing multicultural communities to celebrate their heritage and making tickets affordable. When China played, spectators dressed in red filled the stadium. When Iran played the rest of the country got a glimpse of how strong Iranian immigration had been. Multiculturalism was on full display. Some of Australia's newest citizens demonstrated their dual loyalty by wearing the colours of their country of origin and the Australian colours.

With more than 650,000 tickets sold the tournament delivered a healthy surplus. After the 2005 win against Uruguay in the World Cup qualifiers player registrations spiked. Now an even broader knock-on effect was expected from the diplomatic, cultural and business benefits that had been generated by the tournament in concert with Tourism Australia and Austrade.

Most importantly, however, Australians fell in love with the Socceroos again. In front of their home crowd, the team had come of age. And in front of their adoring fans, for the first time in their ninety-three-year history, they lifted high into the air their first piece of significant silverware. Postecoglou was their hero and he had the respect of the nation. He had kept to his brief to bring generational change and rebuild the team. A short while later the new FIFA rankings came out. Australia was sixty-third. Postecoglou was looking to the future, towards the World Cup in Russia in 2018. For him the Asian Cup was just the beginning.

For Lowy it was the triumphant ending. His youngest grandson, Jonah, had been at every Socceroo match with him and after the final accompanied him into the dressing room where together they raised the new silverware aloft. It reminded

Frank of being with Jonah's father, Steven, in the dressing room at Hakoah decades earlier.

He was aware of time passing. In November 2015 his term would be up and he was preparing to go. The previous twelve months had been a testament to his leadership with the booming popularity of the A League, the FFA Cup, the Wanderers winning the Asian Champions League and now the Socceroos winning the Asian Cup. He had always said the move to the AFC in 2006 had been the game-changing moment that delivered success to Australian football. Hosting and winning this successful Asian Cup took the game to a new level at home and in the region. At home the Socceroos embraced it and captured the hearts of the nation's sports fans. "I'd been hoping for this and when that final whistle blew I could feel it. Football finally belonged to the country," said Lowy. He could also feel the ripples into the region. Football had achieved what governments cannot, a connection between countries at a popular level. You can't overestimate how this will strengthen the ties between Australia and Asia.

For some months a national search had been underway to find a new FFA chairman to replace Lowy and new directors to replace Schwartz and Wolanski, who would retire with him. A board nominations committee had been established, headed by Schwartz, and the executive search company Egon Zehnder had been engaged to produce a shortlist. Ultimately the decision about new directors would be made by the state federations and a representative of the A League clubs.

By the end of 2014 a shortlist was taking shape. While the names were kept confidential, word got out that Steven Lowy was a possible candidate. On the face of it his business credentials, his good working relationship with governments and his passion for the game qualified him as a candidate. Some, however, said his surname was against him.

Lowy senior was acutely conscious of the perception of nepotism. "It's not up to me," he said. "Whoever takes on the job will have to want the job, and be wanted by the stakeholders. And of course they must have the capacity to do the job."

When asked by the *Australian Financial Review* what he thought, Steven conceded that he had been spoken to about the process, but hedged: "We'll have to see if and when the opportunity occurs, I'd have to be desired for the role, I'd have to look at it from a personal perspective, a family perspective, a professional perspective. I do have a passion for the game, and if and when the opportunity is there, I suppose I would consider it, but I'm not considering it at the moment."

By the time he left the sport Lowy's aim was to have a strong management platform so that, in common with other professional sports, the role of the chairman was not as onerous as it had been for him. The management would do the job with board supervision. "The leadership will take a different form of maintaining the momentum and then increasing it, rather than building from a zero base. We don't just want to be the best in Asia, we want to hold our own in world football.

As this book was going to press in May 2015, FIFA was in disarray. Senior FIFA officials were arrested in a dawn raid on a Zurich hotel to face extradition to the US on federal corruption charges. The US warned of further charges. At the same time, Swiss authorities launched criminal proceedings related to the award of the 2018 and 2022 World Cups. A couple of days later, FIFA held its scheduled presidential election in Zurich and Blatter was re-elected.

Westfield
Matters

30

The core

In 2000 Westfield's eighty-seven shopping centres were worth $20 billion.

In 2015 the brand's eighty-seven centres were worth $70 billion.

What happened in between?

For Frank Lowy sharing power is not easy. He shared it for the first twenty-five years at Westfield and then privately celebrated when his co-founder John Saunders retired. Frank was where he wanted to be, at the top. But when he looked down he saw his three sons on their way up. He had groomed them for this and while he took parental pride in how fast they were moving, it wouldn't be long before they reached him. Relinquishing power would be complex but he expected his mixed feelings would be mitigated by his pleasure in seeing them take it up.

After John Saunders departed in the mid 1980s Westfield's upward trajectory continued, and more steeply. Frank was in his element and although he consulted widely, his business style was autocratic. He didn't imagine, however, that he would occupy the top spot for long and on the eve of his sixtieth birthday in 1990 he told a journalist he couldn't see himself working beyond the age of sixty-five. Around the same time he told Rob Ferguson of Bankers Trust that he was planning to be more inclusive at work. Ferguson, who considered him a control freak, laughed out loud. It seemed impossible. "I saw him like a builder of the Sydney Harbour Bridge who had to make sure the two sides touched. Shopping centres were giant logistic exercises and he had to be on top of every detail to make sure that the sides touched perfectly. He had complete control, every road led to Frank. Other corporations were not like that at all."

But Frank was true to his word. As a member of the Westfield board for a decade from 1994, Ferguson observed the transition. "I watched as he relinquished that intense control to the point where, around the board table, the boys would say, 'Dad, that's not right.' That was the signature event. He allowed them to contest what he said because they knew more about the things that he used to know." The sons were growing more assertive and the father was providing space.

From the outside, it seemed that the Lowy sons had enjoyed a dream run and were on their smooth and inevitable way to success. They had had privileged access to the business but once on the inside, their father had driven them hard. The standards he applied to himself he applied to them. They found themselves in situations where they had to stretch to succeed and where they often had to take flak from others who thought they shouldn't be there.

A day or so after David took his final university exam, he was in the car with his father. "How would you like to work in America?" Frank asked. It wasn't really a question. It was 1977 and Westfield's first US mall, in Connecticut, was being managed by an Australian who was something of an old-fashioned disciplinarian. He thought David too young to be assigned the role of trainee manager and they clashed. After nine unpleasant months the disciplinarian returned to Australia, leaving David in sole charge.

David was also tasked with growing Westfield's US business. Whenever he heard mention of a mall for sale somewhere in the US, he'd be on a plane chasing it down. He worked relentlessly with his father encouraging him to do more, including finding a new CEO for the US business.

Peter was put in over his head too. After working in investment banking in New York and London he came home in 1983 to run Westfield Trust. That was a steep learning curve and just when he was comfortable, Westfield moved into the television business and he was sent across to take financial control of it. Frank was acting on advice from Rupert Murdoch, who had urged him to put one of his sons in the business. Peter knew nothing about the media industry. Some at the network thought the boss's son was too closely involved. With financial but no operational responsibilities, Peter found himself in the middle, fighting battles without authority. When Channel Ten failed, blame was sheeted home to him for a period before rightfully going to his father.

Peter took his family to Los Angeles and downscaled. After being the corporate head of a television company that employed a staff of 1500, he took charge of the Westside Pavilion mall which had a staff of fifteen.

Steven was just twenty-four when his father pulled him out of First Boston Corporation in New York and sent him to become general manager of Garden State Plaza, a centre Westfield had just bought in New Jersey. Steven had been with the investment bank two years and would like to have stayed longer, but that wasn't an option.

The day in 1986 that he walked into the new job, the secretary to his predecessor took one look at him and said, "I can't do this," then walked out. The previous general manager had been in his sixties. Steven didn't feel equipped to make the leap from high finance in Manhattan to a major mall in suburban America. "It was no picnic for him," chuckles his father, who in 1988 had him back in Sydney running the Westfield Trust. The task was daunting, but Steven says his business knowledge and experience grew quickly as a result. "That's the way my father works. He doesn't push us, he extends us."

For Frank and his sons an inevitable transition was underway and in 1997 a formal step was taken. David had been the managing director of Westfield's corporate international business for a decade. Now his two brothers became managing directors too; Peter of the US business and Steven of the Australian and New Zealand businesses. The top of Westfield was so tight with Lowys that one commentator said they made a rugby scrum look soggy.

Around this time, Ferguson called Frank to say there was a man in town who he should meet. A lunch was arranged at Westfield's headquarters to which Ferguson brought Mark Bieler, global head of human resources for Bankers Trust. "There was an explosion of understanding between the two of us," said Frank. "We were sparking off each other. Whenever I feel that energy and that understanding in a person, I try and pull them in." Bieler came in willingly as a global consultant to Westfield on HR and over time helped the company move from a family base to an institutional one.

While Bieler's warmth and commonality of background with Frank brought him close, he became highly prized for his ability to speak his mind without fear. He could see what was coming and told Frank that he would have to start taking more of a back seat and let things take their course. Foremost for Frank was the issue of succession. "While I recognised the reality, I also recognised that succession is a process that requires patience all round. It's a slow but inevitable process and it takes a lot of understanding," he said.

In the year 2000 Westfield celebrated its fortieth anniversary as a public company. As one of the largest shopping centre groups in the world, it had a portfolio of eighty-seven centres spread across Australia, New Zealand, the US and the UK. It had been a favourite with investors and its annual report for 2000 featured a letter from the Australian Stock Exchange congratulating the company on its growth and stability and quoting an enviable metric. It noted that "an investment of $1000 in Westfield shares in 1960 would be worth approximately $109 million today (assuming all dividends and other benefits were invested in additional Westfield shares)". This pleased Frank deeply because he regards having others grow rich with him as one of the most rewarding aspects of success.

As the century closed six men formed the core of Westfield, four of them Lowys. The other two were finance director Stephen Johns, who worked closely with Frank on financial and capital structuring matters, and Richard Green, who worked with Peter in America. But within a couple of years two members of this core would be gone.

First to go was David. He had been with the company since he was twenty-two and his interests had changed. He had never wanted to occupy the position of the entitled eldest son, preferring instead to be on par with his brothers. Among other things, he now wanted to take charge of the family's private wealth and in 2000 he peeled off to do so. When he went, the traditional succession pattern went with him. Both Peter and Steven stepped into the vacated space, becoming joint managing directors. They were not quite their father's partners yet, but early signs of a partnership were there.

That a family succession was being played out within the confines of a publicly listed company was unusual. Westfield had been listed since 1960 and despite its size and presence in the market, until the end of the century it was still being run very much as a family-controlled public company. By 2000 it was impatient for change. The company needed to broaden to meet changing corporate governance requirements and, as it was growing so fast, it also needed more executives to fill in the spaces. Bieler was on board and the challenge was to institutionalise without losing entrepreneurship. Frank began talking more about "the Westfield family" and bringing more people into the inner circle.

In the past ambitious executives had left because they could see their career path being blocked by the presence of Lowys. By now an aggressive shareholder element had begun emerging too. These shareholders accepted that the success of Westfield had been achieved through Frank's leadership, but complained that in return he and his family were taking what they perceived to be excessive remuneration.

Although Westfield belonged to thousands of shareholders, the popular perception was that Frank's heart beat at the centre of the company. The media persisted in referring to it as 'Frank Lowy's Westfield' and it was so much a part of Sydney's culture that the phrase 'going to Westfield' was synonymous with 'going shopping'. Later, when the company built mega-malls akin to mini-cities, urban planners would talk of the 'Westfield effect'. This described the phenomenon of shopping precincts being a bigger draw for people than beaches or other natural attractions.

Westfield has two sides. While shoppers see the glamorous malls, the investment community sees the capital structure that underpins them. The operational side of the business looks after these bricks and mortar assets, ensuring they are in excellent working order and on the cutting edge of the industry. The financial side keeps adjusting the capital structure to ensure it is always the best form of ownership for the centres. While Frank has long experience on the operational side, his real interest lies in financial structuring. "Conditions continually change and because we are always growing and huge amounts of money are needed to develop the centres, the capital structure needs to be adapted to the new conditions. We constantly look for new ways to finance our operations – we are highly pragmatic and probably, we do this more than most." He is as proud of the company's invisible "financial brain" as he is of its visible shopping centres.

When David left, operations and financing were carried by his two brothers. Although they both worked across the spectrum of the business, each gravitated towards a different end. Steven tended towards extracting the best possible results from redeveloping existing centres, managing them harder to ensure they were at the forefront of trends and building new ones. Peter tended towards Westfield's financial structuring and investment banking activity.

Smart and tenacious like his father, Steven wanted to drive change across the portfolio in all geographies. This required long hours, long-haul travel and unrelenting attention to detail. He rarely revealed the strain, maintaining a high standard of business etiquette and control. He occupied an office next door to his father and they would be in and out of each other's space all day, mindful not to intrude if a meeting was underway – although Frank could be less mindful than his son.

Peter is described by his peers as restless, financially brilliant and personable. As he was based in Los Angeles and as he was the senior person for Westfield in the United States, he dealt with finance and was involved with operations there. While he didn't see his father every day, on most days they spoke at least once. When Frank woke at dawn in Australia he would head for his study to make the first call of the morning, always to Peter and often disturbing his lunch.

In 2002, the inner circle lost another member when Stephen Johns retired from his position as group finance director. He had begun working for Westfield as a young man in 1970 and felt it was time to make a change. He had had such an integral role that the circle took some time to adjust to his absence and get comfortable again. It was fortunate that Peter was ready and able to close the gap and work more closely with his father on financial strategies and capital structuring. A couple of years later Peter Allen returned to Sydney from London, where he had been establishing Westfield's UK business. He took up the role of chief financial officer and as Stephen Johns' eventual replacement he had immediate admission to the core group.

Fastidious about position and the power it implies, Frank doesn't rest until he is comfortable in his executive environment. Nuances matter and he will work and rework things long after others would have signed them off and gone home. While Peter and Steven had settled into their respective roles which gave them each a responsibility for an area of the business, their jobs were enmeshed. With Frank as a role model, they were not shy about taking control.

Having grown up so close to their father, having prayed with him, worked with him, sailed with him and watched thousands of hours of football with him, they had more or less internalised him. They know how he thinks, what he would say and what he would do in most situations. And they don't necessarily agree. Just as he asserts himself, so they assert themselves and when this happens in front of others, people don't know where to look. Once a journalist asked Peter what it was like to have such a powerful father. "Why don't you ask him what it's like to have such powerful sons?" he shot back.

The power at the top of Westfield had begun to triangulate between the father and his sons, and there were moments when Frank had to discipline himself and lean back. Always with an eye to the future, he could see a triumvirate forming and knew that ultimately its effectiveness would outweigh any sense of personal difficulty he might feel at sharing. But complete sharing was a few years off. In the meantime, he would continue to spearhead the company's strategy, consulting intensely. Transactions that resulted from these decisions would then be driven by Peter or Steven, depending on where in the world they took place. Although his sons were now also doing the transactional work he used to do, they were extending his reach.

Elliott Rusanow, who joined Westfield in the late 1990s after working for Bankers Trust funds management, considers having his uncle Frank as a mentor as a privilege beyond price. Over a few years he gained seniority and moved naturally into the inner circle. From close in he observed the interactions between his uncle and cousins and says it was like watching a football game:

> While they have tremendous respect for each other, the outcome is more important than what each of them brings onto the field. How they relate to each other is less important than the need to succeed. There's a lot of shouting but no possessiveness of ideas. The culture is that there is no single owner of the best idea. What happens on the field is not carried over into their private lives. There's no kiss and make up because there's no upset.

Should there be an upset, they swallow it. While they will pause to deal with hurt feelings in their private sphere, there is no pause in the professional one. After one exchange, an executive reported hearing Frank say to one son: "Okay, I know I've upset you but you upset me too and we both know this is not the last time this will happen."

Inside Westfield there is a culture of trust. It starts with the trust between Frank and his sons and filters down. This stability makes it an excellent environment for disruptive thinking. Indeed, Frank encourages it. He surrounds himself with people willing to challenge the orthodoxy and say exactly what they think. From senior executives he expects "loyal opposition". Based on the premise that no one knows it all, loyal opposition allows for all views to be heard, even when they are in conflict with that held by the leader. It carries the understanding that whatever is said will not be held against the individual.

In Lowy's mind Mark Ryan, who joined Westfield in the mid 1990s to manage its public affairs, typifies the concept. A former adviser to prime minister Paul Keating, Ryan is unafraid of speaking his mind plainly. "He accepts seniority but always says what he thinks regardless of whether it is in conflict with what I or others think. This makes him highly valuable in the circle," says Lowy. After six or seven years Ryan's ability and solid dependability saw him too become part of the magic circle.

There were two more members of the circle to come. In 2002 Simon Tuxen joined as corporate counsel and a couple of years later, Michael Gutman, who had been at Westfield for just over a decade, moved closer in. By the first years of the new century, Westfield had renewed its core. A new synergy was emerging among the senior executives and the challenge for Frank was to be open to their fresh ideas, while keeping his head and relying on his instinct to lead the business.

31

As a dream materialises

By the year 2000 Frank Lowy had been in the mall business for forty years. From time to time he would stop and look back in disbelief at the distance he had travelled. When Westfield built its first small collection of shops in the outer-west of Sydney in 1959, he and John Saunders had basically collected the rent and supplied real-estate services. "But we had an edge. We knew about customer engagement," says Frank. Both had worked behind the counter of the delicatessen where the objective was to sell as much as possible to each shopper. They knew the importance of personal interaction and of creating an environment conducive to shopping.

As time went by and their malls became enormous buildings, John and Frank behaved like hosts. They focused on the comfort and convenience of consumers. It wasn't enough for people to shop and leave, they wanted them to stay. So they provided places for them to meet and sit, as people once did in the village square or the town piazza. They developed food courts and brought in movie theatres to keep people there even longer. They were creating small Westfield worlds in the suburbs.

As these worlds became increasingly sophisticated, so did the underlying business of Westfield. But like the tip of an iceberg, only the bricks and mortar could be seen above the waterline. The financial brain below, which gave Westfield its stability and drove its growth, was not visible to consumers.

When he looked back Frank saw Westfield as an innovator and an adaptor. He remembered the challenge of television shopping and how he had brought in the corporate advisers McKinsey and Company to determine the size of the threat and what Westfield should do about it. It was never a serious competitor but then internet shopping became a concern in the 1990s. Westfield built an internet mall but it was premature, and it closed. It would take another decade before Steven Lowy launched the company powerfully into the digital age.

In 2000 Frank reached across 'the ditch' and brought New Zealand into the Westfield fold by acquiring ten of its malls that the company had previously managed. Then he turned his gaze northwards and looked longingly at London.

For most of his forty years at Westfield, Frank had nursed a private dream and in 2000 it finally began to materialise. While it was a dream with a good commercial engine, it was powered by an old emotional attachment.

The British had made a deep impression on him as a boy and he had always wanted to find a place among them, particularly in London. Whenever he was there on business he would catch something of an accent that gave him comfort,

370 Frank Lowy: A Second Life

an accent he remembered from occupied Budapest, where as a boy he and others had huddled around a radio to wait for the BBC broadcasts. The BBC repeatedly broadcast news of the deportations and urged Hungarians to obstruct them in the name of humanity. No one else spoke of humanity in the context of Jews, and for this alone Frank's heart would be in sympathy with the British forever.

Indeed, when he later found himself interned by the British on Cyprus, he was consoled by their humanity: "We didn't fear them because they were not cruel like the Nazis or the Russians. They observed us from watchtowers around the camp but we were never afraid they would shoot us. There was no hatred: we knew they were just doing their job as fairly as they could." Confined in that camp, Frank observed the British officers as they issued and executed orders, and when he looked into their faces he sensed an air of decency he would not forget.

In the early days he and John Saunders often sat in their shared office in Sydney talking about mythical London and wondering whether it was possible to coax British shoppers off the windy high street and into a climate-controlled mall. They tried to buy into the UK market in the 1970s but were thwarted by the oil-induced economic crash. By the late 1980s their partnership had broken and John wasn't there to encourage Frank on his next sortie into London. Then the establishment didn't have much time for Frank but he persisted and eventually listed a Westfield entity in London to own US malls. It failed to thrive and was swiftly privatised. Although Frank left London in 1989, it never left his mind.

In the mid 1990s Frank's board seat at the Daily Mail and General Trust made him a frequent visitor to the city. Before board meetings, he would spend a couple of days scouting for opportunities. But the very thing that made England an attractive prospect – the shortage of shopping centres – made finding a suitable one all the more difficult. Then in 1996 something came up in west London. It was White City, an extraordinary development site at Shepherd's Bush.

It was the brainchild of two British developers, Elliott Bernerd and Godfrey Bradman. They had cobbled the site together from odd pieces of industrial and contaminated land that in recent times had been home to a greyhound track and a railway siding. It was a classic brownfield site that, in the modern spirit of urban regeneration, they planned to reconfigure into a buzzing hub of activity based around a shopping centre.

As soon as he heard about it, Frank had Westfield's signature on the shopping centre. He approached Bernerd with a proposition for a joint venture. The price was high, negotiations were tough and when the parties failed to agree Frank walked away, resolving to keep watch because things often come back in unexpected ways.

Later on his visits to the UK he often met with Peter Allen, an Australian working for Citibank in London. At the time Frank was annoyed with Citibank over its recent restructuring of Westfield's American debt. Citibank was keen to restore good relations and Allen was perfectly positioned to do so. His job, to find real-estate investment opportunities in the UK and Europe, happened to be exactly what Westfield was looking for. Allen could navigate his way around the local property scene and knew the main players. In those days, there were some characters Citibank was reluctant to deal with, and some with whom it exercised caution. Allen would share this information with Frank and they enjoyed the easy rapport that often exists between Australians abroad.

It wasn't long before Allen had changed jobs and was a roving executive for Westfield, based in Sydney but searching for opportunities in Europe and the UK. He moved regularly with his family following, and their furniture always a couple of months behind them. By 1998, nothing was happening and Frank realised the only way to get a foothold in the UK was to have an executive on the spot, full time, looking for opportunities. Just as Westfield had done in the US, he wanted to start with an existing shopping centre, preferably in an under-shopped part of the retail market. By redeveloping an existing centre the company would not have to get to know the population or build new habits. It would just have to get the tenant mix right and make the mall so attractive that people would be drawn in.

Allen was despatched to London where he set up a 'no frills' Westfield operation in a serviced office. It was tough representing a company no one had heard of, and even though he put together a book showing Westfield's standing in Australia and the US no one was interested. During this period he was in constant contact with Frank, who was steadfastly encouraging. "From the work we had done, we knew we could make money in this market and Frank gave me confidence that the opportunity was out there," says Allen. While the chairman's optimism was a tonic, it also created frustration because from time to time Frank would try to help by talking to his contacts, who operated in a higher sphere to those Allen was dealing with. This complicated things and sent Allen off on a number of tangents that yielded no business. But, through this period he began to understand something of Frank's ability to get the best out of people. "He's not only encouraging but he sets very high goals, offering success in something you never thought was achievable."

In June 1999, while Allen was knocking on the doors of
the British property establishment, Frank was taking one of his
regular mid-year breaks in Israel. Typically, he would take a suite
at the Hilton Hotel in Tel Aviv from where he and Shirley would
conduct a rich social life. They loved being in Israel. Frank easily
switched to Hebrew, soaked himself in Middle Eastern politics
and debated with friends into the small hours. He was close
to Ehud Barak and shortly after arriving on this trip, went to
Barak's offices to congratulate him on his recent election as prime
minister. The office door opened and a smiling Barak emerged
with an Englishman, Michael Levy, whom he introduced as
a member of the British House of Lords. They exchanged
pleasantries for a few moments and the Englishman left.

By the time Frank returned to the Hilton a couple of hours
later Lord Michael Levy, having done his homework, phoned
Shirley to make a social arrangement. Surprised and curious,
Frank accepted the invitation. The conversation was pleasant
and other meetings followed. On one occasion Frank visited him
in London and on another Levy, who happened to be travelling
in the south of France, was a guest on Lowy's boat. It became
apparent that Levy was well connected in the UK and could
possibly help Westfield identify business opportunities and advise
on potential partners. Although he had never been involved in
property development, he did know many people in the business
and in the Jewish community who had links to the business.
Levy was known to be a friend, tennis partner and adviser of the
then British prime minister Tony Blair.

Within weeks Levy was engaged as a consultant to Westfield
and went on to arrange introductions to a number of people in
the London real-estate business. Over the next two and a half
years he worked with Peter Allen, who did not regard him as

particularly useful. "Michael was close to the prime minister and talked a good game, but he had no understanding of the property business. He saw his role as a facilitator to open doors, which in some respects was a negative. It cut across my way of doing things. While I would work up a path to get somewhere, he would come in over the top. Every couple of months we would have a meeting where I would update him on what we were doing and he would see if there was a role he could play to help facilitate it. He would also proffer that he had heard this or that." In the end, a great deal of controversy would arise from the consultancy, but no tangible business.

In the meantime, as the year 2000 approached, Allen's spadework was beginning to pay off: a shopping centre in the relatively affluent city of Nottingham about two hundred kilometres north of London emerged as a possibility. The Broadmarsh Centre was in the middle of the city, next to a train station, above the main bus interchange and ripe for redevelopment. For the past year Hermes, one of the UK's leading fund management organisations, had been seeking a joint venture partner to redevelop it.

This was Westfield's opportunity to gain a foothold in the UK and Steven led the bid. He assembled a team from Australia and the US to work with Peter Allen. "The full horsepower of our company went into a single presentation to Hermes," says Steven. Westfield had to fend off four other competitors including fellow Australian company Lend Lease, which was well known in the UK. In partnership with Hermes and others, Lend Lease had recently opened Bluewater, a much-praised shopping centre and leisure development in Kent. However, its next development underway in Dundee, Scotland, was not drawing accolades and this was Westfield's opportunity to slip in.

With German Chancellor Angela Merkel in Sydney at her first public address in Australia, November 2014. *(Lowy Institute/Peter Morris)*

With the head of NewsCorp, Rupert Murdoch, at the latter's delivery of the Lowy Lecture to mark the Lowy Institute's tenth anniversary, Sydney Town Hall, October 2013. *(Lowy Institute/Peter Morris)*

With former Prime Minister Paul Keating outside the Westin Hotel, Sydney, after Angela Merkel's speech, November 2014. *(Lowy Institute/Peter Morris)*

With then Prime Minister John Howard, who delivered the inaugural Lowy Lecture in March 2005. *(Lowy Institute/Peter Morris)*

Greeting then Prime Minister Julia Gillard before she delivers the Asian Century White Paper at the Lowy Institute, October 2012. Dr Michael Fullilove, Executive Director of the Lowy Institute, looks on. *(Lowy Institute/Peter Morris)*

With Prime Minister Tony Abbott at a party to celebrate both Shirley's eightieth birthday and the Lowys' sixtieth wedding anniversary, Sydney, March 2014. *(David Mane)*

Steven, Frank, Peter and David Lowy outside Westfield's old headquarters in William Street, Sydney, before the sign came down in 2011. *(Westfield/Dean Moncho)*

The board of Westfield in 2013 prior to the restructure the following year that saw the company split into two: an Australasian company and an international company. Standing (left to right): Mark Johnson, Steven Johns, Roy Furman, Professor Judith Sloan, Peter Lowy, Frank Lowy, Steven Lowy, John McFarlane, Peter Allen, The Rt Hon Lord Goldsmith, Professor Fred Hilmer. Seated (left to right): Brian Schwartz, Ilana Atlas. *(Westfield/Stephen Ward)*

Cutting the ribbon at the opening of Westfield London with the Mayor of London, Boris Johnson, October 2008. *(Westfield)*

Frank and his adviser Mark Ryan in the chairman's office, Sydney, 2015. *(Westfield / Peter Morris)*

Michael Gutman, Elliott Rusanow and Simon Tuxen at Westfield headquarters, Sydney, 2015. *(Westfield / Emily Baker)*

Above: With Mark Viduka, captain of the Socceroos, after Australia qualified for the 2006 FIFA World Cup for the first time in thirty-two years. Sydney Olympic Park, November 2005. *(Football Federation of Australia/ Carlos Furtado)*

Left: With Sepp Blatter, president of FIFA, at Sydney Olympic Park June 2013. *(Getty Images/Robert Cianflone)*

Frank Lowy and David Gallop, CEO of the Football Federation of Australia, signing Ange Postecoglou as the Socceroos' new coach, Sydney, October 2013. *(Getty Images/Matt King)*

An exuberant Frank Lowy as Australia scores the winning goal, defeating South Korea to take the Asian Cup, Sydney, 2015. Left to right: Khalid Hamad Hamoud Al Busaidi, chairman and president of the Oman Football Association, Sheikh Salman Bin Ibrahim Al-Khalifa, president of the AFC, Frank Lowy, Governor-General Sir Peter Cosgrove and Lady Cosgrove. *(Hamza Yassin Photography)*

At Sydney Olympic Park in June 2013, congratulating Socceroos captain Lucas Neill on beating Iraq to qualify for the 2014 FIFA World Cup in Brazil. Tim Cahill (hugging Archie Thompson), Rob Cornthwaite and Michael Zullo look on. *(Getty Images/Mark Kolbe)*

Falling off the stage after the A-League Grand Final in Melbourne, May 2015. Frank Lowy was about to award the trophy to Melbourne Victory FC when he slipped. *(Top: Getty Images / Robert Prezioso. Bottom: AAP / Tracy Nearmy)*

After a few minutes on the ground, attended by paramedics, Frank Lowy climbed back onto the podium and awarded the trophy to Mark Milligan, captain of Melbourne Victory. The grass had stained his hair. *(Getty Images / Quinn Rooney)*

Steven's team worked relentlessly for the final 'beauty contest' and emerged thinking it had impressed Hermes. To improve Westfield's position, Steven and Peter Allen persuaded the chairman of Hermes, Richard Harrold, and a senior executive to have dinner with them. For the occasion Allen selected an elite restaurant and, knowing that Harold was a wine enthusiast, he ordered two £600 bottles of 1990 Penfolds Grange. "Steven hated the price and afterwards threatened that I would have to pay for the wine if we didn't get the transaction – but we got it!" says Allen. Westfield got the transaction by paying a top price and by sweetening the deal with stock options for Hermes. When on 14 February 2000 Westfield was formally selected Frank, who rarely over-celebrates, felt pleased. His dream was just beginning to materialise.

For this first venture Frank wanted the company to put the best expertise in place and outperform itself. With the serviced London office comprising only Allen, his PA and Peter Miller – a senior development executive based in Australia and recently relocated to the UK – there was suddenly a lot of work to be done and people to be found. This was not easy. As a rank outsider, the company had struggled to find a reputable British law firm willing to take it on as a client. This difficulty was overcome when some Australian lawyers working in London vouched for Westfield's standing and stability.

Within a couple of months another deal involving nine shopping centres was coming into focus. This deal would help to establish Westfield in the UK market but there was a note of caution from Frank. They should take care not to "do a Lend Lease" and lose credibility by following a good first acquisition with a poor second. The new deal for Westfield was a joint venture with MEPC, a leading UK developer, to purchase a portfolio with nine assets in prime locations across the country. The deal went ahead, the package of nine centres was bought and three, deemed to have little growth potential, were quickly sold. This was a considerable leap for Westfield. From a standing start in January 2000, the company was ending the same year managing a portfolio of seven centres valued at $2.1 billion.

As it urgently tried to build up its workforce the old barriers came up. With no history in England Westfield wasn't considered an employer of choice, and recruiting talented local executives was slow. Locals had no guarantees the company would stay the distance, and persuading them to join took time. To help shoulder the burden Westfield executives were flown in from Australia, the US and New Zealand. Apart from lending a hand, they were there to infuse the new office with the company culture. This cross-fertilisation characterises Westfield's global strategy, combining the skill and experience from its established markets with the invaluable local knowledge of executives in new markets. At any time there may up to thirty expatriate executives working in the outer reaches of its commercial empire.

As Westfield's new UK business began to build, an event across the Atlantic shattered all confidence in the market. The 9/11 attack on the World Trade Center, WTC, in 2001 created nervousness everywhere. Westfield had bought into the WTC six weeks earlier. While Lowy told shareholders that in uncertain times it was important to be strong, privately he was anxious about the US and the UK investments. In the context of the new global uncertainty, had he overspent? Had he put Westfield in danger?

A few months later this anxiety turned into anger when he opened the newspaper to find himself at the centre of a new controversy in the UK relating to Lord Levy, who was known to be a major fundraiser for the British Labour Party and Tony Blair's envoy to the Middle East. The press claimed this background made his involvement with Westfield improper. It was alleged that Lowy had paid him at least £250,000 ($670,000) over a three-year period for what was described as 'cash for access' and 'cash for foreign policy'.

There were suggestions Lord Levy had arranged for Westfield representatives to visit 10 Downing Street and meet important government officers and ministers with influence in property development. Lowy replied that any contact between Westfield and governments in the UK had been arranged and conducted by Westfield alone in the normal course of its business. He vigorously rebuffed suggestions that he was paying Lord Levy to gain political influence in Britain's dealings with Israel. Back in Australia Lowy dealt with this controversy at an annual general meeting, with the comment: "Entering a new market is a tough business. I don't simply arrive at Kennedy Airport in New York, or Heathrow in London or Amsterdam Airport, and hang out a sign saying: 'We want to buy shopping centres' and sit back waiting to be bowled over with offers. It doesn't quite happen that way."

He said the company spends years getting to know the market, forging relationships and establishing potential associations that might one day lead to an opportunity for Westfield. To do this it invests considerable sums of money to retain a wide range of consultants, advisers and bankers, but not all the deals work out: "Lord Levy was one such consultant and we asked him to explore business opportunities for us."

The press eventually lost interest but some four years later, Lord Levy was back in the headlines over allegations of 'cash for peerages'. He denied any wrongdoing and there was no mention of Westfield. Lowy, who watched from the sidelines, was unconcerned: "I was completely comfortable because he never solicited me for Labour Party funds and he never offered me a knighthood." Finally in July 2007 it was announced there would be no prosecutions in the cash-for-honours affair.

In the meantime Lowy got wind that the legendary Elliott Bernerd was in trouble and his White City site might be back on the market. Bernerd had tried to ride the dot.com boom around the turn of the century by developing 'technical real estate' to cater for the specialist needs of IT and telecommunications companies. When the dot.com bubble burst he was left with substantial losses. To add to his troubles, he was just beginning a devastating battle with jaw cancer.

With Peter Allen at his side Frank made his second approach. This time the discussions reached the point where Frank and Bernerd shook hands on a fairly straightforward deal that would deliver half of White City to Westfield, which would then be responsible for the development and management of the new shopping centre on the site. But the bonhomie of the handshake didn't last through the negotiations. Although they had settled conceptually on a price, when it came to agreeing the term sheet, they couldn't agree on who would do what in the partnership. The deal was still in the realm of a friendly agreement and as Westfield hadn't invested much, Frank walked away. He knew something was going to happen with White City soon and he would wait.

32

An American surge

On a Caribbean cruise in the mid 1980s, Frank Lowy took a seat at a blackjack table and fell into conversation with an American sitting next to him. There was something familiar about Norman Hascoe and they soon discovered they had much in common. Apart from being of an age and both enjoying commercial success, they shared a passion for Israel. Hascoe, an entrepreneurial engineer, and his wife Suzanne, a biochemist, had a natural rapport with the Lowys and for the rest of the cruise the two couples spent time together.

When Frank was next in New York Norman introduced him to his old friend Larry Silverstein, who was the same age and had similar interests. This trio would regularly dine together. When the Lowys bought an apartment on Park Avenue it was in the same building as the Silversteins'. Frank counted himself fortunate to have found such friends and his visits to New York were the richer for them. As president of Silverstein Properties, a real estate development and investment firm, Larry was a fount of information, particularly about the New York property scene. He was also a good candidate for a board seat on a new entity Westfield was about to list on the New York Stock Exchange. In 1997, when invited to the board of Westfield America Inc, he accepted warmly. Frank and Larry got on so well it was difficult to imagine that this might not continue.

During the dot.com boom that began in the late 1990s the American retail market began to heat up. By 2000 it was on fire, with retailers expanding at unprecedented rates. Top brands were opening hundreds of stores a year around the country. They needed somewhere to put these stores, and malls welcomed them with open arms. The mantra at Westfield was 'growth, growth, growth'. Shopping centres were providing an initial return of 9 to 10 per cent and although funding costs were high, there were major gains to be had.

Westfield wanted to upscale its investment and become a mainstream participant in this market, but it was hampered by its capital structure. It needed more capital to go into US machinery so it could acquire more malls. As Australia was the best source, it needed to export capital from there to grow the US business. To achieve this, a capital restructure was necessary.

Westfield was no stranger to major restructurings. This was its form of evolution and while not every attempt worked, its willingness to evolve had seen it survive extremely tough times. It bought its first US mall in 1977 and over the next two decades, it morphed five times. In 1988 its US business was floated on the London Stock Exchange; in 1989 the US business was privatised, but in 1993 Westfield bought the US business back. Three years later the Westfield America Trust (WAT) was spun off and listed in Australia, and in 1997 Westfield America Inc was listed on the New York Stock Exchange.

Now it was about to morph for the sixth time. In 2001, Westfield America Inc, which was trading below expectations, was delisted and its shares were bought back by Westfield America Trust, making it a subsidiary of the Australian business.

With more capital available Frank, Peter Lowy and Richard Green were on the lookout for opportunities. As it happened, the World Trade Center was languishing. The stock crash of the late 1980s had left it with high vacancy rates and business was slow. In 2001, as a cost-cutting measure, the New York and New Jersey Port Authority decided to offer a ninety-nine-year lease for the WTC buildings. When the winning bidder fell away Silverstein and his partners were next in line. The lease was theirs for US$3.2 billion. Larry had discussed the deal with Frank, who was understandably interested in the retail space. Silverstein Properties took him on as a partner and for US$420 million Westfield was given control of the 40,000 square metres of retail space on the concourse. The friends shook hands and at the end of July 2001, they had their prize. It was described as one of the richest transactions in the history of New York.

Lowy planned to make the mall a showcase, but six weeks later the story was over. In the worst terrorist attack in US history the WTC collapsed, killing 2753 people and searing the date of 11 September into the American psyche. Among the dead was one Westfield executive. There were other attacks that day and no one was sure what would happen next. The commercial life of New York stopped, the international skies emptied of planes and markets around the world fell. The globe went into shock.

Despite Lowy assuring Westfield shareholders that the company was fully insured, investors wiped 5 per cent off its value. There was one insurance policy for the whole WTC and Westfield had a share of it. Although the claim became contentious, insurance wasn't the only issue that concerned Lowy. He worried about the potential long-term effects of the attack.

The devastated site became known as Ground Zero and was regarded as hallowed ground. The country was in agony over it and Frank and Peter quickly realised that no one needed to hear an Australian voice on the subject. Anyway, Westfield's stake was too small to be relevant to the debate about what should be done with the site. So they came to an arrangement with the Port Authority that owned the land. They agreed to quit on the proviso that Westfield would have the first option on the retail space when all the issues had been resolved and redevelopment began.

In December 2003 Westfield announced it had sold its portion of the WTC to the Port Authority for a little more than it originally paid. In addition it had put down $1 million for the first option when the premises became available again. In a smart move and for no extra cost, it also agreed to make available retail consulting services for the development of these premises.

"There was a strong element of pragmatism in the decision to sell," says Frank. "The complexities had been absorbing too much of our energy and we needed to get on with life. Our stake was not big enough to be influential and we were a minor irritant in the process. Further, we didn't want to get tangled up in the politics of the reconstruction, which took a decade to resolve."

When the matter had been resolved and Westfield was invited back, there was a personal cost. Larry and Frank found themselves at loggerheads. In planning to redevelop the best possible office buildings, Silverstein Properties didn't think it important to provide for the kind of retail space Frank and Peter thought appropriate. When Frank tried to share his vision no one was listening. "With a bit of flexibility and capacity both could be achieved, but they didn't seem to be able to conceptualise what we were talking about. They overlooked a tremendous commercial opportunity," he says. No one in Westfield's team could make Silverstein Properties understand how much value could be added by creating a major retail hub downtown.

In the end Frank Lowy didn't get the space he wanted and his relationship with Larry deteriorated to the point where litigation between the companies was considered. For the sake of the significance of the site, they held off, but the friendship was over. "After that things were cordial when we met, but nothing was left of what we had," said Frank.

A large component of Westfield's business has grown through the personal relationships Lowy established. He works at these connections and goes out of his way to keep them alive. He'll take an extra flight, delay his departure a day or get up at 4 am to make a call if it maintains a connection. "Personal relationships between principals are always preferable because you know each other and you can predict the reaction of the other side," says Lowy. "This works both ways." But ultimately these relationships are secondary to commercial realities. "Your responsibility to the business and to your shareholders takes precedence. Sometimes, as regrettably happened with Larry, these relationships get damaged. But mostly it's just a deal, it is understood that both parties have commercial obligations and any conflict is taken in that context. There is a buyer and a seller and it's just a matter of price."

By the time the WTC was ready to welcome Westfield back in 2011, the volume of commuters predicted to be passing through the transport hub around which Westfield would be built was estimated at 200,000 to 400,000 a day. In addition there would be tourists and the growing number of people living in lower Manhattan would shop there too. In negotiations led by Peter, Westfield bought half the mall space in 2011 and the other half in late 2013 for a total cost of $1.4 billion from the Port Authority. While pleased with the purchase, the restricted size continued to rankle with Frank: "I still can't get over the lack of vision. It still hurts me," he said years later.

Back in 2001, in addition to its original stake in the World Trade Center, Westfield picked up more retail space through the acquisition of two major US shopping centre portfolios. One of these was a textbook acquisition, the other involved warfare.

Peter led the textbook negotiation with the Richard E. Jacobs Group and bought a portfolio of nine centres for $1.45 billion. The warfare involved Rodamco, one of the largest property investment funds in the world and one of Westfield's old friends. Since the early 1990s Westfield had enjoyed partnerships with this Dutch giant, first in Australia and then in the US. Frank worked hard to develop and maintain warm relationships with its principals and would visit when he was in Europe, or would be their host on the Mediterranean.

In 1999 Rodamco went through a fundamental restructure of its international property portfolio and split into four geographical entities, each having to report back to Holland. As Australia didn't fit into its geographical region, Westfield bought its Sydney assets. This happened around the turn of the century and the relationship was sound.

But Rodamco's North American entity, RNA, did not trade well. Managers and shareholders were not happy with one another and a major stakeholder, the Dutch pension fund ABP, wanted out. Both Frank and Peter happened to have warm relationships with ABP too and in 2001 bought its 25 per cent stake. Their declared plan was to use this stake to take over the management of the RNA malls.

ABP worried there could be flak for potentially passing control of a Dutch entity to a third party. To safeguard shareholders it insisted that Westfield provide a strategic plan showing exactly how it would extract better value than the existing management in the US.

The existing management did not want Westfield to come in and take over. It defended its position fiercely and made a series of allegations against Westfield, particularly about its extraction of too large a profit as a manager. Westfield countered that it charged market rates and pointed out that RNA's centres were underperforming because they were underdeveloped.

The battleground for this was Holland so Frank set up headquarters in Amsterdam, in the gracious Amstel Hotel overlooking the Amstel River. Over the next six months he, Peter and several executives shuttled between Holland, Australia and the US. While full of old-world charm this hotel hadn't quite entered the new century. Westfield took over its meeting rooms and rewired them with fast internet, telephone and video conferencing services. When international travel stopped in the wake of the 9/11 attack on the World Trade Center in 2001, Westfield's executives were the only guests in the hotel.

Just after purchasing the ABP's 25 per cent stake Frank and the team spent two weeks holed up in the hotel, meeting with investors. When they went home for a break, Elliott was left to hold the fort. No sooner had they gone than news broke that RNA management had issued 25 per cent of new stock to a foundation it had set up itself. This 'phantom stock' would neutralise Westfield's holding.

The situation was dire. Elliott called Frank, who couldn't believe what he was hearing. Neither could the other executives as they repacked their bags for Holland. Within a couple of days the team had reassembled at the hotel with ranks of local lawyers and advisers. In Australia Frank would have applied for an injunction but the legal system in Holland was different. After getting through the first round of court proceedings successfully, Westfield was told the next round – which involved the appointment of three expert assessors – would take three months. In the meantime, its shareholding remained neutralised.

As the team tried to cope with that, a new front opened. They received word that the US management of RNA had set up a due diligence room in New York, having opened their books to try and lure a white knight or elicit a good bid. But they wouldn't give Westfield access to the room. So Frank went back to court in Holland. RNA denied the existence of the room. The judge ruled that there had to be an open process and there should be no closed room. Despite this, RNA continued to run the closed room in New York.

The lights in the Amstel Hotel burned through the night as the Westfield team strategised. Lawyers from two different firms were present and had different views on how best to proceed. This led to energetic discussions between Frank and Peter. A leading corporate lawyer from the Dutch firm advised that Westfield should rely on the elongated court process. While Frank concurred with his advice, Peter wanted to follow the advice of a lawyer from one of America's biggest international mergers and acquisitions firms. His view was that RNA's actions in setting up a due diligence room, together with the length of the Dutch legal process, would greatly increase the risk of a competing offer being made. The process was fraught but a consensus was reached and a pragmatic solution evolved. Peter would return to the US to negotiate with the potential competing bidders, two US property companies, the Simon and Rouse groups, and agree to work with them.

In the meantime, Frank decided to call a shareholders' meeting in Holland where he could present his side of the story. Frenzied preparation followed and just as the team was ready, RNA pre-empted it by calling its own shareholders' meeting in Rotterdam.

On the morning of the Rotterdam meeting the Westfield team had a strategic session at its lawyer's office, where a new battle plan was developed. It involved Simon and Rouse. Both were keen to be part of the RNA deal. The plan was to divide up the thirty-five malls among the three of them in advance, agree a price and move forward. The documents were bundled into Frank's black leather satchel and the Westfield team left for Rotterdam.

The meeting, at the Rotterdam concert hall, yielded no new information and afterwards Frank and the team went to the airport to fly home. Elliott remained and was looking forward to unwinding and having the evening off when some thirty minutes later his phone rang. It was Frank's unmistakable voice. "Elliott, I don't have my satchel." He was at the airport and wanted Elliott to go back to Rotterdam and look for it.

Elliott found a hire car and by 8.30 pm he was at the concert hall. He raced in to find a concert in progress. It was due to finish at 10 pm so he used the time to check all the rubbish bins he could see in the foyer and those in the surrounding streets. There was no satchel. When the hall eventually emptied there was no satchel in there either. Frank had called several times from the plane and on hearing the news he asked Elliott to inquire when the concert hall cleared its garbage and where it was dumped. This happened at 5 am the next morning so Elliott sped back to Amsterdam, slept fitfully for a couple of hours and then returned to Rotterdam in time to go through the bins – again without success.

Frank, who hadn't slept, instructed Elliott to file a report with the Rotterdam police and then go back to the concert hall and review its CCTV footage. At 8 am, when the security guard arrived, they spent hours watching the tapes. "We saw Frank walk in with the satchel under his arm and later we saw him walk out without it," said Elliott. The pursuit was over and a despondent Elliott flopped into the car for the return journey to Amsterdam. As he arrived, the security guard called: "I think we found it!" The car turned around and raced back with Elliott now in high spirits. But the bag the guard was holding was nothing like Frank's soft leather satchel. So the car turned around again and Elliott finally crawled into his hotel at 5 pm. There was one thing he was pleased about. He had been scheduled to attend a compliance meeting by teleconference at 3 pm that afternoon and as he had missed it, he could go directly to bed. But his phone went. The meeting had been delayed until his return.

The lost papers with the war plan were never found. It was presumed someone had liked the look of the satchel, emptied it and gone off with it. During a bleak cold week that December, the team returned to the Amstel and carefully went through the RNA portfolio, deciding which malls they wanted. Frank would look at a centre and say, "We must have this one." Peter, who had a good sense of what to save for their prospective partners, found himself saying, "Sorry, Dad, that one is out of the question." Once they had divided up the portfolio Peter was despatched to the US to make it a reality. He negotiated with

Simon and Rouse, reached agreements and a bid to buy RNA's portfolio for $10.5 billion was launched.

RNA agreed to the price as long as it was held blameless for the wrongs of the past, such as issuing phantom shares and running the room. A few hitches delayed the deal and by March 2002 Westfield had acquired some 40 per cent of the RNA portfolio for $4.5 billion. This added another fourteen centres bringing its new US total to sixty-one malls – and making Westfield the number two mall operator in the country, after the Simon Property Group. "We are well and truly in the mainstream of the US shopping centre industry," a smiling Frank told shareholders.

There were important lessons from the RNA deal. Westfield had bought only a part of RNA because it feared it didn't have enough capital for it all. As it turned out, it was able to raise more money than it needed through the Westfield America Trust. The key lesson was that if it had combined the balance sheets of the Westfield America Trust, Westfield Trust and Westfield Holdings, it would have been able to execute the transaction in one swoop, on its own.

33

Star chamber

When a deal is in progress, executives who see the Lowys in action for the first time are always surprised. While the daily interaction between father and sons is mostly unremarkable, in the heat of battle all limits fall away. With the implicit understanding that solving the issue is paramount, their interactions are often explosive.

This struck Simon Tuxen when he joined Westfield as corporate counsel in 2002. He had grown up in the sedate atmosphere of a large Australian law firm and later spent time in the quiet upper echelons of an old Chinese hong. When he accepted the Westfield position he packed up his household in Singapore and while the container was on its way to Australia he took his family on a holiday to Spain. Then his phone rang. It was Steven Lowy calling to say they had all gathered in London to talk about a wholesale UK fund. Although he wasn't officially on board yet, they wanted him to join them right away, A surprised Tuxen agreed, but explained he didn't have appropriate clothes because they were in transit. "Well, retailers have to live too," was Steven's reply.

When Tuxen turned up in London in his new suit and squeaky shoes, he was appropriately dressed for his baptism. Frank, Peter, Steven and a few others were about to interview two groups of investment bankers who had also flown in. The first group entered politely and with due deference, presented the meeting with an eighty-page booklet. Peter said, "I've only got one question. Go to page sixty-two. What does that figure mean?" It was duly explained and after an audience of less than twenty minutes the bankers were dismissed. Tuxen felt for them. "These were senior guys who had come all the way from Australia and they were out of the room before they had time to settle in." The same pattern was repeated with the next group. As soon as they left, decorum disintegrated.

Westfield's CFO stood up at the whiteboard but before he could complete his point father and sons let loose. They disagreed with each other, they argued, they shouted, they banged the table and talked over one another to such an extent that Tuxen didn't know where to look. "It was as vigorous as anything I had ever seen in my life and I'm sitting there thinking what have I got myself in for, this is crazy." When it was over and a consensus had been reached, the Lowys gave each other a hug and a kiss and happily went their separate ways. "At that point I realised this was perfectly normal for them. There was no carry-over and I figured they must have some fundamental family rules about business matters." They were passionate about business and had developed the sophisticated art of quarantining the emotion of their professional life from that of their family life.

Frank was now at the height of his executive powers: seasoned, strong and soon to become involved in a major shopping centre war in Australia. It began in around March 2003 when, around midday on a Monday, Elliott took a call at work. He was told that the rival shopping centre company Centro had just bought 19.9 per cent of the AMP Retail Trust. This was big news. If malls were going up for sale Westfield wanted to know. It had built most of its malls from scratch and was keen to get its hands on some ready-made ones. Elliott called Frank, who was nearby, and then Steven, who was a couple of hours away on his boat on the Hawkesbury River. By mid afternoon Westfield's senior executive team was around the table at company headquarters with Peter on a video link from Los Angeles, figuring out what should be done.

That night Steven went to meet AMP to offer Westfield's friendly services. He also talked to Lend Lease. "But by the next day we had formed the view that we had to get in control," says Steven. "Within a couple more days we had put a paper together that fully analysed the business. We put it to the board and by Thursday afternoon we bought 16 per cent of the company. The next day we cleaned up to 19.9 per cent." This was extraordinary given that 20 per cent was owned by AMP and another 19.9 per cent by Centro.

As often happens, Westfield was criticised for overpaying. "We could pay so much because we knew those assets so well. We also knew they were superior assets that had been managed inferiorly. We had the confidence in ourselves to pay up to get in control so we could end up where we wanted to be," says Steven.

Historically AMP was the premier property firm in Australia, and because of its solid and long-standing relationship with Westfield and the healthy respect between the two companies,

Frank would never have initiated such an attack. Once its assets were in play, however, he was in the fray. He knew AMP couldn't win and he wanted to get ahead of other rivals.

At the time, Hamish Douglass was in his early thirties and about to have a front row seat in the strategising to take over the AMP Retail Trust. He represented Deutsche Bank, which was handling the transaction for Westfield, and remembers Frank holding daily meetings in a room packed with lawyers, their associates, bankers and advisers. Although Frank's style was not to take the limelight, his presence dominated the room, which became known as the Star Chamber because of the way the problem was being interrogated. "I had never seen anyone act like this before," says Hamish. "Age was no barrier and Frank would literally go around the table and ask everyone's opinion. At random he'd ask juniors from Westfield, associate lawyers and senior people for their view. He wanted a diversity of opinion and would let the banter run. Suddenly, after five days of this, he said, 'Okay, this is what we are going to do.' He had this ability to assimilate generational views, make a decision and have everyone lock in behind him. I had never seen a leader work like this."

But Hamish was in for a bigger lesson. On Sunday 18 May 2003 his mobile rang next to his bed. "Hamish," came Lowy's deep early-morning growl. "I am very nervous someone is going to make another bid next week and I want to close this transaction down tomorrow."

Hamish couldn't believe what he was hearing. In the world of takeovers this was virtually impossible because Lowy had not yet opened his bid. It was only due to open the next day and now he wanted to close on the same day. In response Hamish immediately began listing the complex problems inherent in such a strategy but was stopped abruptly by Frank's irritation: "Hamish, I haven't rung you up for you to tell me what the problems are, I have rung up for you to tell me what the answers are. I will call you back at 5 pm."

Hamish looked at his watch. It was 8.05 am. Giving up weekends is par for the course in investment banking culture and while his family prepared for a day at Palm Beach he drove to the office. "Frank wasn't joking about 5 pm. It wasn't as if he was saying to me 'Hamish, try your best, see what you can do.' It was almost an instruction. Unlike other clients of mine, he didn't rant or rave or shout down the line, he just lowered his voice and made it clear we would find a solution." In dealing with Lowy Hamish says, "You hit rock quickly. Once he's made up his mind there's an underlying hardness. It's not aggressive, just an uncompromising and unwavering belief that there will be a way."

Once the team had gathered at Deutsche Bank Hamish explained the problem. Had such a request come from most other clients he would have told the team they were in Alice in Wonderland territory and the task was to find a way to dissuade the client from such a course. "But because of Lowy's success and because he thinks it's possible, you kind of think there must be a way. And you don't want to let him down."

The team got to work. "It forced us into a spot of thinking very creatively about our options within the law, about how we could accelerate the process. When the call came at 5 pm we had a strategy to deliver. We couldn't promise it would work, but we had found a way to play it," says Hamish. It was a lightning strike. The head trader at Deutsche got all the stock and on Tuesday morning 20 May 2003 Westfield Trust announced its takeover offer of $1.9 billion for the AMP Shopping Centre Trust.

"That would not have happened without Frank's compression of time, his lateral thinking and his belief that it was possible," says Hamish.

Once the news was out, Westfield's bid trumped the bid by Centro. As part of the strategy, and pre-empting any potential competition concerns, Westfield agreed to cut Centro into the deal by selling it three assets, one from AMP and two from Westfield's existing portfolio.

Having seen how much Westfield paid for the shares, the investment community again questioned the price. The comment that Westfield always overpays is a recurring theme that always elicits the same response from Frank Lowy: "When we buy an asset I don't see what we pay for it, I see what we can make out of it. Quite often it looks like we overpay but, in addition to current value, we are buying potential others don't see." His favourite example is Garden State Plaza in New Jersey, which had one floor of retail space. Underneath were a storage reservoir and truck docks, an area that Westfield knew could be transformed into another full floor of retail space. Competition for the centre was heated and when Westfield won there was talk of how crazy Australians had overpaid. In reality, they had bought double the floor space and would very soon realise the centre's full potential.

While Frank led the AMP strategy Steven drove the process throughout. The transaction resulted in complex arrangements between the AMP and Westfield, including some joint ventures that AMP completely controlled. When concerned advisers pressed for the structure to be sorted out Frank told them not to worry, this would happen over time. A month later the Australian Competition and Consumer Commission decided not to intervene in the takeover, saying that given the distribution of control the deal was not uncompetitive.

When Mark Bloom joined Westfield as deputy chief financial officer in 2003 he was just in time to observe the AMP transaction. Like Hamish he was struck by the inclusiveness and correctness of the Star Chamber gatherings. The process was civil and encouraged creative thinking. "The meeting starts off with the problem and the opportunities. Everyone keeps putting in ideas and at every subsequent meeting there is an incremental increase in understanding, everyone goes to the next step. It's an evolutionary process. All options are open to the last minute but when the decision is made it is absolute."

Keeping the options open is a Lowy hallmark, and it requires considerable effort. Typically, Frank will note that a deal can go three ways and will want to keep all three strands alive for as long as possible. The lawyers have the challenge of keeping all the options running. So does the finance department. But this gives Westfield agility. If something unexpected happens the company will be in a position to take another path quickly.

But away from the cultivated atmosphere of the meeting rooms the finance department was a sweatshop. An aggressive culture of intense analysis produced world-class best practice but wore people out in the process. While property and retail were the company's enablers, finance drove its destiny. Every three months the finance department would produce a finely detailed forecast of five years ahead. Later this forecast was reduced to three years. These snapshots kept the projections on track and helped to calibrate progress, to accelerate or slow where necessary. Few companies manage their business this way. "Westfield never missed earnings forecasts because we were always looking forward and managing the business," said Bloom. As the decision makers at the top need proper numbers coming up, the ethos permeated the business.

Bloom had come from South Africa where, as finance director of the Liberty Group, he had worked for a character not dissimilar to Frank. Sir Donny Gordon was the same age, also Jewish and one of that country's richest men. As an innovator of insurance products, property and shopping centres, he had expanded his business internationally with great success, particularly in the UK. Bloom had learned the value of listening very carefully to what his elderly chairman would say. It was a skill that prepared him for Frank, who could make a casual observation rich in insight that could be easily missed.

While there was much to learn from Frank, there were some things that could only be grasped by experiencing them with him. One was his passion for business. At the end of the AMP transaction Tuxen felt it. On the final night he went across to AMP's headquarters to sign legal documents. The lights in the building were out and he was led across a dark floor to a conference room at the back where the pages were laid out. Only the lawyers were at work. When Tuxen got back to Westfield at 11 pm, the lights were blazing. Frank and the executive team were waiting for him with some rare single malt whiskey on the table. They were there in case something went wrong and in case something went right. There was no question of Frank going home and waiting for a phone call. He thrived on the drama of transactions, on taking responsibility and on making the big call. And he loved Westfield.

The long relationship Frank built with AMP was deep in the roots of a shopping centre phenomenon that was about to appear in the well-to-do eastern suburbs of Sydney. Bondi Junction was an important commercial and transport hub connecting the city, the suburbs and the beaches. In 1994 Westfield bought its first stake in the hub from AMP. It grew from that. Ten years later, after considerable opposition from local councils and subsequent government intervention, it opened a shopping centre on a scale never seen in Sydney before. Driven by Steven and Bob Jordan, then chief operating officer for Westfield in Australia, it created such a sensation that during its first few months of operation it was blamed for a 30 per cent trade downturn in surrounding shopping areas.

Westfield Bondi Junction became the company's first flagship centre. "It changed our entire approach to the assets we build," says Steven. "We reinvented how we designed and built shopping centres. It was the first time we built a mall in an upmarket suburb with luxury retailers." In Australia Westfield had always been seen as a brand of middle-market shopping centres and had never seriously attracted fashion's top end. Now it changed its red logo to black, created a 'platinum' sensibility and moved the mall up the social scale, from classy food courts to valet parking.

When Frank walked through the centre with Steven at his side he registered it as a game changer. "Steven was extending what I'd done. He'd broken through to a new level and as he showed me around, we both knew this was the beginning of a new generation of iconic malls. Seeing it created by the next generation amplified my sense of pride."

By now, with his father's blessing, Steven had begun accumulating sites in the heart of the city. He began with AMP's landmark Centrepoint complex and then acquired the adjoining Imperial Arcade and Skygarden and began to consolidate them into what would become Westfield Sydney City, the most valuable Westfield asset in the country. "Time would show that Bondi Junction and Westfield Sydney City would not only be our trophy assets in Australia, but we would make more money out of them than anything else in the country," said Steven.

34

Radical change

In the first few years of the new century Peter and Steven would drive radical change in the company. Initially their father would resist it, but, being as persistent as he was, they worked tirelessly to convince him to share their vision.

The first radical move came from Peter. For some years he had wanted to overhaul Westfield's capital structure, not just individual parts of it but the whole business. When he put his ideas forward the finance department pushed back. After the Rodamco North America transaction in 2002 he became more determined. That had been a perception-changing exercise: Westfield found itself in no man's land. While it obtained a major equity position in RNA, it didn't believe it had the capacity to take it all over by itself, and shared it with two other parties. The lesson was that if Westfield reconfigured its structure and merged all its entities into one, it would have a big enough balance sheet to swallow the next huge opportunity on its own.

With that lesson well learned and with a change in Westfield's finance department, Peter's ideas began to get currency. He wanted to merge the three entities – Westfield Holdings, Westfield Trust and Westfield America Trust – to create one of the largest shopping centre companies in the world. This would simultaneously be an aggressive and a defensive move. It would create a massive balance sheet for acquisitions in a good market while creating a fortress in the event of an economic downturn, where one huge entity would be more likely to withstand hard times than three separate ones.

Peter worked up the idea internally, refined it with the help of advisers and then spent months selling it. Frank needed a lot of convincing because it meant the family would have to dilute its control of Westfield from 29 per cent to roughly 8 per cent. Peter pushed hard, saying the family didn't need such a large controlling stake. He repeatedly argued the merits of the merger, insisting it was strategically the right thing to do for the company. To his father's objection he observed that it was better to have a small share of a big safe vehicle than a large share of a vulnerable vehicle that could be damaged. After long debate it was concluded that if this was good for Westfield it must be good for the Lowys too. "Control is important but it is not everything. Success is everything," said Frank.

There was another potential benefit from a merger: it would overcome a vulnerability within the group. While Westfield Holdings controlled 40 per cent of the Westfield America Trust, it had no control over the Westfield Trust. As its income was substantially derived from managing both these trusts, its lack of control over Westfield Trust was seen as its Achilles heel. At the time, 2003, private equity firms and others were looking to buy property trusts and if they got their hands on the Westfield Trust, Westfield Holdings would suffer a significant reduction in revenue. A merger would eliminate this possibility. Frank was finally convinced and a paper was prepared for the board's consideration.

Deciding on this merger was one thing, but how would they do it? If Westfield simply put up a transaction, there was a possibility that others would put up counter proposals to stop it. The press suggested one possible way it had been done. It reported that Westfield had 'bought the street', hiring virtually every investment bank in the country so each would be conflicted. Should another party want to have a go at Westfield, there would be no banks left to fund or to act for them. This, the press said, was unprecedented.

Later it was revealed that the idea of buying the street had come from Peter and that his father had had the audacity to do it. Matthew Grounds, who heads UBS in Australia, has another view of why Westfield bought the street then and did so again later. He says the company usually picks one or two people it trusts and can rely on. These people give the key advice and then, near the end, the Lowys announce they are going to have to bring a few others in. This is not to conflict them; rather, it is because of the high volume of debt required to fund the transactions. All the banks participate in the debt and they genuinely want to reward those banks. Further, they value particular banks for particular things: for their brains, for their relationships in foreign exchange markets or for their capacity to deal with US debt. "They just use different banks for their different capabilities," says Grounds.

When the merger was first announced in April 2004 it was presented as a change in the company's structure, not its

philosophy, a change designed to generate growth and create
long-term value. At briefings Frank Lowy shared the credit.
After answering a complex question at an analyst briefing, he
turned to the Westfield team behind him and asked: "Did I do
okay?" They nodded enthusiastically. One newspaper noted how
much the sons appeared to trust their father. It reported that as
Peter and Steven followed Frank out of that briefing and into
the press conference, Peter caught Steven's arm: "We should stay
down here [with the journalists]. He's okay."

In July 2004 the three entities merged to create the Westfield
Group, with $34 billion in assets across Australia, NZ, the US
and the UK. While many didn't quite grasp what it meant, there
was a sense of awe at the size of the transaction. The press that,
as usual, attributed the strategy to Frank, said he had created a
leviathan. Then they watched as the monster built a large sea
chest for itself.

The merger made sense in many ways. It eliminated that
vulnerability and it pleased the market, which by then wanted
trusts internalised rather than being held in external management
arrangements. The market had developed a fondness for stapled
entities and Westfield provided them.

Had Frank moved earlier he might have had an opportunity
to keep control of the merged entity through the issue of non-
voting shares, as Rupert Murdoch had done in the US. Murdoch
used preferred non-voting shares as acquisition currency,
allowing the real power to remain within his family. But he
had faced an upward battle in getting approval, and for the
Lowys replicating that model seemed fraught with difficulty.
The merger was the principal issue and they didn't want to
distract attention from the main game by creating controversy
about control.

Some commentators described the consolidation as the beginning of the end for the Lowys. One said Frank Lowy had engineered his own exit and warned him that after all those years of unfettered decision making he was about to experience the challenges of corporate democracy. He was not fazed. While the dynastic element had been removed, the family presence on the new board remained. But Frank did have to acknowledge the ever-growing pressure of corporate governance and step aside from the chairmanship of Westfield's remuneration committee.

Commenting on the merger, one columnist said "size counts alright" and noted that it had delivered Westfield "sheer bulk, market power, acquisition muscle, cost saving, probably a superior credit rating and perhaps a valuation premium for size", as well as eliminating some vexing conflicts of interest. Lowy was then seventy-three and as fit as a mallee bull, with no qualms about charging at shareholder activists who tried to provoke him.

At the time, the US market was overheated with a great deal for sale, and the Lowys had set their heart on a particular portfolio of thirty-seven malls. It belonged to the Rouse Company, which had been credited with reshaping the American landscape. Rouse had been one of Westfield's partners in the RNA deal, during which it had acquired some high-prestige malls. Peter knew these malls and believed they could take Westfield to the next level in the US market. He had kept watch for four years as Rouse built its portfolio. In expectation of the portfolio coming to market, he and his father had courted the chairman of Rouse.

Westfield was still bedding down its merger when this portfolio was put up for sale. The timing could have been better. A six-week period was allowed for due diligence and although

Westfield gave itself to the task there was a new problem. In addition to the malls, the portfolio contained many thousands of acres of vacant land that could be developed for housing. This component was valued at around US$3 billion. As it wasn't Westfield's core business an investment bank was engaged to see if it could be sold. No buyers were found. Because Westfield wanted the malls so much, the question was whether it could or should stretch anyway. It was prepared to pay US$9 billion for the malls but could it reach US$12 billion without being over-leveraged? There was also a question of human resources, with all the executives still fully engaged in the practicalities of settling the merger.

Frank and Peter kept negotiating. They knew General Growth Properties, their major competitor, was prepared to put up a very large sum. Frank recalled his early experience in owing expensive non-income-producing land in Sydney and warned that this acreage could become Westfield's albatross. After the usual rounds of intense consultation, father and son reluctantly decided it was too big a stretch and too expensive. They had been waiting for this for four years: now it had arrived they needed to exercise discipline. The financial risk was too high and the night before the bidding was due to take place in New York Westfield withdrew. At about 3 am Los Angeles time Peter rang New York to say neither he nor his father would be there the next day. "It was like losing an FA Cup final," said Peter. "But then the final arbiter is economics, not emotion."

The investment bankers couldn't believe that Westfield had pulled out. There had only ever been two serious bidders. Now what? The next day, General Growth was placed in one room and was led to believe Westfield was in the other. A charade ensued, with the bankers appearing to go between rooms. When told an acceptable price had been reached the General Growth team packed their bags, assuming Westfield – with its reputation for overpaying – had won. On learning that in fact he had won a triumphant John Bucksbaum, the chief executive of General Growth, described the victory as, "One plus one equals three." He had agreed to pay about US$12 billion, which was more than a 30 per cent premium on the share price.

A few years later, when the global financial crisis hit, that cost him dearly. He had borrowed short-term money and was in strife. In early 2009 General Growth filed for Chapter 11 bankruptcy protection. As Frank watched the proceedings unfold he thought, "There but for the grace of God ..."

Meanwhile, having swallowed his disappointment over the Rouse portfolio and acknowledged the consequences of a ruined relationship with Rouse's principals, in 2004 Frank took his sea chest across the Atlantic to see what he could do to fulfil his long-term ambition to become established in London. There would be plenty to occupy him there.

For more than forty years Frank had been pushing to acquire more shopping centres in all territories. He aspired to reach 100 and when that was achieved, he wanted more and the company got more. By 2005 it had 128. The formula was simple. More centres brought more shoppers who brought more money that brought more growth. But Steven, who knew the assets intimately, could see that the formula was running out of steam and that the return on capital invested was more important than the number of shopping centres the company held.

Steven began to drive philosophical change through the company. Growth for growth's sake should no longer be the goal. Steven forced the recognition that unlike malls graded A in terms of quality and return, B and C malls no longer had the same potential. Shifts in population, new technology and other factors meant these malls might stagnate or even go backwards. Westfield needed to shed them and concentrate on A malls only. Frank baulked. This was anathema to him. All his life the goal had been to buy centres, not sell them. "You want to reduce the size of the business, are you crazy or something?" he asked. There was plenty of support for Steven's position and after the usual debate Frank grasped it, accepted it and became a convert to the cause.

With the new philosophy in place Westfield aimed to own the best-quality shopping centres in the best markets. Poorer-quality assets would go and only superior assets would be sought. Embedded in this change was the understanding that high-quality assets not only produced better returns but could better withstand market volatility.

The change dovetailed with the classic principles Frank had embedded in the company for decades. One is having geographic diversity as a natural buffer against the varying impacts of different markets. This allows retail resilience in one country to buoy the company during a low in another market. Diversity among retailers is another safeguard. Another is creating strong, stable cash flows based on long-term leases that are not affected by short-term movements in retail sales. The basis of the Westfield business model is that short-term fluctuations should not affect long-term decision making.

By 2006 the price of malls in the US was skyrocketing, and even poorly performing centres were selling at unimaginably high prices. It was clear the cheap easy capital that was driving asset prices would not last so, while everyone else was buying, Westfield entered a period of active selling. It had sixty-eight US malls and, in line with its new philosophy, sold fourteen over the next two years. Most were challenged or were in locations, such as the Midwest, that were oversupplied with malls. If Westfield could get a reasonable price for a challenged asset, it took it.

In this period it raised $8.3 billion through asset sales, joint ventures and the issue of equity. It raised long-term debt and issued common equity, including $3 billion through a rights issue in 2007. As it was spending so much on development, it needed this to maintain its credit rating.

With all this activity the leviathan had built itself into an extraordinarily strong and stable position. With paternal pleasure Frank looked at the factors that had achieved this. "My pride is heightened by my sons' initiatives," he said.

When, in late 2007 the GFC sent its first shudder through the market, Westfield stood firm. To the outside world it seemed the company had been extraordinarily prescient.

35

The ashtray

With Westfield now a giant in the international mall industry Frank was in London in 2004 looking for opportunities. He had been waiting for the White City portfolio to come back into play and he was in luck. Elliott Bernerd – with whom he had negotiated twice before over White City – was in a less fortunate position. Under pressure from shareholders he had delisted the company that held White City.

It was now in the hands of a new consortium that looked like a mini United Nations, with investors from the UK, Germany, Israel, Saudi Arabia, Hong Kong and Australia. As could be expected, all was not well within this new consortium. It had £1.6 billion in debt and its members were unable to agree on what to do with the various assets. When reports of its squabbling reached Frank's ears he began to plan.

On the face of it the consortium looked unassailable. Most

of its investors had pre-emptive rights and at first glance there seemed no crack through which an outsider could squeeze. Frank's enthusiasm to lead a raid on it was not shared by others in Westfield. The numbers didn't add up and they questioned the wisdom of entering an expensive battle in a foreign country for a prize of uncertain value.

Frank argued that numbers are only one part of the equation. The other is vision. "The numbers will turn positive because circumstances will be different," he said. While executives appreciated his far-sightedness they fought him, saying this battle was likely lost before it began. Frank often defers but this time they couldn't shift him. This was Westfield's big chance to stake a claim in the heartland of the UK and he passionately believed it could be done. While he couldn't exactly articulate what he envisaged everyone understood that his instinct, informed by half a century of experience, could not be discounted.

After spirited debate he prevailed and, as is characteristic of Westfield, once the decision had been made everyone fell in behind it and presented a united face to the world. While Frank drove the deal Steven took immediate control of the property side and Peter took charge of the financial and transactional side. Now that they and the other executives had agreed, they were converted to the cause and looking forward to a red-blooded raid.

Frank set up headquarters in a suite at Claridge's Hotel in London. From there Westfield surveyed the opposition. At the centre of the consortium sat the formidable Bombay-born brothers David and Simon Reuben, with a 35 per cent share. They had made their fortune through metal trading in Russia and although they had known Bernerd for decades, they had never worked with him before. There was a view that Bernerd, who still held 14 per cent, had mistakenly perceived the brothers as 'passive capital'. They were the antithesis of passive, focused on every issue from the hiring of butlers to the appointment of board members. It was said the brothers, who have a reputation for frugality, were out of sympathy with Elliott's flamboyant style of running the business and that they clashed on numerous fronts. The relationship quickly deteriorated and the word on the street was that litigation had been threatened. Little did Frank know that the Reuben brothers would later prove to be the toughest opponents of his career.

Once settled in Claridge's Frank called Beny Steinmetz, a billionaire diamond, mining and property magnate he knew from Israel. Beny held a 5 per cent share of the consortium. They talked and Beny agreed to support Westfield's initiative. "All that remains now is for us to get support from the other 95 per cent," a smiling Frank told his executives.

His next call was to John Roberts, the Australian founder of Multiplex, which held a 7 per cent share. Roberts came along to Claridge's for lunch and after a long discussion drawing on their common background Frank came to the point. Roberts, who had the contract to build White City, admitted he was disturbed by the tensions in the consortium and suggested he wouldn't mind getting out as long as he could keep the building contract. Frank was ready with a proposal. What if they combined forces and took on some of the assets together? Multiplex would build while Westfield looked after all the commercial aspects of projects. As Multiplex would have a secure construction pipeline it would not need to hold a share. For Roberts this was attractive because it meant retaining the building contracts, his core business. He left in good spirits, promising to get back to Frank.

Things were looking hopeful. When Frank saw Bernerd a day later he got the feeling that he would probably support Westfield too. The sum was easy: $5 + 7 + 14 = 26$ per cent. Westfield was on its way.

But in the meantime Roberts changed his mind. It was rumoured that he had spoken to his sons, who suggested that Multiplex didn't need Westfield. Without informing Frank, Roberts pressed on alone, and according to the press put in a bid rumoured at £485 million for all the consortium's assets. Then he upped it to a rumoured £515 million.

Soon it became evident that the Reuben brothers had quietly joined forces with Roberts, delivering them a combined holding of 42 per cent to support the bid, which they thought was a controlling stake. However, Westfield had been through the documentation word by word and found that because of a technicality the consortium had hybrid status and was still in part a public company. This status obliged it to abide by rules regarding takeover provisions. Once Multiplex had made a bid, the pre-emptive rights of the other consortium members fell away and the door was ajar for an outsider to come in. By making the bid, Multiplex had effectively let Westfield in.

In September 2004 London's *Telegraph* reported that the £515 million offer had been rejected and there was an expectation that a higher offer would be made by Westfield. The expectation was fulfilled: without the promise of majority support, Westfield countered with a tactical bid of £585 million. It was doing this to flush out the other side and see where it stood. As Peter Allen explained, "We wanted to see if they would split or work as one. We knew they were not going to accept our bid because some of the parties were very keen to keep the assets and grow them. We were forcing the issue – trying to find a place for ourselves."

Frank could see the prize and was not going to be deterred. As Allen observed, "Frank doesn't care about what others are doing, he just cares about Westfield being successful. He won't fail. This doesn't mean he will win, it means if he sees he won't triumph, he'll walk away."

By now the troubled consortium had become so dysfunctional that Rothschild was called in to facilitate its sale. It had to deal with two potential buyers. From the inside the Reubens and Multiplex wanted it, and from the outside Westfield wanted it.

Rothschild's job was to maintain a level playing field. Importantly, it had to guard against the insiders using their position as major shareholders to block a deal from the outsiders, and then securing the assets for themselves at a lower price.

Robert Leitão from Rothschild suggested the parties join forces, buy the assets together and divide them. By now the consortium's debt stood at £2.1 billion. After much consultation, Westfield was good for £1.2 billion while the Reubens and Multiplex would be good for the remainder. This would result in a new company comprised of Westfield, Multiplex and the Reubens.

Experience told Frank that threesomes are hazardous, and he sensed trouble brewing. Two could gang up and leave the other in the cold. He insisted that the other two should act with one voice. They agreed and formed a new entity called R&M. As Multiplex could 'speak Australian' it became the representative of R&M.

The younger generation led the negotiations. John Roberts' son Andrew led the R&M team, while Peter Lowy and Peter Allen led Westfield's team. Over three gruelling days and nights they hammered out an agreement that would allow them to buy the assets as one parcel and immediately split it synthetically. The actual breakup of the assets would take place over the next twelve months, when open issues such as accounting and tax would be dealt with.

From this exercise, Allen learned more about Frank's strategy.

He removes himself from the day-to-day and focuses on the
endgame. This means he is never overwhelmed with issues
that people on the ground face. It is as if he is standing on
a hill watching the battle below. For the troops this can
be a source of frustration because he doesn't appear to
understand what they have to go through. Even though he's
on the hill, you feel him firmly behind you in the endgame.
He has an edge in that he thinks things are possible, where
others walk away. His expectations are unrealistic but
realisable.

The synthetic split, so convenient at the time, was to become
a source of interminable negotiation. It uncovered significant
differences in interpretation and the matters would take five
years to settle. Westfield nicknamed this process 'project flake'
and when it was finally settled, Peter Lowy was presented with a
giant two-metre model of a Cadbury's Flake chocolate bar.

In the carve-up of assets, some were assigned in total and
some were shared. Westfield acquired three shopping centres on
its own and shared two other assets with R&M. One of these
was the jewel, White City. But the consortium had only owned
50 per cent of White City and this share was now split to give
Westfield and R&M 25 per cent each.

The parties also got an equal stake in a mixed development
site in East London called Stratford City. Westfield's 25 per cent,
which was assigned to it almost as an afterthought, would come
to represent the major windfall of the deal.

Once the deal had been announced Westfield was dubbed the
new Wizard of Oz, having taken the prime position from the

other big Australians Lend Lease and Multiplex. Indeed, a couple of weeks later, the UK magazine *Property Week* euphorically described Frank as "without question, the most successful person" the publication had ever interviewed. However, it noted that eyebrows had been raised at the price: 45 per cent more than Bernerd's management buyout team had paid six months earlier.

Used to such criticism, Lowy dismissed it: "People can say what they like. So what? We believe we have paid [for] value. I am very excited about the opportunity." Suddenly there was a buzz about Westfield and even the big legal firms from the so-called magic circle – the leading law firms headquartered in the UK – began offering their services. Five years earlier Westfield hadn't been able to get them to return a call; now their partners were asking to have lunch.

Once Westfield got inside White City things didn't look so good. By Westfield standards the development plan and design were poor, and it wanted to make major changes. But its proposals were blocked and no matter how much it explained them, it could make no headway. In the initial negotiations it had been agreed that Westfield would be the development manager and the centre manager, while Multiplex would be builder. But any Westfield proposals to fix the project had to be approved by R&M. Now, this approval was not forthcoming. Westfield was being blocked.

As it happened the other half of White City was held, as 'passive capital' by the German finance company Commerz Grundbesitz Investment (CGI). Frank figured it could be the kingmaker in this dispute and instructed his executives to cuddle up to it on the quiet. For weeks they wooed CGI, displaying Westfield's past successes and detailing their proposed changes to the plans.

In the meantime Multiplex was already building White City according to the existing plans. The old design was becoming more expensive to correct. Rather than waiting for all this to reach its unsatisfactory conclusion, Frank took action. He engineered a crisis. In private CGI was told that the project was reaching a tipping point beyond which it would become uncommercial to reverse. The present activity had to be halted immediately and new plans implemented.

Then Frank scheduled a meeting with Simon Reuben. His aim was to persuade Simon to allow Westfield to take full charge of the development – which would be good for everyone – or to sell it. Simon arrived alone at the Berkeley Hotel, where Frank was then staying. It was mid morning and he found Frank ensconced in the living room of his suite with two Westfield executives, Michael Gutman who headed the business in the UK and Elliott Rusanow, UK head of finance.

After cordial greetings the men settled in around a coffee table on which was a large and heavy crystal ashtray. Frank opened by establishing their common ground and explaining where they diverged. As he saw it, R&M thought of White City as a short-term financial transaction while Westfield considered it a long-term business. Simon wasn't buying, so Frank restated his position in bald terms: "What do you really want to do? As you don't have the expertise to build a shopping centre and we do, why don't you take your capital profit now and we'll pay you for it? Or if you want to stay on, stay by all means but remove the shackles that are preventing us from building and implementing the changes ..."

Simon interjected. "But we *do* have the expertise! We can do it ourselves!" Still reasonably affable, Frank explained that Westfield had fifty people in the UK focused on shopping centres as well as thriving businesses in the US and Australia, while the Reuben brothers had a mere handful of people in their office and Multiplex was facing major problems of its own. There was no comparison. "Let's agree where the expertise lies and then the natural solution will emerge," he said. But whatever he said, Simon insisted their expertise was equal. After three or four rounds of this Frank became flustered. He had never been in such a negotiation – Simon was steadfastly unyielding.

An argument then ensued about a side issue and Simon protested he was unfairly outnumbered in the room. He became stroppy, and so did Frank. They were stuck and the temperature was rising. It was unpleasant but Frank got them back onto the main issue. Pushed to the limit of self-control and exasperation, he begged: "Simon, please listen to me, just listen."

Simon wouldn't. In a climax of frustration, Frank lifted the Baccarat style ashtray above his head and crashed it down on the coffee table. There was stunned silence. Simon blanched. Then he sprang to his feet and fled.

Frank looked at the other two. "Go after him! Bring him back!" they said. Frank ran into the corridor and called out. Simon took one look back over his shoulder and ran down the fire escape. Frank took the carpeted stairs but by the time he reached the lobby Simon was gone. That was the last time they met. Sometime later Frank tried to restore civil relations but was unsuccessful. After their next obligatory transaction, the relationship froze over permanently.

When the Westfield team analysed the 'ashtray meeting', they took the view that Simon's intransigence meant that the brothers really wanted to be paid out, but were holding out for a big sum. It was all about price. Multiplex, with its own troubles, had good reason to exit, but couldn't afford to go cheaply.

Suddenly it seemed likely that Westfield could have half of White City to itself and with CGI's blessing, could have its own design, its own brand, its own management. It could be run in accordance with its own style. To this end, Rothschild was re-employed and Leitão was back. He was the only person they knew who could get through to Simon.

By now some eight years had passed since Frank first tried to get a piece of White City, and he was fed up with waiting. "It could take whatever I had, it could take all my power, but I was determined. I might change course in the middle and I might walk away but I wouldn't lose. This prize was too big," he said.

Leitão buzzed backwards and forwards between the parties and in May 2005 M&R finally blinked. Together, Multiplex and the Reubens were willing to accept £65 million for their 25 per cent stake in White City. The markets were so high and money was so easily available that the number didn't seem so big to the merged Westfield, now a year old.

On the same day that this agreement was signed Westfield signed another with CGI giving Westfield permission to redesign, redevelop, brand and manage White City. Leitão, who oversaw the negotiations, was impressed with Frank's resolve: "The only way this centre was going to get developed was if Westfield took complete control of the site."

By now, Steven Lowy had taken control of implementing the project and together with Michael Gutman began to review its construction. Multiplex still held the building contract and when the pair saw how it was unfolding they concluded things had to change. They left the site and went directly into a meeting with Frank, Peter Lowy and Peter Allen. "Unless we get control, this project will never be finished and we will never be able to afford it. We have to buy the construction," Steven said. That was a key decision, giving Westfield the impetus to take charge of this last piece of the project.

Peter Allen was given the job of relieving Multiplex of the contract. It had had big problems in the UK and Frank wanted it taken to the brink. Allen remembers holding it up until the last minute to extract the best price.

> Multiplex was wounded and was trying to work out what it should leave in the UK. We were managing them very closely on the corporate side, trying to get them off the building contract. The night before Andrew Roberts [son of John] had to deliver his results in Australia we agreed around three or four in the morning to buy out the contract. This enabled Roberts to announce that Multiplex was out of White City and had not made a loss.

Frank had his prize. White City would be modelled on Westfield's Sydney flagship Bondi Junction and was scheduled to open in three years. It would be up to Steven and Michael to deliver and they knew they had to build something beyond expectations because this centre was three miles from Marble Arch and had a wealthy trade area. "It was close to one of the most important retail precincts on the planet, the West End of London with Harrods, Selfridges, Harvey Nichols, Oxford Street and Bond Street. We needed to create something out of the ordinary, something competitive and very different from the traditional high streets," says Steven. "There were many detractors with people saying Londoners didn't like US-style shopping and wouldn't shop in malls. We needed to put something in place that would knock their socks off."

36

Olympic gold

In 2004 Westfield acquired a small asset it wasn't particularly enthusiastic about. It involved a piece of vacant land on the east side of London on which a mini-city was slated to be built over the next twenty to twenty-five years. There was no infrastructure in place and for Westfield, which traditionally completed its developments in five to ten years, this timetable was not attractive.

Westfield had acquired a share in the development rights for this site during the carve-up of Elliott Bernerd's property portfolio. As these rights had been shared equally among four parties Westfield found itself in a new consortium with four equal partners. It didn't know much about the site and estimated its share to be worth £5 million. The site was in Stratford, close to the area earmarked for the 2012 Olympic Games should London win its bid to host them. It was generally believed, however, that the city had little or no chance of this.

The land was government owned but London and Continental Railways, LCR, had taken control of it in the mid 1990s, intending to build a new international station linking London to Europe. Around this station it planned to create Stratford City, a £3 billion (later £4 billion) mini-city with residential, commercial and retail components. Westfield planned to confine its interest to the retail precinct.

But in July 2005 London took the world by surprise. It outdid Moscow, Madrid, New York and Paris to win the right to host the Olympic Games. Its celebrations, however, were short-lived. Less than twenty-four hours later the city went into lockdown. Three suicide bombings in the Underground were followed by an explosion on a bus. Any euphoria Londoners might have felt swiftly dissipated.

When Westfield's London office shook itself back to life it began to absorb the Olympic decision. The land was not only adjacent to the Olympic site but slightly overlapped it. It was a toehold but in Frank's forward-thinking mind it was already a substantially developed part of the Olympic site and flying a Westfield flag.

The land suddenly had huge political significance and with the Games seven years away its development was a national priority. Frank's blood was up. That he was seventy-four was irrelevant. Although he felt his years on the tennis court, in business he felt ageless. Those on the receiving end of his relentless attention understood that time had not tempered his drive. Indeed, with Michael Gutman in London as lead negotiator for the Olympic site Frank was constantly on the phone. He was there last thing at night and first thing in the morning; Gutman's wife, Karen, eventually remarked that her husband "goes to bed with Frank Lowy every night and wakes up with him" – a sentiment shared, at one time or another, by most of the wives of senior Westfield executives.

But any sense of urgency Westfield was feeling contrasted starkly with the inertia of the consortium of which it was part. Nothing had happened for the past six months because there was no clarity among the new partners about who was responsible for what. Westfield's new partners were Multiplex, the Reuben brothers and the development firm Stanhope. Rather than paying for its share, Stanhope had originally received it in exchange for sweat equity. This was a flashpoint in the new consortium. The Reuben brothers wanted Stanhope to put in money too. When Stanhope couldn't or wouldn't the brothers turned off the tap. As Stanhope was not being paid, it would not continue working.

The group was stuck, and it couldn't afford to be. If it wasn't functional and solvent it could risk losing its development rights. Frank came up with a temporary solution using loans and pulled in senior Westfield executives to create a structure to keep the consortium functioning. It was already clear that the four of them could not complete an Olympic-class development on time.

Frank, of course, wanted sole control. He already knew he couldn't work with the Reuben brothers. Elusive and deeply private, they are said to work brilliantly together, with David as trader and Simon as investor. Little is known of them publicly but they reportedly finish each other's sentences and in business have a reputation for never having overpaid for anything. As they had 'allowed' Westfield to take White City, there was an unexpressed expectation that as a quid pro quo Westfield should now allow them to take Stratford City. There was no chance of that.

When business in London closed for the traditional August break in 2005 the partners took a welcome break. From his boat in the Mediterranean Frank continued his holiday routine, remaining in his study in the morning and joining guests on deck in the afternoon, breaking occasionally to take a call. *Ilona* has a fully equipped office with teleconferencing and a professional assistant, so when business calls Frank is always available.

During that holiday he spent many hours figuring out how to create an 'event' where all the major elements of Stratford could be dealt with once and for all. He had created a crisis over White City that had brought things to a head, and he thought the same strategy might work here. It could be a funding crisis, which was almost upon them anyway, but it would have to be handled delicately because of the risk of the consortium breaching its obligations and losing everything.

It was also important for Westfield to restrain its enthusiasm. It was rearing to go but the more effort it put in, the more value it would create and the more it would have to pay to buy out its partners. Frank guessed there was a good chance the Reuben brothers would not be there for the long haul and if Westfield used its expertise now it would be scoring an own goal. At the same time the Reuben brothers could be expected to hold out because the value of the site was going up every day.

While on holiday the consortium partners learned of a new threat. Government agencies were exploring the option of using a compulsory purchase order to obtain the site. When the partners reassembled in September, despite this threat they still couldn't agree on how to proceed. Frank called in his 'special forces' to prepare a crisis. Meanwhile he remained on the case, questioning what money was being spent and suggesting where and when to go slow. Peter Allen observed Frank in action:

His strength is that he knows what he wants at the endgame. He can visualise the three-dimensional pieces

and what has to happen to get to that endgame. There is
a lot of debate about how to mould the pieces and there
is a lot of hurry to get it done, but not much haste. He deals
with each party, builds a relationship, demonstrates what
he can do for them, articulates what they can do for him
and exerts pressure so the right decision is made.

That same month Frank went to see Ken Livingstone, the mayor
of London and an important player in this game, and laid out
his credentials. He explained that Westfield could develop the
shopping centre and some areas around it but had no aspirations
concerning the residential and other components of the Olympic
village. Lowy provided a history that demonstrated his company's
capabilities and came away feeling he had given it his best shot.
"I think I impressed him with my straightforward approach, my
record and my clarity about the limits of what Westfield could
do. From then on we got on well. He was committed and we
were committed, and that created a relationship."

When there was still no progress Livingstone worried
that the project could be derailed and intensified the threat to
intervene. If the consortium couldn't settle agreements with
the government he would carry out a compulsory purchase
order. As the consortium couldn't agree on anything within
itself, the prospect of agreeing with government seemed beyond
reach. Frank couldn't remember ever having been in such a
dysfunctional organisation. Weeks passed without progress.

Finally, by November, Frank managed to wring some
consensus out of the consortium, but he was not sure it would
hold. It was given a deadline to reach a resolution, losing its rights
if the target date were missed. While externally things appeared
settled, internally the consortium was a mess. Multiplex and

Stanhope were not strong enough to assert themselves and Westfield and the Reubens had their horns locked.

At this point Peter Lowy decided to recall Robert Leitão who, through his previous involvement at White City, had good relationships all round. This time things were tougher and Leitão found it highly stressful trying to mediate between two parties, each adamant to buy and refusing to sell. He tried various permutations but whichever way he sliced the asset, he made no progress: "The only way out was a shootout! The tactic was to propose a set of rules where partners would bid against each other, where the higher bidder would win and would be compelled to buy out the lower bidder."

By now the government was anxious and worked with Leitão. Once the grounds for the 'shootout' were settled all parties would commit to agree to a set of rules and sign a piece of paper formalising their agreement so that twenty-four hours later there could be a resolution. But as Leitão explains, it wasn't that simple.

> There was a view the Reuben brothers' negotiating tactic was to purport to be buyers when they were really sellers and that way to push the price up.
>
> Officials at all levels of government were keen not to be seen to be taking sides or making value judgments as to who would be the better developer, but behind the scenes there were concerns that the Reuben brothers were not really developers, certainly not on the scale of Westfield.
>
> There was a view that if the Reubens took control of the site there would be a degree of execution risk and the chance the site would not be developed to the standard expected for the Olympic gateway.

While the parties needed a shootout because they couldn't agree, things were so bad they couldn't even agree on its terms. More than a hundred hours were spent on its finer details and the sniping between Frank and Simon Reuben became vicious. Although Frank's age made him a more measured negotiator, it also made him more aggressive and in Simon Reuben he had met his match. "Simon was the most unreasonable business opponent I have ever had!" he said. Fortunately, Peter Lowy provided a buffer by handling much of the planning.

Public authorities remained scrupulously neutral about the hostilities until early 2006, when Ken Livingstone broke ranks. When asked about this dispute he replied he wasn't sure how serious the Reubens were about staying with the project. Then, to everyone's surprise, he praised Westfield.

This caused a furore but Livingstone wasn't finished. A few days later he openly attacked the Reuben brothers, implying they were destabilising the consortium and even suggesting they "go back and see if they can do better under the ayatollahs". When asked to clarify where they should go, he said, "To Iran, if they don't like the planning regime or my approach." The brothers are not Iranian. They were born in India of Iraqi Jewish parents. They were raised in the UK and are philanthropists of note.

Understandably furious, they responded by saying the mayor's comments were "totally inaccurate" and that they remained completely committed to Stratford City. When asked to apologise Livingstone deepened the insult by saying: "I would offer a complete apology to the people of Iran for the suggestion that they may be linked in any way to the Reuben brothers." The press went to town, with the *Times* thundering that Ken Livingstone was a fool.

Frank was in full battle mode. "I could taste the potential and I disregarded all this as noise. Shopping centres are in our blood, this was an opportunity not to be repeated. In spite of the difficulties I felt we would win, but we would have to pay dearly for it." Westfield consulted with LCR and the Olympic Authority, who consistently favoured neither side. But Frank did get the sense they would prefer Westfield to develop the shopping centre part of the site. "A hallmark of our policy is to get on with authorities at all levels of government, across all parties. We state the facts of what we can do and where we can add value, without exaggeration. I think our directness and determination get us ahead," said Frank.

By Easter 2006 there was still no progress. Then Multiplex signalled that it was in dire straits. It had been in trouble for some time over the construction of Wembley Stadium and was about to breach its lending covenants again. It appeared it would complete the stadium eight months behind schedule at a loss of £200 million. Its chances of surviving as a construction candidate for Stratford were now remote.

The authorities took action. They set 28 April 2006 as the deadline for an auction to resolve the conflict. When the day came and went with no shootout a law firm was instructed to terminate the consortium's development rights. But the notice stipulated a remedial period of six weeks, which allowed the parties one last chance. The Reuben brothers immediately declared themselves ready and willing for the shootout. Frank held his ground, keeping such a tight grip it was exhausting for his executives, even for Gutman who is twenty-five years his junior. As he explains:

During intense periods, Frank's tenacity is unbelievable and his energy levels are remarkable. There is no way I could keep up with him. At the height, when the Reubens were driving us mad and we were trying to find a way to separate, Frank would be there like a machine until it was done. He just attacked the issue until it was nailed. It was hugely challenging because the brothers are used to being in a commanding position and using that position to extract high margins and penalty rates. In Frank they came across someone who wasn't going to lie down.

David Higgins, chief executive of the Olympic Delivery Authority, would later describe negotiations with the consortium as exhausting and note that Frank was critical in gaining agreement. He was in there "with his sleeves rolled up". From his earlier days as CEO of Lend Lease Higgins knew Westfield and had dined with Frank. He also knew Michael Gutman who had once worked for Lend Lease.

At this point Higgins thought the dispute would never resolve and steadfastly maintained a neutral line: "We couldn't play favourites or try and manipulate the process. It was Russian roulette. Both parties wanted to do it, both had loads of money and both wanted to buy each other out at roughly the same price."

37

Changing tactics

In May 2006 Lowy's boat was spotted sailing up the Thames. It was there as Frank's base for the Stratford negotiations and for the World Cup, which was to be held in Germany the following month. He was spending an inordinate amount of time in London and, despite trying a different hotel every time he couldn't get comfortable. Being on the boat was like being at home. He knew the crew, the surrounds were familiar and the main cabin had the same bed and bed linen as in his home in Sydney. He had planned to moor the boat somewhere along the Thames and slip into London unnoticed.

The river, however, is tidal and due to its size his boat could be safely moored only at Canary Wharf, in full view of all the lawyers and bankers who work there. Westfield executives in the London office received a running commentary about the goings-on at the wharf. When *Ilona* docked the Westfield office was flooded with text messages and telephone calls. 'Is this Lowy's boat?' 'Is Frank in town?' 'Who is that on deck?' There were ongoing accounts of life on *Ilona* and when the aft deck opened and a helicopter rose to the surface there were more astonished calls describing it taking off. When it returned, landed on deck and Frank stepped out, the phones went crazy. Frank was unaware he was being watched.

By now, Leitão had agreement on some terms for the shootout. The parties would enter a room where each would write their price on a piece of paper. Frank wanted both parties to write their price simultaneously; the brothers wanted Westfield to go first and then they would decide. Frank argued this was ridiculous and would change the exercise from a shootout to a pre-emption. Then he realised their suggestion unmasked their real intention. They were traders, not long-term investors. Far from wanting to buy out Westfield, he deduced they clearly wanted Westfield to buy them out – otherwise they would have put their money where their mouth was.

Where earlier in the year the consortium's development rights had been growing in value every day, now they were diminishing as the deadline approached and it stood to lose everything. With the death knell a couple of weeks away Westfield tried to console itself that it had initially valued its share at £5 million.

During conflict Frank shows no weakness. Nor will he allow anyone in his team to flinch. If there is a suggestion they might, he is at their side, holding them up and urging them to stand firm. In personal matters Lowy is known to show vulnerability, but in business, never.

Time was running out and Frank changed tactic. He surprised everyone by announcing he wanted to sell. He didn't really want to, but thought this might jerk the deadlock open.

Rather than stating a price he waited for the opposition to put one on the table. Had he received a very high price, he would have considered it, but nothing happened. There was no offer.

So he changed his mind and announced he was no longer interested in selling. "I think this tactic unnerved them," said Frank, privately predicting the brothers would not show up to the shootout. He was right. To everyone's complete surprise, with a week to go the brothers blinked. They wanted to sell.

The consortium's life was due to expire at midnight on 12 June 2006 and negotiations were stretched to the last minute, with the Reubens extracting an enormous price. Westfield paid £110 million for the 50 per cent held by the Reubens and Multiplex. It paid Stanhope £32 million for its share. With its initial £5 million valuation of its share, its total outlay for the site was £147 million. This was a large payment, but the economy was booming and optimism was high. Characteristically, Lowy was buying potential. "It's just a matter of seeing more than others do," he said.

On the morning of 13 June Westfield announced it had taken full control of the Stratford City development. The site had planning approval for 13 million square feet of mixed-use development, including 2 million square feet of retail.

For Leitão, Stratford was all about Frank:

He was highly visible in this deal. Frank is of a type, a very decent man but it is his resolve that strikes me. It's quite remarkable. So is his vision. It was never a question of whether he was paying the right price for the assets today but whether this was an opportunity to get assets that can't often be bought. When you reflect on the overall economics of the site, Westfield bought out the other partners for quite a lot of money. This wasn't in the financing plan and was a relatively brave thing to do.

A week after the deal was finalised the Greater London Authority published a report of its investigation into Livingstone's conduct in relation to the Reuben brothers. It concluded Livingstone had not used his position improperly. His intention had been to send a clear message that the public authorities would act robustly, in accordance with their legal rights, to secure the achievement of the Games and the redevelopment of Stratford.

Some say Livingstone's outbursts played a role in the brothers' decision to sell. Although they extracted a king's ransom, they did very much want to be involved in the Olympics and were disappointed at having lost the opportunity.

Once he had secured the prize Frank turned to repairing relationships and called David Reuben. He asked if he could come over. David reluctantly agreed. "I went to his offices hoping to restore cordial relations," says Frank. "I tried to say it was business, it was nothing personal and wasn't World War III, but he wasn't swayed. That's how it remains."

When the next mayoral elections were held in May 2008 Livingstone lost office to his arch-rival, the conservative Boris Johnson. Once Johnson was installed Frank made an appointment to see him and again laid out his wares. This time he could show how well Westfield had served London. It had created 10,000 jobs at White City, which was only months from opening and would create a further 20,000 at Stratford.

Westfield's policy of dealing with authorities had served him well with Livingstone and it served him with Johnson. With age, Lowy had become easy in all company. His white hair and success gave him a natural authority and as Gutman observed, he could sit down at a table with powerful people and say things others would choke over: "Of course, there are some things only the chairman can ask and get away with, but he's prepared to ask. He's candid and upfront about what Westfield can achieve."

Westfield had assembled one of the pre-eminent portfolios in the UK in eight years. It had taken decades to do the same in the US and Australia. Were the situation reversed, and had a UK company attempted to push into Sydney, Westfield would have resisted it gaining that kind of market share.

In the end Westfield kept a little less than one-third of the Olympic site. Well before a series of thirty complex agreements covering the site could be negotiated and signed, Frank agreed to start building the shopping centre. This was an act of faith as Westfield didn't yet hold the freehold. Although it did have a safety net of a licensing agreement, Higgins regarded this act as extraordinary.

> It's a remarkable commitment of the trust in the
> relationship that Westfield was prepared to invest hundreds
> of millions of pounds on the strength of the original
> agreements before it owned the freehold in its own name.
> It was unusual, but was well recognised and a few days
> before signing, I arranged for Frank and Steven to come to
> 10 Downing Street so the level of investment that Westfield
> was prepared to make was recognised. I remember waiting
> for the Lowys to arrive and Steven getting out of the car
> and saying, "You know the level of commitment we are
> making to this project is very unusual. We are relying a
> lot on the trust of the government to deliver what it has
> promised." I remember replying, "Well, that is why we are
> meeting the prime minister."

As he entered 10 Downing Street Frank was overawed, not because he was about to meet Gordon Brown but because the building for him was living history. Some sixty years earlier he had been in Budapest straining to hear Churchill's broadcasts; now he was walking into the very building that was synonymous with this great man. That morning he had taken a tour of the Churchill Cabinet war rooms, and his heart was full of the past: "I remembered hearing Churchill on the radio, and all the things we hoped for and expected from him. As I walked up the stairs past the portraits my head was swimming with the meaning of it all. And having my son Steven with me made it all the more significant." The officers ushering Frank Lowy into No 10 would just have seen an older man in a suit. But for a few heightened moments Lowy was a boy back in the Budapest ghetto.

Lowy predicted that Westfield London and Stratford would become the two highest-grossing malls in the United Kingdom. He could hardly wait another moment. After more than three decades, Westfield would finally be embedded in the commercial life of London, and he would have a place there.

38

After the GFC

When the global financial crisis first began to take hold in late 2007, Frank wasn't too perturbed. He'd been through many downturns before and this time Peter and Steven were at his side. They were in their forties, they knew the business inside out and together with him they would form a powerful arrowhead to try and take the company through the downturn, with the guidance of the board.

After the merger of 2004 Westfield's shares were trading at around $15. They kept rising and peaked at $23 in the lead-up to the GFC. It took time before anyone realised the depth of this crisis, that it would be the world's biggest financial shock since the Great Depression of 1930. In the beginning, it seemed no more than a property problem caused by the issuing of sub-prime mortgages, expensive loans to people with poor credit histories in the US. In mid 2007, the US housing market collapsed, banks found themselves with a liquidity crisis and credit was crunched.

Although debt markets were badly affected, initially the equity markets were not. There was a view, or rather a hope, that the crisis would remain confined to the US property sector. In October 2007, when Westfield opened its £340 million UK shopping centre in Derby, retail sales were still strong and the company was enthusiastically looking forward to opening the centre at White City in a year's time. But two months later, Australia woke to the reality of the crisis when the shopping centre company Centro hit the rocks. The real estate investment trust market was badly shaken.

Frank, who had been through innumerable slumps, now counted back on his fingers and realised that Westfield had survived four major downturns. Months after Westfield floated in 1960 it was hit by a severe credit squeeze. A recession in the building industry followed and the new company was saved only by the good relationships Frank and John had with their stockbroker. He underwrote an issue of debentures and when it was only 50 per cent subscribed, he wrote a cheque for the balance.

In the mid 1970s Westfield, like everyone else, took a knock over the oil shock. With oil prices quadrupling and inflation peaking in Australia at just over 20 per cent, bank bills hit 17 per cent and the short-term money market was paying up to 25 per cent for overnight cash. Westfield took its medicine on the short-term market and learned to stay away from it.

Then came the stock crash of 1987, and this hit Frank hardest. He had made some poor decisions and the message was clear. Rather than straying from core business he should have strengthened it. His foray into the fashionable media sector was disastrous and eventually he had to pay to have someone take his television network off his hands.

In the late 1990s Westfield was caught up in the Asian contagion that spread to real estate markets in the US and Australia. It had previously made a brief foray into Malaysia and pulled out. It learned not to expand into developing markets.

There was always pain but with each episode the company had emerged a little stronger. And after each event Westfield had conducted a postmortem to see what could be learned. Now Frank Lowy was ready to revisit these lessons.

By January 2008 the global economy was plainly in crisis, but geography was on Westfield's side. It operated in four countries that had different strengths and weaknesses. While the values of its UK properties fell, rental income in Australia grew strongly. As about 98 per cent of its income came from long-term leases, initially the company wasn't too concerned and Frank wasn't losing more sleep than usual:

> It didn't keep me awake at night but of course we were
> under pressure. If we hadn't merged the three entities they
> would have been far weaker on their own and might well
> have suffered damage. In my mind I saw us as a large heavy
> ship going through some very unfriendly waves. From time
> to time there would be a shudder, but we ploughed on. But
> I was anxious about the family's private wealth and about
> how low the level could drop. I worked closely with David
> to protect LFG's assets.

When Bear Stearns collapsed in the US in April 2008 the financial world looked on in disbelief. When Lehman Brothers – with $600 billion in assets – filed for Chapter 11 bankruptcy protection in September 2008, the global financial system convulsed. This was and remains the largest bankruptcy filing in US history.

It was against this background that a month later Frank's prized Westfield London shopping centre had to open. The centre, which had been leased in bright times, would be opening as economic gloom settled on London. There was no option. Westfield was locked in. Some 99 per cent of the shops had been leased, hundreds of people had been employed and the machinery of the centre was geared up and ready for the button to be pushed. Unaware of these logistics, many expressed astonishment that in such a severe downturn a £1.6 billion mall was preparing to open for trading.

Just before it opened the *Evening Standard* newspaper exhorted its readers in West London to take a last look around: 'Only a week to go now until you are hit by the retail equivalent of the neutron bomb, leaving your area physically intact but destroying all organic shopping life within a five-mile radius.'

On the morning of the official opening observant shoppers could have glimpsed four Lowy men standing to one side with red remembrance poppies on their lapels. With his perfectly cut dark suit, his silver tie and white hair Frank looked a picture of prosperity. None of his inner concerns were evident. It was a week since his seventy-eighth birthday and although he was feeling his age, his old ability to compartmentalise issues was still strong. His son Peter had just come through the fire of a US Senate tax investigation and now, sealed tightly in one compartment of his brain, was disquiet about a tax investigation underway in Australia. For Frank celebrations are rarely free of concerns. There is always something that needs attention. But when the mayor of London, Boris Johnson, swept in with his entourage, Frank stepped forward, full of charm, to greet him.

Westfield London opened to acclaim. Some described it as the only bright spot in the British Isles, an act of faith in the future. It was built on a mesmerising scale, with vast curves of glass and light and Londoners were irresistibly drawn to it. One commentator said it wasn't a shopping centre, it was a new planet glowing in the gloom. It offered novelty and adventure to the crowds surging out of four adjoining stations and teeming over its forty-three acres of shops, restaurants and other facilities. Others came by bus or, in a new experience for Londoners, drove conveniently into one of the centre's 4500 parking spaces. It drizzled all day, but the press said London had been taken by storm. The new Westfield was front-page news. Despite the inevitable critics, the consensus was that Westfield London was a five-star destination, not just for retail but for recreation too.

Frank called it a groundbreaking mall for the company. By building in the centre of London, in the midst of dense population and high activity, the company saw what an impact could be made. But although Westfield London outdid expectations and began to change Westfield's exposure to the world, the financial crisis couldn't be escaped.

Values had changed. That Westfield had an A credit rating meant nothing. How was it going to refinance? "In a normal world we were not over-leveraged – in fact, we were quite modestly leveraged – but now there were no markets for a bond issue, and the banks, under pressure too, were difficult to negotiate with," says Stephen Johns. "This was a new experience for everyone at Westfield. When we looked around, we saw other perfectly good companies staring at the reality that there was no market for refinancing or getting new debt." The only option was equity raisings and fortunately, the Australian investment market was liquid enough to take them up. Many top companies raised equity at bargain prices.

During the crash Westfield's stock price hit a low of $8.80. "Normally, when the share price drops in the Westfield Group it doesn't change anything because the balance sheet is what it is and assets don't drop. But now all the asset values were impaired and we didn't want to be an unwilling seller of any of them," says Johns.

The accounting standards required asset valuations and revaluations to go through the profit and loss account. "In good days when you have massive increases in valuations everyone ignores it because it's not a real profit, it's a book profit. Now it was going the other way and suddenly we had billions of dollars of asset devaluations. There were headlines about the Westfield Group losing billions. Red ink was everywhere. It affected our balance sheet ratios and how the credit rating agencies looked at us. We needed to have more equity and in 2009, during the peak of the GFC we did raise equity at $10.50 a share," says Johns. The shares were readily taken up.

By now Westfield had curtailed all major new developments and begun to conserve its cash. In early 2009 Steven Lowy and Michael Gutman analysed the Stratford project and concluded that in this environment they would have difficulty leasing it. "We came home and told Dad we believed we should slow the development and push out the opening by six months, otherwise we would have to open with big vacancies," said Steven. Although the delay cost £50 million it proved to be a wise move. The expense was largely offset by lower costs due to the slowdown in London's construction industry and the delay would allow Westfield to lease the building in an improving environment.

There was a view that the Australian economy was more insulated than other countries during the GFC and did not suffer as much. By world standards Australia, with its good prudential practice, two government stimulus packages, a responsive Reserve Bank and a resources boom, did manage relatively well.

By the end of 2009 the GFC was more or less over and Westfield emerged in good shape. Having delayed new developments, it had an $8 billion line of credit and was ready for the opportunities that would inevitably arise in the wake of so much financial distress. Peter Lowy was again thinking about how the company's capital structure could be modified to best benefit from what lay ahead.

It seemed 2010 would be a celebratory year. It was the year Westfield turned fifty and Frank turned eighty. It was also the year the BRW Rich List, for the first time, declared Frank the wealthiest man in the country. Worth $5.04 billion, he sat atop one of the world's largest listed retail property groups. At the 2010 AGM he stood for re-election to the board for another three years and such was his confidence that from the podium, rather than engaging in the usual battle with shareholder activists, he enjoyed himself.

When the meeting was open to questions, first to his feet was the journalist and self-described shareholder activist Stephen Mayne, who congratulated Lowy on reaching the top of the Rich List and cheekily asked what took him so long. Mayne then noted that Frank, Peter and Steven Lowy took home a combined annual pay packet of $31 million, of which $15 million went to Frank. He calculated this was $40,000 a day and suggested it might be time for Frank to follow the lead of the Packers and begin working for nothing, or at least for much less.

Frank reminded Mayne that he made this same observation year in and year out. Why, he asked, should anyone lump the three Lowys together? They didn't live together. On his own salary he was clear. "I don't work for nothing. I know I can afford it, but I believe I'm entitled to get paid. And just on the sideline, I don't keep that money that I get paid from the company. I give it away, and a lot more, to deserving causes. I don't believe that the Westfield shareholder is a deserving cause." Then having seemingly enjoyed the encounter he thanked Mayne and said he hoped to see him the following year. "You keep me on my toes!" he said.

A few months earlier Westfield had surprised the market by raising a $2 billion debt issue in the US, demonstrating support for the company by the global capital markets. But it also began to recognise a tension in the way it worked on four continents. While this had advantages there was an investment disincentive. Lately the UK and the US had been underperforming. Why should those who wanted to invest in Australia, which had been doing well, have simultaneously to invest in another country that was doing less well? The group was also working in four currencies and the complexities of this made some investors uncomfortable.

These ideas were motivating Peter to think about ways of lightening the company's capital structure. He believed it was time to split the Westfield Group's Australian assets in two, arguing that this would better serve stakeholders by allowing them to choose how much they wanted to invest in Australia relative to other markets.

But should they split? Experts were brought in and the debate went back and forth. Elliott Rusanow, always a close observer of his uncle, watched how Frank dealt with the noisy meetings.

"People are throwing advice at him, but he's able to silence the noise and see the order things need to be addressed in. He sorts through the mess, picks up things very quickly and at the end of the meeting, breaks them down to three or four points to move forward."

The idea was to return to a model reminiscent of the one that had generated so much growth in Australia in the past. That model involved a holdings company that managed properties held in a separate trust. The plan was to spin off a trust to be known as Westfield Retail Trust, which would hold half the Australian and New Zealand assets. The Westfield Group would keep the other half and all the overseas assets. It would be responsible for all management and development too. What started as an idea in early 2010 became a reality by the end of the year, when the company's Australian properties were split.

The newly created Westfield Retail Trust, WRT, with $12 billion in assets and little foreign exchange risk, had no exposure to other economies around the world. At the same time the Westfield Group was better placed to invest in larger projects, including the new World Trade Center, and to expand into Brazil and Italy. In previous decades it had explored expanding into Japan, India, China, Russia and Turkey but for various reasons had decided not to proceed.

The press, the public and the shareholders were thoroughly confused. To some it looked as if Frank was trying to unscramble the egg. Why was he partially undoing the great merger of 2004? Frank went on television to explain that the structure had been a good one but it had served its purpose. Conditions had changed and a different capital structure was needed.

The new structure would allow the company to grow just as it did before, but with less capital, which should have the effect of increasing the shareholder return. "We are looking at capital management very seriously all the time," Frank told ABC TV's *Lateline* program. "What makes this company successful is not just the property and development business. It is the capital management."

In the end this restructure didn't deliver what had been hoped for. WRT performed in line with its peers but below expectations, and it continued to trade at a big discount to its net asset backing. Local investors couldn't grasp why some domestic assets were held by WRT and some by the Westfield Group.

International investors were not charmed either. They were deterred by the weight of the Australian holding. Sitting in New York or London, investors were unlikely to spend much time thinking about Australia. If they wanted to buy good US or European retail assets they might look at Westfield and think that for every pound of European retail they bought they would have to take a dollar of Australian retail. Australia is on a different cycle, and they may know little about it and its currency.

It seemed the Australian side of the business was pulling down Westfield Group's valuation overseas, and the overseas business was pulling its share price down in Australia. This imbalance needed to be corrected. The Australian assets had to be better valued at home, just as the international assets had to be better valued abroad.

When Frank looked across at the US he saw Westfield's peers selling at much higher multiples. Although Westfield had a recognisable brand it had no identity as an American company. It was seen as Australian and that didn't fit with what a proportion of investors wanted. The company had an identity crisis, and it needed to be addressed.

39

On the brink

For almost four decades Frank had conducted business from Westfield Towers just outside Sydney's CBD. Although there was a slight dissonance about its location and the building was somewhat dated, it was his home from home. He could get there from his house in fifteen minutes, it had easy access to the airport and if he felt like it he could stroll up the hill to the city. But it was time to move. Over Christmas 2010 company headquarters shifted into the heart of the city, to an office block that stood on top of the brand new shopping centre, Westfield Sydney City. From Frank's new office he could see beyond the harbour to the open sea. When he turned around he could almost touch the huge steel cables that held up Sydney Tower. Although spectacular, it would take some adjustment.

It was to this new office that Frank returned in February 2011 after taking a battering abroad. In December 2010 in Zurich he had endured profound disappointment when he failed to win the right for Australia to host the FIFA World Cup in 2022. He had secured funding from the government, he had put in his best effort and he had lost on the world stage. The following month he had been in Qatar for the Asian Cup, watching with white knuckles as the Socceroos made it to the finals. He had hoped for some restoration in football's standing, but in extra time Japan had scored, defeating Australia 1–0. It was heartbreaking.

Back in Australia in early 2011 Frank surprised everyone by tapping himself on the shoulder. It was time, he said, to move from being executive chairman of Westfield to being its non-executive chairman. At eighty he was finally letting go of the levers[3]. He had held them for half a century and knew this change would require considerable adaptation and personal discipline.

He kept these thoughts to himself and at the annual general meeting in May, with no fanfare, his executive status formally changed. The next day he planned to fly to Brazil with Steven to finalise a joint venture there. Instead, he found himself in hospital facing a possible cancer diagnosis. After a hectic few days, he was diagnosed with early bile duct cancer which, left untreated, could become pancreatic cancer.

Frank's only chance of surviving was to have an operation known as a 'whipple'. It is so radical that people whisper its name. Among those who knew he was on the brink there was a view that this might be the end of his career.

But his survival instincts are strong and, although extremely frail, he persuaded his surgeon to discharge him from hospital a week early. He wanted to attend a pre-arranged mediation with the Australian Tax Office over a matter in Liechtenstein and

---

3   See detailed account in the 'Personal Matters' section.

wouldn't hear of it being postponed. At the end of it, his neck was so weak he was unable to hold up his head, but managed to sign and settle the matter.[4]

Then he persuaded his surgeon to allow him to fly to London to open Westfield's new shopping centre, Stratford City, on the site of the forthcoming 2012 Olympic Games. Some ten weeks later, he and Shirley were on their way under strict instructions. They had to make two long stop-overs en route.

He arrived a couple of days early in order to chair a Westfield board meeting in London. At the meeting Steven put forward a new operating strategy. After the GFC, he said, retailers wanted less space in better locations and Westfield's focus should be on creating, owning and operating flagship malls in major global markets, such as Stratford City. Taking the company's 2006 philosophical change to the next level meant disposing of lesser quality assets and further reducing the size of its portfolio. Peter then put forward a complementary capital structure to utilise the proceeds from the sale of those assets for investment in better-quality centres, and return excess capital to shareholders through a buyback of shares. Elliott Rusanow was there too, to make a presentation to the board, and observed how Frank seamlessly took control of the agenda. "It was a momentous occasion: the chairman was well and truly back!" he said.

Stratford City opened in September 2011, on budget and more than 95 per cent leased. Economic hard times had returned but it shone as Europe's largest and most ambitious urban shopping centre. It was a virtual city serving a catchment with more than four million people. As the Olympic gateway, 70 per cent of visitors to the Games would pass through it every day.

---

4   See detailed account in the 'Personal Matters' section.

The *Guardian* described it as "a world within itself ... Beyond the walls of Westfield and its offshoot, the 2012 Olympics, lies a very different London. Old streets, old terraces, old businesses. People without the wherewithal to indulge in the mall's 300 and more VIP shops. This was once the hub not of intense luxury shopping, but of manufacturing."

It was all about urban renewal. Some time later two Westfield executives, Michael Gutman and director of development John Burton, each received an OBE for their work at Stratford and other sites.

On opening Westfield Stratford mayor Boris Johnson noted that not since the Middle Ages had anything triggered such regeneration in London. When the Games were over, the Olympic site would be re-engineered for a second life. It would become the new metropolitan centre of east London and Westfield would be its major retail precinct. At the opening Frank said it was expected that twenty million people a year would visit the centre and it would be there for generations to come. (The number would actually approach forty million.) Standing there, with fifty years of experience behind him and a month away from his eighty-first birthday, Frank looked to be master of both himself and this latest retail universe. But to those there who knew him something had changed. He had a sense of his own mortality. Although he had largely healed physically, emotionally he was still in the shadow of his health crisis.

But business rolled on. By now Westfield had formed a joint venture in Brazil with Almeida Junior Shopping Centres SA, which held five properties in the southern part of the country. There was great enthusiasm for the venture. Brazil had the sixth largest economy in the world with a population of 190 million, more than half of whom belonged to the rapidly expanding middle class. Although the retail industry was in its infancy the population was culturally similar to that in Westfield's other markets, and Westfield invested $440 million in the venture as an entry point. Just as it had done in the US and the UK, it was trying to get a toehold with a view to becoming established.

Following its philosophy of building the best centres in the best markets Westfield had identified potential sites in Brazil that could fit the bill, but the partnership was not compatible. Frank, Steven, Elliott and Michael flew over to look at the centres and the operations and decided it would be best for Westfield to withdraw. And it did.

That same year, 2011, Westfield had also announced its expansion into continental Europe. It had acquired a 50 per cent interest in a site in Milan, on which it expected to build a centre similar in scale and quality to Westfield London. In a press release, Frank said although world markets were volatile this was a unique opportunity to establish Westfield's franchise in one of the wealthiest population centres in Europe. As it happened the partner company, Gruppo Stilo, GS, was owned principally by Antonio Percassi, a former Italian football star. With their mutual enthusiasm for business and football he and Frank got on very well.

By 2012 Frank had regained much of his strength and was ready for a new battle on English soil. The last time he had been intensely engaged in a hand-to-hand corporate fight had been in London over White City and the Stratford site. This had enabled the company to draw a line of latitude across the great city of London from Westfield London in the west to Westfield Stratford in the east. Now Frank was back in the fray, trying to win a third site in the south, at Croydon. Westfield had tried to get a foothold there some years earlier without success.

For a long time there had been a question mark over Croydon, a neglected area that had been the site of a protracted property war. No one knew what to do about it. The prominent UK property company Hammerson owned the Centrale mall and Croydon's oldest educational charity the Whitgift Foundation owned the Whitgift Shopping Centre.

Through Peter Miller, Westfield's chief operating officer in the UK and Europe, the company managed to create some understanding with the Whitgift Foundation and Westfield began trying to build a position. It was tough going and little progress was made. Around that time, Frank happened to be having a meeting with Boris Johnson over some other business. Johnson was a fan. While many other property developers in London talked a good game, he said no one delivered quite like Westfield, which he described as London's biggest foreign direct investor in bricks and mortar. Standing next to Frank, he had felt the company's pulse as they cut ribbons at the official openings of Westfield's malls in west and in east London. Now, as their business meeting came to a close, Boris mentioned Croydon. In a frustrated aside he asked: "Why can't you just sit down and do a deal with Hammerson?"

"Because it would be like asking you to sit down and do a deal with Ken Livingstone!" said Frank. Johnson took that to mean as clear a "no" as one could possibly give.

But Frank heard the message. He, Steven and Michael got deeply involved in the push into Croydon. "But we couldn't budge Hammerson," says Frank. "We had nothing but a plan and some understanding from Whitgift. At times it looked as if the negotiation was out of control, but we fought on. It was acrimonious and highly competitive." Michael Gutman, who was on the front line, said Frank's leadership cut through the whole process and, as it was clear they couldn't have Croydon alone, took them to a joint venture with Hammerson. Over the summer of 2012, Westfield and Hammerson held their own little "Camp David in London" where they nutted out an agreement.

With this done, Frank went to see Johnson, who didn't know why he was coming. At City Hall, Frank was shown into Johnson's office and after a pleasant exchange announced he was bearing an early Christmas gift. Johnson had forgotten all about their casual exchange and there was Frank, quietly announcing he had done a deal with Hammerson over Croydon. "It was indeed a gift," said Boris Johnson.

> The two great mastodons had mated in this extraordinary way and retail had never seen anything like it. London was absolutely amazed and it happened because Frank Lowy decided that is what Westfield would do, and then it did. He has that characteristic of the brilliant businessman, which is of remembering every detail of what you said in an apparently mundane conversation in which you made a few throwaway remarks – and then going off and investigating some detail of it, doing something about it – and then playing it back to you.

Johnson said that from their very first meeting he had been bowled over by the ambition of Westfield for London and the potential it saw. "What you feel with Westfield is that it is bubbling under with new things it wants to do."

In January 2013, a joint venture that would return the rundown London borough of Croydon to its former glory was made public. Later there was another deal with Whitgift. The hope was that this retail renaissance of Croydon would reposition it as a premier place to shop, work and live in South London. While it wouldn't be Westfield's alone, it would greatly expand its presence in London.

No sooner was the Croydon deal signed than Frank was onto the next thing. In February 2013, he was back in Australia to oversee the sale of the family's holding in the Westfield Retail Trust. During the creation of this trust in 2010 the Lowy family had been allocated just over 7 per cent of the shares. Now they employed UBS to handle the sale.

Matthew Grounds and Guy Fowler from UBS knew it would be a difficult gig because it was obvious the identity of the sellers would need to be disclosed. When their clients heard it was the Lowys they would probably ask whether the family was in possession of some special knowledge. Commentators would likely see their proposed divestment as a lack of confidence in WRT's future. When people asked the family why they were selling down they explained that their investment in WRT doubled up their Australian exposure as they held a similar interest in the same assets through the Westfield Group and they wanted to diversify.

It was a decent transaction for UBS, carrying some $700 million of risk. "We would have to buy the stock without knowing how much we could sell it for," says Grounds. "It was a judgment call and being left owning the stock would not be good for us."

As the family's shares were held in the Lowy Family Group, Matthew dealt with David. The process went smoothly and they quickly agreed on the documentation and settled the timing. Frank joined occasionally. After the date and time had been decided, David announced he would be in Perth, playing in his band.

"But who will we deal with?" asked Grounds.

"Oh don't worry, you're going to be dealing with Dad."

"Ooookay," said Grounds. While he and Guy enjoyed Frank's company, Frank was the toughest negotiator they could get.

"Don't worry, it'll be fine," replied David.

The day arrived for UBS to disclose its price. It would give Frank the number in the morning and if he agreed the sale would be announced in the afternoon. That morning LFG called, inviting them over. "Guy and I were thinking we didn't really want to have a negotiation with Frank. So we would just put forward our best price," said Grounds. The two walked the few blocks from Chifley Tower to Westfield Sydney. Frank was nowhere to be seen. The executives at LFG listened carefully to the price and said they would consult with Frank and call later.

The two walked back to their offices at Chifley Tower and waited. There was some tension in the air but soon the call came. Frank wanted to see them right away. "So we walked back and met the executives again," said Matthew. "Then we saw Frank walking down the corridor towards us. We assumed he was coming to see if we had any room to move on price."

Frank walked in, greeted them politely, sat and summarised the situation. Then he announced he only had one question. He looked at Grounds and then he looked at Fowler. "I just want to know that you are going to be okay with the price," he said.

This was not what they were expecting. "What do you mean?" asked Grounds. Frank replied that as a family transaction this was different from a Westfield deal. In this case, he was concerned about them too and wanted to be sure that they were comfortable with the price they would have to sell at.

"Guy and I got goosebumps. I said, 'We don't know if we are going to be okay but we have come here with this price, we hope we'll be okay, but we are going to stand behind it.'"

"Good, that's all I wanted to know," said Frank, closing the meeting. In the lift, Guy and Matthew look at each other in disbelief. "How wild was that? It was really nice. But did we go too high?" They walked back in silence, each trying to process what had happened. In the end, they sold the shares to institutional investors. The papers reported UBS bought the stake at $3.09 a share in a block trade after the market closed, representing a 3 per cent discount to WRT's closing price in Sydney. In the end the Lowys received $663.7 million. "It went okay. I wouldn't say it went well but we didn't lose money and afterwards it traded up, so investors made some money," said Matthew.

The market took the sale as a vote of no confidence in Westfield Retail Trust. JP Morgan noted, "The decision of a long-term and wise investor to reduce its exposure to Australian shopping centres raises questions about the future direction of capital values." The shares did drop about 3 per cent but soon settled back to their previous long-term trading levels.

Frank Lowy has always been an early adapter of technology. From the days when Westfield had one of the first commercial fax machines in Australia to the latest generation mobile phone in his pocket, he goes to great effort to keep up. While he is not afraid of change, by the time he was in his eighties the pace of digital change had become exponential. While he could book his own movie tickets online and download a biography he wanted to read on his Kindle, what concentrated his mind was the possible impact the internet would have on Westfield. Catalogue, radio and television shopping had existed for many years but this was in a class of its own. It was disruptive technology and there was a high probability that over time, the internet would take business away from physical shops. At a cost of $20 million, Westfield had built an internet mall in the late 1990s but it had been ahead of the market and it decided to shut it down before it opened. "That was the best $20 million we ever pissed away because had we opened it, it would have cost us a lot more money," said Steven.

Now Steven was bringing it back with great force. Embracing the digital world required a change in thinking and the creation of a new model for Westfield. To drive this Steven formed Westfield Labs in San Francisco as a global digital laboratory focused on innovation in the retail environment. Its mission was to make Westfield's malls places where the physical and digital converged. This later became known as going "phygital".

Steven explained that this convergence was just beginning and that Westfield had the advantage over online retailers because it had physical real estate close to the consumer. It was going to give retailers and consumers a new experience.

"But how?" asked Frank. Although retailers were online they needed somewhere to display their wares. They still required physical space in malls and although they probably needed fewer outlets, each outlet would have to be bigger. Rather than having a scattering of small shops they would have a few large showrooms. Iconic malls could accommodate these. This was exactly what Westfield was planning. Back in 2006 it had changed its philosophy from accumulating malls to focusing on A-quality malls and shedding those at the B and C levels. In 2011 it had intensified this concept in anticipation of the internet claiming a bigger share of shopping.

Westfield's relationship with consumers was changing too. In the past it had catered for retailers who then engaged with consumers. Now, in order to succeed in the digital age, it had to shift and engage directly with consumers. This took a lot of thinking. Given the malls were like mini-cities, Westfield would move to enable shoppers to go online and plan their shopping trip before they arrived. From home they could make a shopping list and search online for items among the hundreds of stores and millions of products in the centre. In this process they would receive up-to-date information about products and services.

Their plan and their shopping list would be on their phone when they arrived at the mall. As soon as they entered, the mall would register their arrival and reward them if they happened to be frequent shoppers. They could get points which could entitle them to an offer such as extended free parking. Once inside they could have a traditional experience of strolling and browsing or go efficiently to the place where their desired item was for sale.

At the mall, Steven said, as soon as shoppers arrived, they would be instantly connected to a new world of personal shopping and retailers could broadcast special products and services available at that time. If they didn't want to know, they didn't have to engage. Westfield Labs was also reinventing 'way finding' with a mapping mechanism on shoppers' phones that also showed the products in the vicinity.

The point was to make Westfield a 'great host', a concept Frank was entirely familiar with. In his private and business life he is a highly skilled host, with his guests' needs anticipated and usually generously met. He's also a service junkie. When he goes into a shop and the assistant focuses on him and is personable, he says he'll buy three or four times the amount of merchandise he would have purchased from an indifferent sales assistant.

Drawing on his own experience, he understood that while so much was changing in the digital world, in essence things were really the same. Back in the 1950s when he first opened that legendary delicatessen, he had drawn enormous enjoyment from interacting with customers, giving them a taste of this or that delicacy, serving them well and seeing them buy more. At heart, he was a salesman. Many years later, when he took his family on holiday to Surfers Paradise, he found himself waiting to be served in a crowded deli. He offered to help, the owner agreed and gave him an apron and Frank spent a happy hour behind the counter.

Steven explained that malls of the future would offer hands-free shopping, with parcels delivered to shoppers' cars or homes. If people wanted food their phones would tell them what was on offer at the various outlets in the food court and they could order online, either to be served at a fixed time or have the food delivered to their car or home. All this technology, he said, would be good for retailers too.

Frank listened carefully. When he opened Westfield's first mall in 1959, the fact that it made provision for parking was hailed as a major innovation. Since then hands-free shopping, valet parking and home deliveries had become par for the course, but it seemed the internet was adding a new dimension. It could make the process less clunky, more transparent and far more efficient. It also enabled the mall to reach into people's homes. He was right behind the initiative.

He was particularly impressed when, in March 2015, he opened the latest issue of the respected online publication *Fast Company* and scrolled down to read the list of the fifty most innovative companies in the world. There he saw the likes of Apple and Alibaba, Instagram and Google, Toyota and Virgin

America. At number 36, his face broke into a wide smile. There was Westfield Labs. In just two years, its crew had grown to more than fifty-five employees and he was pleased to read it was putting into motion "several ideas to show how malls don't have to be a relic of late–20th-century American commerce".

40

Major split

The restructure of Westfield in 2010 had not produced the success that had been expected and it was not in the company's culture to sit back in the hope that things might improve. Something had to be done and while no one inside the company welcomed the prospect of yet another major overhaul, it seemed necessary. One of the problems was that the investment market continued to value the Westfield Group at a discount to its listed peers globally. Westfield had an identity issue. Rather than being perceived as a global company, it was perceived as an Australian company with global interests.

Another problem was that at home, although Westfield Retail Trust was performing well at the operational level and in line with its peers, its stock market performance was below the company's expectations.

Peter had been thinking about these problems throughout 2013 and had written a paper proposing a plan for change. He sent a copy to Robert Leitão, now head of Rothschild in the UK, and asked him to come to Australia to discuss it. Peter, Steven and Robert spent a day holed up in a Sydney hotel going through the plan. They came up with a variation on it and the following day met with Frank, where the strategy was dissected. "When the family caucuses, the level of debate is incredibly vigorous," says Leitão. "In part, my role was to keep the conversation on track. Frank doesn't impose his will. Through a subtle interaction, they slowly migrate towards a common view. While he has more influence in the thinking, it is not authoritative but rather the result of natural deference."

For Leitão this creates an environment for innovative thinking, for eureka moments that can emerge from collective energy. "It's a much more thorough decision-making process than I have come across before. When David [Lowy] is present, it's a synthesis of at least four people with lot of other views underlying it. Frank is in command and they make a small leap of faith, riding on his experience and leadership."

The next step was to put the plan on the table for analysis within Westfield, where it was again pulled apart, tested, modified and improved. "In the end it was the product of a 'collective think', there was no ownership of the idea," said Leitão. That the debate could be so fluid and reactive impressed him. "In my experience large corporates sometimes suffer because there is too much structure in the system and people think in boxes. In this case it was agile with no limits." Rather than one person going to the board with a paper containing a fresh idea, this idea had already been through the machine and was ready for a new level of consideration at board level.

Press suggestions that the board is dominated and controlled by Frank and that its discussions are about the taste element, not fundamental principles, are not accurate. "Frank is far more deferential to his board and his executives than most chairmen I know," said Leitão. While his relationship with the board might have been different in his younger days, as a mature chairman Frank is venerated. After fifty years at the head of Westfield, his perspective and confidence are unmatchable. Stephen Johns sat on the Westfield board for decades and when he was elevated to the chair of Brambles, he reflected to the press on what he had learned from Lowy. "One of his great qualities — and this may not be perceived publicly — is to include all of the board in the decision making, making sure that the boardroom is fully informed and seeking their advice as to the strategic direction of the company."

By the end of 2013 an audacious plan to split the company along geographical lines had been finalised. It was to split the $70 billion Westfield cleanly into an Australasian business and an international business. The restructure in 2010 had partially achieved this and now it would be taken to its natural conclusion. From the split, two distinct independent businesses would be created. The international business would hold all the assets abroad and would be called Westfield Corporation. The Australasian business would be named the Scentre Group and have all Westfield's local assets merged with the assets of WRT, which were all local too.

Throughout the protracted period of preparation for this split, Frank was steadfast about one thing. On a corporate level he would not sanction the domestic business keeping the corporate name Westfield. It could be kept at the consumer level. On the ground, the Australian and NZ malls would still be branded

Westfield to benefit from the goodwill and to draw shoppers, but beyond that its corporate identity had to be different. Frank fought everyone to make sure this happened. "If there is anything that Dad was insistent about and got away with, to the exclusion of everyone else, it was his gut feeling not to have the domestic business called Westfield," says Steven. "We debated everything about the split but that was the no-go zone throughout the entire transaction. Staff went to see him and investors argued the case but he would not shift."

It was a matter of vision. Frank wanted to keep the corporate identities separate. It was not inconceivable that in ten or fifteen years' time Westfield could find itself in competition with Scentre group in a new territory. Were that to happen and were they to have the same name, there would be confusion, as there had been with Woolworths and others that had different ownerships but the same name in different parts of the world, and sometimes in the same country.

In the split the Lowy executive firepower would go with the international business, which would account in US dollars only and over time might be listed outside Australia. Frank would be its chairman and Peter and Steven would be its joint chief executives. Peter, however, signalled that in eighteen months' time he would likely want to go non-executive. This would leave Steven – or Stevie, as his father calls him – at the helm of the international business.

The levers of the local business would be firmly in the hands of Peter Allen as chief executive. Scentre would start out as the pre-eminent shopping centre company in Australia, three times the size of its closest rival. It would have 47 malls, $4.9 billion of development work from which to improve earnings and Westfield's 2000 local staff – a purely Australasian play for local or foreign investors who wanted to make an investment in Australia. With Frank as chairman and Steven as a non-executive board member it would retain some Lowy expertise. The press reported, however, that some held the view that their board positions and their $700 million shareholding in Scentre would not be long-term propositions.

When the plan was first announced in December 2013 many people scratched their heads. Westfield had merged in 2004, it had split in 2010; what was it doing now? There was talk of 'restructure fatigue' and little clarity about why it was necessary. People wondered why Westfield hadn't gone all the way in 2010. The answer was that back then the financial capacity of the international business would not have been great enough for it to stand on its own. It could, however, be argued that had the company waited another few years for the overseas assets to grow, the 2010 exercise could have been avoided.

The confusion highlighted a characteristic difference between the market and management. While management takes a long-term view to create long-term value, shareholders want to know what is happening in the next six months. This restructure was about creating greater value over the next decade. But communication about the deal was cloudy.

The Lowys are concerned about what people think. The public's relationship with the family swings between awe and envy. Some complain there are too many Lowys in Westfield and that it is run like a family company; but if the Lowys leave, people complain that the family is abandoning the company because it knows something others don't know. The Lowys' corporate governance practices are criticised, as are the salaries they draw. Share activists want to see Frank working for Westfield, but don't want to see him paid. The family is observed so closely that it has to fight for its privacy. Wherever Frank goes in Australia, his distinctive features and his shock of white hair make him instantly recognisable. He's always under scrutiny.

In the case of this restructure, he worried that because the family had 8.4 per cent of the international business (later this was upped to 9.5 per cent) and was putting its executive power behind it, people would imagine the family had some private knowledge. There was speculation in the press that the family thought Australia was shopped-out and that all the growth opportunities were overseas. Whenever he was asked, Frank would say this was not so. While Australia was a mature market, it still had plenty of growth opportunities. "Australia's population is twenty-three million. Over the next decade it's projected to grow at least another four, maybe five, million. That's four to five million extra shoppers!" he said.

The idea was to split the business in two to give both halves the best possible chance of growth. "They can't achieve their optimum value under one roof, and the objective is always to create shareholder value," Frank said. The offshore business would achieve this by concentrating in future on flagship malls in major cities, which would combine physical shopping and lifestyle with the digital world.

The market had five months to digest the plan before shareholders voted on the proposal in May 2014. While investors in Westfield liked the strategy some disliked the numbers, and it soon became evident that there was a backlash from a small but powerful group of vocal institutions. They were concerned that Scentre's gearing would be high and would require partial asset sales that would dilute its underlying asset portfolio. They wanted the deal sweetened. Frank rejected any suggestion of sweetening. Peter was vehemently against it.

There was a perceptual problem. Some investors appeared not to grasp that Scentre was a fully fledged operating company that owned the assets, developed and managed them, which would generate more income than the trust it was incorporating. The detractors said they liked the trust, WRT, and did not want to change it. They saw it as a safe vehicle with very low debt that earned money from its malls and paid a good dividend. Scentre group, on the other hand, would be loaded up with debt and risk. They threatened to vote it down unless the deal was sweetened and they used public relations agencies and other funds to make sure their voice was heard.

It was a long time since Frank had been out and about selling Westfield to investors, but now he was doing roadshows back to back, trying to shore up the numbers. The institutions were surprised to hear he would be in the room and while they gave him due respect they also gave him mental exercise. Frank argued that a vocal minority had been obscuring the positive aspects of the proposal.

Passing the plan required 75 per cent shareholder approval from both Westfield and WRT and as the AGM drew closer, there was a real risk WRT wouldn't get its part of the proposal over the line. Three weeks before the vote, a pragmatic decision was made and the deal was sweetened by $300 million. But it wasn't enough and the detractors lobbied for more. This time the Lowys wouldn't move an inch.

To pass the plan the two groups of shareholders had to vote in two AGMs held on the same day in late May 2014. From the proxies there was confidence the morning meeting of Westfield Group shareholders would vote the plan in. But the proxies indicated that the afternoon WRT meeting was on a knife-edge. Despite the board's recommendation, an independent expert's report favouring the proposal, the roadshows, the sweetener, the investment banks and the Global Proxy Solicitation firm hired to promote the plan to undecided shareholders, it seemed not enough sentiment was on its side to gain the required 75 per cent of WRT shareholders' votes.

If the afternoon WRT meeting did not approve the transaction the Westfield Group had a Plan B. It was an aggressive option. The plan was to go it alone without WRT. This meant it would proceed with forming Westfield Corporation as an international company. The aggressive part was that it would keep its local assets separately listed. This new listed entity would then compete with WRT for capital on the stock market. This plan had been foreshadowed in the memorandum for the meeting, but it seemed no one had taken it seriously.

The rationale for Westfield Group to split off and create an exclusively international company always made strategic sense, with or without WRT. But as the vote grew closer a view began to emerge that the Westfield Group couldn't achieve its international aim without the agreement of WRT. This was wrong but nevertheless the view persisted. As the meeting drew closer people thought that, as the Westfield Group could not afford to have WRT vote down the proposal, it would improve the terms of the deal again.

Although the Westfield Group had said it could go it alone, the WRT shareholders didn't seem to take notice of this. Via proxies the Westfield Group knew it had the support of 98 per cent of its shareholders, and the day before the meeting its board resolved to pursue separation alone if the WRT meeting did not vote in favour. This was communicated to the WRT board that day. That same day, the *Australian Financial Review* outlined the four alternative proposals in the investor booklet should the split not go ahead. It reported Lowy having previously said that if the proposal were not approved by security holders, Westfield Group would 'move on'. It also quoted a Macquarie Securities analyst saying the most likely alternative would be the demerger of Westfield Group's Australian and NZ business, but without any merger with WRT.

41

Payoff

By the time the day arrived for the two AGMs the ballroom at the Wentworth Sofitel hotel was packed. The morning meeting would be for shareholders in the Westfield Group and after a lunch provided by the company, the afternoon would be for shareholders in Westfield Retail Trust.

There was plenty of press, as a particular story had been gaining momentum: after more than half a century in the business, Frank Lowy was about to falter. It was expected that his great new scheme would not achieve the requisite support and he would be defeated. Thursday 29 May, 2014 was to be the day that this particular tall poppy would be cut down.

The first meeting began with unpleasant news for Frank. Some 9 per cent of shareholders voted against his re-election as chairman. Other chairmen might glow at a 91 per cent acceptance rate but it wasn't enough for Frank and he swallowed his initial disappointment. However, during the proceedings, rather than remaining cool, he took the bait from the Australian Shareholders' Association. There was naked hostility in the room and the exchanges became uncomfortably personal. When a shareholder activist became particularly aggressive, Frank replied in kind, plus some. An ABC commentator reported that the atmosphere was electric and that many were astounded by Lowy's performance.

In his prepared address Lowy delivered a message of reassurance for shareholders in the Westfield Group which, for formality, he referred to by its ASX code 'WDC'. Some interpreted the message as a warning for the afternoon meeting of Westfield Retail Trust, WRT.

Lowy told those present, "If the WRT meeting this afternoon does not approve the proposal it will not diminish our determination to proceed with WDC's strategic objective of separating the two businesses. We will pursue that separation – but without WRT."

In simple terms, he was telling the meeting he would activate Plan B. This effectively meant WRT would be cut loose. While this was a crucial piece of information, it didn't affect the morning meeting, which went on to vote overwhelmingly for the proposal. Some 98 per cent of those voting wanted an exclusively international Westfield separate from an exclusively Australian Scentre.

By the lunch break, however, Frank's 'warning' had gone nuclear. People buzzed around the foyer trying to make sense of it as they ate the sandwiches that had been provided. The memorandum for the meeting had provided alternatives, but they had never been considered the main game. This new plan had serious implications. If the WRT stakeholders voted down the proposal in the afternoon, Westfield would spin its local assets into a company to compete with it on the stock market. In frenzied conversations people questioned whether Frank could do such a thing. They were incredulous because it seemed he was turning on his own. He loved Westfield. He was Westfield. Why was he now willing to lop off a large part and disown it? It made no emotional sense. At this point many in the crowd were in the realm of emotion, not commerce. Had they focused on the commercial realities and realised how much steel Lowy has in him, it would have made sense.

The afternoon's meeting was keenly anticipated. How would WRT's chairman, Dick Warburton, handle it? With his twenty-five years on boards Warburton is a man of great experience. He and his board knew what was coming. The night before they had seen a copy of Frank's address, promising to go it alone if necessary, and they had had a little time to prepare for this.

Over lunch the WRT board caucused and took more advice. When Warburton opened the afternoon meeting, the contrast in style between his chairmanship and Lowy's was stark. Where Lowy was instinctive, engaged and full of fire, Warburton was straight down the rails, a consummate professional who couldn't be ruffled. He knew the proxies showed a narrow defeat and when he put them up they were 0.9 per cent short. Just 74.1 per cent had voted for the proposal prior to the meeting via proxy.

He referred to the earlier meeting and Lowy's statement that if WRT didn't pass the motion, Westfield would demerge and form a listed company separate from WRT to hold its Australian and New Zealand management rights and assets. This was obviously a negative for WRT and before the meeting voted he opened the floor to discussion.

During the discussion a representative of a major institutional shareholder rose from the floor and suggested the vote be postponed because Lowy's statement signified "a material change" to the transaction. Warburton agreed the change was material and said the board would leave the podium to discuss a possible postponement and to seek legal advice. In the board's absence – which seemed to last an eternity – the room was alive with small discussions. Although Warburton had the necessary power under WRT's constitution, postponing the vote was unprecedented. People felt they had front-row seats in the making of corporate history. When the board returned, Warburton said he would take a poll of the meeting to see if the meeting itself should be deferred. After further heated discussion, the room voted for a deferral. Taking that vote into account, Warburton then took the controversial decision to adjourn the meeting to allow members time to consider the new information.

Although Lowy had been entitled to raise Plan B, just as Warburton had been entitled to defer the meeting, the whole issue became toxic. It not only disrupted the day's proceedings but radiated through the press over the days that followed. All the aggression was directed at Lowy. In his long career he had never experienced such a response to a corporate manoeuvre and couldn't understand it. Why was the media playing the man, not the ball? he asked.

Some said he had been too successful for too long and was finally getting his comeuppance. It was the most contentious play in Westfield's history and they said Lowy had shifted the goalposts and muddied his reputation. The press described Westfield as a shambles, they called Lowy a bully, an oppressor and an intimidator and described the manoeuvre as a breathtaking lapse in corporate behaviour. They almost ran out of adjectives trying to describe just how far he'd fallen. In their estimation the restructure was doomed and they predicted there would be legal action. They judged the process an outrage and wailed that minority rights had been trampled. It was the end of a great empire.

Back at Westfield Frank and the others watched this outpouring. They were particularly surprised by the words of Robert Gottliebsen, the prince of commentators who for three decades had been one of the most respected voices on Australian business and finance. "Today I feel very sad. One of Australia's great business heroes and icons, Frank Lowy, has clearly stayed on as Westfield Group chairman too long," he wrote in *Business Spectator* and the *Australian*. "Frank Lowy is 83. When you get older sometimes you can become less tolerant of opposing views. I think that may have happened to Frank." He said Lowy's hero status had been tarnished at the very time of his life when his achievements and skills should be celebrated. "Whichever way the battle goes, the loser is Frank Lowy."

Even in this free-for-all, hardened members of the press were astonished at Gottliebsen's attack on Lowy's judgment, and his suggestion that Lowy was impaired by age. Frank wrote him a private letter, suggesting that perhaps Gottliebsen was affected by age and should retire as a commentator. Gottliebsen responded privately and publicly backtracked a couple of days later: "Were we too tough on Westfield chairman Frank Lowy when our heading suggested that he had experienced a spectacular fall from grace?" Even though Westfield was a mess, Gottliebsen wrote, to put all the blame on the 83-year-old chairman was too tough.

The *Australian Financial Review* reported the fracas differently, with its front page declaring "Lowys impose their will", followed by a report on how the chairman had stared down a shareholder revolt over the restructure. As it happened the Supreme Court of NSW approved WRT's decision to adjourn, and set a date for the next meeting three weeks later on 20 June.

Frank always keeps all his options open and now every one was being examined in fine detail. He called a family meeting to debate whether they could or should buy shares in WRT to tip the balance in favour of the separation – after all, it involved less than 1 per cent of the capital of WRT. After some robust discussion they decided that they didn't want to win that way, and in any event the Supreme Court and ASIC had decided that only those who'd held shares during the first meeting would be able to vote in the second.

As Frank had no role in the forthcoming meeting and as the Socceroos were about to play at the FIFA World Cup in Brazil, he left the country. He would participate in the debate and watch the proceedings unfold from Brazil.

During the three-week wait the issue heated up. The superannuation fund UniSuper, which owned 8.49 per cent of WRT and had pushed for the sweetener or for a material change in terms, was the plan's most powerful antagonist. A couple of days into the waiting period its chief investment officer, John Pearce, went on television and challenged the Lowy family to carry out its threat. He said he would welcome a rival to WRT and dared the family to "bring it on". UniSuper had bought into WRT because WRT was a landlord – not a developer or manager – of high-quality retail assets, which delivered attractive yields. He said that under the proposal the vehicle would change and become highly leveraged. "All of a sudden it also takes on property risk, development risk and we're being asked to pay an exorbitant price for the privilege!" he said.

Steven Lowy, who had steadfastly held the family line in the afternoon meeting of WRT of which he was a board member, appeared opposite Pearce on the same TV show. He pointed to the hysteria in the press and defended the decision to defer the vote. "Where is the crime in giving investors a few more weeks to consider this?" he asked. "This is a minority subverting a majority." In describing the focus on his family as ridiculous he said he was very proud of his father and the achievements of the company over the past fifty years.

Warburton used the waiting period. He declared a "call to arms", asking retail shareholders to get behind the proposal. Because many small shareholders supporting the deal were not willing to put their heads above the parapet, he said the debate around the deal had been one-sided. He and the board supported it and it was not certain it would make it over the line.

For Elliott Rusanow as deputy CFO of the Westfield Group this restructure – which he had worked on for a year – took him to the extremes of his career. The new meeting was scheduled for a Friday morning but by the Tuesday afternoon, with only three days to go, WRT hadn't reached the requisite 75 per cent. Elliott called the executives of WRT and their bankers again and desperately recounted the numbers. He was growing increasingly despondent, believing they were headed for failure. He drove home utterly miserable and at the kitchen table did the figures for the last time before composing an email he had dreaded writing. To the top echelon at Westfield he wrote that it looked as if they had fallen just short and that he would be shocked if they ever got over the line. He pushed 'send' and was sitting with his head in his hands when his phone went. It was UBS, the principal investment bankers for WRT.

"Are you sitting down?"

"Yes, I am," Elliott responded.

"There's been a change of mind. A major stakeholder won't be lodging its million votes against the proposal."

Elliott exploded out of his chair. As he almost hit the ceiling so he hit the highest point of his career. He started shouting. "We are going to win!"

In a state of "absolute elation" Elliott tried to call Steven. But as he dialled, Frank called, having just read the email. Elliott had to repeat what he had heard twice: Frank couldn't believe the transaction had pulled back from the brink. Then Steven called and was equally stunned. On Wednesday morning, with the vote nervously sitting at the 76 per cent mark, WRT was keeping the number under wraps.

This winning margin held. By Friday the issue had run its course and the meeting was an anticlimax. After six months of overexcited debate, the matter was settled in twenty minutes. The proposal went though and everyone shook hands. Pearce congratulated Westfield on its effective campaign and added that he would do the same again. "We got the sweetener and our members know that we stand up for their rights."

It had been a case study of institutional activism in Australia. Investors led by a superannuation fund had almost derailed a proposal by two of Australia's great businesses. It seemed that in future large super funds would be more likely to play a more active role in key corporate decisions and that their size would enable them to flex their muscles.

At a press conference signalling the start of the post-Lowy era of the Australian shopping centre business, Steven described it as a "bitter-sweet day". Excitement about the future was tinged with the sadness of parting. Peter found himself having to counter scepticism about the family's motives. He rejected speculation that the split had been driven by the family's desire to shift its wealth offshore and set up the new entity for an overseas takeover. "If we wanted to leave we would have sold our eight per cent and left," he said. "We are mature enough as a family to look to the next step to grow the business, and this is another clear step of succession planning. We now have a debt book to restructure, figure out where to list and new markets to explore."

Steven's sadness carried over to a small drinks party following the press conference. The Australian business that had been part of him for twenty-six years was in fine shape and now he was leaving it in good hands. He turned to Peter Allen and asked him to take good care of it. With that, he went to the airport to fly out to join his dad.

In the end, none of the press's dire warnings came true. There was no legal action – the court vindicated what Warburton had done – and the share price in both companies went up. By December 2014 a total of $8 billion in value had been added to both entities and the number was rising. No one needed to report Frank's vindication. The numbers did it for him. So did the fact that, in an extraordinary vote of confidence, UniSuper immediately upped its stake in Scentre Group by a reported $200 million. Pearce argued that this was not a backflip because he had never said UniSuper didn't like Scentre; it just liked WRT on a relative basis. UniSuper also bought into Westfield Corporation.

This deal had transfixed the corporate sector. According to the *Australian Financial Review*, "it spoke to all the big threads of Australian corporate life: the growing power of Australia's super funds; the transfer of wealth from a generation of entrepreneurial titans to their children; the future of the crucial retail sector in the face of dramatic technology change; and the ability of Australian companies to crack overseas markets."

When the noise died down it became clear that during the event, the ambivalence towards the Lowy family had tipped into the negative. Scepticism fed the notion that the family was acting in its own interests and that its plan had been to cut its Australian heritage loose to achieve its aim.

For a few weeks Frank felt bruised. He couldn't figure out why the press had rounded on him. Why had it not seen the corporate play for what it was? Why hadn't it portrayed UniSuper as an aggressor rather than a victim? UniSuper, as everyone acknowledged afterwards, had done very well indeed for its membership. As a minority stakeholder it had been the tail wagging the dog and had done so to great effect.

Frank told friends he had had plenty of criticism in his career. "It comes with the territory, but I don't recall ever encountering such vengeance and so much misreporting. There were times I wondered if there was some latent animosity that led them to try and crucify me. The press didn't know the facts and didn't see the benefits. I guess in the final analysis the facts speak for themselves. The restructure created shareholder value of $10 billion plus."

During the post mortem Frank realised a weakness lay in having given the market five months to consider the deal. It had created an information vacuum in which much speculation took place. Misinformation filled the space and gained a life of its own. "We lost control of the narrative," he said. "The period between the announcement and the release of the explanatory memorandum should have been kept closer to the obligatory minimum of six weeks."

When Peter Allen began working on this restructure he believed he was effectively working himself out of a job. As it happened, he was working himself into the chief executive's chair of Scentre Group. In eighteen years in the presence of the master he had learned a few things that would be useful in his new role.

In his early Westfield days he had noted Frank's extraordinary capacity to tolerate uncertainty and the benefits it brings. "He is highly focused and knows what the endgame will be but doesn't know the journey. He's comfortable with that journey being all over the place and having lots of balls in the air. His ability to tolerate ambiguity creates flexibility. He'll always take an option but he'll never give one away. At the last moment he'll make his decision."

Allen also learned not to be first to put a price down in a negotiation because it would set the base. Rather, he would do as Frank does and see where the other person stands first. But mostly he understood how Frank extracted the best from people: with a mix of active listening, empathy, encouraging self-belief and then using inspiration to drive them hard.

He had heard Frank talk about the value of family and had seen, in his later years, how good he was at creating balance in his life. He had also heard Frank encourage his executives to value family life but had seen how he didn't always understand their need to take the time to do so. "But if you are comfortable and confident enough and you make a stand, he understands family language," he said.

Over more than half a century, Frank had grown Westfield to the point where the overseas business could be split off, leaving the local business so strong that it was unassailable. In 2015 the value of the two new entities continued to grow at a rate that outstripped all expectations. Most of the $17 billion worth of development in their pipelines was there, Steven said, largely because of the big deals his father had done in the past thirteen or fourteen years.

But rather than looking back, in his eighty-fifth year Frank felt grateful to be functional and to be deeply embedded in the core that was driving Westfield to new challenges.

In the past decade this core had lost a highly valued member in Richard Green, who died of a protracted illness in 2006. He had been with the company for twenty-six years. As a result of the 2014 split Peter Allen was lost too, but to Scentre Group. At the same time it seemed the core was about to lose Peter Lowy as an executive. When the split was first announced, Peter let it be known that he would be relinquishing his executive role in eighteen months. Then he changed his mind. In February 2015 he said he would stay on as joint chief executive with Steven.

The press asked Peter who had persuaded him to stay, his father or the board. "If it was my dad, he would not have asked, he would have told me to stay," Peter answered. Robert Harley, associate editor of the *Australian Financial Review*, didn't bite. He said a move to reverse such an announcement would have been well canvassed in the family. It would not have come out "of the blue as a request from the board – more likely it was a meeting of minds."

Being one of these 'minds' is fundamental to Frank's life. He continues to go to the office every day, he continues to travel for business. For him Westfield remains a work in progress.

Epilogue

Everything Matters

Scholars of the ageing process say older men can protect themselves from a great deal but there is one thing they can't defend against. It is a philosophical change. While many ambitious men maintain their motivation for decades, others find their drive dissipates. It happens imperceptibly and, rather than continuing to strive to reach the top, they begin to realise they are content with the view from where they are. Something within them has relaxed.

By his eighty-fifth year, Frank Lowy had not relaxed; he was still pushing. Nevertheless, there were times of respite when he looked back at the sweep of his life and felt an unfamiliar sense of tranquillity. "Occasionally I have a fleeting appreciation of the privilege I have had through my long years with my wife, my family and my position – I only wish this feeling would stay," he said.

When he stepped back from executive life at the age of eighty and became the non-executive chairman of Westfield, he made a conscious effort to embrace his new position: "It took a measure of self-discipline. Others assumed there was no difference but they didn't know how I restrained myself." After a while he recognised the benefits of relinquishing day-to-day responsibility but still having his feet under the table. Being the elder statesman, at least in business, wasn't so bad.

Towards the end of 2013 a Sydney fund manager received a rare invitation. Would he like to take lunch with Frank Lowy and two of his sons in their dining room at Westfield? Hamish Douglass had a strong business history with the family and had worked closely with David. He counted himself fortunate to be invited and, for an hour or so, sat between David and Steven and was able to get a sense of what it must be like to have a father such as Frank.

Douglass was relaxed as the conversation ranged loosely over many issues but he didn't want to leave without a nugget of insight from the *éminence grise* and towards the end of the meal, he asked: "Frank, I am trying to build Magellan, a global business. What lessons can I learn from you?" After thinking aloud about generalities, Frank hit the essence. "Be paranoid," he said. David looked at Steven. "That's it!"

He could equally have added, "Have vision." When Frank was pushing to create his first major shopping centre in London and his senior executives opposed him, saying the numbers didn't stack up, he responded that there was much more to business than numbers. "I also told him it didn't stack up," says David. "Later when it was being built I went there for the first time and got onto the roof. I looked around and suddenly I saw what Dad saw. This was going to be the most valuable piece of real estate in Europe one day. It hadn't been evident from the figures."

For most of his adult life Frank has been a passionate Australian. Through all his activities – from malls to medical research, from football to foreign policy – he has promoted Australia abroad, always wanting more recognition for his country. For him there is no conflict in having Australia as his national home and Israel as his spiritual home. Rather than feeling tension between the two, he feels fortunate to have Jewish heritage and Australian citizenship.

David Gonski, who has known him for decades, notes that even into his eighties Frank's passion for Australia is obvious. "We had a long discussion about why the Australian government would buy submarines from anywhere other than Adelaide. Frank's points were cogent, with a generosity about his adoptive home that brought a tear to my eye. Here was a shopping centre magnate who has nothing to do with submarines arguing strongly for the benefit of the people of Australia. It meant so much to him that, with foreign expertise, the manufacturing could be done here."

To Gonski, Frank remains intellectually curious and inventive. Whatever the subject of discussion he is immediately engaged. When, for example, the issue of funding for universities arose, he wanted to know what the sector was planning, whether it was prepared for the changes and whether the solution was viable. In 2013, as chancellor of the University of NSW, Gonski held an armchair conversation with Frank in front of an audience of 250 guests. It was a Philanthropy Australia event and Frank was there to talk about what motivated him to give money, particularly to universities and research. He disclosed that in the past decade the family had donated more than $350 million to various causes. Unlike in Israel, where the family's name was rarely seen on its donations, in Australia he said the family had been encouraged to use the Lowy name in the hope that others would be inspired to contribute.

But far from the public eye, Frank gave not only materially but of himself too. On Jewish New Year in 2013 he was sitting in synagogue, listening to the prayers he had known since childhood. It was almost time for the Unesaneh Tokef, one of the most stirring prayers in the liturgy, which speaks of the book of memory being opened and everything forgotten being remembered. Under the praying he became aware that someone nearby was sobbing and when he looked around he saw it was a young boy overcome with grief. A man in the next row whispered that the boy's father had committed suicide in the year just passed. Frank got up, went over to the boy and brought him back to sit next to him.

The Unesaneh Tokef resonates with Frank. It draws him back to the fearful days of his boyhood when the Nazis were drawing closer and his community was racked with anguish. They knew what was coming. Frank had been standing next to his father in their small wooden synagogue when, in preparation for this prayer, Hugo drew his son under his own prayer shawl and held his hand tightly. The rabbi began the incantation, "All men will pass before You like members of the flock". From under the soft shawl Frank could feel his father trembling as the rabbi continued "... who will live and who will die ... who by fire, who by sword ..."

Now here he was some seventy years later, hearing the same prayer and feeling the boy's anguish. "It was as if I was my father and he was me. It was a moment of pure identification, the moment when two souls meet," he said.

As is customary, Frank went back to synagogue on the second day of New Year. Part way through the morning he went out for a while and in the foyer he saw the boy. The boy looked as if he wanted to approach but hesitated, and Frank encouraged him. The boy had a question. He wanted to know how Frank had felt when his own father passed away. "I told him it was very sad and that I still feel very sad. The terrible pain of it is always with me." The encounter remained with Frank and a couple of days later he called the rabbi to find out more about the boy's circumstances. He planned to do something for him, both materially and to enrich his life in other ways. He put plans in place for the boy and his family and then stayed in touch with them.

Acutely aware of the importance of fathering, Frank had taken youngsters under his wing before and given them all manner of assistance, from paternal guidance to tuition fees and even jobs. Through the spontaneity of these gestures and the responsiveness of the young people, he touched something much greater than himself.

In his later years he discovered another source of richness. It came through developing relationships with his grandchildren, unfiltered by their parents. In their younger days, he didn't know them well. Frank had never been the kind of grandfather to collect them from school or help with homework. Had they been stuck for a lift they wouldn't have called him. Now they were calling.

Concerned about the passage of time, Steven's eldest son, Josh, was prepared to cancel arrangements should an opportunity arise to spend time with Frank. "My grandfather seems harsh at times, but he is compassionate and I have seen how hard he has worked, and how much he has copped on the chin to ensure the family remains as the unit it is seen to be. I think that it is probably his masterpiece. I never realised until recently that it is such a tough gig. Everything would be nothing if that didn't exist."

In his late teens Josh decided never to decline an opportunity to be privy to family meetings where he could see the machinery of unity at work. During his university years he would study at the office and join the lunches, where he noted that trivial issues were rarely discussed. "It's always business or family matters. There's always some conflict somewhere in the family because our lives are so intertwined." Sometimes he would sit in Frank's office chatting, unaware of time until the secretary put her head in to announce an appointment.

With his interest in technology, Josh went to work for Westfield Labs in San Francisco after he graduated. On trips home he would talk to Frank about innovation on the internet and sometimes take a whiteboard over to his grandfather's home to explain the dynamics of using it in business. Later, if Frank wanted more information, Josh would talk to him from the US, via a beam (a mobile video conference robot). The family has beams in their homes. By inhabiting these from afar, they can have a virtual but mobile presence in one another's space. While in San Francisco, Josh could arrive in his grandfather's study, 'sit' at his desk and, if necessary, move around to take a closer look at his computer screen and guide him on the keyboard. Then he could navigate himself into the family room to chat to his grandmother.

Josh is a year younger than David's son Noah, and the two of them are so close they may as well be brothers. "We are so affected by the dynamic between our dads that we have probably emulated that relationship between each other," says Josh. While at university, Noah would study at the office and attend the lunches too. After graduation he went to work in investment banking in New York, where he quickly experienced the unrelentingly gruelling hours demanded by the industry.

These were the same hours his grandfather had put in for decades but Noah recognised the difference. For Frank this work was all-absorbing. On his visits to New York Frank would talk to Noah about work demands, not about what he was or wasn't achieving but about the internal requirements of meeting them. Noah had thought deeply about the need to achieve, and he knew the pressure he felt to do so came from within himself.

In his teens, Noah too had begun gravitating to his grandfather. "I was able to speak to him about personal matters. There was never any judgment. He would just 'get it' and his advice would inevitably be good. He's realistic about human nature. I've seen how he sacrifices what needs to be sacrificed to maintain relationships with those he cares about."

Whenever asked, Frank would say the most important work he had done in his life was the emotional work he did as a father. Initially impossibly controlling, he learned the value of loosening his hold. "In football there are players who play 'off the ball'. I developed a sense for that. It's nuanced and with my adult sons, I try not to instruct, I comment." Did that early control harm or help his sons? While it laid the foundation for unity, he is deeply grateful he had the wisdom to change. Where that wisdom came from he does not know.

Having married David in 1979, Margo has a unique perspective on family dynamics. She joined the Lowys when they were still an intact nuclear family and saw something she had never seen before. "There was a powerful bond between the three brothers. Even though Peter and Steven were still in their teens, there was something unbreakable between them. It went beyond family loyalty. David would explain that from their formative years, unity was ingrained in them. It was 'all for one and one for all', regardless of the circumstances. This continues today and while it makes for great strength, it can be a source of tension. There are times when they need to juggle their own family's interest with the interests of their family of origin."

Over time, Margo has seen Frank change. "He is able to adjust. He holds on, he's steely, but he does know when he's got to be malleable and when he has to move on."

On marrying Steven in the 1980s, Judy also saw something for the first time. "When I came into this family, they were all wearing rose-tinted glasses and no one could criticise anyone or anything, not even constructively." She says her father-in-law is far more realistic these days. "One of his more outstanding attributes is his ability to self-evaluate, revaluate the personalities in his sphere and accept the need to change."

The change is often hard won. While Frank gets the credit for the family unity, much is due to Shirley, who took a traditional role of homemaker at a time when many of her peers, propelled by feminism, were building professional lives. That she didn't seek a dual role freed her husband to focus on his career. She did go to university as a mature-aged student but always returned from lectures in time to ensure that no one came home to an empty house. "She was our centre of gravity," says Frank.

While the unity of the immediate family was unassailable, by the next generation the cohesion had loosened. While Frank was now wise enough to know when to keep his wisdom to himself, he wanted to be consulted should "one of the sheep wander off". At his private eightieth birthday celebration, he looked from Daniel, who was thirty to Jonah, who was just seven, and realised this was more than one generation of Lowys. These eleven grandchildren were each a universe unto themselves and driven by forces he couldn't conceive of. While he couldn't lock them into the family, he hoped he could persuade them to stay within reach.

At this gathering, he wanted to give them something for the future. He told them, among other things, that marriage is a difficult institution and many factors should be taken into consideration. Commonality of background was one. "You may want to consider that the Jewish people are connected by a chain that stretches back more than two thousand years," he said. As he spoke the words he did not imagine that anyone would remember them. But a year or so later, well after he'd forgotten providing such counsel, Noah casually reassured him that he had no intention of breaking the chain.

At the time of the party Frank didn't realise that Steven's daughter Rina, who was fourteen, was also listening carefully. While she didn't fully understand the significance of what he was saying, she felt she was hearing something important and the words remained with her. That they had an impact was evident a few years later, when she made a presentation to her fellow school students at which her grandparents were present. In it, she reflected on her desire to keep the chain intact.

Frank was closely bound to David's oldest son, Daniel. As the first grandchild he occupied a special place in his grandfather's heart. His early months had been spent physically very close to Frank and their connection was deep and warm. It was also bracingly honest. That Daniel chose to become a devoutly observant Jew was a source of ongoing tension between them. Frank would have preferred him to be traditional – to take part in communal activities, have faith, but not be constrained by the limits of orthodoxy.

Religion wasn't the only issue over which they disagreed. When Daniel wanted to do an MBA at Wharton in Philadelphia, Frank asked, "What for?" Daniel went ahead anyway. When Daniel wanted to expand his New York day-surgery business into a healthcare services network, he spent hours talking to Frank and taking him around Queens, showing him the environs and the potential. Frank was sceptical. Then Daniel organised a meeting with his bankers and consultants to persuade Frank of the merits of the enterprise. Frank remained sceptical. It was his way of making sure Daniel was fully committed. Daniel went ahead anyway. And when he made headway, Frank became his advocate in the family. The business was analysed and later LFG came on board as a partner. For all the creative tension, Daniel feels his grandfather is behind him. "He believes in me; it's wonderful!" By the time Daniel married Elana Nogid in a full religious ceremony in New York, Frank had stopped bothering him about being strictly orthodox.

When Peter and Janine's oldest daughter, Simonette, married Leo Grifka in Los Angeles, Frank was the sole living grandfather and gave a blessing as a representative of a receding generation.

"Now that my father is not here, Frank's presence is a reminder for me of a past that has now changed," said Janine. "I look at Frank with a greater sentimentality and he has an added meaning for me. He understood my father and he understands the loss."

Unlike her Sydney cousins, Simonette never had regular contact with her Sydney grandparents. When they did meet, her memory is of Frank always working. While completely comfortable in his presence, sometimes she wished he would put the phone down and be a little more present in family situations. But when she started her own fashion business, she developed a new respect for his dedication. "I understand his story and admire him so much for the way he grew his business. Unlike him, I speak perfect English, I have an education and I have all the resources in the world but I am finding it so hard. Almost every day, as I am struggling along, I think if he can do it, I can do it too!"

Of the four Los Angeles grandchildren, it seemed only Simonette intended to go into business. Benjamin had other aspirations and was interested in history and the arts. He went to New York to study in order to fulfil his ambition of becoming a theatre producer. Jacqueline spent three and a half perspective-changing years in the Israeli Army while the youngest, Caroline, wanted to explore everything "outside of the little bubble" they lived in. She keeps a journal and dreams of studying different cultures, writing about them and taking photos, like those she admires in *National Geographic* magazine. She has often heard that her grandmother, Shirley, would spend hours in the school library lost in the exotic photographs in *National Geographic*, never imagining she would have the means to travel to such places. Caroline, growing up in privilege, was acutely aware of the homogeneity of her school and the importance of having courage to go beyond into the world.

Although not light-hearted by nature, Frank is not always the solemn patriarch. Steven's daughter Claudia can bring out his playfulness and is one of the few to describe him as "cute". It gives her great pleasure when, in his Hungarian accent, he endearingly says, "Vopeedoo!" in response to something she might tell him.

When she was young, Claudia formed a sweet link with him. Together with her cousin Jacqui she taught him a complicated handshake. It has a number of steps before ending in a fist bump, an exploding hand and the word 'Kaboom'. Frank, of course, can't remember the whole sequence but whenever he sees Claudia he greets her with his own version of it and they laugh together. She reminds him of the past. When he looks across the Sabbath table at her, something in her always makes him think of his mother.

Every day of his life, Frank looks directly into the smiling face of Steven's youngest son, Jonah. A photograph of this happy child serves as the desktop on all his screens and he often taps him hello on the nose.

By 2015, with twenty-four immediate members of the Lowy clan, there was usually some discord somewhere in the realm. While Frank could feel the dissonance, these conflicts tended to be beyond his influence. However, the family calendar was filled with birthdays, anniversaries and other significant happenings, which Shirley conscientiously marked by sending congratulations and gifts. An important milestone, to which Frank was looking forward, was the last bar mitzvah among his grandchildren. In 2016 Jonah would perform this rite of passage and Frank and Shirley would have seen two complete generations enter "traditional adulthood".

In his later years, as Frank returned to the geography of his past, the only person left who could remember as far back was his oldest brother, Alex. So much had been lost. After long illnesses, their sister Edith and their middle brother John had passed away. Through those difficult years, Alex and Frank had visited them weekly. They would sit around a table of fruit and cakes, reminiscing and singing old Slovakian songs to cheer up their ailing siblings. These gatherings of the original family were as painful as they were precious.

As Frank was becoming closer and more sensitised to the meaning of things, so, paradoxically, he was looking at the world from 50,000 feet up in the air. The first time he held the hand of a great grandchild he had a striking realisation. This child would likely live into the twenty-second century. He remembered holding the hand of his father, who had been born in the nineteenth century. Could it be that he had loved people whose lives would stretch into four centuries? The span was beyond belief.

So was the fact that Shirley was turning eighty and growing frail. In 2014, the year of her eightieth birthday, she and Frank were celebrating sixty years of married life. To mark these events Steven and Judy put up a marquee, filled it with flowers and invited people from around the world. For the first time, four generations of Lowys were present. Shirley walked to the podium, smiled broadly and proceeded to deliver what could only be described as a love song to her husband – with a little humour.

She explained how, after their first date in 1952, she came home, entranced, to find her father waiting up for her.

"So how did it go?" he asked.

"Lovely," she said.

He seemed pleased and went to bed. A short while later she heard her parents arguing. "What do you want already!" came the raised voice of her father. "Who are we that we should expect a doctor or a dentist?"

Shirley talked of the actuality of their lives, of how Frank constantly worked and how he lived with such intensity that everything mattered. He was away very often and she was lonely. "That was our reality, but it was held together by the magic between us. The magic is in the moment when I feel Frank take my hand – when I feel his arm around me and when I know there is nowhere else in the whole world I would rather be. We don't know what the future holds, but we are going into it, holding hands."

Frank, as usual, had planned to wing his response but for the first time in his life, he stood at the podium lost for words.

It is customary among Jews that every year on the anniversary of the passing of a loved one men go to the synagogue to recite Kaddish, an ancient Aramaic prayer for mourners. Frank holds to this tradition. The date of his father's passing is so deep within him that he can feel it approaching. In 2015 he was in New York awaiting this date, as well as the birth of his third great-grandchild. In quiet moments he found himself preoccupied with the possible intersection of these two events.

On the day of the birth, he and Shirley went to the hospital. They found themselves there alone with the baby's mother, Elana, and embraced her. Then Frank went to the nursery and asked the nurse to bring the baby into the room. In the soft, late afternoon, with the new mother resting peacefully and Shirley at his side, he sat holding his great-grandson. The boy in the crook of his arm was four hours old.

When they got home, evening was approaching and Frank lit a memorial candle for his late father. Then he went to the Fifth Avenue synagogue to say Kaddish. Seventy-one years had passed since he last saw his father and blended with the tragic loss of his passing was the scent of the little being he had just held. "As I prayed, this intersection of sorrow and joy lifted me beyond myself," he said.

Postscript

In May 2015, Frank Lowy was on a stage at the centre of a football stadium in Melbourne. Just as he was about to award a large trophy to the winning team, he missed a step at the edge of the podium and fell off.

People gasped as he appeared to hit the ground head first.

The stadium fell silent. The television commentary stopped and, all around Australia, fans leaned forward in quiet horror to watch the drama unfold.

Some couldn't look as – for a few moments – he lay motionless on his back on the field.

When he sat up, the stadium erupted with applause. When he got to his feet, the spectators were exuberant.

They cheered loudly as he climbed back onto the podium and, his white hair stained with grass, resumed the presentation.

Because of his age, the nature of the fall and the way he managed himself, this episode became a national talking point.

It happened on a Sunday evening just after Melbourne Victory FC had defeated Sydney FC, 3–0, in the A League Grand Final.

Two days later, on Tuesday morning, Lowy described the event and its impact on him:

> Before the match, I was in a dilemma. Over the weekend I had a commitment in Israel I was keen to meet but the chairman of Melbourne Victory, Anthony Di Pietro, made a special request for me to be present at the Grand Final. "I want you to give us the trophy if we win," he said.
>
> It would have been good to get away, but his words kept ringing in my ear. As it would also be my last Grand Final as chairman, I decided to stay and leave for Israel immediately afterwards.
>
> The atmosphere in the stadium was electric and I believe the play would have fitted into any top European game. I was particularly pleased Melbourne Victory had made it to the Grand Final because some eighteen months earlier we had recruited its coach for the Socceroos. In his place, Melbourne Victory had the courage to elevate his assistant, Kevin Muscat, and as a result we have another young, top ranking Australian coach.
>
> About five minutes before the end of the match the official party began to move down to the field for the prize-giving ceremony. Out on the field, as they hurriedly put up the stage, we hung around congratulating and commiserating with players and coaches.
>
> Then David Gallop and I went onto the stage to present medals to officials, players and coaches. All was going well and it was time to present the trophy to the winning team. The stage was crowded, the announcement was made and David and I moved towards the trophy.

I don't recall what happened next but I do remember lying on the grass thinking that hundreds of thousands of Australians are watching and I need to steel myself so I don't spoil the night for them and for Melbourne Victory. I also remembered what my son David always says: "Above all, look good!"

Although I never lost consciousness, I have no memory of getting up and climbing back onto the stage. When I saw a video clip of the event this morning, for the first time, I was surprised to see myself smiling, waving, helping to hand over the trophy and clapping. I was talking, too.

I do, however, remember leaving the podium and others being with me. As we walked into the tunnel I saw a chair. It was such a welcome sight. All I wanted to do was sit on it. As I sat, well-wishers and football officials came up. The state premier, Daniel Andrews, came too, and offered help.

But what I most remember are the paramedics, Kelly Liels and Peter Bailey. They made such a great impression on me. Peter never left my side. As I sat, he continually asked me questions like, "How many fingers can you see?" He was so calm, so reassuring and so friendly that he kept me in good spirits. We walked to the small bus and I asked whether he would mind coming to the airport. He stayed with me all the way and onto the plane and even offered to fly with me. These paramedics are unsung heroes. They don't look for accolades, they just do their important job quietly and excellently.

In the bus I kept getting SMSs. I answered them, both to satisfy myself that my brain was working and to let others know I still had my faculties. I wasn't concerned about my body, just my mind. On the plane I fell into the

arms of Shirley, who had been waiting for me. As going
to Israel was out of the question, we flew home to Sydney.
At the airport, David and Margo were waiting to take us
to emergency at St Vincent's Hospital, where a team was
expecting me.

After being examined, tested and scanned, I was asked
to stay overnight for observation. The doctors noted that I
wasn't complaining. Physically I wasn't hurting that much,
and was concentrating on proving to myself that I was
okay mentally. They said it was only my agility, developed
through continual exercise, swimming and walking, that
kept me uninjured.

Meantime, my phone hadn't stopped. Calls and messages
were coming from everywhere, even abroad, and as I
couldn't sleep, I responded from my hospital bed. It seemed
everyone thought I'd fallen on my head, but I'd actually
landed on my shoulder and then my head hit the grass.

I had some other good luck that night. The surgeon
who had operated on me a few years ago — and literally
knew my body inside out — was on call and came to the
hospital. When he returned in the morning — at 6.25am —
I was waiting for him. He said I could go home. It was such
a relief. So was coming home to a household of love and
care. I have also been touched very much by the sentiment
that Australia showed towards me. I received calls from
people in high places and felt the genuineness of their
pleasure that I was okay.

The first day home I didn't look at the newspapers, the
photos or the videos because I didn't want to be reminded
of what had happened. But early this morning, I watched a
YouTube clip and as I did, something happened to me. I felt

overwhelmingly grateful to have survived the way I did.
I've had some close shaves in my life and this seemed to be
a sign, a sign from a power above that it is time to accept
the reality of being eighty-four. It's time to depressurise.

My business activity has been lessening for a little while
now and my term at football is coming to an end soon.
I guess I had been concerned about being "unemployed",
so to speak. But as I watched that video clip I recognised I
ought to be thankful for what I have achieved and shift the
balance to less activity and more appreciation. I want to try
and appreciate the journey that is left with my life partner,
Shirley.

The big question is whether I will be able to keep to
this resolution. It may be the hardest challenge for me yet.

Acknowledgments

With so many thanks to Emanuel Klein, Veronica Sumegi, Helen Garner, Shelley Kenigsberg, Pat Jacobs, Carolyn Stone, Anne Wyndham, Vita Palestrant, Lucy Chipkin, Sybil Pliner, Joanne Cooper, Elisabeth Agostino, Julia Clarke and Andras Berkes for your gracious support. To Jacqueline Kent, Catherine Milne and Denise O'Dea, thank you for your patience and professionalism. To my dear family, Jonathan, Emily, Sarah, Sally, Richard and Peter, I am so grateful you stay close.

Index

Tel Hashomer Medical Center 130
television shopping 369
Telstra 241
Telstra Stadium 268
Temarii, Reynald 304–305
Temora Aviation Museum 63–64
10 Downing Street 432–433
Thailand 277, 316
think tanks 98–100, 112, 119, 122
    see also Jaffee Center for Strategic
    Studies; Lowy Institute for
    International Policy
Tinkler, Nathan 329, 330, 331
Tobago 297, 321–322
Top Ryde 34
Tour de France (2011) 271
Tourism Australia 351
Transport Museum in Budapest
    174
Trinidad 297, 321–322
Trumbull (Connecticut) 37, 359
Turkey 442
Tuxen, Simon 193, 367, 390–391,
    397

U
UBS 208, 401, 451–453, 473–474
UCLA, Jules Stein Eye Institute 72
UEFA (Union of European Football
    Associations) 292–293
Ukraine 124
Ungar, Rami 149
UniSuper 472–476
United Arab Emirates 115–116
United Nations 21, 94
United Nations Security Council 121,
    123, 285, 321
United States
    American malls 34
    Australian alliance with 106
    China, ping-pong diplomacy with
        260
    FIFA World Cup (2022) bid 303,
        306, 310
    Fifth Amendment 212–213
    global financial crisis (2007–2008)
        207, 434–440
    tax issues see Internal Revenue
        Service; Senate Committee
        on Homeland Security and
        Governmental Affairs
    Westfield in see Westfield in United
        States

University College London 79
university funding 481
University of New South Wales 95–96,
    481
University of Pennsylvania 119
University of Tel Aviv 127, 135–137
Uruguay 261, 263, 266–271, 314, 337
US News & World Report 141

V
Valcke, Jerome 313–314
valet parking 456
values, transmission of 60
Venglos, Dr Jozef 243
Verbeek, Pim 278–279, 280
Veszprém 12
Victor Chang Cardiac Research
    Institute 74–75
Victoria 36
Vietnam 277
Villa, David 345–346
Vision Asia 285

W
Walker, Ron 229, 239, 240, 242
Wallenberg, Raoul 94
Wanderers of North Parramatta 333
Warburton, Dick 469–470, 473, 475
Warner, Jack 313, 321, 322
Warren, Johnny 228
Washington DC 98
Washington Institute for Near East
    Policy 104
'way finding' 455
Wellington, Duke of 98
Wembley Stadium 426
Wentworth Sofitel, Sydney 467
Wesley, Dr Michael 116–120
western Sydney 332–333
Western Sydney Wanderers FC 324–
    325, 332, 333–334, 344–345,
    348–350
Westfield America Inc 380–381
Westfield America Trust 48, 380–389,
    400–403
Westfield Bondi Junction 59, 397–398,
    418
Westfield Capital Corporation 47–48
Westfield Corporation
    Frank Lowy as chairman 461
    as international arm of Westfield
        460
    Lowy family stake 463, 475–476